Orientalism, Aramaic and Kabbalah
in the Catholic Reformation

Studies in the History of Christian Traditions

Founded by

Heiko A. Oberman†

Edited by

Robert J. Bast
Knoxville, Tennessee

In cooperation with

Henry Chadwick, Cambridge
Scott H. Hendrix, Princeton, New Jersey
Paul C.H. Lim, Nashville, Tennessee
Eric Saak, Indianapolis, Indiana
Brian Tierney, Ithaca, New York
Arjo Vanderjagt, Groningen
John Van Engen, Notre Dame, Indiana

VOLUME 137

Orientalism, Aramaic and Kabbalah in the Catholic Reformation

The First Printing of the Syriac New Testament

By

Robert J. Wilkinson

BRILL

LEIDEN · BOSTON
2007

On the cover: The Sephirotic plate from John's Gospel.

Brill has made all reasonable efforts to trace all rights holders to any copyrighted material used in this work. In cases where these efforts have not been successful the publisher welcomes communications from copyrights holders, so that the appropriate acknowledgements can be made in future editions, and to settle other permission matters.

This book is printed on acid-free paper.

A Cataloging-in-Publication record of this book is available from the Library of Congress.

ISBN 978 90 04 16250 1

Iris Wilkinson
28. 2. 1925–15. 2. 2006

John Henry Wilkinson
22. 7. 1925–24. 5. 2006

in piam memoriam

CONTENTS

CONTENTS

LIST OF PLATES

PLATES

Plate One. Title page of Teseo's *Introductio* (Padua 1593) proclaiming the mystical and kabbalistic significance of his alphabets.

CHALDAEORVM LITERAE, QVI
Syriam incolunt, quæ etiam Syriacæ dicuntur, & quibus Antiochęna Patriarchalis Ecclesia in sacris vtitur, duę & viginti sunt, quę his figuris atqǝ nominibus exprimuntur. Caput. Primum.

V.   H.   D.   G.   B.   A.
Vau.   He.   Dolad. Gomal. Beth. Olaph.

L.   C.   I.   T.   HH.   Z.
Lomad. Coph. Iud.   Teth. Hheth. Zain.

P.   Ga.A. S.   N.   M.
Phe.Pe. Gain.Ain. Somchath. Nun. Mim.

Th.   Sc.   R.   Q.   ZZ.
Thau. Scin. Ris.   Quoph. Zzodé.

Legútur autem Hebræorum more, à dextro, in sinistrū latus. Habét pterea Chaldæi & Syri, alias quoqǝ minores literas, quarum figuræ sunt infrascriptæ.

Plate Two. Specimen page of the *Introductio* to illustrate the estrangela type.

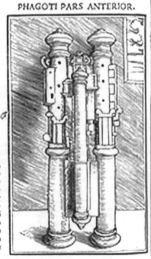

Plate Three. Teseo's plates illustrating the Phagotum.

Plate Four. Title page of Postel's *Linguarum duodecim characteribus* to illustrate the difficulties of printing oriental and particularly ligatured script.

Plate Five. Widmanstetter's arms, with Syriac text and kabbalistic word play (explained in the text).

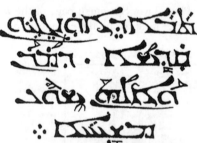

Plate Six. Title page of *editio princeps* 1555.

Plate Seven. *Obtestatio ad lectorem* from *editio princeps*.

Plate Eight. Specimen page from *editio princeps* (Hebrews 1), illustrating its similarity to an eastern book.

Plate Nine. Festal list from *editio princeps* in Syriac and Latin. The presence of liturgical material in the Syriac New Testament proved of significance for confessional polemics.

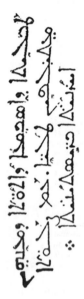

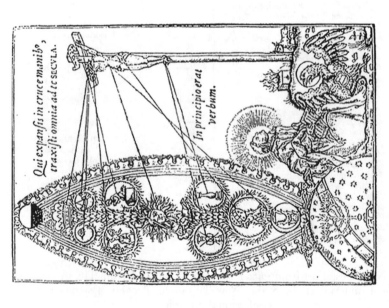

SYRIACÆ LINGVÆ.
IESV CHRISTO, EIVSQVE MATRI
Virgini atq; Iudæis omnibus, Chriſtianæ
redemptionis Euangelicæq; prædicationis
tempore, Vernaculæ & popularis, ideoq; à
Noui Teſtamenti Scriptoribus quibuſdam
Hebraicæ dictæ.

PRIMA ELEMENTA.

Quibus adiectæ ſunt Chriſtianæ Religionis
ſolennes, quotidianæq; Precationes.

VIENNÆ AVSTRIÆ,
ANNO M. D. LV. XXI.
NOVEMB.

Plate Eleven. Title page of Widmanstetter's *Syriacae Linguae...Prin-
cipia Elementa* (Vienna 1556) often bound with the *editio princeps*.

Plate Ten. The Sephirotic plate from John's Gospel
discussed extensively in the text.

INTRODUCTION

Historians often allow themselves the imprecision of speaking of 'the Bible'. But 'the Bible' (dare one so put it?) is a theological abstraction. What we encounter empirically are bibles—and they are all different. They differ in canon, order of books, language, and text. If they are translations, their relationships to their original may differ considerably. Nor do they come naked into the world. Most bibles provide guidance instructing the reader how to read them—their own hermeneutic key, as it were.

The following pages seek first to recognise the specific features that characterise the first sixteenth-century edition of the Syriac New Testament. My description of this book, however, does not seek bibliographic precision and may, I fear, irritate the purist. My remarks extend no further than those features for which I feel I am able to give some sort of explanatory account. Nevertheless I have taken seriously the task of explaining the reasons why this bible—considered as an artefact—is as it is. I hope I have given proper attention to its typography and text, to its layout and apparatuses, to its prefaces and appendices. Certainly I have sought to explain why it was produced in terms of the ideology and motives of the editors, and to locate those in turn in a broader cultural context, and that within the history of the sixteenth century. Such an attempt will appear in some respects patchy and uneven, but the desirability of such a project—even if total success eludes us—will surely be granted by those who wish to place the specific and technical discourses of Bibliography, Philology, Text Studies, and Oriental Languages (or any such like) within a broader historical account as a way of writing Intellectual History that transcends the technicalities of the narrow discipline and contributes to a broader more accessible, but also more comprehensive, account.[1]

---

[1] I hope the following work will also be of interest to scholars turning their attention to the Bible as a book (in the relevant sense) as exemplified by the programmatically titled ed. K. van Kampen & P. Saenger, *The Bible as a Book. The First Printed Editions* (British Library, 1999). There is also a growing body of work addressing sixteenth-century biblical exposition, to which I believe the following work may make a contribution: ed. D. Steinmetz, *The Bible in the Sixteenth Century* (Duke UP, Durham 1996); eds. R. A. Muller & J. L. Thompson, *Biblical Interpretation in the Era of the Reformation*

In this respect the following pages seek specifically to articulate a technical appreciation of this New Testament edition from the perspective of Syriac Studies within a broader Early Modern history, and thereby to make a contribution to both. Syriac specialists, not surprisingly, concern themselves in general with the language, literature and history of the Eastern Churches. They have not given extended consideration to the reception of Syriac language and culture in the West. That is not to say that such topics have been ignored, merely that the field has not yet been fully worked.[2] My debt to certain giants in the field, most notably Giorgio Levi della Vida, is enormous.[3]

But Semitists working on the Early Modern period (and not on the Old Testament or its 'World') are still rather rare, certainly in the United Kingdom, and the story of these bibles has not yet been told with any degree of completeness. Early Modern historians, on the other hand,

---

(Eerdmans, Grand Rapids 1996); ed. R. Griffiths, *The Bible in the Renaissance* (Ashgate, Aldershot 2001).

[2] The best introductory account of Syriac studies to date is S. P. Brock "The Development of Syriac Studies" in ed. K. J. Cathcart, *The Edward Hincks Bicentenary Lectures* (Univ. Coll. Dublin, Dublin 1994) pg 94–113 on pg 96–97. W. Strothmann, *Die Anfänge der syrischen Studien in Europa* (Harrasowitz, Wiesbaden 1971) is not much more than a list of editions with descriptions of their immediate circumstances. Its reproductions are quite outstandingly poor. A van Roey, *Les Études syriaques de 1538 à 1658* (K.U. Leuven—Faculteit der Godgeleerdheid Bibliotheek [Documentaria Libraria] 1988) is essentially an exhibition catalogue. Earlier accounts specifically of printed Syriac New Testaments are: Anon. "The Printed Editions of the Syriac New Testament" Church Quarterly Review LII (1888) pg 257–294; Alfred Durand "Les Éditions imprimées du Nouveau Testament syriaque, Recherches de Science religieuse" (Paris) XI 1921 pg 385–409; E. Nestle "Literatura Syriaca" in *Syriac Grammar with Bibliography, Chrestomathy and Glossary* (Reuther, Berlin 1889) pg 1–39. R. Contini "Gli Inizi della Linguistica Siriaca nell'Europa rinascimentale" Rivista degli Studi Orientali LXVIII (1994) pg 15–30 discusses early Syriac studies from the perspective of modern linguistics, but does not share our interest in the kabbalistic interpretation of the language. J. Perles, *Beiträge zur Geschichte der hebräischen und aramäischen Studien* (Ackermann, Munich 1884) is an important source of relevant observations. Bibliographically, R. Smitskamp, *Philologia Orientalia. A description of books illustrating the study and printing of Oriental languages in Europe* (E. J. Brill, Leiden 1976–1992: three volumes), despite being a sale catalogue, is a most helpful work in the area of typography and written by a master. There is, of course, also Cyril Moss, *Catalogue of Syriac Printed Books and Related Literature in the British Museum* (B.M., London 1962). K. Austin, *From Judaism to Calvinism: the Life and Writings of Emmanuel Tremellius*. Unpublished Doctoral Thesis St. Andrews University 2003 gives some consideration of Tremellius's Syriac New Testament. I offer a technical assessment of Tremellius's work in Robert J. Wilkinson "Emmanuel Tremellius' 1569 Edition of the Syriac New Testament" Journal of Ecclesiastical History 58/1 January 2007 pg 9–25.

[3] Principally to his fundamental *Ricerche sulla formazione del più antico fondo dei manoscritti orientali della Biblioteca Vaticana* (BAV, Vatican City 1939), though other works are also used below.

rarely have the necessary interest or competence in oriental languages to attempt an account of oriental philology in their period. I hope to be able to persuade them that the story of the printed editions of the Syriac New Testament is an interesting one, and that, far from being a mere recondite footnote to a story about something else, it is in fact an index of a broader ideological and cultural stance that was not marginal in its significance.

I have endeavoured below to explain the *editio princeps* of 1555. However, the greater part of this work is given over to a reconstruction of the world of Catholic Orientalism in the High Renaissance within which the first Western knowledge of Syriac was contextualised and out of which the *editio princeps* arose. The distinctive nature of that Orientalism has not previously been used to explain the features of the *editio princeps*. Nor has it been appreciated that this distinctive world-view is characteristic of *all* sixteenth-century Catholic editions of the Syriac New Testament. My reconstruction of this world-view thus forms a necessary prolegomenon to a longer account of all sixteenth-century Catholic editions that has already been written and appears as a companion volume to this: *The Kabbalistic Scholars of the Antwerp Polyglot Bible*.

The social context of this distinctive Catholic Orientalism is provided by the small group of scholars, related closely to each other by friendship, collaboration and correspondence, who studied Syriac in the sixteenth century. These men are not unknown to contemporary historians, though the story of their sustained cooperation on the production of Syriac bibles has not previously been told.[4] Syriac was conceived in a distinctive way by its first Western student, Teseo Ambrogio, and this particular apprehension, inspired by Egidio da Viterbo, determined the understanding of the language entertained by Widmanstetter, Masius, and later by Guy Lefèvre de la Boderie. The consistent presence behind all these bibles, in both linguistic and typographic expertise, was however Guillaume Postel and though his own sense of mission was to develop to a point of such singularity that he was most conveniently treated as insane, he may be fairly said to have both inspired and enabled the Syriac editions of the others. I believe the full significance of Postel's role is made clear here for the first time. The importance of Postel for

---

[4] It will be evident to what extent I am dependent upon the work of previous scholars in characterising Egidio, Widmanstetter, Postel, *et al.* I trust however that my presentation will be helpful to those not intimately familiar with the specialised literature on each of these scholars.

the production of the Antwerp Polyglot and his influence upon the 1584 Paris edition (brought out three years after his death) when realised only strengthen the case made here.

It is not surprisingly amongst scholars (often *these* scholars) that such traces as remain of the reception of successive Syriac editions are generally to be found. Syriac, though not an unreasonable expectation of a biblical scholar in the seventeenth century, was rare in the sixteenth and has never in any sense been popular. It was, of course, the achievement of the editions we are to examine to have facilitated the access of later scholars to the Syriac New Testament, its text and its language, though knowledge of very much else had to await the subsequent growth of Maronite scholarship in the West. Nevertheless, Syriac studies in the sixteenth century had a missionary motive that was as strong as any more speculative or arcane interest. The intention behind the *editio princeps* was not only the provision of liturgical books for the Eastern Church, but also the evangelisation of Moslems. Widmanstetter (as well as Tremellius and Guy Lefèvre de la Boderie) thought their work would serve to convert the Jews. Though we do not have as much evidence for the reception of these editions as we would like, there is some material for us to review and enough to keep us attentive to the wider usefulness the editors hoped for their work.

I have characterised the work of the scholars who produced the Syriac New Testament editions in two ways—both of which may need some explanation. I have generally referred to their productions on the one hand as a type of Orientalism, and on the other (perhaps more controversially) as kabbalistic.

Orientalism is a familiar term. But it is not generally used in sixteenth-century studies, and there is no developed typology for this early period. It has been my concern, however, to link the voyages of Postel (the only one of our scholars to visit the East) that were distinguished by the benefits and fruits of his extraordinary linguistic facility, and the arcane tradition that found the secrets of Aramaean antiquity from the time of Noah mediated through the local histories of Viterbo, Rome, Florence, France or Spain. Characteristically the Oriental 'Other' was found not only in a Biblical past, but also in a local tradition. Postel then found this same local antiquity out East. The linking of the domestic past and Oriental present was based upon a Mediaeval Biblicism, but developed in his case by a well-informed acquaintance with contemporary Easterners and their language. Postel could cope with the languages, could describe with considerable detachment the singularities of the East, but still relegated the whole to share a mythical past that he would reintegrate in the proclamation of his Gospel—that of the One Shepherd and His One Flock. It seems to me that there is a distinctive Orientalism here that is more than Mediaeval Biblicism, yet falls short of the objectivity of, say, Jones's descriptions of Sanskrit.[5] Certainly it is worthy of our attention, however we seek to place it within a wider schema.

I have used the term *kabbalistic* to characterise the notions and books of both Jews and Christians.[6] Although where it seemed necessary I

---

[5] Now discussed in M. J. Franklin, *Sir William Jones* (University of Wales Press, Cardiff 1995).

[6] The founding article of the modern study of Christian Kabbalism was Gershom Scholem "Zur Geschichte der Anfänge der christlischen Kabbala" *Essays presented to Leo Baeck* (East & West Library, London 1954) pg 158–193. An English translation appears in J. Dan, *The Christian Kabbalah* (Harvard 1997) pg 17–51. J. L. Blau, *The Christian Interpretation of the Cabala in the Renaissance* (Columbia UP, New York 1944) was superseded by F. Secret, *Le Zohar chez les Kabbalistes chrétiens de la Renaissance* (Librairie Durlacher, Paris 1958) and *Les kabbalistes chrétiens de la Renaissance* (Dunod, Paris 1964: 2nd edition Arma Artis, Neully's/Seine 1985). General surveys exist in L. Gorny, *La Kabbale. Kabbale juive et Cabale chrétienne* (Pierre Belfort, Paris 1977) of which Part III is devoted to Christian Kabbalah; F. Secret "L'Interpretazione della Kabbala nel Rinascimento" Convivium XXIV (1956) pg 541–552; G. Javary, *Recherches sur l'Utilisation du Thème de la Sekina dans l'Apologetique chrétienne du XV au XVIII siècle* (Champion, Paris 1978). Various, *Kabbalistes chrétiens* (Cahiers de l'Hermétisme, Albin Michel, Paris 1979); Moshe Idel "The Magical and Neoplatonic Interpretation of the Kabbalah in the Renaissance" in ed. B. D. Cooperman, *Jewish Thought in the Sixteenth Century* (Harvard U.P., Cambridge Mass. 1983) pg 186–242; W. K. Percival "The Reception of Hebrew in Sixteenth-Century Europe: the impact of the Cabala" Historiographa Linguistica XI 1/2 (1984) pg 21–38: ed. J. Dan, *The Christian Kabbalah. Jewish Mystical Books and their Christian Interpreters* (Harvard Coll. Library, Cambridge Mass. 1997). S. A. Spector, *Jewish Mysticism An annotated Bibliography of the Kabbalah in English* (Garland Publishing, New York 1984) pg 309–357 treats of non–Jewish Kabbalah—and includes rather a mixed bag. There is a considerable bibliography devoted to Pico della Mirandola and the origins of Christian Kabbalah. Though I do not treat of Pico in detail below it may be helpful to note: Heinz Pflaum "Leone Ebreo und Pico della Mirandola" Monatschrift für Geschichte und Wissenschaft des Judentums LXXII (1928) pg 344–350; Bohdan Kieszkowski "Les Rapports entre Elie del Megido et Pic de la Mirandole (d'après le ms. lat. 6508 de la Bibliothèque Nationale)" Rinascimento IV (1964) pg 58–61; G. dell'Aqua & L. Munster "I Rapporti di Giovanni Pico della Mirandola con alcuni filosofi ebrei" in *L'Opera e il Penserio di G. Pico della Mirandola nella Storia dell' Umanismo* (Instituto Nationale di Studi sul Rinascimento, Florence 1965) Vol. II pg 149–165: also F. Secret "Nouvelles Précisions sur Flavius Mithridates Maître de Pic de la Mirandole et Traducteur de Commentaires de Kabbale" *ibid* pg 169–187; C. Wirszubski "Giovanni Pico's Companion to Kabbalistic Symbolism" *Studies in Mysticism and Religion presented to Gershom Scholem* (Jerusalem 1967) pg 353–362; C. Wirszubski "Giovanni Pico's Book of Job" Journal of the Warburg and Courtauld Institute XXXII (1969) pg 171–199; Herman Greive "Die christlische Kabbala des Giovanni Pico della Mirandola" Archiv für Kulturgeschichte LVII (1975) pg 141–161; Moshe Idel "The Throne and the

have spoken of *Jewish* or *Christian* Kabbalah, I have generally used the same word of Jewish mystical writers and of Christians. I have (after experimentation) found it not possible to preserve, say, one spelling for Jewish books and authors and another (perhaps a Latinised *Cabala*) for Christians. I am aware the Kabbalah was originally Jewish, and that Christians borrowed Kabbalah (with different degrees of erudition) from Jews. I have no wish to deny the proprietary claims of Judaism, but neither do I seek to belittle the spiritual content of the Christian authors (should anyone wish to claim there is one), even though they naturally understood kabbalistic texts in a sense radically different from that of their authors or Jewish readers. Since the Israelites built their Tabernacle from the spoils of Egypt, we have been familiar with the place of both *récuperation* and *bricolage* in the construction of the sacred. Personally I have no investment in either Jewish or Christian reading. It may be objected that more than the presence of a superficial Hebrew *jeu de mot* is needed to make a Kabbalist and that I have not sought rigorously to define how much knowledge of (*'real'*) Jewish Kabbalah a Christian Kabbalist needs to qualify for the title. I would however argue that *by any standard* the knowledge of Jewish kabbalistic texts shown by Egidio da Viterbo, Widmanstetter, and Postel is extensive and far from trivial. They read, annotated and translated these difficult texts themselves. That their reading of these texts was a monument of Chris-

---

Seven-Branched Candlestick: Pico della Mirandola's Hebrew source" Journal of the Warburg and Courtauld Institute XL (1977) pg 290–292; Klaus Reichert "Pico della Mirandola and the beginnings of Christian Kabbala in ed. K. E. Grözinger & J. Dan, *Mysticism, Magic and Kabbalah in Ashkenazi Judaism* (W. de Gruyter, Berlin 1995). On Pico's teacher Alemanno: E. I. J. Rosenthal "Yohanan Alemanno & Occult Science" in ed. Y. Maeyama & W. G. Saltzer, *ΠΡΙΣΜΑΤΑ Naturwissenschaftsgeschichtliche Studien (Festschrift für Willy Hartner)* (Frank Steiner Verlag, Wiesbaden 1977) pg 349–361, and Moshe Idel "The Anthropology of Yohanan Alemanno: Sources and Influences" Annali di Storia dell' Esegesi (Bologna) VII/1 (1990) pg 93–112. On the important figure of Flavius Mithridates see: ed C. Wirszubski, *Flavius Mithridates Sermo de Passione Domini* (Israel Academy of Sciences and Humanities, Jerusalem 1963) preceded by U. Cassuto "Wer was der Orientalist Mithridates?" Zeitschrift für die Geschichte der Juden in Deutschland V 1934 pg 230–236 and F. Secret "Qui était l'Orientaliste Mithridates" Revue des Études juives XVI (CXVI) 1958 pg 96–102. Two very important earlier articles are R. Starabba "Guglielmo Moncada, Ebreo Convertito siciliano del Secola XV" Archivio Storico siciliano n.s. III (Palermo 1878) pg 15–91 and I Carini "Guglielmo Raimondo Moncado" ibid. n.s. XXII (1897) pg 485–92. For reviews of Wirszubski's Hebrew works: Micheline Chaze "Trois chapitres sur l'Histoire de la Kabbale chrétienne" Revue des Études juives CXXXIV (1975) pg 137–140; G. Vadja "A Christian Kabbalist reads the Law" Revue des Études juives CXXXVII (1978) pg 258–259 with bibliographic reference to Hebrew volumes.

tian eisegesis—*plunder*, surely, from a Jewish perspective—is of mainly confessional moment. The text becomes Christian once incorporated within a Christian world-view, just as we suspect passages of Canaanite poetry became Israelite by their incorporation in the canonical Psalter. The Christian Kabbalists however did not seek to conceal the Jewish origin of their texts, though they drew from that conclusions that were generally anti-Judaic. To the marginal extent that their conclusions were less anti-Judaic than the prejudices of the majority, they do perhaps have some historical significance. Sadly however we shall find that though a reverence for the arcane wisdom preserved in Hebrew books did practically seem to lead to more cooperative and constructive relationships with some Jewish scholars, not even Postel will be free of the dreary traditional Christian denigration of Judaism. What I insist upon here, however, is that Christian Kabbalah is a most significant component of the world-view of the Catholic scholars who produced the printed editions of the Syriac New Testament. This has not been systematically observed or described before, and whether or not one likes the labels, the reality is inescapable.

I make no claim to have contributed to the study of Jewish Kabbalists.[7] My contribution to the study of the Christian Kabbalists, I would claim, is to have recovered Widmanstetter's real attitude to the Kabbalah and refuted the common view of him as a man who believed that Kabbalah entered the Church as a Trojan Horse. That point however serves merely to clear the ground for my major claim that what has been missing from previous accounts of printed editions of the Syriac New Testament is precisely their background in the varied kabbalistic speculations of their editors. I use the term widely—of both Egidio's books and Postel's fantasies—but the continuities are real, whether or not (once again) one likes the labels and in that my usage of the term conforms to that of the *doyen* of Christian kabbalistic studies, François Secret, it may scarcely be called eccentric.[8]

---

[7] I have therefore not sought to offer bibliographic orientation for this vast and difficult area. The works of Gershom Scholem are the founding documents of the modern study of the subject, though his legacy is at present being re-evaluated. A modern developmental synthesis may be found in Moshe Idel, *Kabbalah, New Perspectives* (Yale U.P., New Haven 1988).

[8] My indebtedness to Secret's work is apparent upon every page. Apart from major books mentioned above, there are innumerable technical articles and notes. Ed. Sylvain Malton, *Documents oubliés sur l'Alchemie, la Kabbale et Guillaume Postel* (Droz,

The Orientalism that I have characterised as kabbalistic was not confined to Syriac studies. Indeed though its use by Christ and His Mother and the arcane content of the Aramaic tradition perhaps gave Syriac an edge over Arabic, one cannot but feel that, had they been able, our scholars would have given priority to the publication of an Arabic New Testament as better able to fulfil their missionary plans. The knowledge of Arabic in the West grew apace with that of Syriac and the same scholars were involved. Widmanstetter we shall see was able to find a kabbalistic core in the Teachings of Islam, and Postel has recently been treated in a study that has given a proper technical assessment of his Arabic philology.[9] Beginnings were being made in the study of Ethiopic, Samaritan, Armenian and other exotic tongues: scripts were published, lexical items recovered and rudimentary morphological features isolated. I hope I have shown how these varied attempts are to be seen as characterised by the same kabbalistic motivation as early Syriac studies. My concern to show that what I am describing is not merely a feature of Syriac studies but is of such a wider generality as to deserve being labelled as an Orientalism has led me to include some account of studies of these other languages. This entailed certain expansiveness both in the text and particularly in the footnotes. I have sought to offer an initial characterisation in these areas that is not misleading, to indicate the most important evidence and to give essential bibliographic information—while at the same time seeking to prevent the whole digressing into unreadability. I cannot claim consistent success, but do hope that the attempt to mark out a whole area will be serviceable to those whom I may convince that what I describe here is of more than marginal significance in the study of sixteenth-century Intellectual History and who may wish themselves to read in this area.

The initial definition of my kabbalistic oriental scholars has been essentially pragmatic, being based upon the documentary evidence of what they wrote. Such an approach may give us some confidence that we are talking about something real rather than merely an imaginative construct. I have however further sought to define this type of scholarship by contrast. I have taken the burning of the Talmud in Rome in

Geneva 2001)—the Festschrift for Secret's ninety-sixth birthday—has an invaluable bibliography up to 2001 on pg 1–29.

[9] Hartmut Bobzin, *Der Koran in Zeitalter der Reformation* (Franz Steiner, Beirut 1995) pg 365–498.

1553 as indicative of a Papal policy towards Judaism and Kabbalah that was both different from that entertained by the High Renaissance Pontiffs and inimical to the work of our scholars. Certainly they thought and said so. We are thus able to use this change in the Curia's attitude to Kabbalah negatively to define the movement that interests us. It also explains to some extent the subsequent suspicions of heterodoxy that attach to the editors of the Syriac New Testament, and indeed why the Syriac New Testament was not first printed in Rome.

Finally I should remark that in the interest of accessibility I have avoided the use of oriental type, but have provided reproductions of significant book pages so that typographic points do not become incomprehensible for lack of illustration. For a similar reason transcriptions of Syriac or Arabic names are ruthlessly anglicised and diacritical points suppressed. I regret that it has not been possible to offer translations of all passages in Latin or other European languages, but decisive considerations of space prevent this. I have however tried to ensure that the sense of the main text can be followed by the reader without ancient or oriental languages.

While this book was in the press J. P. Coakley The Typography of Syriac (British Library, 2006) appeared. It is now the authorative catalogue of Syriac types. Also A. Turo "Un codice ebraico di cabala appartenuto a Egidio da Viterbo" Bibliothèque d'Humanisme et Renaissance LXVIII 2006 pg 535–543 now discusses Egidio's notation on the kabbalistic manuscript Montefiori 319.

My most sincere thanks are due to my two teachers, the late Dr Trevor Johnson (University of the West of England) and Dr Sebastian Brock (University of Oxford) who supervised the doctoral research upon which this book is based. I am also indebted to the learned remarks of E. J. Brill's anonymous reader and their helpful editorial staff. The recent news of the sudden death of Trevor Johnson robs me of my closest academic companion and the warmest of friends. His death will impoverish Early Modern History for decades to come.

FIRST BEGINNINGS: TESEO AMBROGIO AND THE MARONITE DELEGATION TO THE FIFTH LATERAN COUNCIL

Probably the first European scholar to acquire any significant knowledge of Syriac was Teseo Ambrogio (1469–1540). He belonged to the family of the Counts of Albonese in the Lomellina in Italy. Born in Padua, he trained as a lawyer, was ordained a priest, and entered the community of the Canons of St. John Lateran. Later in 1537 he became Provost of S. Pietro in Cieldoro in his native city.[1] Teseo's introduction to Syriac came at the time of the Fifth Lateran Council (1513–1515) to which the forty-first Maronite Patriarch, Sim'an ibn Dawud ibn Hassan, sent a delegation at the invitation of Pope Leo X.[2] The Fifth Lateran Council was thus the occasion for the introduction of Syriac into the West. We shall have cause to return to the Council, Leo X, and his learned cardinal Egidio da Viterbo in due time. First, however, we must consider the Maronite delegation and the Church they represented.

The Maronites

The union of the Maronite Christians in the Lebanon with Rome had been a long process that began with the arrival of the Franks in the Levant in 1099. The Crusaders had found eager supporters amongst the Maronites on the coast and ecclesiastical conformity developed from this amity.[3] The Maronites of the mountain fastnesses however seem

---

[1] Properly: Teseo Ambrogio degli Albonesi. Full biographical details in Levi della Vida's article in *Dizionario Biografico degli Italiani* (G. Ernest and S. Foa, Rome 1960) vol. II, pg 39–42.

[2] For the Maronite delegation see: N. H. Minnich "The Participants at the Fifth Lateran Council" Archivum Historiae Pontificae XII (1974) pg 157–206, especially pg 166–167.

[3] For what follows, see: the Lebanese scholar Kamal S. Salibi "The Maronites of Lebanon under Frankish and Mamluke Rule" Arabica IV (1957) pg 288–303; also his "The Maronite Church in the Middle Ages and its Union with Rome." Oriens Christianus XLII (1958) pg 92–104 with full bibliography to that date; Jean Gribomont "Documents sur les Origines de l'Eglise maronite" Parole de L'Orient V (1974) pg

rather to have resented Frankish rule and to have opposed union with Rome. Their opposition to the union championed by the Patriarchs made its realisation a long drawn out business. William of Tyre records the community's abjuration of its heresy—which he portrays explicitly as Monothelitism—and their submission to Almeric of Limoges, Latin Patriarch of Antioch (1142–c. 1196), around 1180.[4] That submission however was violently contested by the anti-union Maronites.[5]

Peter of Capua (1150–1209), Cardinal-priest of the Church of St. Marcellus, was sent by Innocent III with the Fourth Crusade (1202–1204) as his Legate to the East to correct (as Rome saw it) Maronite doctrine and practice and the Oath of Union was renewed to him. A subsequent bull of Innocent however had to reinstate Peter's corrections and shows that the matter of conformity remained controversial.[6]

The Maronites trace their origins to St Maron, a Syrian hermit of the late fourth, and early fifth centuries, and to St. John Maron, Patriarch of Antioch (685–707), under whose leadership the invading armies of Justinian II were routed in 687. In spite of William of Tyre's accusations of Monothelitism, their own traditions assert that they have always been orthodox.[7]

95–132; Charles Frazee "The Maronite Middle Ages" Eastern Churches Review X (1978) pg 88–100. For a good general introduction: Matti Moosa, *The Maronites in History* (Syracuse U.P., New York 1986). A helpful modern overview and with more recent bibliography is Jean Meyendorff and Aristeides Papadakis, *L'Orient chrétien et L'Essor de la Papauté* (Cerf, Paris 2001 (English ed. 1994) especially pg 138–152. More specifically: Harald Suermann, *Die Gründungsgeschichte der Maronitischen Kirche* (Harrassowitz, Wiesbaden 1998). The standard modern Maronite history is: Pierre Dib, *Histoire de l'Eglise maronite* (2 volumes, Beirut 1962). An account of Maronite historiography may be found in K. S. Salibi, *Maronite Historians of Mediaeval Lebanon* (Beirut 1959: 2nd ed. Naufal Group, Beirut/Paris 1991) which I have not seen. The Maronite historiographical tradition is criticised by C. de Clerq in *Dictionnaire de droit canonique* vol. 6. pg 811–829 and C. Karalevslij in *Dictionnaire d'histoire et de la géographie ecclésiastique* vol. 3 pg 563–703. The Maronite Research Institute (MARI) today produces invaluable bibliographic listings and the *Journal of Maronite Studies*.

[4] William of Tyre, *Historia Rerum in Partibus Transmarinis Gestarum* Lib XXII cap VIII (Migne P.L. 201 col. 856) *"ad unitatem Ecclesiae Catholicae reversi sunt, fidem orthodoxam suscipientes, parati Romanae Ecclesiae traditiones cum omni veneratione amplecti et observare"*.

[5] It is perhaps in this context of resistance that we should imagine the circumstances that led to the death of the 'mummies' uncovered in the exciting excavations of the Cave of 'Asi-l-Hadat. See: GERSL (Groupe d'Etudes et Recherches souterraines du Liban), *Momies du Liban. Rapport préliminaire sur la découverte archéologique de 'Asi-l-Hadat (XIII siècle)* (Edifra, Beirut 1994).

[6] T. Anaïssi, *Bullarum Maronitarum* (Max Bretschneider, Rome 1911) pg 2ff. This work is the source for all bulls concerning the Maronites that are cited below.

[7] William's accusations are challenged, *inter alios*, by R. W. Crawford "William of Tyre and the Maronites" Speculum XXX 1955 pg 222–8.

The *Fourth* Lateran Council, which began in Rome on 11 November 1215, was the first Oecumenical Council attended by a Maronite Patriarch. Upon his departure he was handed Innocent III's bull of 3 January 1216 reinstating Peter's corrections that we have already mentioned. This bull is our earliest document in the history of the Maronites' relationship with Rome.

Unanimous acceptance of the Union was not achieved while the Franks remained in Syria. Under Mamluk rule and no longer under the supervision of the Latin Church of Syria, the Maronites were suspected in Rome of having relapsed. Rome's missionary activity in the East was renewed by the Franciscans who took up the work of their brothers who had been driven from Beirut when the Latin Kingdom had fallen to the Mamluks in 1291. They returned in 1345 but their efforts were not to bear significant fruit until the Council of Florence in 1439 when the Maronite Church was recognised as having re-accepted Union and the Patriarch John (1404–1445) received the staff from Pope Eugenius IV.[8] Thereafter the Maronites remained loyal to Rome and together with the Franciscans attempted to reconcile their non-uniate brothers, a task which was substantially completed by the beginning of the sixteenth century.

In 1475 Sixtus IV (1471–1484) appointed the Franciscan Vicar-General, Brother Pietro di Napoli, as his commissioner to the Maronites, and subsequent Vicars-General held the office. Thus in 1515 Leo X was able to respond positively to the delegation from the Patriarch Sim'an which came to the eleventh session of the Fifth Lateran Council and

---

[8] Joseph Gill, *The Council of Florence* (CUP, Cambridge 1959) pg 335ff (with a discussion of Maronites in Cyprus). Nicholas V mentions this reunion in his bull of 1447 sent to the Maronite Patriarch Jacob of Hadath (1445–1458). Also Gill *in loc.* for the Union of the Syrians of Mesopotamia (Jacobites) with the Latin Church celebrated in the Lateran 30 September 1444 with 'Abdallah Archbishop of Edessa sent by Patriarch Ignatius, probably as a result of Franciscan activity. The protocols for the last part of the Council are lost, and we are dependant upon the bull *Multa et Admirabilia* of 30 September 1444 for an account of a long discussion with Cardinals and theologians, after which the Archbishop renounced his errors in respect of the Procession of the Holy Spirit, the two natures of Christ, the two wills in Christ and submitted to the Roman Church. Documents were put into Arabic for the Patriarch. For subsequent discussions over union with the Jacobites, see below on Moses of Mardin and the ex-Patriarch Na'matallah. G. Alberigo has edited a collection of modern reflections upon the work of the Council: G. Alberigo, *Christian Unity, The Council of Ferrara-Florence 1438/39–1989* (Leuven UP, Louvain 1991). Similarly: Jean Meyendorff and Aristeides Papadakis, *op. cit.*, pg 455–490.

with which we began our account.[9] The Pope confirmed the Patriarch in his office, but nevertheless took the opportunity to exhort him to reform certain practices in his church.[10]

The Delegation

Teseo Ambrogio names the Maronite delegates as *"Joseph a priest, Moses a monk and deacon and Elias a sub-deacon"*.[11] The priest Joseph requested permission to celebrate Mass in a Roman church after the Syriac ritual and in Syriac.[12] Teseo was commissioned by the Cardinal Santa Croce, Bernadino Caravajal, to instruct Joseph in Latin, to inquire into his orthodoxy, and to examine his liturgy. Teseo was an able linguist and had early been competent in Greek, but knew no Syriac: work on the liturgy was effected with the assistance of learned Jews who knew Arabic, including most probably his teacher Joseph ben Samuel Zarfati.

In 1906 Mercati drew attention to a codex (Estiensis α. R.7.20) amongst the Estense Greek codices in Modena that contains the Liturgy of St. John Chrystostom and a Latin version thereof, and then announces a translation of the Mass from Syriac by Teseo: *"Ritus missae Caldeorum* [sic] *Maronitarum ab Ambrosio Comite. V.I. doctore Canonico Congregationis Laterensis ad verbum servata de industria verborum puritate fideliter translati"*.[13] There follows a Syriac alphabet, a Syriac liturgy set out in

---

[9] For correspondence between Leo X and the Patriarch Anaissi, *op. cit.*, pg 25–35.

[10] The bull dated 1 August 1515 is found in Anaissi, *op. cit.*, pg 32–5.

[11] Teseo's own account is found in his *Introductio* f.14 whence the quotations in the text and notes here. Bibliographic material in Giorgio Levi della Vita, *Ricerche sulla Formazione del più Antico Fondo dei Manoscritti Orientali della Biblioteca Vaticana* (BAV, Vatican City 1939) (Hereafter cited as *Ricerche*) pg 133–134.

[12] Teseo writes: *"quorum sacerdos, cum divinam lyturgiam (quam Missam hebraico nomine Appelamus) celebrare, sacraque Deo offerre munera intenderet…"* Of interest is the Hebrew etymology of *'Missa'*, not least because it is also found in Postel *de Originibus* (Paris 1538 without pagination) where Postel offers: *"Voces Latinis Gallis Hebraeis et quandoque Graecis communes, ut se promiscue offerunt."* Thus: עלמה *alma quo titulo ob insignem integritatem beatam virginem donamus;* ספרה *siffra—chiffre; and* מסה *missa oblatio non a mittendo ut vulgo dicunt"*. Also, Eberhard Nestle "Aus einem sprachwissenschaftlichen Werk von 1539" Monatschrift der Deutschen Morgenlandischer Gesellschaft (Wiesbaden) LVIII (1904) pg 601–616 pg 61. For the obscure term of office *'Acurius'* used of Joseph, see: *Ricerche* pg 133 note 2.

[13] G. Mercati "Ambrogio Teseo primo traduttore e raccoglitore di liturgie orientali" Rassenga Gregoriana V (1906) pg 551–557. Mercati has useful annotations upon Teseo's own account in his *Introductio* f. 14, pg 553–555.

columns, an Ethiopic liturgy and an Armenian liturgy of St. Basil.[14] This is undoubtedly Teseo's translation text and the completion of his work at the end of 1516 assured the orthodoxy of the liturgy. The text was instrumental in enabling the Pontiff, Leo X, to give permission for its use, thereby clearly signalling that he recognised the ancient Oriental rites, a point of great consequence for subsequent Oriental scholarship in Rome as we shall see.[15] Mercati also stressed that the collection of these varied Eastern texts at this time (the copyist dated his subscription 23 August 1517) is itself significant in placing Teseo—most probably himself the collector of these items—at the very beginnings of comparative Oriental and liturgical studies in Rome.[16]

Another member of the delegation, the monk and sub-deacon Elias—twenty years old when he began his two years of study in the Roman house of the Lateran Canons in S. Maria della Pace by the Piazza Navona—was to make a considerable contribution to the beginning of Syriac studies in the West by being the first to teach the language to Europeans.[17]

Some Manuscripts

The first two Syriac manuscripts to enter the Vatican Library came from Elias's hand.[18] The first of these is an octavo parchment codex,

---

[14] See A. Raes, *Anaphorae Syriacae* (Pont. Inst. Or. Stud, Rome 1939) Vol. 1, fasc. I, pg xxviii "Anaphora Ioannis evangelistae". For a general introduction to the Eastern Rites, see Cardinal E. Tisserant's article in *Catholic Encyclopedia* s.v. Teseo's interest in Ethiopic and Armenian will be discussed shortly. The copy of the Armenian liturgy was made 24 October 1519 by David, Armenian Catholic bishop of Cyprus, though it is not known why he was in Rome. He is, however, a likely source of Teseo's Armenian books.

[15] Teseo writes: "*Dataque tum fuit Chaldaeis istis Syris libera in Urbe licentia, libertasque sacra celebrandi*". Nonetheless this work had evidently been forgotten in 1578 when Santoro had a new translation of the Eastern Rite made.

[16] Teseo refers to his collection of Oriental books in f. 15v: "*librorum Chaldaeorum, Syrorum, Armeniorum, Hebraeorum, Graecorum variumque aliarum linguarum gratam suppillectilem, quam magno mihi precio comparatam ex urbe Roma in patriam mecum adduxeram*". As we shall see the poor man lost all these in the sack of Pavia in 1527. Mercati pg 557 further conjectures that Teseo may also have been the owner of the particular codex in question as well as its compiler.

[17] Teseo f. 78: "*[Elias] mihi postmodum in litteris latinis erudiendus in canonica nostra Pacis Romae per biennium Pontificis iussu traditus*". Widmanstetter mentions in the Preface to the *editio princeps* that Elias taught '*litteras syriacas*' to Teseo.

[18] Both sir. 9 and sir. 15 are described in della Vida, *Ricerche* pg 133–9. J. S. Assemani, *Bibl. Apost. Vat. Codicum Manuscriptum Catalogus* (Rome 1758) describes sir. 9 on pg 20–23 and sir. 15 on pg 49ff.

a Psalter (sir. 9) copied in December of 1518 in the subscription to which are mentioned Leo X, Teseo Ambrogio, and also Alberto Pio da Carpi.[19] Count Alberto Pio da Carpi was a humanist bibliophile who took considerable interest in oriental sacred texts and their translation.[20] He has left a very interesting Arabic version of Paul's Letters copied in 1521 by Leo Africanus (who we shall see was Egidio da Viterbo's Arabic master).[21] Moreover Elias collaborated on the subscription to frame the magrebian Arabic in a distinctly Syriac ornamentation.[22] Regrettably we cannot know what Alberto's motives were in collecting New Testament material in both Syriac and Arabic. Levi della Vida made the suggestion that he may have wanted to produce a Polyglot, and the nature of the material collected gives this an immediate plausibility.[23] Agostino Giustiniani had produced his Polyglot Psalter in Genoa in 1516[24] and Potken's Tetraplar Psalter was published in Cologne in 1518.[25] There was also the great work of Cardinal Ximenes, the Complutensian Polyglot that was published in 1520, to act as a stimulus. The matter must remain somewhat conjectural, but it does seem likely that the impulse to produce a Polyglot Bible was present at the very beginning of European Syriac studies.

The second of Elias's manuscripts is Vatican sir. 15, a parchment codex of 180 folios, containing the Four Gospels. It once belonged to Master of Ceremonies Biagio Baroni Martellini da Cesena and contains

---

[19] The ms is attractive and decorated with characteristic red, blue and yellow trellises, though the decoration is not entirely finished. It is vocalised. A Latin rubric occurs at the end of each Psalm and a Latin number at the beginning of each, probably where the scribe left a gap. There are however no real gaps for Latin insertions after pg 72, though there are 174 pages. There is Arabic at the end. The final dedications appear in both Latin and Syriac though there are some gaps in the Latin and ruled but unused sheets at the end. The manuscript was written in Santa Maria della Pace. The bi-lingual nature of the manuscript, though not consistently pursued, is striking. Its frequent Latin intrusions, particularly in isolating and identifying the earlier Psalms, would be helpful for any European who may have wished to read it.

[20] See *Ricerche* pg 103, 134–5. We shall make consistent use of the dedicatory material in mss and printed books. For a general discussion of the importance of dedication in the sixteenth century: L. Voet, *The Golden Compasses* (P. Vangendt, Amsterdam 1972) Vol. 2, pg 283–290.

[21] *Ibid.*, pg 104–6. Widmanstetter *editio princeps* f. 12r.

[22] *Ibid.*, pg 107 also illustration on Tavola 6.

[23] *Ibid.*

[24] On this work which contained Hebrew, Greek, Arabic, Chaldaean (ie the Targum), three Latin versions and scholia, see below.

[25] The work comprised Hebrew, Greek, Latin, and Chaldaean. It is discussed below as is the curious use of the term Chaldaean in this work to refer to Ethiopic.

a letter from Franciscus Muscantius giving it to Pope Gregory XIII at the beginning of his Pontificate. It had been he says: "carefully kept for several years amongst my grandfather's books". The manuscript carries the date 9 December 1519. It is decorated on f. 175 & 176 by three crosses very similar to those that appear in the printed *editio princeps* of the Syriac New Testament of 1555. The manuscript contains Latin glosses and at the end of Matthew one reads *"Explicit evangelus Matei Apostoli qui locutus est et predicavit habrayce in phlestini"* where 'habrayce' renders the preceding Syriac 'BR´YT. The view that Matthew was written in Hebrew or some form of Aramaic, including Syriac, we shall find to be both ancient and widespread in the West.[26] It is interesting however to see the claim made in a Syriac manuscript intended for European consumption.[27] The Gospels are divided in the codex into 251 lections according to the rite of the Maronite Church of Antioch: *"iuxta ritum Ecclesiae Antiochenae Maronitarum"*. Such lectionary divisions became a matter of great interest for Catholic scholars and also of inter-confessional polemic, and it is important to notice that they were marked for their attention in Latin glosses to the very first Syriac Gospels they encountered. This Gospel book also has a certain interest in that we know that Masius consulted it when collecting the material that would eventually end up in the Syriac Dictionary he published in the Antwerp Polyglot Bible, the *Syrorum Peculium*.

In 1968 S. Grill described another Psalter of Elias, now in Innsbruck.[28] It was copied on 11 February 1517 and is thus the first piece of work we have from Elias. In addition to the Psalter, one also finds in the manuscript an Ave, a Magnificat, an Angelic Hymn of Praise, the Paternoster, the Eight Beatitudes, a Hymn of Praise, the Hymn of the Three Children, a Symbolum Niceanum and the concluding prayer of the scribe. The colophon, however, is of particular importance, though its significance was only subsequently noticed by Jean Gribomont who succeeded in deciphering the proper names.[29] Translated it runs: "Written in the City of Rome for our reverend and holy Father of the Monks Egidio (GDY´) of Viterbo (BYTRBY´) in the region of Rome

---

[26] The view is found initially in Eusebius, Ecclesiastical History 3.39.16.

[27] The view is also expressed in Vindob. Syr. 1, the Syriac Gospels in Vienna copied by Moses of Mardin in 1554 for the Emperor Ferdinand I.

[28] S. Grill "Eine unbekannte syrische Handschrift in Innsbruck: Cod 401. Bibl. Univ." Oriens Christianus LII (1968) pg 151–155.

[29] Jean Gribomont "Gilles de Viterbe, le moine Elie, et l'influence de la littérature maronite sur la Rome érudite de 1515" Oriens Christianus LIV (1970) pg 125–9.

and belonging to the monks of Saint Augustine (KWSTYN)". Here in what was the first manuscript copied by Elias, we find a dedication to Egidio da Viterbo. Egidio's interest in Syriac was previously reported only in the Prologue to Widmanstetter's Syriac New Testament of 1555. We shall shortly be arguing for the central importance of this scholar and prince of the Church in determining the understanding of the significance of Syriac both for Teseo and subsequent scholars. Egidio played a major role at the Fifth Lateran Council, as we shall see. It is fitting that he should have received the dedication of the first Syriac manuscript copied in the West.

It may be helpful at this point to review all of Elias's manuscripts in chronological order. Six days after completing the manuscript for Egidio, Elias dedicated another Psalter like it (now Vat sir. 265) to Cardinal Bernadino Caravajal, whose hospitality the three Maronites had enjoyed and who had commissioned Teseo to undertake his first steps in Syriac.[30] Thereafter he produced sir. 9 (above) in 1518 and a fourth Psalter (now Modena α.U.2.6, Or.XIX) in 1525. Elias offered his first Gospel book dated 10 April 1518 to Alberto Pio da Carpi (Modena Estensis J.6.3.104, Or XXI) a few months before he was mentioned in the subscription to the Psalter sir. 9. This was followed by sir. 15 (above) and finally a Gospel book was offered again to Cardinal Caravajal (Paris syr. 17, Zotenberg 44). The dedications enable us to examine the connections of this small group of monks and Western scholars working under the powerful patronage of Leo X, Caravajal and Egidio da Viterbo. For the first time Rome had some Syriac books and some men with access to Syriac scribes who were learning to construe them. How they would understand the significance of the new language was to be very much influenced by Egidio da Viterbo.

Teseo Ambrogio and the first Syriac printing

After the Council Teseo returned to Pavia to prepare a printed edition of the Psalter for which he had obtained a manuscript *"ex Syria advectum"* together with some other comparative material he had collected.[31] For

---

[30] *Ricerche* pg 134 note 2.

[31] *Introductio* pg 15–16: *"Id animo ac mente concepi, ut, si quando (iuvante Deo) mihi facultas unquam data concessaque esset, Psalterium Chaldaicum ex Syria advectum in publicum ederam. Et cum relictis Romano tum penatibus in patriam tandem me contullissem, iamque animo diu conceptus desiderii igniculus in publicum erumperet, aeneis comparatis typis conflatisque ex convenienti metallo*

these he had produced, we know not how, copper matrices and cast type. When we consider the difficulties subsequent editors experienced in obtaining serviceable type, Teseo's initial efforts and his success are quite remarkable. Regrettably we know nothing about them. When in just a moment we encounter his type in his *Introductio*, we shall see that it has no scribal felicity like that which betrays Moses of Mardin's collaboration in the production of the type of Widmanstetter's *editio princeps* of the Syriac New Testament of 1555. One has, I think, to conclude that Teseo drew and cut the shapes himself. Nevertheless his experience was transmitted to Postel and thence to all subsequent printers who thus benefited from this first heroic attempt.

Just as the Psalter was ready to be printed, disaster struck. In 1527, while Teseo was visiting the Chapter of his Order in Ravenna, the French army of François I took Pavia by storm and all Teseo's books and printing materials were lost in the sack.[32] Quite remarkably, seven years later in Ferrara, Teseo came across his copy of the Psalter in a sausage-maker's shop—torn, disfigured, but complete![33] At his death in 1540, Teseo had still not published his Psalter and the manuscript copy so miraculously refound was lost again. The first printing of the Syriac Psalter was thus that of Erpenius at Leiden in 1625.[34]

After the sack of Pavia, Teseo retired to a monastery in Reggio (in Modena). In the autumn of 1529 the Emperor Charles V passed through the city on his way from Genoa to Bologna for his coronation by Clement VII. In his train was the young Johann Albrecht Widmanstetter and his chance meeting with Teseo was to be heavy with consequences for Syriac Studies and the history of New Testament printed editions in Syriac. Widmanstetter was given a Syriac Gospel book by Teseo and apparently felt entrusted by the older man with the responsibility of

---

literum formulis & adiecta pene manu post maximos infinitosque propemodum sumptus ad opus perficiendum", and *ibid "ad linguae illius multarumque aliarum linguarum lectionem notitionem: mutuamque inter se conformationem spectantia"* which sounds very much like the material later found in his *Introductio*.

[32] In *Introductio* f.118 Teseo in treating עמר in Exodus 16 quotes *"Chaldaica vero interpretatio quae Maronitae et Syri utuntur"*. This may possibly indicate a book that had survived the sack.

[33] *"Post septem vero annos (divina ut reor voluntate ita disponente) in manibus publici cuisdam Fartoris reperto iam semilacerto Psalterii libello quem cum caeteris in cineres volcano passim debacchante iam dudum fuisse existimaveram"*.

[34] On Thomas Erpenius (1584–1624) ed. F. Nave, *Philologia Arabica* (MPM/PK, Antwerp 1986) pg 139–169. For this Psalter: Rijk Smitskamp, *Philologia Orientalis* (E. J. Brill, Leiden 1992) pg 69–70 #80.

carrying on his lonely attempts to print Syriac, a commission he was eventually to discharge in the *editio princeps* of the Syriac New Testament of 1555. We shall return subsequently to Widmanstetter's account of this crucial meeting.

Thereafter Teseo moved to the Ferrara of Ercole II where he set about renewing his material and type. He began the printing of his *Introductio* in July 1537 but was moved back to Pavia by his Order in 1538. Thus his book was finally published there on 1 March 1539.

The Introductio ad Chaldaicam linguam

Teseo's rare and fascinating book deserves extensive consideration.[35] Fortunately an ample description has been given by Nestle, so we shall concentrate on those aspects that serve to characterise the nascent Orientalism the book presents.[36]

Teseo dedicated his book to his uncle Afranius who had invented a musical instrument called the *'phagotum'* (a sort of advanced bagpipe,

---

[35] *Introductio in Chaldaicam linguam, Syriacam, atque Armenicam, et decem alias linuas. Characterum differentium Alphabeta, circiter quadraginta, et eorundem invicem conformatio, Mystica et Cabalistica quamplurima scitu digna. Et descriptio ac simulachrum Phagoti Afranii. Theseo Ambrosio ex Comitibus Albonesii I.V. Doct. Papień. Canonico Regulari Lateranensi, ac Sancti Petri in Coelo Aureo Papiae Praeposito, Authore MDXXXIX. Linguarum vero, & Alphabetorum nomina sequens pagella demonstrabit. Pavia excudebat J. M. Simoneta, sumptibus & typis auctoris libri.* At end: *Excudebat Papiae. Joan. Maria Simoneta Cremoneň In Canonica Sancti Petri in Coelo Aureo. Sumptibus et Typis Autoris libri. Anno a Virginis Partu 1539 Kal' Martii.* Discussion in Rijk Smitskamp, *Philologia Orientalis III* (E. J. Brill, Leiden 1992) pg 240–1. I have made use of the copy in the Bodleian. Smitskamp's *Catalogue 632* May 2001 #12 offered a copy for 13, 455 euros. Virgil Strohmeyer "The Armenian Manuscripts in the Personal Library of Teseo Ambrogio degli Albonesi" in ed. H. Palandjian, A. Tonoyan *et al., Festschrift Prof. Dr. Dora Sakayan zum 65 Geburtstag* (Diocese of the Armenian Church of Canada, Montreal 1996) pg 145–158, at pg 150 indicates the existence of two separate printings on the basis of a copy in the Matenadaran in Yerevan. The same authors in "A Prolegomenon to the study of the Armenian material in Teseo Ambrogio's Alphabetical Compendium" in ed. J. J. Wertenberg, *New Approaches to Armenian Language and Literature* (Rodopi, Amsterdam & Atlanta 1995) pg 157–172 consider the help Teseo might give to a reconstruction of the Armenian dialect of Tabriz in the sixteenth century.

[36] Eberhard Nestle "Aus einem sprachwissenschaftlichen Werk von 1539" Zeitschrift der Deutschen Morgenländischer Gesellschaft (Wiesbaden) LVIII (1904) pg 601–616 with generous quotations. See also: Werner Strothmann, *Die Anfänge der syrischen Studien in Europa* (Harrassowitz, Wiesbaden 1971) pg 3–4. The *Introductio* is also curious in being a book set from dictation. Philip Gaskell, *A New Introduction to Bibliography* (OUP, Oxford 1972) pg 49 knows only one similar case in the 1540s in the Basle printing house of Michael Isengrinius who specialised in learned printing. Teseo's account f. 140–141 where he describes himself reading to the compositor and talking to his friends is thus of considerable interest.

bellows-blown with two chanters and no drone).[37] Teseo describes the instrument in depth (f. 336–338) and gives two fine woodcuts of it (f. 178–9). The connection between his uncle's invention and his own work is announced immediately in the introduction. Teseo is interested in Harmony: the congruence between the visible world and the rational world; between the microcosm and the macrocosm; between even the theoretical and the useful. Teseo believes his own work on the harmonisation of letters in different scripts is akin to that of Pythagoras in Music.[38] Thus he can link the phagotum to his own work—both are concerned with Harmony (f. 2b): *"Tu novi & non amplius visi, singularis Musicae facultatis Organi, quod Phagotum vocas, de quo plura alibi dicentur. Et ego praesentis novae et utilis consonantiae, ac variarum linguarum characterum differentium harmoniae"*.

The work offered the first detailed Western account of Syriac and Armenian and substantially contributed to the beginnings of the study of Ethiopic (called 'Indian') and Coptic (called 'Jacobite'). Teseo relates (f. 13b–14a) an important discussion between Potken and himself over the designation of Ethiopic which Potken called 'Chaldaean' and we are also indebted to Teseo for the dating of an important Arabic edition of the Koran.[39] It is however equally important that we notice Teseo's interest in the kabbalistic and mystical properties of the characters. As he says: *"these letters also conceal the Mysteries of Christian Truth"*.

The book opens with the Syriac alphabet in two sizes.[40] Immediately a mystical interest is apparent. In speaking of the ligatures Teseo makes reference (f. 9b) to the ligatures of the letter Tau: "about whose

---

[37] On the *phagotum* see the article by Francis W. Galpin and Guy Oldham in ed. Stanley Sadie, *The New Grove Dictionary of Music and Musicians* (Macmillan, London 1986) Vol. XIV pg 616–17; F. W. Galpin "The Romance of the Phagotum" Proceedings of the Musical Association LXVII (1941–1942) pg 57–72; W. A. Cocks "The Phagotum: an attempt at reconstruction" The Galpin Society Journal vol. XII (1959) pg 57–9 (with Plate III). We know of the use of the instrument by Afranius on two occasions: at a banquet given by Ippolito II d'Este, Archbishop of Milan (and later Cardinal of Ferrara) at Belfiore on Saturday 20 May 1529; and at a domestic meal given by Alphonso d'Este, Duke of Ferrara in Mantua 21 November 1532. See: H. M. Brown "A Cook's Tour of Ferrara in 1529" Rivista Italiana da Musicologia vol. X (1975) pg 216–41, especially the summaries of the music performed at the banquets translated in Appendices I & II (pg 237–9, 240–1). Teseo tells that his uncle played 'divine songs and hymns' rather than 'vain and amatory' songs.

[38] f. 2b; f. 28b; f. 177.

[39] A. Nuovo "Il Corano arabo ritrovato" La Bibliofilia LXXXIX (1987) pg 237–271.

[40] Both are Western. Teseo nowhere appears to have seen Nestorian characters.

mystical sense St Paul spoke at length in a letter to Paula", and later:
"for in these two ways of joining letters mysteries lie hidden" Thereafter he teaches the order of the letters (f.10, 10b) by attaching each to
a Syriac name of God from the liturgy, a pious practice he probably
learned from Joseph or Elias and which Widmanstetter subsequently
copied in his *Syriacae linguae…prima elementa* of 1556.[41] Syriac vowels are
considered together with those of Samaritan, Hebrew, Arabic (Teseo
knows Giustiniani's Psalter), and Punic, though those of more obscure
languages—"*vocales vero Aegypticas, Babylonicas…Magicas*"—are left for a
subsequent occasion. Coptic and Ethiopic vowels are then treated. After
a discussion of Potken's misnaming of Ethiopic as Chaldaean, Teseo
remarks that in fact Armenian (given its location) has a better case for
being given that misnomer—"*quandoquidem Chaldia regio quaedam Armeniae
est*"—and then turns his attention to Armenian (f. 16).

It is at this point that Teseo lets us know that he had been pursuing
his Armenian studies with an Armenian in Venice alongside Guillaume
Postel, and that is how he had learned the names of the 30 letters of
the Armenian alphabet.[42] Postel had at this time just returned from his
first voyage to the East in 1536 in the company of Jean de la Forêt.
Whilst in Venice in 1537, Postel had developed his friendship with the
printer Bomberg in whose home he probably met Jewish scholar Elias
Levita. Postel left Venice on 9 August 1537. This account of Postel and
Teseo sharing their researches is precious. Postel was to be behind every
Catholic printed edition of the Syriac New Testament we shall consider.
He also was the channel by which Teseo's printing experience was to
be passed down, even to Granjon and the great Plantin. Although, as
we shall see, their friendship soured a bit after 1537, this short period
of collaboration between Teseo and Postel marks an important node
in the network of early Syriac scholars.

Not surprisingly Teseo's discussion of Armenian (f. 16) again betrays
his mystical interests. Armenian, he tells us (f. 18b, 19), often transposes
(so to speak) 'au' and 'o', just as Christ is both Alpha and Omega.[43]

---

[41] Thus: "*a. aloho. deus; b. baruio. creator; g. gaboro. potens; etc*" (f. 10–10b).
[42] f. 17b–18. For the names of the Armenian letters mentioned here: R. H. Kévorkian, *Catalogue des 'Incunables' arméniens (1511/1695) ou Chronique de L'Imprimerie arménienne.*
(Craimer, Geneva 1986) pg 172. Postel's crude Armenian wood-cuts in the *Duodecim
Linguarum* of 1538 are discussed on pg 171.
[43] "*Et quam sane optime etiam hoc in mysticum sensum flectitur. Ego enim sum inquit alpha &
O. Ego sum ayp, & aypun, principium scilicet et finis. nam in Ⱎ ayp prima alphabeti Armenici litera
quae a est, tria in unum coeunt pater, scilicet, filius et spiritus sanctus, tres unum sunt & o, aypyn,*

Furthermore the shape of the first Armenian letter (Ⴈ) recalls the Holy Trinity. The vowel interchange au-o however is not confined to Armenian, but has passed from Armenian into Latin where *"pro plostrum, plaustrum; pro plodere, plaudere"*. This is because the interchange was a linguistic characteristic of Noah, who, of course, landed in Armenia. When Noah migrated to Italy he took this curious phonetic trait with him. These remarks introduce us to a mythical linguistic history that we shall soon encounter in both Egidio da Viterbo, and Postel, as well as more generally. It is within such a framework that the linguistic and mystical significance of Syriac was understood.

Teseo then discusses the Syriac Consonants (f. 21) whose names often have an 'o' where Hebrew has an 'a'. (*'Olaph' pro 'Aleph', 'Dolad' pro 'Daleth'* etc.) The 'o' we learn is the more primitive sound—the name of the first man was *'Odom'*—which remained with the Chaldaeans after Babel when the Hebrews changed to 'a', though this does not otherwise prejudice the antiquity of Hebrew (f. 22, 22b). The section is also of interest because it gives evidence of Teseo's initial encounters with Samaritan.[44] There can be little doubt he had discussed this with Postel,

---

trigesima nomina litera alphabetum claudens, nec ad quadragenarium numerum transire permittens, orbis est in se revolutus atque reflexus: principio et fine careens, & quam pulchre perpetuam Trinitatis inextricabilem unionem insinuate, vestigando vestigent atque cum delectione odorentur in quibus mystica sensa placent & imitentur illum qui a Iudaeis quinquies quadragenas una minus accepit (Paul: "five times received I forty stripes save one": 2 Cor 11. 24). *Et numerationem istam minime negligat"*. The assumption of an affinity between Armenian and the Semitic languages may strike us as odd but it was not unknown in the sixteenth century. Konrad Gessner *Mithridates* (10 v) illustrates a supposed affinity between Armenian and Ethiopic ed. Manfred Peters, *Konrad Gessner Mithridates* (Scientia Verlag, Darmstadt 1974) pg 19. Essential now is: Virgil Strohmeyer "The Armenian Manuscripts in the Personal Library of Teseo Ambrogio degli Albonesi" in ed H. Palandjian, A. Tonoyan et al., *Festschrift Prof. Dr. Dora Sakayan zum 65 Geburtstag* (Diocese of the Armenian Church of Canada, Montreal 1996) pg 145–158. I am indebted to Rijk Smitskamp for this reference. Strohmeyer has identified Teseo's use of Codex 178 Miscellanea armena; Codex 179 Miscellanea armena; Codex 346 Diurninum armeniacum; Codex 347 Breviarium armeniacum in the collection of the University of Pavia. All bear Teseo's glosses and annotations. Teseo's font comes from the hand of Codex 347 as do most of his Armenian texts in the *Introductio*. See also V. B. Strohmeyer, *The Importance of Teseo Ambrogio degli Albonesi's Selected Armenian Materials for the development of the Renaissance's Perennial Philosophy and an Armenological Philosophical Tradition* (Yerevan 1998). There is now a useful summary of Armenian biblical matters in: Vrej Nersessian, *The Bible in the Armenian Tradition* (British Library, London 2001).

[44] *"...et anno praeterito in aere conflatam Servatoris nostri imaginem, cum literis Samaritanis, ostendit mihi Matrona illa sanctissimae credita vitae cuius nomen (ne illam castissimasque eius aures offendam) silentio involuam, cum Ferrariam pertransiret, navique Venetias profectura per Paduam veheret, in cuius altera numismatis, parte literae conflatae seu percussae videbantur, quarum sensus talis erat: Messias rex venit in pace, Deus homo factus est vel incarnatus est."* For such 'Jesusmünze'

who had at this point access to a Samaritan grammar in manuscript and some Second Temple coins whose paleo-Hebrew script he took to be Samaritan. We shall discuss Postel's Samaritan studies later.

The chapter *'De literis radicalibus & servilibus'* (f. 89–131) is the longest in the book and is replete with the mystical and kabbalistic observation that the title of the book promises. Nestle gives ample quotations about the Hebrew letter *'He'* (f. 96); *'Vau'* (f. 98); and *'Zayin'* (f. 98b) to enable those unable conveniently to read the book itself to be convinced of Teseo's essentially mystical and kabbalistic approach to both alphabets and languages.[45] Teseo's repertoire includes: Pythagorean anticipations (f. 96, 123b); speculations upon divine names (f. 110b); the numerical values of letters combined with Sephirotic emanations and messianic anticipations (f. 115ff, 127); mystical phonology;[46] and cosmological myth.[47]

Whilst all this is not particularly uncommon, it is of importance that we should observe that the essential harmony and kinship between alphabets enables the Syriac script as well as the Hebrew to carry mystical meanings, and indeed, on occasions, the Syriac script may have unique felicities of its own. Thus whilst observing that the Hebrew He (ה) is made up from Daleth (ד) and Yod (י), Teseo notes that analogously the Syriac He is made up from *"Vau et Dolad"*. Of the Hebrew Vav (ו) he remarks (f. 98) that it is the sixth letter of the alphabet, a sacred number and associated with Creation. He draws attention to the integrity of its form which makes it suitable to be 'a pillar of the world'.[48] The Syriac Vaw, however, is shaped like a circle, lacking either beginning or end, which gives it a particular propriety here.[49] Teseo thus provides evidence of the mystical possibilities of the Syriac script. In the case of

---

cf. Nestle *op. cit.*, pg 616. J. G. Fraser "Guillaume Postel and Samaritan Studies" in ed. M. L. Kuntz, *Postello, Venezia e il suo Mondo a cura di Marion Leathers Kuntz* (Olschki, Florence 1988) pg 99–117 gives a text: משיח מלך בא בשלום ואך מאדם עשוי חי.

[45] *Op. cit.*, pg 606–613.

[46] f. 96b For Aspirates: *"solo spiritu pronuncie[n]tur"* are given special significance by those *"qui cabalistica scripserunt"* (e.g. *Sephir Yesirah*). Also, f. 99b.

[47] On Yod; f. 104.

[48] *"Et praeter id sexta est alphabeti litera, sextam quoque sacram numerationem repraesentat. Quanti in sacris habita sit, qui cognoscere cupit, legat eos qui sex diebus mundum conditum fuisse asseverunt, et illius numeri causas scrutantur. Litera praeterea ista Hebraeorum quia nihil secum exterius admittit, neque a se ipsa prominent, sed in sese constans atque sufficiens, simplex et se ipsa contenta nullius indigne sed absoluta integra atque perfecta mundi columna nominata est".*

[49] *"Quod multo magis in Chaldaico Vau conspici potest cum orbis sit in se revolutus atque (ut de aipium Armenico dictum fuit) reflexus, principio et fine carens. Iccirco etiam perfectorum primis evasit numerus".*

the letter Teth, Persius, Martial and Vergil provide Latin evidence for the letter's special significance. But here again the construction of the Syriac letter Teth from *"Olaph"* and *"Hheth"*, or even from *"Zzode et Vau"* (numerically this would represent 1+8 or 90+6 respectively) has mystical import. The numerical value of Mem gives a similar significance to the letter in either language (f. 113), while the form of both the Hebrew and Chaldaean Caph is significant.[50]

Teseo's comments help us to identify an important source of his speculations. In discussing the composition of the letter Mem, he refers to Egidio da Viterbo's *de Hebraicis Elementis*.[51] He does so again when discussing the letter Samech, a symbol of the Millennium.[52] And again, when discussing the letter Ayin.[53] We have seen the manuscript evidence for Egidio's patronage of the very beginnings of Syriac Studies: here is further clear evidence of his influence upon the interpretation of Syriac which we shall draw in clearer lines when we come to look at his own work. After f. 184 there follow several passages in Armenian and Syriac with Latin transcription and translation.[54]

The *Peroratio et Operis Conclusio* (f. 192b) relates how on 14 July 1537 (though he must have the date wrong),[55] while working on his book, Teseo was visited by a bookseller who brought Teseo a letter and a copy of Postel's *Linguarum Duodecim* which came out in March 1538. Teseo suffered the disagreeable realisation that he had been pre-empted in the publication of his work by the friend to whom he had given generous assistance, and who had sought from him his type.[56] Teseo

---

[50] f. 106b The Hebrew ב represents the moon and the feminine *"Quae itidem mutato ordine, inverses nimirum cornibus, Chaldaeae Hebraeaeque oppositis constituta masculum, scilicet Solem, in sacris ac mysticis sensibus designare valet."*

[51] f. 113 Mem is made from ו and כ, *"sed alio atque alio modo...et istorum elementorum conformem conflatum difformes vero nutus latissime nostris temporibus Egidius Cardinalis in libello de Hebraicis elementis tractavit".*

[52] *"ut ait Egidius".*

[53] Of Ayin he writes: *"De hac litera Hebraica praeter ea quae habent in libro qui Sepher thenuoth i.e. liber figarum inscribitur, Egidius Cardinalis plurima ac scitu digna retulit".*

[54] A Paternoster and Salutio Angelica (used again by Widmanstetter in *Syriacae linguae...prima elementa*); Matthew 22 (The Parable of the Marriage Feast); an Oratio ad Virginem Mariam; a Magnificat; John 1; Luke 2; and an Apostolic Creed. The Syriac text is that of the Peshitta.

[55] *Linguarum Duodecim* was published in March 1538. Similarly August 1538 is the date of Postel's letter to Teseo asking for Arabic characters for his *Grammatica Arabica*. On this see François Secret "Theseus Ambrosius et Postellus 'Ambolateus Doctor Medicinae'" Bibliothèque d'Humanisme et Renaissance XXIII (1961) pg 130–132, pg 131 n2.

[56] Particularly the Arabic for his *Grammatica Arabica*. f. 202. See: J. Balagna, *L'Imprimerie arabe en Occident (XVI, XVII, XVIII siècles)* (Maisonneuve & Larose, Paris 1984) pg 24–27.

likened Postel to John the Evangelist who had run to the Empty Tomb with Simon Peter and because he was younger had managed to reach the Tomb first and look in. Peter came behind. (One recalls, however, from John 20. 5–6 that John 'went not in' whereas Simon Peter did. I doubt Teseo had overlooked this.) Postel, says Teseo, had 'looked in' and seen Teseo's printed Armenian and Syriac and his press, yet though the older man had published his *Introductio* second, he had started first, had by implication 'entered', and had certainly communicated far more of what he had seen.[57] And to make the point quite clear to everyone Teseo then printed his correspondence with Postel and an appendix in which he displayed twenty-four different exotic and fantastic alphabets, with the suggestion of more to come.

Postel's response to the charges raised against him has been found in Postel's own copy of the *Introductio* that is now in the Bibliothèque nationale in Paris. Against the text of Teseo, he entered his handwritten responses in the margin.[58] In the dedication to Petrus Palmerius, Archbishop of Vienne, of the *Linguarum Duodecim*, Postel, who in 1538 had become one of François I's *Lecteurs royaux* in Greek, Arabic and Hebrew at the Collège de France, gave as his motive the glory of France.[59] Postel's haste had clearly hurt the old man. Nevertheless their co-operation remains central. Whatever Postel saw when he 'looked in'

Postel's Arabics in the *Linguarum duodecim* are wood-cuts. The Arabics in the *Grammatica Arabica* are quite different, though their origin is again unknown. They are moveable though without ligatures and were not apparently used again. It would appear that Postel sought from Teseo the Arabics that Alexander Paganini of Brescia would have inherited from his father and that had been used on the Koran of 1537–1538 (See: A. Nuovo *op. cit., supra* for this Koran). Teseo does not actually tell us whether he had purchased the punches and the matrices that Postel was after. However, if he had them he did not use them. The Arabics of the *Introductio* were hand-written in gaps left by the printer. The short passages of the Koran there offered are in Syriac characters (karšuni). Teseo did have a copy of the 1537–1538 Koran. Angela Nuovo "Il Corano arabo ritrovato" La Bibliofilia LXXXIX (1987) pg 237–271 has found the copy with his marks of possession.

[57] f. 193: "*Vidit excussas Chaldaicas, Armenicasq; formas meas. Vidit chalcographum meum mecum*". The passage suggests that Teseo provided considerable help to Postel.

[58] See: F. Secret "La Réponse de G. Postel a Teseo Ambrogio" Bibliothèque d'Humanisme et Renaissance XXVIII (1966) pg 698–699. The volume, Res. x. 701, is interesting because Postel's copy of the *Introductio* is bound with Widmanstetter's *Syriacae Linguae...prima elementa* of 1556 and belonged to Guy Lefèvre de la Boderie as a gift from the will of Barthomaeus Grivellus. It is interesting to know the copy of Teseo Guy read. Guy was to publish his own edition of the Widmanstetter without Widmanstetter's name on the title page.

[59] "*Tu enim aliquando mihi apud te dicebas opus esse istos varios characters edere in luce ut externis nationibus ostenderemus etiam Gallis sua non deesse ingenia*".

upon Teseo's press, what he learned he was to transmit to the producers of subsequent printed Syriac type who were guided by him.

Teseo was the first European to learn Syriac and produce an account of its language and script. He managed remarkably to contrive to print Syriac with moveable type, and shared his expertise with Postel who after his death, we shall see, made efforts to recover the type.[60] It was Teseo who gave to the young Widmanstetter the charge of printing a Syriac New Testament. His book was demonstrably known to Postel, and later to Guy Lefèvre de la Boderie. Widmanstetter refers to it in the introduction to the *editio princeps* (pg 163ff) and borrowed features for his own small Grammar. The reception of Teseo's book, unique and irreplaceable reading for those wishing to learn Syriac, ensured the diffusion of his mystical and kabbalistic approach to the language, an approach learned in large part from the Cardinal Egidio da Viterbo to whom we shall now turn.

---

[60] Teseo's Syriac type thus represents a considerable advance upon woodcuts. However where other Semitic or unusual scripts (Samaritan, Arabic, Coptic, Cyrillic, Ethiopic) are mentioned they are written in with a pen, and consequently throughout the book one may find blank spaces where the copy in hand has not been completed in this way. Teseo generally, as we have seen, copied Arabic by hand, but at f. 25b he has the Arabic text of Luke 3 in Syriac characters. This is in fact the earliest printed karšuni. The alphabets at the back of the book are printed in larger type apparently cast from letters cut in wood. In a tantalising sequel a letter of Postel to Masius from Venice 7 June 1555 (M. Lossen, *Briefe von Andreas Masius und seinen Freunde* (Gesellschaft für Rheinische Geschichtskunde, Leipzig 1886) pg 201, text in Chaufpié III pg 218) tells us that in April 1555 Postel travelled to Pavia to attempt to buy Teseo's Syriac type. We do not hear that he was successful and do not know what happened to the type.

CHAPTER TWO

FIRST BEGINNINGS:
EGIDIO DA VITERBO AND THE KABBALISTIC
CONTEXT OF SYRIAC STUDIES AT THE TIME
OF THE FIFTH LATERAN COUNCIL

We have mentioned Egidio da Viterbo (Giles of Viterbo, or Aegidius Viterbiensis).[1] This remarkable Cardinal and scholar was of great influence in the construction of the Orientalism within which the printed Syriac New Testaments were produced.

Egidio da Viterbo (1469–1532) was for twelve years (1506–1518) General of the Augustinian Order, and the superior whom Luther met on a visit to Rome in 1511. He was a distinguished humanist and classical scholar[2] in whose honour Giovanni Pontano composed his dialogue *Aegidius*.[3] He was the defender of Reuchlin and the protector of Elias Levita. His opening oration at the Fifth Lateran Council with its memorable epigram "Men should be changed by Religion, not Religion by men" is recalled as one of the last appeals for Church reform before the Lutheran Schism. As Bishop of Viterbo he was himself a committed reformer and Leo X made him a Cardinal in 1517 and Latin Patriarch of Constantinople in 1523. Nor was Egidio lacking

---

[1] On Egidio's historiographic fortunes: Francis X. Martin, "The Problem of Giles of Viterbo A historiographic survey". Augustiniana IX (1959) pg 357–379; X (1960) pg 43–60. A somewhat eulogistic biography is: Giuseppe Signorelli, *Il Card. Egidio da Viterbo, Augostiniano, Umanista, e Reformatore (1469–1532)* (Libreria Editrice Florentina, Florence 1929). A useful summary with bibliography is the article in *Dizionario Biografico degli Italiani* (G. Ernest and S. Foa, Rome 1993) vol XLII, pg 341–353. Essential for a characterisation of Egidio's thought is John W. O'Malley, *Giles of Viterbo on Church and Reform. A Study in Renaissance Thought* (E. J. Brill, Leiden 1968). Also: F. X. Martin, *Friar, Reformer and Renaissance Scholar. The Life and Work of Giles of Viterbo 1469–1532* (Augustinian Press, Rome 1992). (Father Martin's 1958 Cambridge doctoral thesis *'Egidio da Viterbo. A Study in Renaissance Reform History'*, provided a major stimulus to subsequent study of Egidio). Important conference papers are found in *Egidio da Viterbo O.S.A. e il suo tempo. Atti del V Convegna dell' Instituto Storico Augostiniano, Roma—Viterbo 20–23 ottobre 1982* (Analecta Augustiniana, Rome 1983). Other works are mentioned below at appropriate points.

[2] See: J. Whittaker, "Giles of Viterbo as Classical Scholar" in *Egidio da Viterbo e il suo tempo* pg 85–105.

[3] G. Pontano *Aegidius* in *Dialoghi* ed. C. Previtera (Sansoni, Florence 1943).

when it came to action: he gathered a force of two thousand men at
Isola in May 1527 to attempt to free Clement VII who was besieged
in Castel Sant' Angelo by the Imperial troops.

Our interest in this fascinating and many-sided churchman lies in his
Orientalism. That, however, we must approach in the context of Egidio's
notion of Concord; his ideas about History; and his eschatology. An
examination of his scriptural and more particularly his kabbalistic studies—seen in the context of his relations with Jewish scholars—will then
provide the setting of his interest in Syriac and help us to understand
the nature of his influence upon the scholars of the next generation
who produced the printed editions of the Syriac New Testament.

Concord

John W. O'Malley gives a very clear account of the importance of the
notion of Concord for Egidio and his equal insistence that orthodoxy
be not compromised.[4] Egidio endeavoured to bring into harmony with
the doctrines of the Church all that he thought valuable in pre- and
non-Christian thought to the extent of being able to discern Christian
truth in authors and traditions that fell well beyond the limits of the
Church. He was not alone in this. Ficino and to a greater extent Pico
della Mirandola[5] were committed to the reconciliation of different
religions and intellectual traditions through a 'divine science' which
would harmonise differences in a simple underlying unity.[6]

The publication of the Latin Hermetic Corpus by Marsilio Ficino
(whom Egidio had met in Florence in the winter of 1494/5) and the
1470 Latin version of Eusebius's *Praeparatio Evangelica* by George of

---

[4] *Giles of Viterbo on Church and Reform* pg 19–38. These pages have extensive references to Egidio's manuscripts. I do not therefore generally refer to these below except
where I supplement them.

[5] Egidio discussed both astrology and Kabbalah with Giovanni Pico della Mirandola.
F. Secret "Notes sur Egidio da Viterbo" Augustiniana XXVII (1977) pg 205–237 quotes
supporting passages. These pages give detailed references to Egidio's manuscript relating to these discussions from the *Historia XX Saeculorum* after the autograph in Naples.
They do not occur in the Biblioteca Angelica copy that has generally been used and
are not therefore mentioned in O'Malley.

[6] For an edition of an extraordinary work of precisely such a synthetic philosophy
by Egidio, called by its editor 'a Christian Pimander', see: John Monfasani, "Hermes
Trismegistus, Rome and the myth of Europa: an unknown text of Giles of Viterbo".
Viator XXII (1991) pg 311–342. There is however some evidence that Egidio was not
entirely happy that Hermes anticipated the Christian Mysteries, *op. cit.*, pg 317.

Trebizond (1395–1484) provided material suitable for such a reading of pre-Christian antiquity and indeed the record of a previous such reading. David Walker's work on the *'prisci theologi'*[7] has long made us familiar with Hermes Trismegistus, Zoroaster, Orpheus, and to a noteworthy extent Pythagoras, as carriers of Primordial Wisdom and Ancient Truth. Inevitably those Hebrew and Aramaic works that were considered of great antiquity (and kabbalistic texts claimed suitably ancient origins with the Patriarchs) received the same treatment. Convinced that such supposedly ancient texts contained a hard core of Christian Truth, Egidio was able to lift phrases and notions from their contexts and impose some pretty exotic connections between them. He was, says O'Malley, "in possession of a hermeneutics which could filter out obvious and disturbing discrepancies between the authors and traditions he was discussing and magnify a slight residue of superficial similarity".[8]

That the Gentiles might share a primitive revelation with the Hebrews that could be traced back to Noah was not implausible, nor were the enlightened borrowings of sensitive pagan philosophers.[9] Controversial to say the least, however, was the notion that Plato might write so explicitly and well on the Holy Trinity by 'Nature' alone and without Revelation.[10] However in purely historical terms (so to speak) what is of greater importance to us is the role Egidio assigns to the transmission of the Ancient Wisdom—and here he means Kabbalah—to the Etruscans: *"...prius in Italia nostra arcana apud Etruscos innotuisse constat".*[11] Nor is the Etruscan connection important for Egidio alone. It engages both Florentine scholars and Postel and forms part of the historical awareness of several of our authors.

---

[7] D. P. Walker, *The Ancient Theology* (Duckworth, London 1972) (embracing earlier essays). Frances A. Yates, *Giordano Bruno and the Hermetic Tradition* (Routledge, London 1971) remains important on the whole tradition. She has a discussion of Pico and kabbalistic magic pg 84–116. See also her *The Occult Philosophy in the Elizabethan Age* (Routledge, London 1979) pg 17–22. An overview is given by Cesare Vasoli, "Ermetismo e Cabala nel tardo Rinascimento e nel primo '600" in ed. Fabio Troncanelli, *La Città dei Segreti. Magia, Astrologia e Cultura Esoterica a Roma (XV–XVIII)* (Franco Angel, Milan 1985) pg 103–118.

[8] *Op. cit.,* pg 22.

[9] For a general discussion of Noah in the Renaissance: D. C. Allen, *The Legend of Noah* (University of Illinois Press, Urbana 1963).

[10] O'Malley, *op. cit.,* pg 24.

[11] F. Secret ed. *Scechina* vol. I, pg 185.

The epistemological basis of Egidio's hermeneutic—proceeding from the enigma of the world to a higher level of integrating intelligibility—was, of course, Platonic. Egidio was hostile to the Paduan Philosophers and approved the Fifth Lateran Council's proscription of them not least because they denied 'the oracles' and sought emancipation from Theology.[12] Egidio on the other hand saw Ficino's revival of Platonism as the return of the Golden Age. Neoplatonism thus forms the matrix of Egidio's speculations. It permits a symbolic and synthetic style of thinking, very different from that which informs scholastic dogmatic formulations.

Annius da Viterbo

In the growing awareness of Etruscan civilisation in central Italy, Egidio, together with his compatriot Annius da Viterbo (Giovanni Nanni, 1432–1502) became an enthusiastic exponent of the importance of Etruria in history.[13]

---

[12] "In maintaining that Truth was derived mainly from sense-impressions, he argued, they not only denied Revelation but also more mystical sources of enlightenment." Marjorie Reeves, "Cardinal Egidio of Viterbo: A Prophetic Interpretation of History" in ed. Marjorie Reeves, *Prophetic Rome in the High Renaissance Period* (Clarendon, Oxford 1992) pg 91–109. Quotation on pg 97. O'Malley makes clear the centrality of Lateran V in this philosophical debate, *op. cit.*, pg 42–45. Relevant discussion of the more philosophical aspects of Egidio's thought is found in: Eugenio Massa, "Egidio da Viterbo e la Metodologia del sapere nel Cinquecento" in *Pensée humaniste et Tradition chrétienne au XVe et XVIe siècles* (CRNS, Paris 1950) pg 185–239.

[13] For Annius: Robert Weiss, "Traccia per una Biografia di Annio da Viterbo" in Italia Medievale e Umanistica V (1962) pg 425–441. Also his "An unknown Epigraphic Tract by Annius of Viterbo" in *Italian Studies presented to E. R. Vincent*, (CUP, Cambridge 1962) pg 101–120; E. N. Tigerstedt, "Ioannes Annius and Graecia Mendax" in ed C. Henderson, *Classical, Mediaeval, and Renaissance Studies in honour of Berthold Louis Ullman (Vol II)* (Edizioni di Storia e Letteratura, Rome 1964) pg 293–310; O. A. Danielsson, "Annius von Viterbo über die Gründungsgeschichte Roms" *Corolla Archaeologica Principi Hereditario Regni Sueciae Gustavo Adolpho Dedicata*, (Humphrey Milford, London 1932) pg 1–16; Walter E. Stephens "The Etruscans and the Ancient Theology in Annius of Viterbo" in eds. P. Brezzi et al., *Umanismo a Roma nel Quatrocento* (Columbia UP, New York 1984) pg 309–322; E. Fumagalli "Un falso tardo-quattrocentesco: Lo Pseudo-Catone di Annio da Viterbo" in ed. Rino Avesani, *Vestigia: Studi in onore di Giuseppe Billanovich* (Rome, 1984) pg 337–83; E. Fumagalli "Aneddoti della Vita di Annio da Viterbo O P." Archivum Fratrum Praedicatorum L (1980) pg 167–199. Further up-to-date bibliography is given in Ingrid D. Rowland, *The Culture of the High Renaissance. Ancients and Moderns in Sixteenth-Century Rome* (CUP, Cambridge, 1998) pg 53–59. Rowland considers the possibilities that Annius was responsible for the scheme of decorations in the Vatican's Borgia Apartments on pg 58–59. A discussion of Annius's commendably high standards of forgery is found in Anthony Grafton, *Forgers and Critics: Creativity and*

Giovanni (fraudulently)[14] claimed that in Genoa he had come across two manuscripts, a Latin version of the (lost) Annals of Berosus the Chaldaean, Babylon's librarian at the time of Moses and a revised version (in the light of that same new Berosus) of Manetho's list of Egyptian pharaohs. This manuscript included lost texts from Fabius Pictor, Cato, Archilochus and a hitherto unknown Persian Metasthenes. These authors offered confirmation of the material in the new Berosus that provided information extending back beyond the Flood to Adam. In anticipation of the Deluge Noah had sought to preserve the sum of human wisdom to date as an inscription on a stone pillar, which had indeed survived the Flood to have its contents summarized by Berosus and recovered at last by Giovanni. Furthermore as Noah and his family set about the repopulation of the earth, the Patriarch gave each of his sons a continent to colonize. Ham got Africa, Shem Asia, and Japheth Europe. Noah then sailed up the Tiber. He disembarked around Rome and walked to found a new city 'Vetulonia', later 'Etruria', and later still—Viterbo! People here spoke in Aramaic and wrote backwards. Their piety was exceptional, but then they were descended from Noah.

Noah invented wine, and from the Hebrew word for wine (יין 'yayin') he became known in Etruscan as 'Janus'. When Noah died he was buried at a site which would subsequently fall within the city of Rome and which would preserve his name: Noah was buried on the Janiculum.

Giovanni supported his textual forgeries with archaeological artefacts[15] and considerably impressed Alexander VI who made him his preacher—*Magister Sacri Palatii*—in 1499. A year before, having suitably modified his name,[16] he had published his book *Commentaria Fratris Joannis Annii Viterbiensis super Opera Diversorum Auctorum de Antiquitatibus Loquentium.*[17]

---

duplicity in Western Scholarship (Princeton University Press, Princeton 1990) mainly in chapters 2 & 3. For a delightful tale of later seventeenth century 'Etruscan' forgery, see I. D. Rowland, *The Scarith of Scornello* (UCP, Chicago 2004).

[14] There is no doubt of this. Weiss's judgment ("Traccia" pg 441) is irreproachable: "Che Annio fosse un falsario senza scrupoli è certo." Fumagalli ("Aneddoti") offers some properly restrained conjectures about his motivation.

[15] See Rowland, *op. cit.*, pg 56–57.

[16] Giovanni adopted the Etruscan name 'Annius' at some stage prior to the publication of the book.

[17] Rowland, *op. cit.*, pg 58 draws attention to the significance of the appearance of this book with its Gothic print, single crude woodcut, and layout. She points out that Silber's typeface resembled that of the Gutenberg Bible. The work looked as if it

With his new texts, Annius had achieved a highly attractive amal-
gamation of biblical and classical mythology that facilitated not only
the construction of a satisfying Viterbian history, but also did the same
for patriots in France, Spain and Germany. In his preface (f. a. IIIr) he
claims: *"pro patria et Italia, immo & Europa tota profiteor"*. Not everyone, of
course, was convinced by the new evidence,[18] but many authors found
the national space imaginatively proffered by the new history liberating:
the Etruscan, Florentine, Celtic, and French use of this new perspective all presuppose the work of Annius.[19] His false history stimulated
all over Europe a remarkable flowering of national origin myths, each
going back to Noah and each with very specific political, religious and
linguistic implications. In different countries and with writers of very
different formation and convictions, this myth helped the slow formation
of new national identities though within a global account of origins
that could be exploited as the basis of a utopian universalistic politics
of fraternity.[20]

   The losers in the new synthesis were the Greeks and (real) Greek
historians.[21] As the new Chaldaean or Aramaean tradition reconnected
Europe with its antediluvian roots, the intimidating weight of the classical Greek tradition could be set aside: the native and vernacular was now

---

belonged to a world older than the neo-Roman elegance of Aldus Manutius. She argues
convincingly that the pseudo-biblical format was a premeditated part of Giovanni's
attempt to supplement biblical chronology. The book was printed widely and repeatedly. There were no fewer than eighteen printings of the original Latin text and at
least three printed translations in Italian. I have myself used the 1515 Paris edition
with the device of Petit in Bristol City Library. Annius claimed (152 v) to have written
an *Historia Hetrusca Pontificia* "*quam iccirco pontificam dicimus quod a pontifice maximo Noa qui
et Ianus in Vaticano coepta, iterato ad pontificem maximum et sedem apostolicam subiecta rediit*".
Whether Annius really did write this work is not known. Either way Alexander VI will
have been pleased by the further legitimisation offered by this myth.

   [18] An interesting example is: Goropius Becanus, *Origines Antwerpiae sive Cimmeriorum
Becceselana novem libros complexa* (Plantin, Antwerp 1569 dedicated to Philip II). See:
F. Secret "Les Origines...de Goropius Beccanus" Bibliothèque d'Humanisme et
Renaissance XII (1960) pg 557–558.

   [19] Specifically for France: R. E. Asher, *National Myths in Renaissance France: Francus,
Samothes and the Druids* (Edinburgh UP, Edinburgh 1993) pg 44–87.

   [20] One can scarcely overlook the unblushing *campanilismo* that underlies Giovanni's
mythology. We shall find later that the type of Orientalism we are seeking progressively
to explore has often more to say about one's own heritage and local western loyalties
than the distant 'Other'.

   [21] One should consider the possibility that there is here also a latent prejudice
against the Greek-speaking Orthodox Church. For the persistence of Annius's views,
see: F. Secret "Postel et la Graecia Mendax" Bibliothèque d'Humanisme et Renaissance XXXIX (1977) pg 125–135.

known to enjoy an even more venerable antiquity.[22] Thus, as we shall see, Greeks often appear as corrupters of the Aramaic tradition.[23]

Egidio's own annotated copy of the first 1498 edition of the *Antiquitates* is now in the Vatican Library (Inc. II. 274).[24] Egidio had intended to write a history of Etruria himself,[25] but was content to rely upon Annius's researches.[26] Repeating Annius's identification of Noah and Janus, he tells us how Noah's teaching was brought to Etruria, thereby explaining the essential identity of Etruscan and Aramaic languages, beliefs and customs.[27] The Etruscans revered the ancient deposit even more than the ancient Egyptians. Their legacy from Noah and the fidelity with which they had preserved it established in effect an independent but parallel tradition to that of the Jews that accounted for the religious destiny of Rome.[28] Rome's religious credentials went back to

---

[22] *Berosi*, edit. Antwerp 1532 pg 580, makes clear the link between the Etruscan tradition and Kabbalah: *"Plinius tradit in disciplina etrusca contineri quo pacto possint evocari dii, fulgura, ignes et eiuscemodi...Hoc autem nullo modo fieri melius poterat quam occultando nomen ipsius dei in cuius tutela urbs ipsa erat. Eius occultandi modus erat Etruscis, mysterio quodam et literis quibusdam ab ipso Dei nomine alterum extrahere cuius ritu ac mysterio nunc soli Talmudistae Caballarii utuntur in disciplina quam vocant Caballa."*

[23] Stephens, *op. cit.*, pg 316 points out that the model for Annius's misohellenism was Josephus in the *Jewish Antiquities* and the *Against Apion*. It was, of course, Josephus's constant evocation of Berosus and Manetho that inspired Annius's forgeries. Josephus also reports, he observes, "that the Chaldaeans were the original ancestors of our race, and this blood relationship accounts for the mention of the Jews that is found in their annals".

[24] An illustration may be found in Rowland, *op. cit.*, Figure 11.

[25] Signorelli, *op. cit.*, pg 214 quoting *Hist. XX Saec.* f. 5, 28, 36.

[26] F. Secret, "Egidio da Viterbo et quelques-uns de ses contemporains". Augustiniana XVI (1966) pg 371–385. On pg 374–76 there is an important discussion of 'Rabi Samuel' whom Annius used as his consultant on Semitic matters. Thus we find (pg 467 of the 1552 edition) R. Samuel responsible for an etymology taken up by Postel and others after him: *"Notandum est quod, apud Hebraeos et Aramaeos, Gallym undam et inundationem significat, ut noster Talmudista Samuel hunc mihi locum exponens dicebat. Asserit enim Gallos dici eos qui inundationem imbriumque excessum passi essent. Ombros vero populum ex his ortum".* A longer passage (pg 616) gives us an indication of the scope of the Rabbi's etymological creativity (Secret, *op. cit.*, pg 376). Or again (pg 31): *"Nam quum Aramaei vocant Tussan Nanam, hanc latina lingua profert Tuscanellam, ut erudite noster Samuel Talmudista interpretabatur".* Samuel is not identified but the etymology of Janus/יין is found in Leone Ebreo's *Dialoghi d'Amore* and Yedaliah ibn Yahya's Chain of Tradition. (*Encyclopedia Judaica* s.v. Noah).

[27] *Scechina* f. 159v makes clear the linguistic identity of the Aramaeans: *"Sic enim nominabo Theologos Hebraeorum qui ex Aram Mesopotamie et Chaldaeorum ora...qui haec arcana prodere orsi sunt: non Hebraica sed Aramaea lingua".* This Aramaic is, of course, the language of the *Zohar*.

[28] O'Malley, *op. cit.*, pg 123ff.

the period immediately after the Flood, and were in no way derivative from those of Jerusalem.[29]

While Egidio shared with Annius and further developed this distinctive view of the past that enabled him not only promiscuously to read Christian arcana into pagan authors of the past, but also show the importance of his bishopric to the providential centrality of the Roman Church, he also entertained lively prophetic notions that addressed again the destiny of Rome.[30]

Prophetic Rome

The prophetic world of the Rome of Julius II and Leo X and Egidio's place therein has been illuminated by recent studies.[31] Marjorie Reeves has sought to unite Egidio's denunciation of corruption within the Church, his reforming zeal, and his enthusiasm for the two expanding

---

[29] Thus we find Roman traditions explained *'ex arcanis'*. O'Malley, *op. cit.* (pg 80) refers for example to Egidio's account of the ancient origins of the papal tiara. The texts can be found in F. Secret, "Notes sur Egidio da Viterbo" Augustiniana XXVII (1977) pg 205–237. They appear on pg 226–229. Egidio believed that Providence had selected the Etruscan site of the Vatican to be the seat of the Church, emphasising the continuity between Aramaean-Etruscans and Christians. The foundation of the new Basilica of Julius had of course just been laid and Egidio considered its construction an important part of the providential design for the Pontificate. He supported Julius II in his refusal to allow Bramante to move the Tomb of Peter. See: O'Malley, *op. cit.*, pg 122–125, 273. On the question of the Tomb, Charles L. Stinger, *The Renaissance in Rome* (Indiana University Press, Bloomington, 1985, new ed. 1998) pg 184–186. Also important for Egidio's view of the destiny of Rome is his discourse edited again by J. W. O'Malley "Man's Dignity, God's Love and the Destiny of Rome: A text of Giles of Viterbo" Viator III (1972) pg 389–416. There are suggestive remarks in Edgar Wind's 1960 article "Michelangelo's Prophets and Sibyls" (now conveniently in ed. George Holmes, *Art and Politics in Renaissance Italy* (British Academy, OUP, London 1993) pg 263–300 that link Egidio to the theological programme behind the Sistine Chapel ceiling. The origins of Egidio's own Order were not allowed to remain outside the web of legendary connections. M. Benedict Hachett O.S.A., "A 'Lost' Work of Giles of Viterbo" in *Egidio da Viterbo e il suo tempo*, pg 117–127, gives on pg 126 n. 32 a bibliography for Augustine's legendary visit to Tuscany and the origins of the Order there.

[30] Marjorie Reeves, *op. cit.*, pg 94–95 considers the question whether Egidio also was influenced by Annius's *Glosa sive Expositio super Apocalypsim* of 1480 and decides against this.

[31] The papers collected in Marjorie Reeves, *Prophetic Rome in the High Renaissance Period* (Clarendon, Oxford 1992) are of particular importance. Also: J. O'Malley *op. cit.*, pg 100–138. The 1995 unpublished Bristol University PhD thesis of Sharon Ann Leftley, *Millenarian Thought in Renaissance Rome with special reference to Pietro Galatino (c. 1464–c. 1540) and Egidio da Viterbo (c. 1469–1532)* beyond its obvious relevance includes a survey of recent research on early sixteenth-century prophecy and millenarianism on pg 315–359.

worlds of geography and letters, with his expectation of an immi-
nent Golden Age and within his prophetic vision of History: "God's
providential purpose for mankind is seen as approaching its climax in
the *renovatio mundi* which fuses the Christian and Humanist visions of
the Golden Age".[32] Egidio approached History as the realisation of the
Divine Providence. History is the providential outworking of the heav-
enly design, and thus contains signs which when properly interpreted in
the light of the Scriptures reveal the meaning of contemporary events
and the direction of History.[33]

Prophetic Preaching

Thorough editing has provided us with reliable texts of several of
Egidio's more important orations—particularly the one given at the
Fifth Vatican Council, and also some of his everyday sermons.[34] All
are characterised by a flood of erudition—classical, biblical and kabbalistic—even his confirmation sermons are heavy with gematria,

---

[32] *Op. cit.*, pg 92.

[33] See: J. W. O'Malley "Historical Thought and the Reform Crisis of the Early
Sixteenth Century" Theological Studies XXVIII (1967) pg 531–548.

[34] Texts and commentaries in: J. W. O'Malley, "Fulfilment of the Christian Golden
Age under Pope Julius II: Text of a discourse of Giles of Viterbo 1507" Traditio XXV
(1969) pg 265–338. This sermon of 1506 was published in 1507 as a tract *De Aurea
Aetate* dedicated to King Manuel of Portugal. For the oration at the Opening of the
Lateran Council: C. O'Reilly, "Without Councils we cannot be saved... Giles of Viterbo
addresses the Fifth Lateran Council". Augustiniana XXVII (1977) pg 184–204, offers an
edition of the oration. On Reform: Nelson H. Minnich S. J., "The Concept of reform
proposed at the Fifth Lateran Council" Archivum Historiae Pontificae VII (1969) pg
163–251. On Egidio and Reform: J. W. O'Malley, "Giles of Viterbo: a Reformer's
Thought on Renaissance Rome" Renaissance Quarterly XX (1967) pg 1–11. On the
issue of prophecy at the Council: Nelson. H. Minnich "Prophecy and the Fifth Lateran
Council 1512–1517" in M. Reeves, *Prophetic Rome* pg 63–88; Nelson H. Minnich, "The
Participants at the Fifth Lateran Council" Archivum Historiae Pontificae XII (1974)
pg 157–206; Aldo Londi, "Prophecy at the Time of the Council of Pisa (1511–1513)"
in M. Reeves *op. cit.*, pg 53–61; Ottavia Niccoli, "High and Low in Prophetic Culture
in Rome at the beginning of the 16th Century" in ed. M. Reeves, *op. cit.*, pg 203–222.
See also her *Prophecy and People in Renaissance Italy* (Princeton University Press, Princeton
N.J., 1990) pg 35ff. For the oration before Julius II and the Emperor Maximilian 1512:
C. O'Reilly, "Maximus Caesar et Pontifex Maximus: Giles of Viterbo proclaims the Alliance between the Emperor Maximilian I and Pope Julius II" Augustiniana XXII (1972)
pg 80–117. Additionally: John Monfasani, "Sermons of Giles of Viterbo as Bishop" in
Egidio da Viterbo e il suo tempo pg 137–189. The sermons are taken from Vaticanus latinus
6320 f.123r–146v where they are found transcribed by Nicholas Scrutellius, Egidio's
assistant and protégé. See pg 142–145 for manuscripts of other sermons possibly by
Egidio or perhaps Scrutellius that similarly offer arcana to congregations.

and etymological points arising from the Aramaean arcana. But their burden is prophetic: the expansion of world horizons and the unfolding of biblical knowledge through the recovery of oriental languages were signs of the new Golden Age. The Church must reform, make a crusade against the Turks, and recover the Holy Places before the Angelic Pope appears to herald the End.[35]

Historia Viginti Saeculorum

The enduring monument of Egidio's prophetic world-view is the *Historia Viginti Saeculorum*,[36] a work of more than 300 folios written during the period of the Council.[37] It offers a reading of the first twenty Psalms that describes Twenty Ages, the Christian era beginning with the Eleventh Age. Ten ages thus precede, and ten follow the Incarnation, and this mystical number thus links history with the Sephiroth.[38] He exploits a series of concords between the eras before and after the Incarnation that he takes from the Old Testament and classical history—not forgetting, of course, the history of Etruria. The myth of Etruscan origins is again used to point to the apotheosis of Rome. God's promises apply to Etruria and Rome, not to Jews; to the Vatican, not Sion or Jerusalem. Just as the Vatican succeeded the Etruscan settlement of the Janiculum, so St. Peter buried in the Vatican has succeeded Janus or Noah buried on the Janiculum.

---

[35] On the Joachimist figure of the Angelic Pope, see: M. Reeves, "The Medieval Heritage" in ed. M. Reeves, *op. cit.*, pg 3–21.

[36] The archetype is manuscript. Lat IX B14 in the Biblioteca Nazionale in Naples, "*Aegidii Viterbiensis Hystoria Saeculorum per totidem psalmos digesta*". The manuscript was dedicated to Leo X and has Egidio's marginalia. On the title page a note by Girolamo Seripando records the loss of the manuscript and its subsequent purchase on a stall in Rome by Cervini. William Hudon, "Marcellus II, Girolamo Seripando, and the image of the Angelic Pope" in ed. Majorie Reeves, *op. cit.*, pg 373–387 raises the possibility on pg 387 that the recovery of Egidio's call to the Pope to lead the Tenth Age of *renovatio*, even though he does not explicitly mention the Angelic Pope, may have inspired Seripando and Marcellus (who we shall discover much concerned with Syriac New Testaments) to respond to that vision. There is no complete printed edition of the *Historia*. In what follows I rely upon J. W. O'Malley and Marjorie Reeves (using ms 502 from the Angelica, not the archetype). Leftley, *op. cit.*, pg 255–307 offers a detailed description of the book. Manuscript references in support of my text above are found in these authors and are not given again here.

[37] Probably between 1513–1518, G. Signorelli, *op. cit.*, pg 214–215 n. 25.

[38] On the number symbolism here, see: F. Secret, *Kabbalistes chrétiens de la Renaissance* (Dunod, Paris 1964) pg 113–114.

The Nineteenth Psalm ("The heavens declare...") prophesies the opening out of God's purpose in the Nineteenth Age. "Their sound is gone out into all the earth" (v4) wonderfully predicts the opening of unknown lands by Ferdinand King of Spain and Emmanuel King of Portugal. Julius II who had begun rebuilding St. Peter's is like the giant (v5) who rejoices to run the course. The Tenth Age (after the Incarnation) however is to be characterised by the fullest understanding of Scripture. All secrets will be revealed: those of the divine world through the Kabbalah, and those of the created world by voyages of discovery. Mankind will be brought into a new intellectual and religious unity under the Papacy. All humanity will be converted before the End and brought as One Flock under One Shepherd. The union of all races and all knowledge that will mark the final period is described by Egidio as *"Plenitudo temporum, plenitudo gentium, plentitudo doctrinae"*. This is the perspective—modified only in detail—within which all the sixteenth-century Catholic printed editions of the Syriac New Testament were to be produced: the parallel expansion of geographical and biblical knowledge in preparation for the union of mankind at the End Time locates these Bibles and their purpose firmly within the Divine Plan.

In the *Historia* Leo X is hailed as the first pope of the Tenth Age. He enjoyed, as a Medici, excellent Etruscan origins. He was to continue the building of St. Peter's and the promotion of reform in the Council. It was, we have seen, precisely at this moment of supreme expectation that the Maronite Patriarch's delegation arrived in Rome. They represented the East that needed to be freed from the Turk; they evoked other Christians who yet needed to be brought, as they had been, into the Flock of the One Pastor. They brought the challenge of the linguistic competence that would be necessary for the Word to go forth from Rome to the ends of the Earth. They also brought with them their own dialect of the mystical Aramaic language that Christ and His Mother had spoken and some precious books. The first reception of Syriac in the West under the patronage of Egidio and Leo X was not therefore a casual business but occurred at a moment of great prophetic significance.

The Sack

The immediate prophetic aspirations of Rome were to be roughly dashed by the trauma of the Sack of 1527. Egidio was subsequently

to see the slaughter and sacrilege as a divine punishment with the
Emperor Charles V, like a new Cyrus, purging the Church of its evils.
Egidio's last and greatest work, the *Scechina*, was written at the behest
of Clement VII who turned to Egidio for the guidance of a prophet
in the dark days after the Sack.[39] The book was however dedicated to
Charles V. It combines a defence of Egidio's new methods of kabbalistic scriptural interpretation with an eloquent appeal to Charles V to
assume the eschatological role of Last World Emperor.[40]

Scechina

We have in *Scechina* finally a veritable *summa* of Egidio's learning acquired
over many years of study and meditation.[41] It is an elaborated Christian
interpretation of Kabbalah and also an apology for its introduction

---

[39] A. M. Voci, "Un 'Ipotesi sulla Genesi della Scechina di Egidio da Viterbo"
Critica Storica XX (1983) pg 130–137 finds a motivation for Clement VII's instruction to Egidio to write *Scechina* in Charles V's Reichstag at Ausburg in 1530 where
Melanchthon was negotiating for the Protestants. She finds the proem reflects the
position of the Curia on the struggle against both heretics and Turks and offers an
appreciation of the providential pairing of Charles V and Clement VII. Consequently
she finds herself in disagreement with O'Malley (*Giles of Viterbo on Church and Reform* pg
135) on the question of whether Egidio approved the idea of the Emperor promoting
the convocation of a Council to bring peace to Germany and reconcile the Church.
It is worth noticing Egidio's caution in explicitly identifying eschatological figures. He
did not press Leo X or Julius II before him into the mould of the Angelic Pope (in
contrast here to Galatinus). Nor, however important his providential role, does he
assert plainly that Charles V was definitely the Last World Emperor. See: Leftley pg
294, 298. J. W. O'Malley, "Giles of Viterbo: A Sixteenth Century Text on Doctrinal
Development". Traditio XXII (1966) pg 445–450 on pg 447 suggests this may have
been due to the importance he placed upon the role of Councils.

[40] Egidio knew Charles V personally from his papal legateship in Spain.

[41] *Scechina* enjoys an excellent modern edition with annotations and a short but
invaluable introduction by F. Secret, *Egidio da Viterbo Scechina e Libellus de Litteris Hebraicis
Inediti a cura di François Secret* (Centro Internationale di Studi Umanistici, Rome 1959).
Reference should be made to pg 65 for a summary of the contents and structure of
Scechina. After a dedication to Clement VII (f. 157), and a general exposition (f. 159–162),
Egidio deals with *De numeris* (f. 162), *De Literis* (f. 182) and *De nominibus divinis* (f. 214).
Also essential is F. Secret "Le Symbolisme de la Kabbale chrétienne dans la 'Scechina'
de Egidio da Viterbo". Archivo di Filosofia (Rome. Instituto di Studi Filosofia 1958)
pg 131–154. His *Les Kabbalistes chrétiens* discusses Egidio on pg 106–125 and gives a
brief characterisation of *Scechina* on pg 118–120. There he writes that: "L'oeuvre de
Giles de Viterbe est sans doute le plus remarquable d'assimilation de la Kabbale dans
le monde des humanistes chrétiens, compte tenu de son interprétation chrétienne".
On pg 15 of his edition Secret writes: "Si…Egidio da Viterbe emploie des thèmes
familiers depuis le Pugio, ou traités par Pic de la Mirandole, P. Rici ou Reuchlin, ce
qui caractérise Libellus et Scechina c'est que tous les ouvrages qui y sont cités ont étés

into Christian thought.[42] Egidio's teaching is in an important sense new:[43] it is a sign of the Tenth and Last Age that all secrets should be revealed and that an enlightenment not previously known should be made available to the Church.[44] Egidio's reading of the Scriptures '*ex fontibus Arameorum theologie*' was the vehicle of the new and definitive understanding. And there is something new in the depth of Egidio's engagement with Kabbalah. Though he had discussed these matters with Pico della Mirandola, and was as we shall see personally much involved in the Reuchlin affair, both the extent of his Hebrew learning and personal exploration of Jewish Kabbalistic texts and the thoroughness of his utilisation of these in his meditations upon the meaning of Scripture—"*scrutandae scripturae*"—mark clearly a new stage in the Christian appropriation of Kabbalah. This depth and consistency of engagement we shall find in Postel and Guy Lefèvre de la Boderie, and to a lesser extent, but still significantly, in Widmanstetter and Masius. It is a common and significant characteristic of all the scholars in the sixteenth century who worked on printed editions of the Syriac New Testament—with the sole exception of the Jewish convert to Protestantism Tremellius. Equally important however is the eschatological framework within which this new learning was acquired. This gave their Oriental scholarship a motivation beyond the merely academic and placed the scholars themselves at a decisive moment of Salvation History. The consciousness of fulfilling a providential role, if not indeed of prophetic or messianic office, again is characteristic of the Catholic scholars who worked on the editions of the Syriac New Testament. This may mark another distinction between them and the earlier Christian Kabbalists.

---

traduits, en tout ou en partie par le Cardinal". The list of sources then given on pg 15 leaves no doubt of this.

[42] Genevieve Javary offers a thematic investigation of the Schekinah over three centuries of Christian Kabbalists in *Recherches sur L'Utilisation du Thème de la Sekina dans L'Apologétique chrétienne du XVème au XVIIIème siècle* (Librairie Honoré Champion, Paris 1978). The absence of an index makes this book, her 1976 Paris IV thesis, difficult to use and the standard of reproduction of the typewritten text beggars belief. Also by G. Javary "A propos du thème de la Sekina: variations sur le nom de Dieu" in *Kabbalistes chrétiens* (Albin Michel, Paris 1979) pg 281–306.

[43] Secret on pg 10 of his edition cites the evidence of Egidio's clear awareness of his place within Christian Kabbalism.

[44] Nor are the importance of world mission and the promise of the One Shepherd and One Flock overlooked: the Apostles had conquered only the smallest part of the world, now it could all be won (*Scechina.* ed pg 160).

Libellus de litteris sanctis

Scechina was never published nor do we know why.[45] It was not however
the only kabbalistic work written by Egidio. In 1517 he produced the
Libellus de litteris sanctis that we have already seen shaped Teseo Ambrogio's understanding of Syriac.[46] Egidio wrote it in the same year as he
received the dedication of Elias's Psalter and dedicated it to Cardinal
Giulio de' Medici.[47] It is based upon Egidio's own translation of the
Hebrew *Sepher ha-Temunah*. The work remains in manuscript and like
Scechina was never published. Its diffusion was achieved by Pietro Galatinus who made extensive use of it in his *De Arcanis Catholicae Veritatis*,
which was a very widely read book in the Renaissance.

The book, a sort of introduction to scriptural study, begins by assert-
ing that names are not man-made but given by God. This had been
taught by Dionysus the Areopagite and of late by Pico, Paulus Rici and
Reuchlin who began the Christian study of Kabbalah.[48] But not only do
names have privileged access to reality, Scripture itself gives significance
to the letters of the alphabet and their order: Lamentations chapters

---

[45] Anyone who has tried to read this long and difficult book, even with the sure
guidance of Secret's edition, will not imagine that even in Renaissance Rome it would
have found sufficient readers to make a commercial success for a printer. The modern
academic publisher omitted Secret's Italian translation. It is however worth noting the
inscription on f.1a: *"Collegii Neophytarum Rom"*. Perhaps it was thought that the Library
of a college for converted Jews was the most appropriate place for the manuscript. On
the College of the Neophytes, see for brief orientation: R. Le Déaut "Jalons pour une
histoire d'un manuscrit du Targum palestinien (Neofiti I)" Biblica XLVIII (1967) pg
509–533, pg 515–523 and M. Fitzmaurice Martin, "The Palaeological Character of
Codex Neofiti I" Textus III (1963) pg 1–35. Paul III by his bull *Illius Qui* 19 February
1543 granted permission to Don Giovanni di Torano, parish priest of S. Giovanni
di Mercato who was acting upon the suggestion of Ignatius Loyola, to erect *"unum
monasterium pro puellis et unum Hospitale pro viris Judaeis"*. Cardinal Marcello Crescenzi was
its first Cardinal-protector. Gregory XIII remodelled the Hospitale by his bull *Vices
Eius* of September 1577 and called it *Collegium Ecclesiasticum Adolescentium Neophytorum*.
Hereafter it housed not only Jewish and Islamic converts, but members of the eastern
Churches. In 1580 the College was transferred to its present site besides Madonna
dei Monti. It was suppressed in 1798 but began work again in the nineteenth century.
Today it is called *Ospizio Pontificio dei Catechumeni e Neofiti*. On the contribution of the
College to Oriental Studies: Levi della Vida, *Ricerche* pg 405–406.

[46] An edition is included in Secret's edition of *Scechina*.

[47] Vat. lat. 5808 is the calligraphic bound copy offered to the Cardinal. On the date
see Secret's edition pg 23. Another ms, Vat. lat. 3146 f. 1–26v, Secret describes as
a rough draft, 'le brouillon'. Secret offers a summary of the book: *Kabbalistes chrétiens*
pg 111–114.

[48] Pseudo-Dionysus was commonly assimilated to the Kabbalah. Secret's edition pg
24 gives authors who do this to whom may be added Jean Thenaud (died c. 1542).

1–4 is an acrostic, like Psalm 119. The alphabets of the Chaldaeans, Aramaeans and Phoenicians—*"quorum una fere lingua est"*—are then compared and contrasted with the Egyptians' mystical script.

Egidio then explains how God was revealed to Moses by *Geura* (i.e. *Geburah*) which is fire, by the Tetragrammaton, and by other divine names that are to be understood as the ten *'numeri'* or Sephiroth, *"ab Aramaeis et Hebraeis, numerationes et mensurae nuncupatae"*. These are called the Ideas in Plato. In Canticles (4. 7), they are the limbs of God. The highest three Sephiroth form the Upper World and are in God. The next seven form the Middle World whence our sensible world was formed. We learn that the three hypostases of the Trinity are found in the Sephiroth. But the Sephiroth symbolise many other things—*"multa praeterea haec decem sortiuntur nomina"*—virtues, powers, acts of God, elements, parts of the body, Patriarchs, Tabernacle ornaments etc. These mysteries had not previously received attention from any Christian, but they are the ten branches of the Tree of Life. It is to these mysteries that the letter forms have reference. Egidio then refers to his *Vorlage*: *"Extat super ea re liber: qui Sepher Themunot: liber figurarum inscribitur: latissime is quidem abdyta mysteria recensens: ea ego omnia vobis, ita iubentibus, silenti sacro involvens: figures tantum perstringo sanctarum litterarum: eius linguae:que utramque Legem: illam Deus Mosi: hanc Apostolis Dei filius tradens, est locutus"*. We must grasp the significance of this last point. Not only was the Law given to Moses in the sacred language, but also Christ gave His Law to the Apostles in the same language. And the *figures* of the script of both languages were the same. Here *in nuce* is a major but as yet unacknowledged part of the significance of the Syriac New Testaments. When we come to the *editio princeps* of the printed Syriac New Testament in 1555, we shall need to recall the sacred nature of the script and its association with the Sephiroth to explain the more puzzling features of that edition.

Egidio's little book then proceeds through the alphabet. Aleph is made of a Waw and two Yods and signifies the Trinity. It is also the first letter of EHYH, the Divine Name given in Exodus 3.14. Beth is the firstborn of Aleph (consider Colossians 1. 15). It is made of a Daleth and a Waw. Waw is the human chest and the Sephirah *Tipheret* and the Sun...etc. In this way the book progresses through the alphabet. What we are to learn from all this is that the sacred letters given to the Chaldaean fathers and subsequently shared with Egyptians and Arabs preserve their mystical forms. Thus even Pythagoras's mystical use of the Greek Upsilon reflects the mysteries of the Semitic *'Zade'*. These forms, as reflected in the various Semitic and other scripts, remain susceptible to kabbalistic manipulation.[49] This observation, of course, is central to the use made of this book by Teseo.[50]

It is important to notice again the providential role assigned to Leo X in stimulating the essential studies that Augustine in *De Doctrina Christiana* had long ago recommended for the resolution of problems in Scripture. At the end of his introduction Egidio observed to the Medici Cardinal that the time of his dedication was most auspicious for the Chaldaeans had brought their letters to Leo X from Asia (he was referring to the Maronite Mission to the Fifth Lateran Council) and Giustiniani's Psalter dedicated to the same Pope had just been printed in Arabic.[51] The dedication thus brings together the arrival of Syriac in Rome and the parallel developments in Arabic and unites them both in a scheme that extends the mystical significance of Hebrew letters to other Semitic scripts. This was the book that determined Teseo's approach to Syriac and in which he was followed by subsequent scholars.

Egidio's Oriental Studies

Good general summaries of Egidio as a biblical scholar[52] allow us here to concentrate upon his oriental languages.[53] It is probable that Egidio began to learn Hebrew during his stay in Florence in 1497 (Pico had died in 1494). Parenti described him in 1502 as skilled in Greek, Hebrew and Latin.[54] It may be that Egidio's printed copy of the rabbinic Dictionary '*Aruk* in the Angelica in Rome that is annotated by him in Latin and not, as was his later practice, in Hebrew belongs to this

---

[49] f. 5 *"Ita litterae sacrae: datae patribus Chaldaeis: Aegyptiis: Arabibus communicare vicinis: servarunt et numerum et vim"*.

[50] It is perhaps as well to be aware of the extent of Teseo's borrowings. These are the long passages in his *Introductio* that are taken from Egidio: f. 96 (He), 98 (Waw), 100v (Heth), 101 (Teth), 104 (Yod), 110 (Lamed), 113 (Mem), 116v (Samec), 119 (Ain), 121v (Pe), 122 (Zade), 124v (Qof) 126ff. (Res, Shin, Tau).

[51] Libellus f. 15 *"Scripsi ego has litteras: quas tuo nomini dicandas duxi: hoc praecipue tempore: quo ad Leonem decimum Chaldaei ex Asia litteras suas attulerunt: alii in Psalmis arabicas impresserunt: rem nullis ante saeculis visam: Leonis tum foelicitati et memoriae reservatam"*.

[52] J. W. O'Malley, *Giles of Viterbo on Church and Reform* Chapter Four pg 67–99 'Scripture and Cabala' is a masterful summary. F. X. Martin, *Friar Reformer*, pg 153–179, similarly.

[53] On Egidio's Hebrew studies: F. Secret, *Kabbalistes chrétiens* pg 107–121. Also F. Secret, "Aegidiana Hebraica" Revue des Études juives CXXI (4ème série, vol. I) (1962) pg 409–416.

[54] F. X. Martin, *op. cit.*, pg 157.

early period.[55] In 1504 Egidio had copied a most important manuscript, which since its discovery by Alejandro Diez Macho in 1956 has been known as Codex Neofiti.[56] It is the sole manuscript of the Palestinian Targum (a Targum is an Aramaic paraphrase of the Hebrew Scriptures) and its recovery has marked an important advance in Targum scholarship in our own time. Egidio paginated the manuscript and his marginalia show he could read the Aramaic. There is perhaps a hint that Egidio was already searching for kabbalistic material. He has a mark at Genesis 5. 24, a verse that concerns Enoch. But this manuscript is not as heavily annotated as the others of Egidio. Of course, being a Targum, it is by and large reasonably close to the Hebrew and hardly of much kabbalistic interest.

Signorelli gives the Jewish convert Felix Pratensis as Egidio's first Hebrew teacher.[57] It seems he was baptised around 1506.[58] Felix's *Psalterium* of 1515 shows considerable interest in Christian Kabbalah that may have influenced Egidio, and he announced (f. 39v) his intention of writing about the Divine Names. A passage of 23 April 1515 quoted by Secret indicates that Felix had translated the *Sepher ha-Temunah* into Latin before Egidio's *Libellus*.[59] The role of Felix in Egidio's production however remains uncertain. The manuscript is certainly in Egidio's hand, though the text may have been dictated to him.[60]

---

[55] A copy of David Kimchi's *Shorashim* copied for Egidio is described in L. G. Pélisser, "Manuscrits de Gilles de Viterbe à La Bibliothèque Angélique (Rome)". Revue des Bibliothèques (1892) pg 228–240, pg 231.

[56] The modern edition is A. Diez Macho, *Neofiti I Targum palestinense Ms. de la Biblioteca Vaticana* (Madrid-Barcelona), *I Génesis*, 1968, *II Exodo*, 1970, *III Levitico*, 1971, *IV Numeros* 1974, *V Deuteronomio* 1978, *VI Apendices* 1979. On the manuscripts, M. Fitzmaurice Martin "The Palaeographical Character of Codex Neofiti I". Textus III (1963) pg 8–11, to be revised by: R. Le Déaut, "Jalons pour une histoire d'un manuscrit du Targum palestinien (Neofiti I)" Biblica XLVIII (1967) pg 509–533 which is also helpful on Egidio's scholarship. Elias Levita used Neofiti I Le Déaut, *op. cit.*, pg 512.

[57] *Op. cit.*, pg 203 n. 8.

[58] F. Secret, ed. *Scechina* pg 11.

[59] *Op. cit.*, pg 12.

[60] Felix also edited the first Great Rabbinic Bible published by Daniel Bomberg and dedicated to Leo X. This was the first Hebrew Bible to carry the verse divisions that were taken from the Vulgate. The Bible also contained the first printing of the Targum *Yerushalmi* or *Fragmententargum*. The edition however was marred by the poor text it offered. It was criticised by Elias Levita and superseded by Jacob ben Hayim's Bible of 1524–5. See: Paul Kahle, *The Cairo Geniza* (Second edition, Blackwell, Oxford 1959) pg 120–124. Also: "Zwei durch Humanisten besorgte, dem Papst gewidmete Ausgaben der hebräischen Bibel" in *Essays presented to Leo Baeck on the occasion of his Eightieth Birthday* (East and West Library, London 1954) pg 50–74. It was Felix who initially persuaded Bomberg to found a printing press in Venice. The first privilege

Widmanstetter claimed that Egidio was responsible for making the Zohar available to Christians.[61] Egidio apparently had a copy made in 1513 by Isaac ben Abraham at Tivoli and translated extracts himself.[62] He discovered however that Abraham had copied from an incomplete manuscript and turned to della Volta to find him a complete copy.

Egidio's competence in Arabic

The extent of Egidio's active cooperation with Jewish scribes and scholars, the richness of his library, and the omnipresence of annotations in his own hand leave no doubt of his technical proficiency in both Hebrew and Aramaic and the extent of his erudition in these

---

was granted Bomberg in 1515. Between then and 1538 Bomberg had produced 186 Hebrew texts, some of considerable size. See: Amram, *op. cit.*, pg 150ff.; Alfredo Cioni, *Diz. Bio. degli Italiani*, vol, X, pg 382–587; Paul Grendler, *The Roman Inquisition and the Venetian Press 1540–1605* (Princeton UP, Princeton 1977) pg 89–93 & 140–145. Justus Jonas in a letter to Luther 12. June 1530 from the Regensburg Reichstag quoted by H. Bobzin, *Der Koran in Zeitalter der Reformation* (Franz Steiner, Beirut 1995) pg 380 says: *"Fuit in diebus nobiscum dominus Daniel Bomberga ille, … qui sumptu suo Venetiis in hunc diem alit Hebraice bene Eruditos et ianmolim edidit nobis bibliam, Concordias etc, solusque habet maximam officinam. Est vir humanissimus multaque officiose et amanter nobiscum contulit, admonit de Cabala etc in vocabula baroschis [בראשית] esse annos a mundo condito usque ad Christum passum et similia etc. Videtur plane ιουδαιζειν more eorum, qui non praemuniti cognitione pietatis nimis hebraicantur, sed alias vir est optimus et humanissimus".* Bomberg also produced the first complete Babylonian Talmud 1519–1523. A most useful survey of Hebrew Bible editions is Herbert C. Zafren "Bible Editions, Bible Study and the Early History of Hebrew Printing" Eretz—Israel: Archaeological Historical and Geographical Studies XVI (1982) pg 240–251.

[61] He refers to a translation of parts of the *Zohar* made for Egidio by Baruch Benedictus of Beneventum: *"Eodem tempore (1532) audivi Baruch Beneventanum optimum Cabbalistam qui primus libros Zoharis per Aegidium Viterbensem Cardinalem in Christianos vulgavit"* (Text quoted J. Perles, *Beiträge zur Geschichte der hebräischen und aramäischen Studien* (Ackermann, Munich 1884) pg 180).

[62] The manuscript of the Hebrew text is in the Biblioteca Casanatense in Rome. (G. Sacerdote, *Catalogo dei codici ebraici della biblioteca Casanatense* (Florence, 1897) n. 178 (I. III. 10: 2971) pg 589). The translation is in Paris (Bibliothèque nationale Ms. Lat. 527 (1) f. 5r) The text has 566 folios and marginalia in Egidio's hand. The title is: *Incipit liber Zohar super Liber mosis: labore magno quaesitus: maiore inventus: maximo rescriptus: longe ac multo multo cimulatione in latinum raptim cursimque excerptus f. Egidio Viterbiensi Eremita.* Fundamental here is F. Secret, *Le Zohar chez les Kabbalistes chrétiens de la Renaissance* (Librairie Durlacher, Paris 1958) especially pg 34–52. Secret traces such previous knowledge of the Zohar as there was (pg 25–30). His remarks about Galatinus's use of the Zoharic material (pg 30–34) are interesting as it displays parallels with Giustiniani's Psalter (pg 31) on which Galatinus was collaborating at the time. Secret also discusses the relation of Egidio's translations to the text of the Hebrew manuscript and the subsequent use of Egidio's work.

languages.[63] His competence in Arabic is also in evidence. We have
Widmanstetter's testimony in his Preface to the *editio princeps*.[64] During
the period from 1518 when he was Papal legate in Spain, Egidio had
a two-volume copy of the Koran with a complete Latin translation (the
first) made.[65] F. X. Martin drew attention to a *Rudimenta Linguae Arabicae excerpta per me fratrem Franciscum Gambassiensem, anno 1519, sic volente
ac iubente Reverendissimo D.Egidio Cardinali meo patrono, qui Latinae Graecae,*

---

[63] It seems Egidio had a library at Rome and one in Venice. The library in Rome
was sacked in 1527 but by 1530 Egidio had again a library in the city as Widmanstetter had access to it. The library at Venice remained untouched and a collection
of sixty-four manuscripts were acquired by Egidio's successor as bishop of Viterbo,
Cardinal Ridolfi. These books eventually became part of the Royal Library in Paris.
Some of these books went to Seripando who bequeathed them to the Monastery of
San Giovanni in Carbonara. Many of these books have since been scattered around
other libraries. See: D. Gutierrez "De Antiquis Ordinis Eremitarum S. Augustini
Bibliothecis" Analecta Augustiniana XXIII (1954) pg 164–174. An important list of
Egidio's books in the Bibliothèque nationale Paris (Grec 3074 f. 74–79v) is given in
Charles Astruc et Jacques Monfrin, "Livres latins et hébreux du Cardinal Gilles de
Viterbe" Bibliothèque d'Humanisme et Renaissance XXIII (1961) pg 551–554. Also:
L-G. Pélissier "Manuscrits de Gilles de Viterbe à la Bibliothèque Angélique" Revue
des Bibliothèques II (1892) pg 228–240, and his "Pour la biographie du Cardinal Gilles
de Viterbe" in *Miscellanea di studi critici edita in honore di Arturo Graf* (Bergamo 1903) pg
789–815. An essential overview of Egidio's manuscripts now in different libraries is
J. W. O'Malley, *Giles of Viterbo* pg 192–197. It is important for our understanding of the
continuity of scholarship amongst the scholars we are studying to recall Widmanstetter's
pleasure at receiving access to Egidio's library (*editio princeps* f. 10). For Egidio's manuscripts in Munich (i.e. those Widmanstetter came to possess) see Steinschneider, *Heb.
H.S. Muenchen* mss: 74, 81, 92, 103, 215, 217–219, 285. For indication of Egidio's
reading beyond the extant manuscripts, see the sources listed by Secret in his edition
of *Scechina* vol. I, pg 9–20. Gabrielle Sed-Rajna "Une Diagramme kabbalistique de la
Bibliothèque de Gilles de Viterbe" in ed. G. Nahon and C. Touati, *Hommages à Georges
Vajda* (Editions Peeters, Louvain 1980) pg 365–376 is of interest as it concerns a parch-
ment copy of a Sephirotic Tree from Egidio's library that is now in the Bodleian. On
this also Désirée Hirst "The Bodleian Scroll: Hunt Add. E.R. (Roll): The European
Background to Clement Edmondes' Gift to Sir Thomas Bodley for his new library of
a large illustrated scroll of the Kabbalah" in ed. G. Sorelius and M. Srigley, *Cultural
Exchange between European Nations during the Renaissance* (Almquist & Wiksell International,
Stockholm 1994).

[64] f. 10 *"factum est, ut Aegydius, postquam et Justinianus [nebiensis Antistes] ex hac vita, et Leo
Eliberitanus Catholica fide cum Punica commutata Tannetem migrasset, Arabicarum literarum dignitatem inter Christianos prope solus tueretur".* On Leo see below. Incidentally Widmanstetter's
remarks remind us of just how few scholars of any competence in Oriental languages
there were.

[65] The ms D.100 inf. in the Ambrosiana (which is a copy) is now described and
discussed in Hartmut Bobzin, *Der Koran in Zeitalter der Reformation* (Franz Steiner Verlag,
Beirut, 1995) pg 87. (Also pg 84–88 for an estimation of Egidio as an Arabist.) The
work was made for Egidio in 1518 by an otherwise unknown Joannes Gabriel Ter-
rolensis and corrected by Leo Africanus in 1525. The format is interesting. It has four
columns: Arabic, Arabic in Latin characters, Latin translation, and Remarks.

Hebraicae, necnon Arabicae linguae scientissimum fuit et mecum multos discipulos his linguis initiavit. There are Arabic notations in Egidio's hand.[66]

Further to promote Egidio's Oriental Studies, Leo X made him a gift of the Tunisian Arabic scholar Leo Africanus who had been captured by Sicilian corsairs.[67] Africanus became his tutor. Subsequently we know of an elementary Arabic grammar from Augustino Giustiniani in a manuscript dated 9 November 1524.[68]

Egidio and Elias Levita

From 1515 Egidio had in his household at Rome the German-born Jewish scholar and grammarian Elias Levita (1468–1549).[69] Their part-

---

[66] *Op. cit.*, pg 173 Bib. Ang. SS. II.II (Item 4). For other Arabic books in Egidio's library see C. Astruc & J. Monfrin, *op. cit.*, #33 (*Tabula alphabeti in Alcoranum in lingua spagnola*), #56–59.

[67] Leo was born Al-hasan ibn Mohammad in 1495 in Granada, moved to Fez, visited Africa and Istanbul, and made the pilgrimage to Mecca. In 1518 he was captured near Djerba, taken to Naples and given to Leo X in 1520. He was baptised Johannes Leo de Medici. He was in Rome until c. 1531 when he returned to Tunis and his ancestral faith. He died in 1550. Massignon has an article in *Encyclopedia Iudaica* (2nd ed.) V pg 723f that discusses Leo's book *Descrittione dell'Africa* published in J. B. Ramusios *Naviagazioni e viaggi* Venice 1550.This made reliable material on Islam available in the West for the first time. Subsequently the collection appeared in Latin (1556), French (1556), English (1600) and Dutch (1665). The English is: *A History and Description of Africa* tr. *John Pory 1600* (3 Vols, Hakluyt Society, London 1896). Leo's other work *De Viris* (1527) is found in J. A. Fabricius, *Bibliotheca Graeca* XIII (Hamburg 1726) pg 259–294. For Leo's metrical treatise see: Angela Codazzi "Il Trattato dell'arte metrica di Giovanni Leone Africano" *Studi orientalistici in onore di Giorgio Levi della Vida* Vol. I, (1956) pg 180–198. For relations with Jacob Mantino: H. Derenbourg "Léon l'Africain et Jacob Mantino" Revue des Etudes juives VII (1883) pg 283–285. Leo wrote an Arabic—Spanish Vocabulary for the instruction of his pupil, the celebrated Jewish physician.

[68] *Augustini Justiniani Genuensis pontificis Nebiensis arabica rudimenta: ad Egidium S. Romanae Ecclesiae Cardinalem.* This is in the Staatsbibliothek in Munich (Cod Arab 920/2 formerly Cod Or 100). It came into Widmanstetter's hands and bears his marks of ownership. It therefore perhaps also documents his progress in Arabic. Finally we may note Secret's report (*Scechina* pg 18 n 47) of a large Hebrew and Chaldaean Vocabulary (*Dictionarium sacrae Legis cum expositione latina per ordinem alphabet: Vocabularium dictionum chaldaicorum cum expositione latina per ordinem alphabet*) Paris B.n. Ms F lat 596) that has more than one hundred and twenty Koranic quotations.

[69] Gérard E. Weil, *Élie Lévita Humaniste et Massorète (1469–1549)* (E. J. Brill, Leiden 1963) is an outstanding work of scholarship from which all subsequent accounts are taken. Also Christian D. Ginsburg, *The Massoreth Ha-Massoreth of Elias Levita* (Longmans, London 1867). Egidio used several scribes to copy Hebrew texts for him but none are as important as Levita. Lists of Egidio's scribes may be found in U. Cassuto, Encyco-

nership was of enormous significance for European Christian Hebrew Studies.[70]

Under Egidio's patronage Elias was able in 1518 to bring out his *Ha-Bahur* that dealt with unusual word-forms in the Hebrew Bible. Thereafter Elias, encouraged by Egidio to work systematically on Aramaic, undertook a five-year project: the last page of the manuscript gives the date of completion as 9 June 1521. The two-volume work is called *Zikhronot*.[71] It is concerned with previous scholars of the Massorah and contains 167 massoretic lists and a massoretic concordance. It was never printed but is the seminal work that underlies both the *Meturgeman* and the *Massoreth ha-Massoreth*.[72]

The importance of the *Meturgeman* has been made clear by Raimundo Griño.[73] It is a dictionary of biblical and targumic (Oriental and Palestinian) Aramaic that because of its arrangement may be used as an Hebrew—Aramaic or Aramaic—Hebrew lexicon. Griño compares the work favourably with the lexicons of the modern scholars Lewy, Jastrow

---

pedia Judaica (1904) vol. I, pg 1041; J. Perles, *Beiträge zur Geschichte der hebräischen und aramäischen Studien* (Ackermann, Munich, 1884) pg 155–158, 163, 171–181, 200–203: F. Secret, *Kabbalistes chrétiens* pg 109; F. Secret "Aegidiana Hebraica" pg 409–416, 414–416. We lack a systematic study of these scribes.

[70] The only reference to Levita in Egidio I can find is *Historia* f. 245: *"Germania nobis praeceptorem exhibuit"*. Egidio's patronage of the Jewish community seems to have extended to arranging a papal audience for the Jewish messiah David Reubeni. There is an excellent account of this in F. Secret, *Kabbalistes chrétiens* pg 115–118 in the context of Jewish messianic expectations at the time. The Hebrew Text of the הראובני דוד ספור is in Ad. Neubauer, *Mediaeval Jewish Chronicles, II* (OUP Oxford 1895) pg 151–223. Jacob Mann offers a letter plausibly identified as from Reubeni in "Glanures de La Gueniza" Revue des Etudes juives LXXIV (1954) pg 148–159. A translation of the Neubauer text is found in E. N. Adler, *Jewish Travellers* (Routledge, London 1938) pg 251–328 (The audience is on pg 271–272). There is also a helpful article in *Encyclopedia Judaica. sub voc.* F. Secret "Notes sur les Hébraisants chrétiens" Revue des Etudes juives CXXIII/1–2 (1964) pg 141–173, pg 142 notes references to Reubeni in Postel.

[71] Now Ms Heb 74 in the Staatsbibliothek, Munich. It is important to note that this manuscript was part of Widmansetter's collection.

[72] G.Weil, "L'Archétype du Massoret ha-Massoret d'Élie Lévita" Revue d'Histoire et Philologie religieuses XLI (1961) pg 147–158. Also published as Offprint no. 2 of the same by Presses universitaires de France, Paris 1961.

[73] Raimundo Griño "Importancia del *Meturgeman* de Elias Lévita y del Ms Angelica 6-6 para el studio del mismo". Revista di Sefarad XXXI (1971) pg 353–361. Also: "Un Nuevo manuscrito del *Meturgeman* di Elias Lévita" in *Homenaja a Juan Prado* (Madrid, 1975) pg 571–583. The manuscript is Ms.Or 84 (A 6–6) in the Angelica which is important as it is the unabridged work. The shorter printed version of Paul Fagius in 1541 is called *Lexicon Chaldaicum*. To these Griño has now added Ms. Heb. 98 (2) in the Bibliothèque nationale, Paris.

and Dalman, mainly because of the number of examples including some 500 from *Yerushalmi*. Griño has also shown conclusively that Elias used Neofiti I.[74] The *Meturgeman* surpassed in scope and design its only contemporary competitor the *'Aruk* of R. Nathan of Rome.[75] The printed version deals with more than 3300 'roots'.

Egidio maintained his patronage and Levita produced his crowning work on grammar and orthography the *Massoreth ha-Massoreth*[76] which Bomberg printed in Venice in 1538.[77] The publication of the work raised a storm that raged thereafter for nearly three centuries. Levita set forward powerful arguments to prove that the vowel points found in Hebrew Bibles were not of the same antiquity as the consonantal text and had been put there well into the Common Era by the Massoretes. This led to a long-running dispute that engaged both Jewish and Christian scholars.[78] The first Jewish scholar to dispute Levita's evidence was Azariah de' Rossi, nearly forty years later, in his *Me'or 'Einayim* of 1574–1575 (Part III ch. 59). One of de' Rossi's arguments was that the analogy of cognate languages, like Syriac, all of which have vowel signs, showed that Hebrew had such signs from the earliest times.[79]

---

[74] "El *Meturgeman* y Neofiti I". Biblica LVIII (1977) pg 153–188. (Replying to a previous denial of this by Michael Klein "Elias Lévita and Ms. Neofiti I" Biblica LVI (1975) pg 242–246.)

[75] *'Aruk ha-Salem* ed. Alexander Kohut, 9 vols. (New York, 1955).

[76] G. Weil, *Élie Lévita* pg 286–341 is given over to a description of this work. See also Ginsberg's edition *cit. supra*.

[77] It was at Venice in 1538 that Widmanstetter visited Levita. We have a letter dated 1543 to Widmanstetter from Levita: J. Perles *op. cit.* 157ff.; Max Müller, *Johann Albrecht v. Widmanstetter 1506–1557 Sein Leben und Wirken* (Handels-Druckerei, Bamberg 1907) pg 32.

[78] A good account in Ginsberg's edition pg 44–61. See pg 52 for De' Rossi's arguments.

[79] A curious, but somewhat later (1577) example of interest in the significance of the variants in the Syriac Text is found in the work which Azariah de' Rossi felt would be of interest to his Gentile patrons. Dr. Joanna Weinberg has drawn to our attention ms 1948, of unknown provenance, in the Bibliotheca Angelica entitled: *"Osservazione di Buonaiuto de' Rossi ebreo, sopra diversi luoghi degli evangelisti, nuovamente espositi secondo La vera Lezione Siriaca"*. The ms contains a letter to the Cardinal Sancta Serverina (Julius Antonius Sanctorius) dated Ferrara 21. 6. 1577 but is dedicated to Giacomo Bonconpagno. It contains a general introduction to Syriac as the language of the Apostles and the Peshitta, and discusses the original sense of difficult passages (thus on pg 52 Matthew's attribution of a quotation to Jeremiah that really comes from Zechariah 11 is made easier by omitting the name of the prophet with the Syriac). Seventeen passages in the Gospels in which one finds Aramaic expressions are also discussed. The work was offered to the Inquisitors for alms. The work is of interest as it shows the facility

Interestingly Elias when arguing for a relatively late date for masso-retic vowel points makes reference to Syriac and the Maronite delegates at the Fifth Lateran Council to support his view that it is possible for a man to learn to read by habit and without points. He gives the fol-lowing account:[80]

> Now when I was in Rome I saw three Chaldeans (כלדאים) from the country of Prester John,[81] having been sent for by Pope Leo X. They were masters of the Syriac language and literature (ספר ולשון כשדים) though their vernacular language was Arabic. The special language, however, wherein the books were written, as well as the Gospels of the Christians which they brought with them, was Syriac (לשון כשדים), which is also called Aramaean, Babylonian, Assyrian, Chaldee, Tursea

---

with which a Jewish scholar (like Tremellius) might turn to Syriac, but the variants are offered to clear away difficulties in the Vulgate and not to replace it. See further: J. Weinberg "Azariah dei Rossi: Towards a reappraisal of the Last Years of his Life" Annali della Scuola Normale Superiore di Pisa 3d ser. VIII (1978) 493–511, especially pg 494–501 on the manuscript which I follow here. Also her "Azariah de' Rossi and Septuagint Traditions" Italia V no. 1–2 1985 pg 7–35; and her "An Apocryphal Source in the Me'or 'Einayim" Journal of the Warburg and Courtauld Institute LVI (1993) pg 280–284. Dr. Weinberg's unpublished doctoral thesis was: The Me'or 'Einayim of Azariah de' Rossi: A critical study and selected translations (London University PhD June 1982) and she has subsequently brought out a translation of the whole work as Azariah de'Rossi The Light of the Eyes (CUP, Cambridge 2001). Dr Weinberg, to whom I am indebted for kindnesses, has now given us an edition of the Angelica manuscript, J. Weinberg, Azariah de' Rossi's Observations on the Syriac New Testament (Warburg Insti-tute, London 2005) which supersedes previous discussions. Also helpful for a general orientation is: Lester A. Segal, Historical Consciousness and Religious Tradition in Azariah de' Rossi's Me'or 'Einayim (Jewish Publication Society, Philadelphia 1989).

[80] Translation and text from Ginsberg's edition pg 130–131. For a discussion of Levita's argument with Azariah de' Rossi here, and within the wider context of the debate over vocalisation see: S. G. Burnett, From Christian Hebraism to Jewish Studies (E. J. Brill, Leiden 1996) ch. 7 especially pg 205–213.

[81] Prester John's kingdom seems to have been located initially in India but then to have moved after about the fifteenth century to Africa and specifically Ethiopia. A recent survey is Ulrich Knefelkamp, Die Suche nach dem Reich des Priesterkönigs Johannes (Verlag Andreas Müller, Gelsenkirchen 1986). Meir Bar-Ilan "Prester John: fiction and history" History of European Ideas XX 1–3 (1995) pg 291–298 makes use of the Hebrew Letters of Prester John most recently edited in E. Ullendorff and C. F. Beckingham, The Hebrew letters of Prester John (OUP, Oxford 1982) and argues that in the letters the kingdom is in India. He cites the passage above as supporting his case, "as it is clear Eliahu Levita wrote of Nestorians". He has doubtless taken this from Ginsberg's edition pg 130 where Ginsberg offers 'Nestorians or Maronites'. Both have failed to make the necessary link to the Maronite delegation to the Fifth Lateran Council.

or Targum, (טורסאי, תרנום, ארמי, בבלי, אשורי, כלדאי) being denominated by these seven names.[82]

Pope Leo X had sent for them in order to correct by their codices his exemplar of his New Testament, which was written in Latin (להניה מספריהם ספרי אוונגליון שלו הכתוב לשון לטין). I then saw in their hands the Book of Psalms written in Syriac character, as well as translated into Syriac; that is to say the text was written with Syriac characters, the origin, pronunciation, and form of which greatly resemble the Hebrew. Now I saw them reading their Psalter without points, and asked them, Have you points, or any signs to indicate the vowels? and they answered me, "No! but we have been conversant with that language from our youth till now, and, therefore, know how to read without points". Thus far their remark".

The three Chaldaeans are undoubtedly the Maronite mission to the Fifth Vatican Council. Though Levita was interested in the question of reading unvocalised texts, we may notice incidentally that the Pope's specific interest was to compare the Syriac texts with the Vulgate.[83] We recall Leo X was the dedicatee of the Complutensian Polyglot and had approved Erasmus's Greek New Testament. He had been the dedicatee of Bomberg's Hebrew Bibles from Venice, of Giustiniani's *Psalterium*, the Arabic Prayer Book from Fano, and of Potken's *Tetraplar Psalter*. He received the dedication of Elias's Psalter (Vat sir. 9) in 1518 together with Alberto Pio da Carpi whom we suspected of interest in the production of a Polyglot. This was a Pontiff who supported biblical studies, and naturally took an interest in the latest and exotic Syriac texts which were now to be found in Rome.

During the winter of 1540–1 Levita travelled over the Alps to Isny on the Danube in Württenberg where he been invited by his former

---

[82] Considerable interest attaches to the variety of names possible for Syriac (of which 'Syriac' is not one). Some denominate peoples and places, but others תרנום (Targum) and perhaps בבלי (Babli) denote texts. This point emphasises the continuity that was perceived between Syriac and other forms of Aramaic in targumic, talmudic and kabbalistic texts. It is because of this that both Egidio's 'Aramaean' arcana and Levita's philology are important for a study of the reception of Syriac. Konrad Gessner's *Mithridates* (1555) uses the terms (in Latin): Chaldaean, Aramaic, Syriac, Assyrian and Babylonian: ed. M. Peters, *Konrad Gessner Mithridates* (Scientia Verlag, Aalen 1974) 15r & 9v on pg 20. I do not know what is '*Tursaea*' unless it refers to '*Tarse*' the home of '*Les Trois Rois tarsensiens*' or the Magi discussed by Postel in *Les Merveilles du Monde* (Paris, 1552) who came from "*la region de Tarse, confinante au Cathay*".

[83] The precise meaning of the relevant verb rendered 'to correct' is not clear.

student Paul Fagius to oversee his press in Isny and later in Constance.[84]
We need not pursue his career and subsequent publications further.[85]

The Reuchlin Affair

The publication of the Christian kabbalist Reuchlin's *Augenspiegel* of
1511 brought controversy on both sides of the Alps.[86] Egidio admired

---

[84] On Fagius: R Raubenheimer, *Paul Fagius aus Rheinabern* (Emil Sommer, Grunstadt,
1957); Weil, *Élias Lévita* pg 238–243. Jerome Friedman *op. cit.*, pg 99–118 offers a
characterisation of Fagius as a 'Christian Pharisee' interested in finding a source not
of arcana but of moral wisdom in post-Biblical Hebrew texts. We may note here
without pursuing the contrast a very different form of Protestant Orientalism to that
we have so far examined. Fagius went to Heidelberg at the invitation of Frederick II,
the Elector Palatine, but as he rejected the Interim Agreement he fled with Bucer to
Thomas Cranmer in 1549 and was given a chair at Cambridge. He died soon after
his arrival and was buried in St. Michael's church. Mary exhumed and burnt his body,
but Elizabeth 'reburied' him. Tremellius succeeded him in his chair.
[85] Except perhaps to notice his correspondence with Masius. The letters are lost
but the exchange of 1547 is reconstructed by J. Perles, *op. cit.*, pg 209–216 from letters
between Masius and Cornelio Adelkind. See Weil, *Élias Lévita* pg 162–163, 247.
[86] The large bibliography addressing the several aspects of the Reuchlin affair
cannot be listed here. A good indication of the literature may be had from: Fausto
Parente "La Chiesa e il Talmud" in ed. C. Vivanti, *Storia d'Italia Annali II: Gli ebrei in
Italia* (Turin 1996) pg 521–643, pg 574–579. Parente also gives a brief indication of
the historiographic fortunes of the question. For earlier works: J. Benzing, *Bibliographie
der Schriften Johannes Reuchlins im 15 und 16 Jahrhundert* (Bibliotheca Bibliographica 18,
Bad Bocket, Vienna/Zürich/Florence 1955). It is perhaps worth remarking that different issues were in question for the several parties. The Cologne Dominicans were
concerned with the question of converting Jews and the impediments to this provided
by post-biblical Jewish literature: thus the initial question was whether Jews might be
allowed the Talmud and other rabbinic literature. Reuchlin's repost was essentially a
legal response (not being Christians their literature could hardly be treated as heretical).
His interest in the Jewish literature, particularly as a Christian kabbalist, was a separate
issue, and the location of the debate within a possible scholastic/humanist polarisation
again a separate issue. (On this latter: J. H. Overfield, Humanism *and Scholasticism in
Late Medieval Germany* (Princeton U. P., Princeton, 1984) pg 247–297.) Leo X's final
decision of 23 July 1520 against Reuchlin seems to be motivated by his fear of Lutheranism. Reuchlin as a Christian kabbalist is discussed by F. Secret, *Kabbalistes chrétiens*
pg 44–72 and Jerome Friedman, *The Most Ancient Testimony Sixteenth Century Christian
Hebraica in the Age of Renaissance Nostalgia* (Ohio UP, Ohio 1983) pg 71–98. There is a
good facsimile and translation of the *De Arte Cabalistica* by Martin and Sarah Goodman (Bison Book Edition, University of Nabraska Press, Nabraska 1993). Moshe Idel's
introduction pg xi–xvi gives a survey of Pythagoras in Reuchlin and other Kabbalists.
A French translation by F. Secret with introduction and notes is *Johann Reuchlin La
Kabbale (de arte cabalistica)* (Aubier Montaigne, Paris 1973). The *De Verbo Mirifico* (1494)
and the *De Arte Cabalistica* appeared in facsimile from Friedrich Frommann Verlag,
Stuttgart-Bad Cannstatt 1964. A convenient description of Reuchlin's grammatical
work is: Hermann Greive "Die hebräische Grammatik Johannes Reuchlins *De rudimentis*

Reuchlin and was later to receive a copy of the *De Arte Cabalistica* (1517) as a gift from the author. Egidio probably sat upon the commission in Rome presided over by the Cardinal of St. Mark's, Domenico Grimani, dealing with the Reuchlin affair.[87] A letter from Egidio to Jacques Lefèvre d'Étaples[88] of 11 July 1516 thanked him for his support in the affair which had apparently just been settled in Reuchlin's favour.[89] Lefèvre's previous letter of support had been read to universal applause by those who supported Reuchlin, *"in conventu praesulum et theologorum quo defendae veritatis (Reuchlini) gratia conveneramus"*.

We have three letters of Egidio to Reuchlin that appeared in the second 1519 edition of *Illustrorum virorum epistolae* and give some indication of Egidio's feelings towards Reuchlin.[90]

A recent article by Joseph Dan helpfully emphasises the innovation of the approach of Reuchlin (and indeed of Egidio) in the Christian use of Kabbalah not primarily for polemical purposes but as constitutive of real Christianity.[91] But he also emphasises the instability of that position: they were finding Truth in the texts of a religious competitor.

---

hebraicis" Zeitschrift für die alttestamentische Wissenschaft XC (1978) pg 395–409. For Reuchlin's own library, indispensable is Karl Christ, *Die Bibliothek Reuchlins in Pforzheim* (Otto Harrassowitz, Leipzig 1924).

[87] Grimani (1461–1523) was the son of a Doge who had bought Pico della Mirandola's library.

[88] Franco Giacone and Guy Bedouelle, "Une Lettre de Giles de Viterbe (1469–1532) à Jacques Lefèvre d'Étaples (c. 1460–1536) au sujet de l'affaire Reuchlin" Bibliothèque d'Humanisme et Renaissance XXXVI (1974) pg 335–345.

[89] "Apparently" because on 23 June 1520, just two years before Reuchlin's death, the Pope revoked the decision and forbade the circulation of the *Augenspiegel* as a book offensive, scandalous and unlawfully favourable to Jews. See further below.

[90] f. Biii.v—Ci.r. Also ed. Ludwig Geiger, *Reuchlins Briefswechsel*, (Tübingen, 1875) pg 260, 261, 271. For bibliography on these letters: J. W. O'Malley, *Giles of Viterbo* pg 76 where Vat. lat. 3461 should be 3146). The first of 1516 expresses Egidio's regret at not having met Reuchlin personally when he was himself in Germany for the Pope. The second of 20 October 1516, after his letter to Lefèvre, is written as Prior General of the Augustinians and admits Reuchlin, his brother and his sister Elisabeth as affiliated members of the Order *"toto corde confratres et consororem per has literas et accepimus et vocamus"*. The third (24 May 1517) acknowledges receipt of the gift of the *De Arte Cabalistica* that had come out that year and was dedicated to Leo X.

[91] Joseph Dan, "The Kabbalah of Johannes Reuchlin and its historical significance" in ed. Joseph Dan, *The Christian Kabbalah Jewish Mystical Books and their Christian Interpreters* (Harvard College Library, Cambridge Mass. 1997) pg 55–96.

Egidio and other Christian Kabbalists

It is not easy to establish the extent of Egidio's connections with Christian Kabbalists other than Reuchlin. Umberto Cassuto noticed that some of Egidio's Hebrew manuscripts in the Angelica had previously belonged to Antonio Flaminio who had been keenly interested in Kabbalah.[92] Egidio would have known of the Dominican Agostino Giustiniani (1470–1536) and of the Franciscan Pietro Galatinus (c. 1464–c. 1540) who cooperated mutually on the apparatus of their respective works, the *Octapla Psalter* and the *De Arcanis Catholicae Veritatis.*[93]

Agostino Giustiniani

Giustiniani was a Genoese patrician who entered the Dominican Order (for the second time) in 1488 and was Bishop of Nebbio in Corsica. He published his Psalter in 1516 in Genoa.[94] It has eight columns across each opening of two pages: the Hebrew text; a Latin translation thereof; the Vulgate; the Greek Septuagint; an Arabic text; the Targum; and a Latin translation of it; and a column of copious scholia.[95]

---

[92] Umberto Cassuto, *I Manoscritti palatini ebraici della Bib. Apost. Vat. e la loro Storia* Studi e Testi LXVI (1935) pg 73. Antonio Flaminio wrote a Latin poem in praise of the *Ensis Pauli* of Paulus de Heredia. See: F. Secret "Pico della Mirandola e gli inizi della cabala cristiana" Convivium I (1957) pg 46. Galatinus acknowledged the use of Flaminius's Hebrew manuscripts in the Vatican Library when writing on the 72 divine Names in the *De Arcanis.* See: Levi della Vida, *Ricerche* pg 161. F. Secret has an entry 'Flaminio Antonio' in *Dictionnaire d'histoire et Géographie écclesiastique* vol. XVII Paris, 1971 pg 354 with bibliography. On the convert Paul of Heredia himself: F. Secret "'L'Ensis Pauli' de Paulus de Heredia" Revista di Sefarad XXVI (1966) pg 79–102, 253–271. His *Epistola de secretis* that contained the *Gale Razeia* was disseminated by the work of both Galatius and Giustinianus. F. Secret, *Le Zohar* pg 30–34 displays these relationships. For evidence of Egidio's borrowing of Mithridates's translation of Eleazar of Worms from the Vatican Library in 1516: ed. C. Wirszubski, *Flavius Mithridates Sermo de Passione Domini* (Israel Academy of Sciences and Humanities, Jerusalem 1963) pg 58–59. Widmanstetter mentions this translation in his Preface to the *editio princeps.*

[93] On both see: F. Secret, *Kabbalistes chrétiens* pg 99–106.

[94] *Biblia Polyglotta Psalterium Hebraeum Graecum Arabicum & Chaldeum cum tribus Latinis interpretatibus & glossis [Edidit Aug. Iustinianus Genuensis Praedicatorii ordinis episcopus Nebiensis]* Genua impressit Petrus Paulus Porrus, in aedibus Nicolai Iustiniani Pauli 1516. 4to. See: J. Balagna, *L'Imprimerie arabe en occident (XVI, XVII, XVIII siècles)* (Maisonneuve et Larose, Paris 1984) pg 20–23.

[95] Darlow & Moule, *Historical Catalogue of Printed editions of Holy Scripture* Part II Division I pg 2 observe that in a note to Psalm 8 the assistance of Jacobus Furnius is acknowledged in correcting the Greek and Baptista Cigala in correcting the Arabic.

This remarkable book, dedicated as we have seen to Leo X, was printed some six years before the Complutensian Polyglot went on sale in the house of Nicolas Giustiniani, in the Republic of Genoa, by a Milanese printer lately from Turin, Paulus Porrus, whom Giustiniani had brought to Genoa.[96] There were two thousand copies, and fifty on vellum.[97]

Following very quickly upon the heels of the 1514 Arabic prayer book from Fano, this is the first polyglot edition of part of the Bible printed with exotic script.[98] The Hebrew type is a little clumsy, not only because this is the first Hebrew printed in Genoa, but also because it was made by Gentiles. Amram emphasises that no Jews took part in the production of the book: the Doge was expelling them from Genoa at the time.[99] The Arabics are the second known (after the prayer book of Fano of which only nine copies are now known). Variants from two Arabic manuscripts are noted on leaves 08, P3, V7 & X1. The role played by this book in spreading knowledge of Arabic was considerable: both Nicolas Clénard (1495–1542) and Wolfgang Musculus (1497–1563) used it.[100] The Targum is also printed here for the first time. A gap is left Q3 where the Vulgate text has *"Tu vero repulisti et despexisti, distulisti christum tuum"*, though generally the Hebrew is followed as *'archetypus'*.

The column of scholia is interesting. It has long quotations from rabbinic and midrashic material. On X2 Giustiniani quotes from the *Cabbalistica Fragmenta* he published in woodcut in 1513—itself taken substantially from Reuchlin's *De Verbo Mirifico* and in turn to be taken

---

The Preface promises the whole Bible in the polyglot format and claims that the New Testament had been completed in manuscript.

[96] For an appraisal of Agostino as an Arabist: Hartmut Bobzin "Agostino Giustiniani (1470–1536) und seine Bedeutung für die Geschichte der Arabistik" in eds. Werner Diem & Aboli Arad Falaturi, *XXIV Deutscher Orientalistentag (Köln 1988)* (Stuttgart 1990) pg 131–139.

[97] Rijk Smitskamp, *Philologia Orientalia III* # 236, pg 231–235. Also: D. W. Aram, *The Makers of Hebrew Books in Italy* (Holland Press, London 1963) pg 225–229.

[98] *Septem horae canonicae, a laicis hominibus recitandae, iuxta ritum Alexandrinorum seu Jacobitarum Alexandrino Patriarchae subditorum Arabicae, editae a Gregorio Georgio Veneto, sub auspiciis Leonis X Pontificis Maximi in urbe Fano.* See: Christian F. de Schnurrer, *Bibliotheca Arabica* (Halle, 1811) pg 231 #235; G. Galbiati "La Prima Stampa in Arabo" in *Miscellanea Giovanni Mercati* vol. VI (Studi e Testi 126, 1946) pg 409–413. The prayer book was produced for the Melchites (Egyptian Jacobites).

[99] *Op. cit.,* pg 227.

[100] Briefly: Karl H. Dannefeldt "The Renaissance Humanists' Knowledge of Arabic" *Studies in the Renaissance II* (1955) pg 96–117 pg 113–115.

up by Galatinus in *De Arcanis*. Secret describes the notes by saying *"fourissent toute une littérature kabbalistique"*.

At Psalm 19. 4 *"in omnem terram exivit sonus eorum, et in fines orbis terrae verba eorum"*, the verse we have seen Egidio make so much of in the *Historia* as a prophecy of the kings of Spain and Portugal, we find Giustiniani claiming that it was fellow-townsman Columbus who had fulfilled the prophecy: *"At vero"*, he continues, *"quoniam Columbus frequenter praedicabit se a Deo electum ut per ipsum adimpleretur hec prophetia, non alienum existimavi vitam ipsius hoc loco inserere..."*. The account of Columbus's life and discoveries which follows is the first mention of his name in print.

In 1517 Giustiniani was called to France by Étienne Poncher the Bishop of Paris, where he remained until 1522 teaching Hebrew and Arabic at the University of Paris.[101] There he published in 1520 Moses Kimchi's *Grammar* (with Levita's annotations); Porchetus's *Victoria adversus impios Hebraeos* dedicated to the King;[102] Philo's *Questions on Genesis* dedicated to Louise of Savoy; and a Latin translation of Maimonides's *More Nebukim* (*Guide for the Perplexed*).[103] The publication of this latter marks a certain distance from Egidio who warmly took against this Aristotelian defence of the Jewish Faith, a work as far removed as could be from Kabbalah.[104]

Giustiniani died sailing to Corsica and his valuable library was dispersed. He had sent however his *Rudiments of Arabic* to Egidio, and in time Widmanstetter had that.[105]

---

[101] L Delaruelle "Le Séjour à Paris d'Agostino Giustiniani" Revue du seizième siècle XII (1925) pg 322–337 and F. Secret "Les Grammaires hébraïques d'Augustinus Justinianus" Archivum Fratrum Praedicatorum XXXIII (1963) pg 269–279.

[102] This work of 1303 acknowledged its dependence upon the *Pugio Fidei* of Raymond Martin (1220–1285). (Martin was a Dominican Friar active in Spain and Tunis and who knew Arabic.) On the *Pugio* see F. Secret "Notes pour une Histoire du Pugio Fidei à la Renaissance" Revista di Sefarad XX (1960) pg 401–407. Many passages in Galatinus's *De Arcanis* are taken from here and a list of them appears at the end of the 1603 Frankfurt edition.

[103] This great Aristotelian defence of the Jewish faith was written by Moses ibn Maimun (Maimonides) 1135–1204, initially in Arabic, but put into Hebrew by Samuel ibn Tibbon.

[104] For a modern account of Kabbalah as a reaction to Maimonides philosophical account of the Faith, see: Maurice-Ruben Hayoun, *Le Zohar aux origins de la Mystique juive* (Noêsis, Paris 1999).

[105] J. Perles, *op. cit.*, pg 177 on ms arab. 920 in Munich; F. Secret, *Kabbalistes chrétiens* pg 101.

Pietro Galatino

Pietro Galatino (1460–1540) was a Franciscan who took his name from Galatina in the diocese of Otranto which he saw taken by the Turks in 1480.[106] Doctor of Philosophy and Theology, he was from c. 1523 Poententiarius Apostolicus at St. Peter's. It is not difficult to believe with Kleinhaus that Galatinus was probably acquainted with Egidio's kabbalistic circle (*"probabaliter etiam consuetudinem habuit cum coetu 'cabbalistico' Romae in aedibus Cardinalis Aegidii Viterbiensis tunc existente"*) though specific documentation of any contact between the two has yet to be found.[107] Links of friendship also associated him not only with Giustiniani but also with Potken who taught him Chaldaean (which in his case means Ethiopic), and Elias Levita who taught him Hebrew. He wrote in support of Reuchlin.[108]

Kleinhaus initially gave a survey of Galatinus's work, much of which remains in manuscript.[109] This has of late been extended by studies of his Kabbalism[110] and also his interest in the *Apocalypsis Nova* of Amadeus.[111] Perrone has addressed his political thought.[112]

---

[106] Fundamental is: A Kleinhaus "De Vita et Operibus Petri Galatini O.F.M. Scientiarum Biblicarum Cultoris (c1460–1540)" Antonianum I 1926 pg 145–179 & 327–356 to which reference should be made. Also: Leftley, *op. cit.*, pg 98–104, 124–194, 197–253. For biographical details: C. Combero in DBI XXVII pg 402–404 s. v. 'Colonna Pietro'. G.Vallone, "Pietro S. detto il Galatino" *Letteratura e Storia Meridionale. Studi Offerti ad Aldo Valone I* (Biblioteca dell' Archivum Romanum CCXIV Florence, 1989) pg 87–105 is based upon Galatinus's own writings. Franciscan and Puglian sources are used by B. Perrone "Il *'De Republica Christiana'* nel pensiero filosofico e politico di P. Galatino." *Studi Pugliese in Onore di G. Chiarelli II* (Galatina, 1973) pg 449–633. See also: Wilhelm Schmidt Biggemann "Political Theology in Renaissance Christian Kabbalah: Petrus Galatinus and Guillaume Postel" Hebraic Political Studies 1/3 2006 pg 286–309.

[107] Galatinus *De Arcanis* f. 21r mentions Egidio: *"Qui ex nostris iunioribus de Cabala scripserunt . . . Egidius est ille Viterbiensis, vir utique eloquentissimus, ac disertissimus, omnique literari genere apprime eruditus, quem Leo hodiernus Pontifex Maximus, ob eius multiplices virtutes ac merita, ad cardinalatus dignitatem sublimavit: ab initio rem orsus, in libello de literis sanctis, elegantissimo quodam stylo, mirifice huiusce divinae sapientiae fundmenta iecit: ut palam ostenderet, a se longe plura, longeque altiora, quae ceteri omnes hactenus hac de re scripserint, cito esse proditura: quae rei tam obscure clarissimam afferent lucem".*

[108] *Illustrium Virorum Epistolae*, Hagenoae 1519. Text conveniently in Geiger, *Briefwechsel* pg 235.

[109] pg 172ff.

[110] A. Morisi, "Galatino et la Kabbale chrétienne" in *Kabbalistes chrétiens* (Cahiers de Humanisme, Albin Michel, Paris 1979) pg 213–31.

[111] R. Rusconi "An Angelic Pope before the Sack of Rome" in ed. M. Reeves, *Prophetic Rome* pg 157–187. Giorgio B. Salviati "Postel, Galatino e l'Apocalypsis Nova" in *Guillaume Postel 1581–1981 Actes du Colloque international d'Avranches 5–9 sept 1981* (G.Trédaniel, Paris 1985) pg 7–108.

[112] B. Perrone, *op. cit.*

Galatino's interest in Kabbalah is indicated by his expressed support for Reuchlin and through his *Expositio dulcissimi nominis Tetragrammaton* (1507). His first published work the *Oratio de Circumcisione Dominica* with its quotations in Oriental languages and its defence of the mystical sense of scripture was delivered before Leo X on 1 January 1515.[113]

Galatinus's major publication was the *De Arcanis* published in Ortona-al-Mare in 1518 with further editions in Basle (1550 and 1561) and Frankfurt (1603 and 1672).[114] It was one of the most widely dispersed books of the Renaissance and remained so until Scaliger damaged its reputation by exposing its plagiarism from the *Pugio Fidei* of Raymond Martin and the *Gale Razeia* of Paul de Heredia.[115] The *De Arcanis* was popular even amongst non-kabbalists as useful for refuting the Jews. Nevertheless the substantial continuities with the Middle Ages that this work displays should not detract from our appreciation of its change in attitude to the Talmud and its appreciation of the substantive and independent value of Kabbalah for Christians. In this respect Vasoli's reconstruction of the circumstances of the work's printing is important.[116] The work itself is a trilogue between Galatinus, Reuchlin and von Hoogstraten, the opponent of Reuchlin. Vasoli suggests that this was part of the effort of a group of Reuchlin supporters in Rome, some German humanists to whom Galatinus was connected, to win support for Reuchlin and that Leo X himself encouraged Galatinus to write. (Subsequent editions of the *De Arcanis* were printed together with Reuchlin's work).[117] If this is so we may add further material to our

---

[113] Kleinhaus, pg 172–173. He writes: *"Galatinus in decursu orationis citat more humanistarum voces graecas, hebraicas atque unam aethiopicam, uti vidimus; contra eos, qui in S Scriptura sensum mysticum nolunt agnoscere invehitur".*

[114] P. Galatinus, *Opus toti christianae Reipublicae maxime utile de arcanis catholicae veritatis, contra obstinatissimam judaeorum nostrae tempestatis perfidiam: ex Talmud, aliisque hebraiicis libris nuper excerptum: & quadruplici linguarum genere eleganter congestum, Orthona maris impressum per Hieronymum Suncinum.* 1518. The work is a small folio of 312 leaves. Hieronymus Suncinus is, of course, Gershom Soncino. Soncino was without doubt the greatest Jewish printer in the history of Hebrew typography (Amram, *Makers of Hebrew Books* pg 89–145). In *De Arcanis* he achieved a milestone of printing with mixed print for Greek and Hebrew quotations (he has no less than five different Hebrews). The privilege of Leo X mentions expressly *"ingenioso chaldaeorum, hebraicorum, graecorum, ac latinorum characterum genere impressum et editum".*

[115] F. Secret, *Kabbalistes chrétiens* defends Galatinus against this charge.

[116] C. Vasoli, "Giorgio B. Salvati, Pietro Galatino e la edizione di Ortona—1518—del De Arcanis Catholicae Fidei" in *Cultura Humanistica nel Meridione e la Stampa in Abruzzo. Atti del Convegno su Cultura Umanistica nel Meridone e la Stampa in Abruzzo* (L'Aquila, 1984) pg 183–210. On Salviati: C. Vasoli, "Giorgio Benigno Salviati". In ed. M. Reeves, *Prophetic Rome* pg 121–56.

[117] Kleinhaus, *op. cit.*, pg 174–179.

growing evidence of the growth and flourishing of a particular form
of kabbalistically motivated bible-study under this Pontiff.

Morisi's[118] work has concentrated upon building up a coherent
notion of Galatinus's ideas in this work and the need he expressed
to go beyond the literal sense to the mystical.[119] Here a contrast with
Erasmus may be helpful.[120]

Beyond Galatinus's Kabbalism, emphasis has recently been placed
upon Galatinus's prophetic notions. Marjorie Reeves identified the
Joachimite influence upon Galatinus and the centrality of the notion of
the 'Angelic Pope' for him.[121] Secret had earlier pointed out that Galatinus, the inveterate collector of prophecies, had come to see himself
precisely in that role.[122] Postel, who, in turn, saw himself as the Angelic
Pope, when reading the manuscripts of Galatinus in Ara Coeli in Rome
in 1544 saw that Galatinus was making that claim.[123] Galatinus had
fallen under the influence of the Commentary on the Apocalypse of
Amadeus (Jo Menesius da Silva 1431–1482 who founded the Order
of the Amadeites) who had taken down the *Apocalypsis Nova* in a cave
on the Janiculum as the Angel Gabriel dictated it.[124]

---

[118] Anna-Morisi-Guerra "The Apocalypsis Nova: a Plan for Reform" in ed. M.
Reeves *Prophetic Rome*, pg 27–50. Full bibliography in A. Morisi, *Apocalypsis Nova: Ricerche
sull' origine e la formazione del testo dello pseudo-Amadeo* (Studi storici 77, Rome 1970).

[119] Rusoni, *op. cit.*, pg 166 notes that Galatinus, like Egidio, developed from a position which grounded the arcana in Neoplatonism (characteristic of Ficino, Pico della
Mirandola and even Reuchlin) to one which laid more emphasis upon the foundation
of Kabbalah.

[120] Galatinus was not only committed to an *Hebraica Veritas* whereby he was prepared
to adjust the apparent inadequacies of the Vulgate to the Hebrew, but also to a notion
of *Hebraica Veritas* which gave every letter its significance. At this point the contrast
with Erasmus is sharp. Kleinhaus, *op. cit.*, pg 215–6.

[121] M. Reeves, *The Influence of Prophecy in the Late Middle Ages: A Study in Joachism* (OUP,
Oxford 1969) pg 234–238, 366–367, 442–447, 503. Also: M. Reeves, *Joachim of Fiore
and the Prophetic Future* (London 1976) pg 101–104.

[122] "G. Postel et les courants prophétique de la Renaissance". Studi Francesi III
(1957) pg 376ff; "L'emithologie de Guillaume Postel" in ed. E. Castelli, *Umanismo e
Simbolismo* (CEDAM, Padova 1958) pg 381–437, pg 390–393. Also his introduction to
his *Guillaume Postel le Thrésor des Propheties de l'Univers* (M. Nijhoff, The Hague 1969) pg
15–17. C.Vasoli, *Filosofia e Religione nella Cultura de Rinascimento* (Guida Editori, 1988)
pg 26–29.

[123] Galatinus was buried in the monastery of Santa Maria in Ara Coeli. His books
were initially preserved there, but were later dispersed to the Vatican library and
elsewhere. Leftley, *op. cit.*, pg 98, 360–363.

[124] The passage on the Angelic Pope was published in 1524 in a prophetic book in
Italian by Paulus Angelus, and Postel (F. Secret, *Kabbalistes chrétiens* pg 103) stated that
versions of Amadeus's prophecy were in the hands of all the Cardinals. Ignatius of
Loyola was later to warn François de Borgia against these predictions.

Finally Roberto Rusconi's work here is of considerable importance for it offers a new appraisal of Galatinus which places priority on the influence of the *Apocalypsis Nova* and thus allows for the integration and extension of a Joachimite apocalyptic system. This helps explain the messianic relevance of the Kabbalah to personal identification with the Angelic Pope who was to reform the Church, abolish the Mohammedan sect, and convert the infidels to Christ in a world under one Monarch, with one Pastor, one Sheepfold and divine worship diffused throughout.[125] The vital immediacy of the eschatological scheme in which these scholars lived drove a few beyond the role of mere spectators of the Last Days to assume more active roles. Galatinus's personal claims to be the Angelic Pope, however, pale beside the pretensions of Postel.[126]

Conclusion

Egidio articulated the most profound aspirations of High Renaissance Rome promoting the mythology, prophetic destiny, and eschatological mission of the Eternal City and offering at the same time, and indeed for the first time, learned philological support for such a programme. He was the Church's major spokesman and scholar in oriental languages, a rapidly expanding new area of scholarship of both prophetic and missionary significance and earned the close cooperation of the Pontiff. The concurrence of the expansion of geographical horizons and Oriental scholarship was itself a Sign of the Times. The oriental scholars of High Renaissance Rome were moreover Christian kabbalists, and it is to emphasise this that we have spent so long in the High Renaissance. The ideological matrix in which the first Western

---

[125] R. Rusconi "An Angelic Pope before the Sack of Rome" in ed. M. Reeves, *Prophetic Rome* pg 157–187.

[126] The prophecy of the Angelic Pope from the *Apocalypsis Nova* appears to have played a determining role in the career of Cardinal Bernadino López de Caravajal, leading him to encourage Maximillian I to take up arms against the Turk, to call and lead the Council of Pisa with its call for Church Reform in 'Head and Members', to seek a crusade against the Turk, and finally to seek his own election to the Chair of St. Peter. He seems subsequently to have transferred the role to his successful rival Adrian VI. See: N. H. Minnich "The role of Prophecy in the Career of the Enigmatic Bernadino López de Caravajal" in ed. M. Reeves, *Prophetic Rome* pg 111–120. Caravajal was of course one of the dedicatees of the early Syriac texts copied by Elias, Vat. sir 265 & Paris syr. 17, described above.

experience of Syriac was received and given meaning was thus both elaborated and central. Syriac studies from their very beginning had their place within a prophetic schema and a mystical hermeneutic that would remain the context within which they would be pursued by the Western Catholic Syriac scholars responsible for the printed editions of the sixteenth century. It was a schema that would survive in the mind of these scholars, even when the Curia no longer maintained its enthusiasm for the Aramaean arcana.

CHAPTER THREE

THE SCHOLARS OF THE *EDITIO PRINCEPS*:
MOSES AND MASIUS

The 1555 Vienna *editio princeps* of the Syriac New Testament was an extraordinary achievement, remarkable for the integrity of its text, the felicity of its typeface and its comparative freedom from typographical errors. Its type marks a clear advance upon that of Teseo and of Postel's *Linguarum duodecim characteribus*, though its production drew upon Postel's technical assistance as the sole living repository of previous experience in printing Syriac.[1] There is however really nothing before it that quite prepares us for its length and its confident, attractive and accurate biblical pages. The particular excellence of the first edition arose from the cooperation in its production of a Syriac scribe, Moses of Mardin, and the German humanist, J. A. Widmanstetter, assisted by Postel. This unique collaboration is responsible for the particular features of the book, for within the volume there is a quite unique juxtaposition of scribal features characteristic of a Syriac Gospel-book or New Testament suitable for liturgical use (and now for the first time in print), and the more familiar characteristics of a Western humanist book. Yet, though intended for two distinctly different sets of readers, the book has coherence that subsumes the utilitarian pastoral purposes of its intended Syriac readers within the larger purpose of Widmanstetter that we shall seek subsequently to describe. It is an outstanding bible.

Properly to understand the circumstances that led to the production of the *editio princeps* we must first consider the mission and experiences of Moses, the motivations of Widmanstetter, and the decisively important development of Postel's scholarship and strange self-understanding. Moreover, in explaining why the *editio princeps* was eventually produced in Vienna rather than Rome, we shall be led to embark upon a broader characterisation of two distinct periods in Curial attitudes to the nascent Oriental Studies of our scholars. There are several matters therefore

---

[1] A convenient table of specimens of all the sixteenth-century Syriac types is found in Rijk Smitskamp, *Philologia Orientalis* (E. J. Brill, Leiden 1992) III pg 202–204.

which we must examine before we turn to the *editio princeps* and we shall begin with Moses.

Moses of Mardin

In the mid-sixteenth century there was no Syriac printing press in the East.[2] The Maronites first printed Syriac at Quzhaya in the Lebanon around 1610,[3] and the Melkite Athanasius Dabbas (1647–1724) had a press with Arabic characters at Aleppo.[4] The first Arabic press in the Lebanon was established amongst the Maronite monks at St. Jean de Choueir by Abdallah Nasrallah Zakher (1680–1748), a man simultaneously goldsmith, engraver, painter, watch smith and author who added printing to his repertoire. Jules Léroy has left us a description of this press that was still extant in the 1950s that gives us some idea of its rudimentary nature.[5] But in 1549 there was not even this. It was

---

[2] It is well to remember that printing was forbidden in the Ottoman Empire in 1483 by Sultan Bayazid and that the ban was not lifted until 1720 when the first Turkish printed book appeared. See: R. H. Kévorkian, *Catalogue des 'Incunables' arméniens (1511/1695) ou Chronique del'Imprimerie arménienne* (Cramer, Geneva 1986). A most useful collection of essays may be found in ed. F. Hitzel, *Livres et Lecture dans le Monde ottoman* (Revue des Mondes musulmans et de la Méditerranée. Série Histoire) (Edisud, Aix-en-Provence 1990).

[3] Franz Babinger "Ein vergessner maronitischer Psalterdruck auf der Nürnberger Stadtbücherei" Zeitschrift für alttestamentliche Wissenschaft (1925) pg 275 for a description of this first Syriac work printed in the East. Also: Jean Muller & Ernst Roth, *Aussereuropäische Druckereien in 16. Jahrhundert* (Verlag Librairie Heitz, Baden-Baden 1969) pg 53. The book is a Syriac Psalter with an Arabic commentary in karšuni. The colophon names the printers as Pasquale Eli (from Camerino in the Italian Marches) and Yusuf (Joseph) ibn 'Amina. The colophon also names Archbishop Sarakis of Damascus as the patron of the project. He wrote the preface and his arms appear on the title-page. Steph. Ev. Assemani listed this work in his Laurentian catalogue (*Bibliothecae Mediceae Laurentianae et Palatinae codicum mss orientalium catalogues… Steph. Evodius Assemanus archiep. Apameae recensuit, digessit notis illustravit, Ant. Franc. Gorio curante, (Florentiae, 1742)* pg 71. He also noted there an earlier Psalter of 1585 from the same monastery and printed also by ibn 'Amina. Simon Assemani echoed this in his catalogue of the Naniana (*Catologo dei Codici manoscritti orientali della Biblioteca Naniana, compilato dall' abate Simone Assemani* (2 vols, Padova, 1789/93) pg 8. The existence of this Psalter has been disputed, particularly by J. Nasrallah, *L'Imprimerie au Liban* (Harissa, 1949) pg 2 who believes that confusion may have arisen between Archbishop Sarkis (1600–1638) and Patriarch Sarkin (1581–1590). All Nasrallah's remarks upon the Psalter (pg 1–7) are valuable. Most important generally for Lebanese printing is: ed. Camille Aboussouan, *Exposition Le Livre et le Liban jusqu'à 1900* (Paris 1990). The catalogue illustrates and comments upon many of the books discussed below.

[4] Nasrallah, *op. cit.* pg 17–25.

[5] J. Léroy, *Moines et Monastères du Proche-Orient* (Horizons de France, Paris 1958) pg 163. See also Nasrallah, *op. cit.* pg 26–45. On pg 31 Nasrallah cites De Volney's famous

probably in this year[6] that the Jacobite[7] (Syrian Orthodox) Patriarch of Antioch, Ignatius III 'Abdallah († 1557),[8] heard of printing in the West and sent a scribe, Moses of Mardin, to Rome to procure printed Syriac Bibles in quantities far greater than he or his fellow scribes could produce.[9] Moses came from the region of Mardin, not therefore from the Lebanon but from Mesopotamia. He was armed with some Syriac manuscripts and a commendatory letter. The motive of his mission was in this respect essentially pastoral: the Eastern Churches never had the number of scribally produced biblical and liturgical books they needed to promote and maintain the spiritual welfare of their faithful.[10] However, the Jacobite Church was not at the time in union with Rome and there may have been weighty matters of ecclesiastical politics to which Moses was also to attend. When Widmanstetter in the preface to the *editio princeps* tells us of Moses's arrival, he says he came

---

description of the press from *Voyage en Syrie et en Égypte pendant les années 1783, 84 et 85*. (4o edition, vol. II, Paris 1807) pg 78–89.

[6] J. S. Assemani, *Bibliotheca Orientalis I* pg 535–536 was in error in placing the arrival of Moses under Pope Julius III rather than at the time of predecessor Paul III who died 10 November 1549. Though the exact date of his arrival is uncertain it was without doubt in 1549, a little before the Pope died. As Moses says himself in the subscription to the Gospels (f. 158) in the *editio princeps*, he was accredited to both popes. The date of manuscript Harley 5512 below is also persuasive.

[7] The Syriac-speaking Christians who followed the teaching of Severus and Dioscurus on the single nature of Christ were called 'Jacobites' by the Greeks after Jacob Baradeus, the organiser of the Monophysite Church in Syria. The Calendar in manuscript vat. syr. 68 gives on 31 July *"the feast of Mar Jacob Baradeus after whom we are called 'Jacobites'"*: F. Nau "Martyrologies et Ménologies orientaux, I–XIII: Un martyrologie et douze ménologies syriaques" Patrologia Orientalis X (1915) pg 131. The Syriac Orthodox Church today finds this term pejorative. I use it merely to simplify nomenclature for readers possibly unfamiliar with these Churches, observing that it was used both by Arab historians and by prelates of this Church in the past.

[8] All Patriarchs since the thirteenth century have carried the name Ignatius. See: Levi della Vida, *Documenti* pg 3 n. 4.

[9] On Moses initially see J. S. Assemani, *Bibliothecae Orientalis Clementino-Vaticanae Tomus Primus de Scriptoribus Syris Orthodoxis* (Rome 1719) pg 535ff. On Mardin: *E.I.* (second edition) Vol III s.v. pg 273–227. For Moses's arrival: Alfred Durant "Les Editions imprimées du Nouveau Testament syriaque" Recherches de Science religieuse XI (1921) pg 385–409, pg 385; Levi della Vida, *Ricerche* pg 142.

[10] This desperate shortage of books is brought home by Leon Abel who was sent East in 1583: [Leon Abel], *Une Mission religieuse en Orient au seizième siècle* (Benjamin Duprat/Challamel, Paris 1866) pg 44: *"Parmi ces nations, il n'existe pas aujourd'hui un livre traitant de la foi dans lequel il n'y ait plus d'erreur que de vérité: il y a un tel manqué de livres de l'Écriture, que dans toute la Syrie, la Mésopotamie et la Cilicie, je n'ai pu trouver que deux corps entiers de toute la Bible en langue arabe, trois en langue chaldéene, et quatorze dans toute la nation arménienne. La fait a été affirmé comme certain par beaucoup de personnes et le patriarche lui-même de l'Arménie mineure"*.

to Rome: *"cum ob alias gravissimas causas, tum ut Novi Testamenti volumen praelo excusorio multipicatum in Syriam reportaret"*. The *'gravissimas causas'* were probably negotiations with a view to the Union of the Churches, and the printing of bibles may in fact have been subordinate to this.[11] Though Moses was only a priest, some such person would be necessary as an ambassador before the arrival of the Patriarch himself.[12] If this were so, it would seem that in all cases we can say that knowledge of Syriac was brought to the West by representatives of the Eastern Churches seeking union with Rome.[13]

We can find evidence of Moses's initial liturgical activity in Rome in the British Museum manuscript Harley 5512 that he wrote.[14] This remarkable manuscript of 186 folios contains the Roman Missal in use thirty years before the Trentine *Missale Pianum* of 1570, in Latin but written in a black Syriac serto script. Some rubrics are in Arabic and there are a few Syriac anaphoras. The first colophon, perhaps in anticipation of Union, juxtaposes the names of the Patriarch, Ignatius 'Abdallah III, and Pope Paul III, though the fact that Paul III died 10 November 1549 makes the colophon's date of 1550 wrong. A third highly elaborate colophon consisting of a circular calligraphic pattern gives a date corresponding to 1548/9 when Moses describes himself as *'taking refuge in God'*, perhaps a reference to his recently begun stay in Rome.

Moses tells us that he wrote the manuscript at the monastery of San Stefano Maggiore (later San Stefano dei Mori) that was situated in the Vatican on the site of the present Ethiopic Seminary. It was here at

---

[11] Union was achieved under Gregory XIII (1572–1585) but did not last long.

[12] The Jacobite Patriarch Na'matallah was in Rome from 1577–1595. In 1578 Gregory XIII was reluctant to negotiate Union with an ex-Patriarch and insisted on contact with the reigning Patriarch. Moses's profession of faith on behalf of himself and his Patriarch could hardly in itself be expected to effect Union.

[13] A partial parallel to Moses's mission may be found in the voyage to Rome of the Armenian noble Abgar T'oxar'c'i in 1564. The object was to repair relations broken after the Council of Florence. We hear of this from the Preface to his 1565 Psalter printed in Venice. See: R. H. Kévorkian, *Catalogue des 'Incunables' arméniens (1511/1695) ou Chronique del'Imprimerie arménienne* (Cramer, Geneva 1986) pg 26–27 (with plate).

[14] W. Wright, *Catalogue of the Syriac manuscripts in the B.M. Vol. I* (London 1870) pg 214–216. Lord Harley's own clear Latin description of the manuscript has been inserted at the beginning of the volume. Other descriptions of the manuscript are found in Levi della Vida, *Ricerche* pg 142 n. 5 which corrects Harley in points. Most important is J. Léroy "Une Copie syriaque du Missale Romanum de Paul III et son Arrière-plan historique" Mélanges de l'Université de St. Joseph, XLVI (fasc 23) (1979) pg 355–382 on which the above relies heavily.

San Stefano in 1513 that Johannes Potken of the Cologne Chapter had produced the first printed book in Ethiopic:[15] *Alphabetum seu potius Syllabarium litterarum chaldaearum, Psalterium chaldaeum, cantica Mosis, Hannae etc.*[16] This was the first ever printing in an Oriental script in Rome[17] and it inaugurated a distinguished history of Ethiopic scholarship within the monastery.[18] The book contains, in addition to the Alphabet and the Psalter, the Canticles used in the Roman Liturgy. If this were an aid to worship it would enable Ethiopic speakers to have the Canticles in their own language, but it is more probably merely a small pedagogic chrestomathy.

What is striking however about Moses's Harley manuscript is that it is a *transliteration* of the Latin text. Its obvious function is to allow a Syriac reader, inexpert in the Latin script, to sound out the words of the Mass in Latin, and not the words of the Mass in his own language. Perhaps that was what Moses was learning to do (or had to learn to do), and he was preserving his crib for others. Whether we should deduce from this that Leo X's permission to celebrate the liturgy in

---

[15] Potken describes the circumstances of his edition in the Preface. We may also learn from the Preface of Potken's theory of the 'Chaldaean' origin and nature of the Ethiopic Liturgy. His usage of 'Chaldaean' for Ethiopic remained characteristic of scholars associated with the Monastery up until Job Leuthof (Ludolf) in his Frankfurt *Grammatica aethiopica* of 1702. A rather bizarre anticipation of this misnomer is found in ed. C. Wirszubski, *Flavius Mithridates Sermo de Passione Domini* (Israel Academy of Sciences and Humanities, Jerusalem 1963) pg 38–39 where it appears Mithridates may have written and taught Ethiopic characters as Chaldaean.

[16] The whole was without doubt printed from the Vatican ms et. 20, a fifteenth-century parchment that arrived in the Vatican Library in the sixteenth century (see: Levi della Vida, *Ricerche* pg 41). Renato Lefevre discusses this manuscript in "Su un codice etiopico della 'Vaticana'" La Bibliofilia XLII (1940) pg 97–102. This was probably the only Ethiopic book in the Library at the time. Potken seems to have been the first scholar to make use of the Oriental manuscripts in the Library (Levi della Vida, *Ricerche* pg 444).

[17] The printer was Marcellus Silber, alias Frank, from Regensberg. The type is moveable and skilfully cut. We do not know the name of the engraver, punch-cutter or type-founder. When he left Rome in 1515–1516, Potken took the Ethiopic fount with him. In 1518 in Cologne he published, with the help of a relative Johannes Soter, the Psalter in Hebrew, Greek, Ethiopic and Latin columns side by side. This was the *Psalterium in quatuor linguis hebrea graeca chaldea latina.* He used the 1513 type for the Ethiopic. In 1522 he added a page with the Ethiopic alphabet, a Paternoster and an Ave in Ethiopic and Latin. On Ethiopic printing in general: H. F. Wijnman, *A Outline of the Development of Ethiopic Typography in Europe* (E. J. Brill, Leiden 1960).

[18] M. Chaîne "Un Monastère éthiopien à Rome au XVᵉ et XVIᵉ siècle" Mélanges de l'Université de Saint Joseph V (1911) pg 1–36; Sebastian Euringer "San Stefano dei Mori (Vatikanstadt) in seiner Bedeutung für die abessinische Sprachwissenschaft und Missionsgeschichte" Oriens Christianus X (1935) pg 38–59.

Syriac given to Elias had been forgotten is uncertain. Perhaps the fact that Moses was a schismatic, if not heretical, Jacobite rather than a Maronite made conspicuous conformity to the Roman rite significant at this stage. One does not know.

The prior of San Stefano dei Mori between 1550 and his departure to the East in 1568 was Giovanni Battista Abissino who acted as official interpreter in Arabic to the Curia during that period.[19] The senior Ethiopic scholar at San Stefano was Tasfa Sejon ('Hope of Zion'; otherwise, Petrus Aethiops, Pietro Indiano) and Moses specifically mentions him as commissioning his work in the first colophon to manuscript Harley 5512.[20] Tasfa Sejon who had come from Debra Libanos via Jerusalem with two other monks (Tanse'a-Wald, otherwise 'Resurrection of the Son', otherwise Petrus: Za-Sellase 'He of the Trinity', otherwise Bernadino) died prematurely aged thirty-six sometime after 1552 yet his achievements were significant. These are succinctly summarised in his epitaph from San Stefano.[21] Tasfa Sejon had brought out an edition of the New Testament in Ge'ez based upon an Ethiopic Bible manuscript he had brought to Rome only the year before Moses arrived in Rome.[22]

---

[19] Unfortunately he could not read it. This caused considerable embarrassment when Abramo the Copt brought a letter from Gabriel VII in 1557 (Levi della Vida, *Ricerche* pg 194–195).

[20] Essential is Renato Lefevre "Documenti e Notizie su Tasfa Seyon e la sua attivita Romana nel sec. XVI". Rassegna di Studi Etiopici (Rome) XXIV (1969–1970) pg 74–133. See Levi della Vida, *Ricerche* pg 142 n. 5 for a discussion of the fact that the colophon makes Tasfa unexpectedly a bishop. Leroy, *op. cit.* pg 369–70 objects.

[21] Sebastian Euringer "Das Epitaphium des Tasfa Sejon (Petrus Aethiops) und Seine Chronologie" Oriens Christianus I (1926–1927) pg 49 for the Latin and Ethiopic text. Kuntz, *Postel* pg 99n 316 notes a previous suggestion that Tasfa Sejon was Postel's unnamed *'noster Niger'* who accompanied him on his first oriental journey. Postel had departed from Venice sometime after 19 May 1549 and was in Jerusalem in August. One questions whether this conjecture would leave enough time for the friendship between Moses and Tasfa to develop between Moses's arrival (before Julius III's death 10 November 1549) and the colophon of the Harley manuscript. But the matter is not certain. Postel did however know Tasfa Sejon whom he mentions warmly in a manuscript gloss: F. Secret, *Guillaume Postel et son Interprétation du Candélabre de Moyses* (B. De Graaf, Niewkoop 1966) pg 24.

[22] *Testamentum Novum cum epistola Pauli ad Hebreos tantum…Romae 1548.* Ignazio Guidi "La prima stampa del nuovo Testamento in ethiopico, fatta in Roma nel 1548–1549" Archivo della R. Societa Romana di Storia Patria IX (1886) pg 273–278 (with the text of two interesting letters). This article (pg 273) gives an interesting insight into why Tasfa was eager to print: the Moslems had destroyed monasteries and libraries and he was eager to preserve the New Testament in print. A short but authoritative introduction to Ethiopic Bibles in general may be found in: Edward Ullendorff, *Ethiopia and the Bible* (Schweich Lectures 1967 OUP London 1968) pg 31–72. For the New Testament: Bruce M. Metzger, *The Early Versions of the New Testament* (OUP, Oxford, 1977)

In addition to his ecclesiastical and diplomatic role, Moses had been sent to Rome to have the New Testament printed in Syriac. Who better to befriend him than Tasfa Sejon.[23]

Before leaving manuscript Harley 5512 we must notice yet more distinguished patrons for whom Moses prays in the (second) colophon (f. 179r).[24] The first is the Cardinal of Santa Croce whom he describes as a friend of strangers, φιλόξενος, like Abraham. This is none other than Marcello Cervini[25] who became pope Marcellus II 9 April 1555 upon the death of Julius III and who had supported Tasfa Sejon.[26]

By 1549 Cervini had already established his reputation as a humanist scholar of distinction with an interest in printing Biblical manuscripts, Patristics and the Lives of the Saints. In addition to his episcopal

---

pg 215–257 (For the deficiencies of the manuscript and the edition see especially pg 228–229); Rochus Zuurmond, "The Ethiopic Version of the New Testament" in eds. B. D. Ehrman & M. W. Holmes, *The Text of the New Testament in Contemporary Research* (Eerdmans, Michigan, 1995) pg 142–156. For the Old Testament text initial orientation may be found in E. Tisserant's review in Revue Biblique (1925) pg 292–296 of A. Rahlfs's "Die aethiopische Bibelübersetzung" in *Septuaginta Studien* (2nd ed., Gottingen, 1965) pg 659–681).

[23] The second colophon also praises the Catholic priest Mariano Vittori da Rieti (1518–1572). Vittori assisted in the production of the 1548–9 Ethiopic New Testament. In 1552 he produced in Rome the first Ethiopic Grammar *Chaldeae seu Aethiopicae linguae institutiones*...that like the New Testament was printed by Valerius Doricus Brixiensis '*opera Angeli de Oldradis*'. Vittori's work was assisted by Tasfa Sejon. Again the names of punch-cutter and type-founder are lost, but most significantly in the dedication we learn that Cervini had commissioned the printing of the Ethiopic New Testament ("*imprimi aedique curasti*") from which it looks as if Cervini had had the fount made at his own expense. Cervini is further described as: "*vir doctus et perhumanus, qui solus ex nostratibus posit errores corrigere...*, *si quidem ante eum nullus ex latinis hominibus hac in lingua legitur profecisse*". This seems remarkable to claim that Cervini could read Ethiopic. If this were so, it would suggest an involvement in Oriental Studies on his part beyond that which has previously been imagined. Vittori's Grammar also managed to find its way into Robert Harley's library (Euringer, Oriens Christianus X (1935) pg 47). Guy Lefèvre de la Boderie in a letter to Scaliger 25 January 1581 speaks critically of this work. The letter is quoted F. Roudaut, *Le Point centrique* (Klincksieck, Paris 1992) pg 54–55.

[24] Before leaving the manuscript we may also note the common quotation that appears therein accompanying a drawn Cross and that is also found in the *editio princeps*. "In Thee we conquer our enemies, and because of Thee we trample under foot those who hate us" (Psalm 44. 5). Léroy, *op. cit.* pg 357. J. Léroy, *Les Manuscripts syriaques à peintures* (Paul Geuthner, Paris 1964) pg 113 discusses the functions, both sanctifying and apotropaic, of the Cross and this text. The same text is found with the engraving at the end of Mark's Gospel in the *editio princeps*.

[25] See generally: William V. Hudon, *Marcello Cervini and Ecclesiastical Government in Tridentine Italy* (North Illinois U.P., Illinois, 1992).

[26] Indeed it seems likely that Cervini used Tasfa Sejon to read the titles of such Arabic and oriental manuscripts as the Vatican Library then possessed (Levi della Vida, *Ricerche* pg 141).

duties which his reforming bent led him to take seriously, his period of service at the Council of Trent and other demands of ecclesiastical administration,[27] Cervini had collaborated closely with both Agostino Steuco of Gubbio (1497–1548) whom Paul III had placed over the Vatican Library in 1538, and also with Guglielmo Sirleto (1514–1585) who became custodian of the library in 1545.[28] Upon Sirleto's death on 15 March 1548, Paul III appointed Cervini as the first Cardinal to direct the Library, a post he held until his death.

Well before his own formal appointment as Director of the Library Cervini had shown himself interested in printing and through the house of Antonio Blado in Rome had sponsored an edition of the Gospel Commentary of Theophylact Archbishop of Bulgaria.[29] He further supported the production of Henry VIII's *Assertio septem sacramentorum*, the letters of Cicero, Theodoret of Cyrrus's ten sermons on Providence, an Italian Suetonius and a Plato with Ficino's commentary. During the Council he had himself worked upon Greek manuscripts in preparation for an edition of John Chrystostom subsequently published by his colleague Genziano Herveto (1499–1584). Also on the margins of the Council, he directed Herveto in his collation of Codex Bezae.[30]

In addition to his interest in printing Cervini also set about the systematic procurement of books for the library. During his tenure he acquired 143 Greek manuscripts and was concerned to produce a new catalogue of the Oriental Collection.[31] Cervini was also eager to find

---

[27] Victor Baroni, *La Contre-Réforme devant La Bible* (Imprimerie La Concorde, Lausanne 1943) pg 114 &117 discusses Cervini in the context of the debates on the Bible at Trent. Cervini showed himself favourable to a new Latin version, though Seripando argued for a Vulgate corrected from the Hebrew and Greek. Both felt the need for renewed and reorganised Biblical studies.

[28] For continuity between Steuco and the syncretistic tradition we have previously examined: Charles B. Schmitt "Perennial Philosophy: from Agostino Steuco to Leibniz" Journal of the History of Ideas XXVII (1966) pg 505–532. The basic work remains: Theodor Freudenberger, *Augustinus Steuchus aus Gubbio, Augustiner Chorherr und päpstlicher Bibliothekar (1497–1548) und sein literarisches Lebenswerk* (Münster 1935). For Paul III's interest in Kabbalah, see: F. Secret "Paul III et La Kabbale" in "Notes sur les Hébraïsants chrétiens" Revue des Études juives CXXIII/1–2 (1964) pg 154–158. The article describes the kabbalistic text of Antonius Hieronymus Lunarius de Recaneto *Discursus de Reformatione Ecclesiae* dedicated to Paul III as the Pope destined to renew the Church.

[29] In 1549 two works put into Latin came from Bado's press: *Missa qua Ethiopes communiter utuntur* and *Modus baptizandi, preces et benedictiones quibus ecclesia ethiopum utitur* in which Tasfa Sejon had collaborated.

[30] V. Baroni, *La Contre-Réforme devant La Bible* (Imprimerie de la Concorde, Lausanne 1943) pg 193.

[31] An inventory of the Library made between September 1518 and 27 July 1519

men capable of using the manuscripts. We have suggested he made use of Tasfa Sejon. Masius was also his protégé.[32] Postel had been in Rome 1544–6 but was absent during the Cervini years.[33] Widmanstetter was in Rome at various times between 1532 and 1550 but knew himself to be as yet inadequate for such tasks, even though after the death of Egidio 13 Nov 1532 and until the arrival of Tasfa there may well have been no one else in Rome other than Widmanstetter and his teacher who could have read these books.[34] Though we shall see Widmanstetter had links with Cervini and Steuco we have no evidence to connect him to the Vatican Library at the time.[35]

Cervini we can see was a scholar deeply interested in bibles, Oriental scholarship and printing, and also the patron of Moses. This alone should render suspicious the received account of his reception in Rome "[Moses] seems to have met with little encouragement from either Pope. No pecuniary help was to be had", and, "the printing of

---

by the custodians Lorenzo Parmenio and Romolo Mammacini on the initiative of the Librarian Zanobi Acciaiuoli (*Ricerche* pg 112) makes no specific references to Oriental books but merely refers to a case of '*libri diversarum linguarum*' which were "*in fragmentis et varii quaterniones inordinati*". There was a slightly more descriptive listing in 1533 (*ibid.* pg 113). At this point there were no Syriac manuscripts and most of the holding was Christian Arabic. In 1548 an alphabetic index was compiled after Cervini's nomination as Protector of the Library (*ibid.* pg 120). It seems he was concerned to develop a system of labelling the Oriental msanuscripts with a view to arranging a new catalogue (*ibid.* pg 130). We have discussed the arrival of the Library's first Syriac manuscripts above. A concise overview of Oriental scholarship in the context of the Library is provided in Alastair Hamilton "Eastern Churches and Western Scholarship" in ed. Anthony Grafton, *Rome Reborn The Vatican Library and Renaissance Culture* (Yale U.P., New Haven 1993) pg 225–249.

[32] H. De Vocht Andreas Masius (1514–1573) in *Miscellanea Giovanni Mercati* (Studi e Testi CXXIV) Rome 1946 pg 425–441, pg 431.

[33] He did however correspond with Cervini about his differences with the Jesuits, and sent him a copy of his kabbalistic *Candelabrum Mosis*.

[34] Widmanstetter in the Preface to the *editio princeps* speaks of a teacher, a certain "*Symeonis Syrorum, qui iuga Libani incolunt, Episcopi Catholici et doctissime viri institutione profeci adeo, ut sentirem Thesei* (i.e. Teseo Ambrogio) *desiderium... leniri iam aliquantum posse*". This appears to be the Maronite bishop to whom Sulaqa sent a brief note of greeting ("*Al vescovo maronita*") appended to a letter written to Julius III from Aleppo 27 December 1553: "*Et ancora damo la pace nostra al vescovo Symeone, maronita...*", see: Giuseppe Beltrami, *La Chiesa Caldea nel secolo dell' Unione* (Orientalia Christiana XXIX vol 83) (Institutum Orientalium Studiorum, Rome 1933) pg148. It is frustrating that we do not know any more about this bishop.

[35] For Widmanstetter's connections here and his attempt to persuade Clement VII in 1534 to have Syriac and Arabic taught in Christian Schools (mentioned in the Preface to the *editio princeps*) see below. We shall also see that Cervini sent the deacon Petrus Ghalinus from Damascus to Germany to help Widmanstetter with his Arabic.

the Peshitto New Testament found no favour at Rome".[36] This is all quite wrong. Two entries in a Vatican register of expenses made under Cervini prove exactly the opposite.[37] The first for 3 December 1552 authorises a payment of thirteen scudi to *'Moyse soriano'*: *"quanti si sono speci per far la stampa da stampar libri in lingua soriana per uso della libraria"*. The second subsequently speaks of *"spesa fatta in polzoni per la stampa di libri sorani"*. Though in the event the Syriac New Testament was not printed in Rome, Moses did not lack the patronage and financial support of the powerful Cardinal Protector of the Vatican Library who was eager to have Syriac books—and these can scarcely be other than Psalters, Gospel Books or New Testaments—printed at his expense for his Library.[38]

It is interesting at this point to ask whether a similar 'Orientalism' was to be found in Rome at this time as was under Egidio. William Hudon has suggested that the Joachimite notions of the Angelic Pope remained alive with Girolamo Seripando who may have applied them to Cervini himself as Marcellus II and we have noted above Steuco's interest in the Neoplatonic tradition.[39] We shall see shortly however that

---

[36] Anon. "The Printed Editions of the Syriac New Testament" Church Quarterly Review LII (1888) pg 257–294, pg 269.

[37] L. Dorez "Le Registre des Dépenses de la Bibliothèque vaticane de 1548–1555" in *Fasciculus Ioanni Clark Dedicatus* (CUP, Cambridge 1909) pg 142–185. On page 166 Dorez discusses another occasion when Cervini had type cut.

[38] Cervini's desire to produce a Syriac press in Rome is recognised in Alberto Tinto "Per una Storia della Tipografia orientale a Roma nell'Età della Controriforma" Accademie e Biblioteche d'Italia Anno XLI (24 n.s.) nn. 4–5 pg 280–303, pg 282–283. This should be seen within the context of his many vast printing projects. See: L. Dorez "Le Cardinal Marcello Cervini et l'imprimerie à Rome (1539–1556)" in Mélanges d'archéologie et d'histoire XII (1892) pg 289–313; R. Ridolfi "Nuovi contributi sulle 'stamperie papali' di Paulo III" La Bibliofilia L (1948) pg 183–197; Pio Paschini "Un Cardinale Editore. Marcello Cervini" in his *Cinquecento Romano e Riforma Cattolica* (Lateranum, Rome 1958) pg 185–217. In English there is S. Morison "Marcello Cervini Pope Marcellus II Bibliography's Patron Saint" Italia medioevale e umanistica V (1962) pg 301–319. Dorez's vital "Registre…" *supra* stresses Cervini's interest in Syriac and Ethiopic printing as the initial steps towards the establishment of a polyglot press in Rome and the subsequent work of the Congregatio de Propaganda Fide. More specifically he notes that in 1540 after discussion with Sirleto, Cervini planned to print a Polyglot—a critical revision, accurately printed, of the Hebrew, Greek and Latin texts of the whole Bible. We have discussed Cervini's interest in Ethiopic above. For much later developments: Willi Henkel "The Polyglot Printing Office of the Congregation: the Press Apostolate as an important means for communicating the Faith" in ed. J. Metzler, *Sacrae Congregationis de Propaganda Fide memoria Rerum* Vol. 1/1 1622–1972 (Herder, Rome 1971).

[39] William Hudon "Marcellus II, Girolamo Seripando and the Image of the Angelic Pope" in ed. M. Reeves, *Prophetic Rome* pg 373–387 offers evidence for continuity here.

such notions did not long survive the changes in Papal policy towards the Jews after 1553.

Cervini was a friend of Reginald Pole (†1558) who had received Cervini's promotion to the College of Cardinals 19 December 1539 with warm enthusiasm.[40] (Shortly afterwards at the end of December, Cervini was to be equally warmly greeted in Paris by Cardinal Jean du Bellay who served as Bishop of Paris from 1532–1551) Whilst it is true Cervini had in 1553 to inform Pole of the suspicions entertained by the Holy Office about his views on Predestination, Cervini had died before formal charges were laid and the enduring friendship of the two men seems to have been unaffected. Part of the burden of William Hudon's recent biography of Cervini is to soften the usual distinction between the 'spiritual' and the 'intransigent' legates at Trent and to show how people like Pole and also Seripando applauded Cervini's reformist tendencies, welcomed his elevation and feared only his successor in the Chair of St. Peter.

Such a revaluation of the relationship between the two men prepares us to read, again in the second colophon of manuscript Harley, that Pole, "the Cardinal of Angleterre (d-NGLTRRʿ) renowned for his goodness and kindness among men" was also a patron of Moses. It will come then as no surprise when we learn subsequently that Moses on his way to Germany accompanied Pole as the Cardinal left Italy on his way to his cousin Mary's England. A third Cardinal is mentioned in the second colophon—"blessed, generous, merciful and full of Charity, Afaris (PʿRYS)". Levi speculates that this was Jean du Bellay returned to Rome from his Paris bishopric in 1549.[41]

At this point we may reflect upon the excellent connections Moses had established for his diplomatic and printing missions. Lodged at San Stefano he enjoyed the friendship of the two foremost Ethiopic scholars who had worked on biblical and liturgical projects and were probably able to speak to him in Arabic and help him with his Latin. Through

---

Seripando (c. 1493–1563) was Cardinal General of the Augustinians after Egidio and maintained his predecessor's kabbalistic interests, see: F. Secret "Girolamo Seripando et la Kabbale" Rinascimento (second series) III (1963) pg 251–268.

[40] On Pole see D. Fenlan, *Heresy & Obedience in Tridentine Italy. Cardinal Pole and the Counter-Reformation* (OUP, Oxford 1972) and now Thomas F. Mayer, *Reginald Pole Prince and Prophet* (CUP, Cambridge 2000); William V. Hudon, *Marcello Cervini* pg 32–33, 143, 155, 164–5 on the relationship of the two men.

[41] Levi della Vida, *Ricerche* pg 144. Léroy "Une Copie syriaque b" pg 381 remains unconvinced.

them Moses had established contact with the Pope's confidante, the Cardinal Protector of the Vatican Library who was eager to print a Syriac bible and two of the influential Cardinal friends of Cervini, one just from Paris and the other shortly on his way to London. By 1549, Moses could not have been better placed. The question naturally arises: why was the *editio princeps* of the Syriac New Testament not produced at this time in Rome?

The answer to this question lies initially, I believe, in an appreciation of the inadequacies of the 1548 Ethiopic New Testament (of which Tasfa Sejon was only too aware). The book was printed by the brothers Valerius Doricus and Ludovicus who could not read the script and therefore needed the constant supervision of Tasfa. In one of the several colophons seeking the reader's indulgence he remarked that the compositors could not read the script, and he did not know how to compose. The result was a book stiff with typographic errors.[42] A similarly flawed edition is not likely to have commended itself to the scribe Moses nor would it have served his Patriarch's purposes at all. In addition, though the Ethiopic script is not joined by ligatures, the Syriac script is. There was no one in Rome with the technical skill to tackle this problem. In fact the only person at all with any experience of this matter at the time was Guillaume Postel. The production of the *editio princeps* would be delayed until these problems could be addressed.

Moses therefore systematically sought out the very few men in Europe who knew some Syriac, the group of scholars who form the focus of our study of the production of the Syriac New Testament. Moses was able to establish productive scholarly relations with all of them, but initially the prospects for an edition cannot have looked good. The technical difficulties were matched by the commercial certainty that no profit but only a considerable loss would accrue from such an edition. Moses was to produce the edition finally with Widmanstetter in Vienna in 1555. Before that he was to cooperate with Cervini's protégé Masius but that liaison did not apparently begin until 1553. What has not been sufficiently appreciated in accounts of Moses's career is that

---

[42] The edition is also defective in its text. The text of *Acts*, as a colophon acknowledges, is a hodge-podge being mostly the editor's translation from the Latin by reason of the lacunae in the Ethiopic he had. The manuscripts used were Vat et. 25 (XV cent), Vat et. 68 (XV cent), and Vat et. 5 (XVI cent). These are discussed Metzger, *op. cit.* pg 230 & 227. Moses did not face similar problems in this respect: the manuscript he had brought from the Patriarch was quite adequate for a printed edition.

subsequent to Postel's return to Venice after his second visit to the East in the autumn of 1550, Moses had at some point joined him at Bomberg's house in Venice.[43]

Moses and Postel: Postel's early work on the Syriac New Testament

Postel had brought back good manuscripts for an Arabic New Testament and was discussing these with Iohannes Renialmus, the editor of Bomberg (Bomberg had just died in 1549). But, as we learn from a most important passage, he was also working on a Syriac New Testament at Bomberg's expense when Providence brought him Moses of Mardin.[44]

In the Preface to *Cosmographicae disciplinae compendium* (Basle 1561), also addressed to the Emperor Ferdinand, we have (sig. a 3) another reference to Bomberg's support and the contribution of Moses who had brought older manuscripts.[45]

The first passage *"cuius aere Syriaca ipsa exemplaria paraveram"* acknowledges Bomberg's financial support in the provision of the manuscript. The second passage *"ad mei collationem"* indicates that Postel had prepared a text for print and was glad to collate this with the manuscripts Moses had and that he saw were older.

---

[43] Postel left Venice shortly after his return. For his movements in Paris and Basle between then and his return to Venice in August 1553 see Kuntz, *Postel* pg 99–115. The passage from the *Cosmographicae disciplinae compendium* quoted above has 'vix rediissem' and 'statim'. This may indicate that Moses was with him in 1550 rather than later in 1553. Cervini made his first payment to Moses in December 1552. It is perhaps more likely that Moses had returned to Rome at that date, in which case this would be before Postel's return to Venice in 1553.

[44] British Library, Sloane ms. 1413 f. 87. *"attuli Venetias multa vetustissima fidelissimaque exemplaria Arabici novi testamenti, de quibus utrisque per typos multiplicandis ut in Orientem referantur aut deferantur, et dum maxime de hac re cum Ioh. Renialmo Dan. Bomberghi curatore, cuius aere Syriaca ipsa exemplaria paraveram, pertractarem, Ecce (o admiranda Christi providentia) se offert utrique Moses ille Syrus sacerdos, cui, pridem Romae a suo Patriarcha misso fuerat idem studium atque mihi et quem ea de re tandem ad Widmanstadium quasi huius linguae perdiscendae cupidum (nam nesciebam adhuc illud aut patria pulsum, aut tibi esse Cancellarium) mittere utrique nostrum visum est"*. Postel is here writing to the Emperor Ferdinand.

[45] *"attuleram inquam exemplar fidelissimum novi Testamenti quam ad rem meo succurrens desiderio pridem etiam eiusdem linguae manifestandae studio incitatus Daniel Bombergus, curator curatore suarum rerum Iohanne Renialmo impensas suppeditaverat: a cuius conquirendi peregrinatione quum vix rediissem, se statim mihi Venetiis obtulit Cassis ille sacerdos ue T. M. notus, Moses Mesopotamius Syrus, vestustis exemplaribus instructus, cuius opera sum usus ad mei collationem, eo quod meum erat recentius scriptum..."*

This is an important notice as it establishes that Postel was at work on a Syriac Gospel in 1549. We shall however shortly review, in this chapter and the next, two further pieces of evidence which show that Postel was working on the Syriac Gospels as early as 1537 when Bomberg had shown him a manuscript, and that he wrote to Masius in 1547 recording his progress. These three pieces of evidence together will give us a pre-history of the *editio princeps* that has not previously been perceived because the sources have not been properly understood. It is also a story that, as we shall see, Widmanstetter for his own reasons omitted from his account of Syriac studies in his introduction to the *editio princeps*. The recovery of Postel's early work on the Syriac New Testament is one of the new perspectives offered by the present work, and we shall return on occasion to its significance.

One has, however, no reason to believe that Postel had actually at this stage produced punches or matrices. We know of his collaboration with Teseo that resulted in the *Linguarum duodecim characteribus* of March 1538 and we know later that after Teseo's death Postel had made an attempt to come by his type. But we have no reason to believe that he was successful. Further, it was after Moses's return to Rome that Cervini in 1553 had made his first payment precisely for the cutting of new type. All this would have been unnecessary if Postel actually had some cut. And there is the question of time: H. D. L. Vervliet has estimated that the time required in the sixteenth century to make a new cutting and casting of type was between four and six months.[46] Postel was not in Venice long enough.

We do not then know the precise time, duration or specific details of Moses's work on an edition of the Syriac New Testament with Postel, yet it seems quite probable that this was the context in which Cervini was prepared to pay for type to be cut. We should therefore imagine continuity between the work in Venice and the production of the *editio princeps* in Vienna when Moses again was working with Postel, this time in the company of Widmanstetter with whom Postel claims to have put him into touch himself. Once again we see that Postel is the technical conduit of Syriac printing expertise.

However there were ominous developments in the world of Hebrew printers in Venice. A rivalry was developing between Bomberg's com-

---

[46] H. D. L. Vervliet, *Sixteenth Century Printing types of the Low Countries* (Amsterdam 1967) pg 344.

petitor Marco Antonio Guistiniani and Alvise Bragadoni that was to have catastrophic effects and bring the Hebrew presses of Venice to a standstill. In spite of its initial progress therefore, it would not be the house of the late Bomberg in Venice that produced the *editio princeps* of the Syriac New Testament.

Masius

After his return from Venice, Moses began collaboration with Masius.[47] Though Masius was not involved in the production of the *editio princeps*, he is an exceptionally important figure amongst the early orientalists and made a substantial contribution to the Antwerp Polyglot. Before examining Masius's collaboration with Moses, it will be convenient to examine here his earlier career.

Andreas Maes (Masius, Linichus or Liniacensis) came from the village of Lennick (Linniacum) to the South of Brussels where he was born on St. Andrews' Day, 30 November 1514, in circumstances of which we know nothing. He studied with distinction at Louvain. He attended lectures at the Collegium Trilingue that had been founded by Erasmus in 1517 in execution of the will of Jerome de Busleyden. He purified his Latin under Conrad Goclenius and learned Greek with Rutger Rescius. Balenus taught him Hebrew.[48] These were exciting times in the life of the new institution before the political troubles of the 1570s and Masius made friendships that were to last through his life and have left their traces in his correspondence. The majority of these were young humanists who made their way to Italy.[49]

---

[47] Fundamental is M. Lossen, *Briefe von Andreas Masius und seinen Freunden 1538 bis 1573* (Publikationen der Gesellschaft für Rheinische Geschichtskunde II, Leipzig 1886). This excellent edition unfortunately does not contain previously published correspondence (pg vii). Lossen also wrote the article on Masius in the *Allgemeine Deutsche Biographie* (Leipzig, 1884) Vol. XX pg 559–562. Also: H. De Vocht "Andreas Masius (1514–1573)" in *Miscellanea Giovanni Mercati* (Studi e Testi CXXIV) (Rome 1946) pg 425–441. J. Vercruyst "Un humaniste brabançon oublié: Andreas Masius Bruxellanus" Le Folklore Brabançon CLII (1961) pg 615–621 adds very little. Most important are: A. van Roey "Les Études syriaque d'Andreas Masius" Orientalia Louvansia Periodica IX (1978) pg 141–158; his "Le début des Études syriaque et André Masius" in ed. René Lavenant, *V Symposium Syriacum 1988* (Orientalia Christiana Analecta CCXXXVI) (Pont. Institutum Studiorum Orientalium, Rome 1990) pg 9–11; and Jan Wim Wesselius "The Syriac Correspondence of Andreas Masius" in the same volume pg 21–30.

[48] See H. de Vocht "Andreas Masius" pg 427 for sources.

[49] Martin de Smet, Stephanus Pighius (who worked in the Vatican Library and like

Masius left Louvain in 1537 and for the next ten years he became
Secretary to Johann van Wese until the latter's sudden death at the
Diet of Augsburg 13 June 1548. (It was at the Diet that Masius met
Widmanstetter). Though the peregrinations of the Court left Masius
little time to study, he nevertheless maintained correspondence with the
leading semitic scholars and his status is apparent from the accolades of
that formidably learned circle. In 1539 Sebastian Münster[50] dedicated to
Masius his Latin translation of Elias Levita's work on Hebrew accents as
a reply to at least four letters written from different places, some in Latin
and some in Hebrew.[51] It is clear from the wording of the dedication that
the men only knew each other through correspondence. Münster again
refers to this correspondence in his *Dictionarium Trilingue*. Paul Fagius
at Isny in July 1542 dedicated his Latin translation of the ספר אמנה
Liber Fidei to Masius, again as a man personally unknown to him but as
thanks for letters *"hebraice scriptae et tam docte, quales ab homine christiano ad
me antea numquam datae sunt".*[52] We possess a letter in Hebrew written by
Masius to Widmanstetter in 1541.[53] Hebrew correspondence was the
celebrated achievement of only a few of the most learned humanists
of the sixteenth century. Masius alone of these scholars would go on
to correspond not only in Hebrew but also in Syriac.[54]

Masius enjoyed Cervini's patronage), John Visbroeck (Secretary to Cardinal Morone),
Laevinius Torrentius etc.

[50] On Sebastian Münster, Karl H. Burmeister, *Sebastian Münster* (Helbing & Lichtenhahn, Basle, 1963). Jerome Friedman, The Most Ancient Testimony: Sixteenth-
century Christian-Hebraica in the Age of Renaissance (Nostalgia Ohio U.P., Athens
Ohio, 1983) pg 212–251 offers a characterisation of Münster which should now be
revised in the light of Stephen G. Burnett "A Dialogue of the Deaf: Hebrew Pedagogy
and anti-Jewish Polemic in Sebastian Münster's *Messiahs of the Christians and the Jews*
(1529/39)" Archiv für Reformationsgeschichte XCI (2000) pg 168–190. Münster's
Chaldaica Grammatica (Basle 1527) may claim to be the inaugural document of Christian
Aramaic studies in Germany. It is an Aramaic not a Syriac Grammar. See Burmeister,
op. cit. pg 47–50. Guy Lefèvre de la Boderie used Münster extensively in his Grammar
in the Antwerp Polyglot.

[51] *Accentuum Hebraicorum liber unus* (Basle 1539) taken from Levita's טוב טעם (Venise
1518) and מסרת המסרה (Venise, 1518). The dedication referring to the letters is quoted
in J. Perles, *Beiträge zur Geschichte der hebräischen und aramäische Studien* (Theodor Ackermann,
Munich, 1884) pg 205 and L. Geiger, *Das Studium der hebräischen Sprache in Deutschland*
(Breslau 1870) pg 74–75.

[52] J. Perles, *op. cit.* pg 205.

[53] J. Perles, *op. cit.* pg 203–4. References to Widmanstetter by his name 'Lucretius' are
found in Masius's correspondence: Lossen, *op. cit.* pg 8, 160–163, 199, 262, 351, 438.

[54] For Buxtorf's work on Hebrew Correspondence see: S. G. Burnett, *From Christian Hebraism to Jewish Studies Johannes Buxtorf 1564–1629 and Hebrew Learning in the
Seventeenth Century* (E. J. Brill, Leiden 1996) pg 138–145. For later Hebrew letters and

Masius developed a warm relationship with the nephew of his employer Johann van Wese, Henry-Rudolph up ten Haitzhovel whom Masius had taught before the young man went up to Louvain to study at the Trilingue between 1544–1546. Their friends knew them as the '*fratres*'. Masius accompanied Henry-Rudolph to Italy between 1544–1546 when both were promoted *Doctor Utriusque Iuris*.

It was in Italy that Masius was able to meet Postel and be instructed by him in the rudiments of Arabic. He had written to Fagius 8 May 1545 mentioning the publication of Postel's *De Orbe Terrae Concordia libri IV* in which both he and Fagius were mentioned but he had not yet met the man.[55] This was the period of Postel's sojourn with the Jesuits. He had abandoned his benefice and situation in Paris and was in Rome until early 1546. He parted company with the Jesuits in December 1545 but remained in Rome for a few months more. Not only did Postel teach Masius Arabic but also shared with him his interest in Kabbalah.[56] Postel kept Masius informed of his own publications and their problems and at times sought his help.[57]

In 1545 in Rome Masius was able to indulge his passion for rabbinic texts. In the Preface to his ספר צורת האריץ (*Sphaera Mundi* Basle 1546) Sebastian Münster mentions Masius's trawl of Hebraica from the previous year.[58]

---

some eighteenth-century Syriac correspondence, Wesselius *op. cit.* pg 21. The Hebrew correspondence of Johann Stephan Rittangel (1606–1652) is discussed in P. T. van Rooden and J. W. Wesselius "J. S. Rittangel in Amsterdam" Nederlands Archief voor Kerkgeschiedenis LXV (1985) pg 131–152. That of Antonius Hulsius is found in P. T. van Rooden and J. W. Wesselius "Two early cases of publication by subscription in Holland and Germany: Jacob Abendana's *Mikhal Yophi* (1661) and David Cohen de Lara's *Keter Kehunna* (1668)" Quaerendo XVI 2 (1986) pg 110–130.

[55] The letter is not found in Lossen but appears in M. Raubenheimer, *Paul Fagius aus Rheinabern* (Emil Sommer, Grunstadt 1957) pg 136. The letter is dated Rome 8 March 1540, but F. Secret has shown that it was written in 1545. "La Rencontre d'Andreas Masius avec Postel à Rome" Revue d'histoire ecclésiastique LIX 1964 pg 485–489. See also: F. Secret "Notes sur Guillaume Postel (VII G. Postel et Sébastien Munster)" Bibliothèque d'Humanisme et Renaissance XXII (1960) pg 377.

[56] Letter of Masius to Postel 13 April 1554 (Lossen, *op. cit.* pg 161) making reference to Postel's *Grammatica Arabica* (Paris 1538/9). Masius clearly did not have his own printed copy. Postel attempted a reprint in 1549 but significantly could not find characters. Letter to Masius 19 May 1549 Chaufepié, *Nouveau Dictionnaire* III pg 220: "*Nostra grammatica arabica non potuit secundo edi ob characterum penuriam*". For Masius's lack of an Arabic lexicon, see: A. van Roey "Les Études syriaques" pg 143.

[57] F. Secret "La Rencontre" pg 487–489.

[58] J. Perles, *op. cit.* pg 206. One notices the presence of kabbalistic works in this list. J. Perles, *in loc.* describes Masius's passion for Hebrew Books as "*eine rege Fürsorge*". This was to be apparent in the dark days of September 1553 when Hebrew Books

Notice of Postel's continuing work on the Syriac New Testament

On 22 January 1547 Postel wrote a letter to Masius from Venice where
a letter sent to him previously by Masius and awaiting his attention at
Bomberg's house had been brought to his attention by Nicolas Stopius.[59]
Postel wrote about his work *Opus de restitutione humanae naturae* (*"In eo est
basis Evangelii aeterni"*) that he sent ten months previously to Oporinus
in Basle and which was now lost (*"interceptum est"*). The text does not
appear in Lossen but only in Chaufepié and may for this reason not
have previously appeared in accounts of Syriac Bibles.[60] The passage
indicates that Postel was preparing a text of the Gospels in Arabic
and Syriac for publication in 1547, two years before Moses arrived in
Rome.[61] There is nothing improbable in this, rather it corroborates the
evidence we have seen above that Postel had an edition underway when
Moses visited him. We shall see in the next chapter that Bomberg had
shown Postel a Syriac Gospel in 1537. This passage thus constitutes

---

were burned in the Campo dei Fiori. Every page of Masius's great commentary *Joshua*
of 1571 displays his knowledge of Talmud and Midrash, Jewish commentators and
philosophers. The volume ends with a list of Hebrew books and manuscripts with bibliographic annotation attached. See: J. Perles, *op. cit.* 206–207. These annotations reveal
Masius's view of rabbinic literature. He believed it contained evidences of Christian
truth. Thus of Midrash Rabbah he writes: *"illa רבות quae Moses hadarsan composuerat sunt
a Judaeis, quantum apparet, abolita, quod nostris mysteriis viderentur favere in multis locis"*. In the
commentary upon Joshua 1.4 we have: *"in commentariis quae vocant בראשית רבה non illis
quidem quae a R. Mose Hadarsan hoc est concionatore sunt conscripta, haec enim, ut nostrae crebro
doctrinae consentanea, videntur Judaei conspiratione quadam suppressisse, sed in alteris quae R.Osaïas
nisi fallor congessit…"*. And of kabbalists (on Joshua 7. 7); *"diviniores Hebraeorum Philosophi
quos Cabbalistas vocant"*; (on Joshua 22. 22) *"Cabbalistae, philosophi apud hebraeos non sane
prorsus vani neque semper superstitiosi sed saepe etiam arguti et fructuosi"*. J. Perles, *op. cit.* pg 207
gives the list of kabbalistic manuscripts referred to by Masius at the end of the Joshua.
These give a good indication of the width of his kabbalistic knowledge.

[59] "Stopius noster" see: J. Perles, *op. cit.* pg 210.

[60] Lossen, *op. cit.*, refers to the letter pg 23. It is printed in full in Chaufepié III pg
219.

[61] *"De Volumine Evangeliorem* (sic) *Arabico-Chaldaeorum nil est quod te torqueat, in nostra enim
potestate est. Eo solo nomine me Christus Romam deduxerat, ut multos illos annos, quos decreveram
expendere pro eo aut simili nanciscendo inter barbaros, alio converteret, curareturque ut in utraque
lingua aut saltem in Arabica prodiret, quod antequam sit mihi concessum, non facile patiar a me, nisi
eo nomine, divelli. Eo nomine ut faciam publicum accepi Romae. Nec mihi sane videtur tanta esse
varietate aut diversitate a nostris exemplar Graecis, ut opus sit nova versione. Satis esset per annotationes etymorum rationem in linguae sanctae characteres deducere, ob magna nominum propriorum
mysteria & praecipue ubi dicitur Hebraice, autem etiam pro Alcoranismo in Lingua Arabica, pro
Judaismo in Chaldaica est edendum, mutato in linguam Adami charactere hoc novo. Quum ad te
venies de hac re agemus"*.

one of the three important pieces of evidence for Postel's early work on the Syriac New Testament.

The new text Postel had compared with the Vulgate, it is interesting to note, and did not think his books required a new translation (*"nova versio"*) into Latin other than the Vulgate. However he seems to think that annotations should display the etymology of proper names in Hebrew Script on account of their hidden mysteries (*"in linguae sanctae characteres deducere"*). He seems to have intended to address Moslems in Arabic but the purpose of the Syriac seems to have been to evangelise Jews *"in Chaldaica"* (i.e. the Syriac version) *"mutatato in linguae Adami characteres"* put into Hebrew characters. This last point helps us to understand a significant feature of several Syriac New Testaments. In Tremellius's case there was no chance of using Syriac Type. There was Syriac type at Antwerp and in Paris, yet in both Bibles the 'Chaldaean' Syriac text is also printed in Hebrew characters. Raphelengius's 1574 Plantin edition *only* had Hebrew script, though the house did not lack Syriac type. This, says Postel, was to evangelise the Jews. We should take this remark seriously when looking at the later versions. Finally we should notice the remarks about the mystical etymological meaning of names that was an interest of later editors of Syriac New Testaments and the letter's final passage of letter mysticism.

Masius's further contacts with Postel and other scholars

Johann van Wese died at the Reichstag in Ausburg 14 June 1548. Masius mourned him in sixty-eight elegiac lines.[62] Henry-Rudolph succeeded his uncle as administrator of Waldsassen Abbey and wished to transfer that preferment to Masius but the Elector Palatine, intent upon introducing the Reformation into the abbey, did not grant this. Masius thereupon became a councillor of Duke William IV of Cleve. In 1549 Masius was in Rome in the service of the Duke. A letter to him there from Postel, again from Venice, confirms receipt of a letter sent to him by Masius through Remalinus Bomberg's agent.[63] Postel sent Masius his book *'De ultimo adventu'*. In addition he received the Latin edition

---

[62] Gaspar Bruschius, *Chronologia Monasteriorum Germaniae Sulzbaci Georgi Schenreri* 1682 pg 50–52.
[63] Chaufepié III pg 220 (19 May 1549).

of Postel's *Candel. typici interpretatio Venetii 1548*.[64] Postel further tells him
he had just sent *Revelationes matris mundi seu Chavae novae* to Oporinus
in Basle. This highly controversial book treats of the role of Mother
Joanna. Masius was asked to keep the secret. Postel's next letter was
dated from Zion Cloister Jerusalem 21 August 1549.[65] It contains an
interesting insight into Postel's linguistic philosophy at this time and
also speaks of the books he has seen.[66] A letter of 10 June 1550, written from Constantinople, reports that Postel had been copying Syriac
New Testament Books.[67]

There are extant two letters from Israel (or Cornelio) Adil chind
(or Adelkind) ben Baruch in Venice to Masius in Rome dated 21 May
and 11 June 1547 that deal with Masius's Hebrew studies and his
quest for editions.[68] Adelkind was agent and corrector for Bomberg
and other printers in Venice and Sabionetta (1524–1554). He wrote
in difficult Italian betraying his German origins and signed the first
letter in Hebrew.

Adelkind did not know Masius personally (a fact for which he apolo-
gised) but mentions as common friends Elias Levita who was eager to
see Masius before he died (*"in ante che il vada a patrem"*: Levita died in

---

[64] This work will be discussed subsequently.

[65] Chaufpié III pg 216.

[66] *"Magna copia librorum hic est, Librorum Chaldeorum dico, in ea lingua qua Christus usus est, conscriptum, quos non aegre usuro concredunt, aegre quantumvis tenues vendunt. Post illa nostra IV Evangelia repperi iam reliquum Novi Testamenti, praeter Apocalypsin, & Epistolam alteram Petri & Johannis, & tertiam similiter, una cum ea quae est Judae, quae desiderantur in hoc satis alioqui avito volumine"* (i.e. the normal Syriac canon).

[67] Chaufepié III pg 216. Lossen pg 56–57. The letter describes the sight of *"varia & Novi Testamenti & multarum admodum traditionum volumina in Syriaco sermone"* in Jerusalem that Postel had been unable to buy. Postel was assisted by the Royal Legate Gabriel Aramontius who helped him see books in Damascus *"Sed re vera omnia ista debentur Legato, viro incomparabili: Damasci curatum est, ut quidquid habent Syri Christiani de sacris, sive sint Maronitae, sive sint Suriani habuerim. Ferebatur quod Lex extaret. Sed re vera de veteri nil praeter Psalmos potuit cum sumus Legati indagine haberi. Totum novum Instrumentum, praeter illa quae desiderari dixeram meis ad te literis, est illi oblatum, sed re vera nullus vendere unquam voluit, nisi dum partim authoritate, partim precibus, partim precio tria volumina mihi comparavit, Psalterium & Evangelia, quae iam in duobus voluminibus ad nostrum Renialmum, cum Epistola ad Hebraeos, a me transcripta, misi. Apud me supersunt in pervetusto Exemplari Pauli Epistolae cum Actibus, ut solent apud eos partiri"*. Postel continues with a description of Maronites and Druze. The Druze he believed were remnants of the Franks: *"& vocantur Dreusi a celebri Gallorum urbe, quae in finibus Carnutorum est* (i.e. Dreux), *ubi olim fuerat Druidarum schola"*.

[68] The letters are taken from Munich Latin ms 23736 (*Catalogus Codd. latin. Bibl. Monac. tom: II, pars IV* pg 88–89) that contains 207 items including many of Masius's letters edited in Lossen. These letters are items 204 and 156 of the manuscript. The text appears with comment in J. Perles, *op. cit.* pg 209–211.

1549), Postel and of course Bomberg himself. Masius who had obtained a Talmud from Bomberg speaks of his friendship with him and tells us in a passage in his *Joshua* that Bomberg had given him an Israelite shekel as a gift.[69] In the correspondence Adelkind asks Masius on Bomberg's behalf to pass an opinion upon the work of a monk, Fra Paduano, who had undertaken to produce a translation of Maimonides's *Guide*. Bomberg was uncertain whether to reprint the translation of Augustino Giustiniani of Paris 1520 or this new work. Adelkind however did not think the monk up to it and wanted Masius to check the work. He refers in this context to a Jewish friend of both Bomberg and Postel in Rome—Benjamin ben Joseph Arignano who could provide Masius with a Hebrew text of the מורה and the necessary commentaries of which he considered the commentary of Narboni the best.[70]

This correspondence is also noteworthy because it shows the keen interest of both parties in kabbalistic texts. In response to Adelkind's request Masius sent an impressive list of the kabbalistic books he possessed. In return Adelkind indicates what kabbalistic books Bomberg had and others he knew of in Jewish hands in Venice that could be borrowed or copied for Masius.[71]

Thus we can see from the evidence of this Roman period that Masius had contacts with Postel and was aware of the development of the latter's thought. We also see close working contacts not only with Bomberg but also with other Jewish scholars in Venice and Rome in pursuit of rabbinic and kabbalistic learning. We may thus now better appreciate Masius's bitterness when the blow fell in 1553.

Moses and Masius

Moses was back in Rome by the end of 1552 when Cervini gave him funds for printing. Masius was in Rome from at least 29 March 1549[72]

---

[69] Masius's *Joshua* on 7. 20–21.
[70] Widmanstetter f. 12 (J. Perles, *op. cit.* pg 189). On Arigiano, who was clearly on good terms with Christians and prepared to teach them: J. Perles, *op. cit.* pg 190.
[71] #156 in ms (J. Perles, *op. cit.* pg 210): *"Jo ho visto la vostra poliza deli libri de* קבלה, *per mia fe che stati bene e aveti de belle cose. Li libri che noi avemo sono questi,* היסוד שער, היסוד, מאירת, שפרי אמר, ספר הבהיר מעשר שער וסתרי תורה ונם סוד רזיי ספירות עשר ספירות, הקנה, תמונות עינים, ספר יצירה *e poi qui sene trova altro fra ebrei che se poderia aver perimprestido per copiar".*
[72] Lossen, *op. cit.* pg 39.

until at least 27 May 1550[73] and then from the end of 1551[74] until April
1553.[75] For a few months at the beginning of 1553 Moses and Masius
collaborated. Cervini was no doubt instrumental in bringing them
together. Moses taught Masius Syriac and also helped to improve his
Arabic that he had begun under Postel in 1545–1546.[76] We know about
this period of collaboration from comments in Masius's subsequent
publications and his correspondence, including that which he conducted
with Moses in Syriac.[77] No doubt Masius's considerable knowledge of
Hebrew and Aramaic made his progress in Syriac swift. Moses had
brought with him from Mesopotamia a dictionary and Barhebraeus's
Grammar, which would no doubt have been of considerable assistance
to Masius, but Moses had left them in Venice.[78] In return, Masius was
to translate into Latin Moses's 1552 Confession of Faith before the
Pope and Cardinals made on behalf of himself and his Patriarch.[79]
This Masius says had not been made immediately on arrival but had
only been offered when Moses had fully grasped it. What needed to

---

[73] Lossen, *op. cit.* pg 56.

[74] Lossen, *op. cit.* pg 77.

[75] Lossen, *op. cit.* pg 121–122.

[76] Lossen, *op. cit.* pg 161: 13 April 1554, Masius writing to Postel about Moses: "*illo
usus sum praeceptore, tum in hac* (id est arabica) *tum in Syra lingua*".

[77] On Masius's Syriac letters G. S. Assemani, *Bibliotheca Orientalis Clementino-vaticanae*
(*Tomus primus de Scriptoribus Syris Orthodoxis*) (Rome 1719) pg 535–536; Levi della Vida,
Ricerche pg 142 n. 5; and now Jan Wim Wesselius "The Syriac Correspondence of
Andreas Masius" *cit. supra.* Two letters were published in A. Müller, *Symbolae syriacae,
sive I Epistolae duae amoebeae…(Berolini s. a.) II Dissertationes duae de rebus itidem Syriacis*
(Coloniae Brandeburgiciae, 1673) that contains summaries of five others. These were
all taken from a manuscript (Syriac 342) in the Staatsbibliothek Preußischer Kulturbe-
sitz in Berlin (E.Sauchau, *Verzeichnis der syrischen Handschriften der königlichen Bibliothek zu
Berlin II* (Berlin, 1899) pg 910) that contained in all six letters from Moses to Masius,
one letter from Moses to Rignalmo, Bomberg's agent in Venice, and one draft of
a letter from Masius to Moses. A copy of the unpublished letters was made by G. S.
Bayer and was deposited in Glasgow University Library (J.Young, *A Catalogue of the
mss in the Library of the Hunterian Museum in the University of Glasgow* (Glasgow 1908) pg
456. Jan Wim Wesselius (pg 23) reports the discovery of two more letters from Moses
to Masius not known to Müller in private hands that he intends to publish.

[78] On this see A. van Roey "Les Études syriaques" pg 145, 156 n. 84. *De Paradiso* 42:
"*Est etiam apud Syros, ut mihi meus doctor dixit, Grammatica absolutissima de syriaca lingua…*".
On the identification of the Grammar (Barhebraeus wrote two) see: R. Contini "Gli
Inizi della Linguistica Siriaca nell'Europa rinascimentale" Rivista Studi Orientali
LXVIII (1994) pg 15–30, pg 2.

[79] *De Paradiso* pg 257–262: *Fidei professio, quam Moses Mardenus, Assyrius, Jacobita,
patriarchae Antiocheni legatus, suo et Patriarchae sui nomine est Romae professus anno 1552; exipso
profitentis autographo syriaco traducta ad verbum per Andream Masium Bruxellanum.* Assemani,
Bib Or. I pg 535 notes: "*cuius tamen fidem Ignatius eiusdem Patriarcha nequa quam ratam habuit
postmodum compertum*".

be grasped, of course, was the Procession of the Spirit *ab utroque*, the two natures in Christ according to Chalcedon, and the Supremacy of Rome. Masius also translated a short *Contemplatio Theologica* on the Holy Trinity that Moses had composed the previous year.[80] Masius was subsequently to print both of these in his translation of the *De Paradiso* in 1567.

Masius and Mar Sulaqa

During the early months of 1553 and before Masius left Rome, a Nestorian (Chaldaean) monk from Rabban Hormizd near Mosul in what is today Iraq arrived in Rome. He was Mar Shem'un Sulaqa.[81] Like Moses he had been drawn to the Chair of St. Peter—but in somewhat more complicated circumstances.

---

[80] *De Paradiso* pg 273–276: *Moses Mardeni Theologica de sacrosancta Trinitate contemplatio, scripta ab ipso anno 1552, et ex autographo syrico ad verbum translata per eundem Andream Masium.* Assemani, I pg 536, pointed out that the work was derived from the Liturgy for the Feast of the Trinity and not original (*"quae tamen Mosis non foetus est, sed ab eo Ecclesiasticis Syrorum officiis descripta"*).

[81] Of fundamental importance: J. Habbi "Signification del'Union Chaldéenne de Mar Sulaqa avec Rome in 1553" L'Orient syrien XI (1966) pg 99–132, 199–230 which reviews previous partial accounts, straightens the matter out and gives a full bibliography. (Habbi wrote in the spirit of Vatican II: he deals fairly with the fact that the previous Patriarch Shem'un was still alive at the time of Sulaqa's consecration, and he is not without criticism of Rome's attitude to the Chaldaean Church at the time). S. Giamil, *Genuinae Relationes inter Sedem Apostolicam et Assyriorum Orientalium seu Chaldaeorum Ecclesiam nunc maiori ex parte primum editae* (Rome 1902) is a most important collection of relevant texts. Also essential is: W. van Gulik, "Die Konsistorialakten über die Begrundung des uniers-chaldaischen Patriarchates von Mosul unter Papst Julius III" Oriens Christianus IV (1904) pg 261–277, to which may be added: L. Lemmens "Notae criticae ad initia unionis Chaldaeorum" Antonianum I 1926 pg 205–218; and his "Relationes Nationem Chaldaeorum inter et Custodiam Terrae Sanctae 1551–1629" Archivum Franciscanum Historicum XIX (1926) pg 17–28. For an overview: Giuseppe Beltrami, *La Chiesa Caldea nel secolo dell' Unione* (Orientalia Christiana XXIX vol 83) (Institutum Orientalium Studiorum, Rome 1933). Finally: J. M. Voste "Mar Johannan Soulaqa, premier patriarche des Chaldéens, martyr de l'union avec Rome († 1555) Trois poesies inédites de 'Abdisho' de Gazertha." Angelicum VIII (1931) pg 187–234. Abisho shared Sulaqa's Roman visit and was chosen Patriarch of those in Union with Rome after Sulaqa's death. His election was confirmed in Rome in 1562 (Giamil, *op. cit.* pg 31–77). His poems recount Sulaqa's election, visit, and Martyrdom (J. M.Voste, *op. cit.* pg 218–222). They also give us a delightful account of an eastern ecclesiastic's visit to the pilgrim sites and relics of Rome. The Patriarch of Greater Armenia (the Catholicos of Ečmiadin) had earlier visited Rome in 1548. See: Gisseppe Messina "Notizia su un Diatessaron persiano tradotto dal Siriaco" (Biblica et Orientalia X) (Pontificio Istituto Biblico, Rome 1943) pg 13–16.

Sulaqa had been chosen Patriarch by a section of the Chaldaean Church and in the absence of a suitable Metropolitan had come to Rome to seek consecration from the Pope. He was accompanied as far as Jerusalem by seventy ecclesiastics and other faithful and had celebrated Easter there in 1552. At Pentecost he was in Beirut and after landing at Venice arrived in Rome 18 November 1552 and was lodged in the Ospizio di Santo Spirito near St. Peter's. Naturally he was concerned to visit the holy places and the relics of the saints.

Sulaqa brought three documents with him: a letter from the Nestorians of Mosul asking the Pope to consecrate Sulaqa as Patriarch;[82] a letter from the seventy Nestorians who had accompanied Sulaqa from Mosul as far as Jerusalem;[83] and a confession of Faith though this he may have produced when asked in Rome. Masius befriended Sulaqa and translated the texts.[84] Nobody else in Rome was up to it.[85]

On 15 February 1553 Sulaqa made his profession of Faith *ore et scriptu.*[86] In a Consistory of 17 February Cardinal Bernardino Maffei proposed the confirmation of Sulaqa but the matter was postponed until a Consistory of 20 February on account of the gravity of the matter.[87] The petition of the Chaldaeans was there confirmed by the bull *Divina disponente clementia.*[88] Sulaqa was then made a bishop on 9 April and consecrated Patriarch 28 April, this being confirmed by the bull *Cum nos nuper.*[89] Sulaqa was installed quickly so that he might return home as soon as possible. He was however able to contact the Portuguese ambassador and raise the subject of Chaldaeans in Malabar. There was sent back with him Ambroise Buttigeg, a Maltese Dominican, who was created titular bishop of Orans 5 May 1553 and Nuncio to the Province of Mosul 23 June.[90] The proposal was made

---

[82] Giamil, *op. cit.* pg 12–14.

[83] Giami, *op. cit.* 1 pg 475–476.

[84] Masius, *Dictionarium* pg 54.

[85] *De Paradiso* pg 229. Moses, as a representative of a Church considered Monophysite and not formally in Union with Rome at this point, could hardly be asked to conduct the negotiations with repentant Nestorians!

[86] Giamil, *op. cit.* pg 23.

[87] Made a Cardinal 8 April 1549 and for a time private secretary of Paul III. He was a lifelong friend of Cervini and a colleague on Julius III's Reform Commission.

[88] Giamil, *op. cit.* pg 15–23.

[89] Giamil, *op. cit.* pg 24–27.

[90] Beltrami, *op. cit.* pg 144–145. The essential text is: M. Vosté "Missio Duorum Fratrum Melitensium O. P. in Orientem saeculo XVI, et relatio, nunc primum edita, eorum quae in istis regionibus gesserunt" Analecta Ordinis Praedicatorum XXXIII (fasc. IV) (1925) pg 261–278.

by Cardinal Giampero Carafa who was to become Paul IV.[91] He took with him a fellow Dominican Antonin Zahara and other companions whose purpose we shall consider shortly.[92]

The End of Sulaqa

Sulaqa and his colleagues left Rome at the beginning of July 1553 and made their way to Constantinople to seek recognition by the Sublime Porte.[93] Unfortunately the Sultan had left a fortnight earlier and they had to pursue him towards Diarbekir where he stayed a while. It was at this point that events caught up with Sulaqa for—in spite of statements to the contrary in all the Roman documents—Sulaqa had been consecrated Patriarch whilst the previous Patriarch was still alive![94] Rome had unwittingly created a second Hierarchy in Union with itself and the old Patriarch Shem'un bar Mama took steps to rectify the problem. He bribed the Governor Hussein Beik. In January 1555 Sulaqa was imprisoned and murdered.

J. Habbi's important study has made it clear that Sulaqa supporters brought him to Rome with the clear intention of getting their (scarcely canonical) Patriarch confirmed as a way to deal with the (canonical) Patriarch they considered scandalous and tyrannical. Rome, of course, not only knew nothing about this stratagem but also took a quite different view of the mission of Sulaqa. The Chaldaean Church had been considered heretically Nestorian for a millennium. Though the question of Union with Rome had been raised in the Patriarchate of Sabrišo' V (1226–1256) and his successor Yahbalaha III (1283–1318) nothing conclusive had emerged and the difficulties of their times and the problems of communication had prevented further progress.[95] Julius III was a Pope of missionary fervour not only in the New World but also in the Orient. However he could not have been expected to receive the Chaldaean delegation as anything other than repentant heretics. His appointment of Ambroise Buttigeg was to ensure the conformity of the Chaldaeans who supported Sulaqa to Roman doctrine, law and liturgy.

---

[91] Beltrami, *op. cit.* pg 7.
[92] Beltrami, *op. cit.* pg 10ff.
[93] Beltrami, *op. cit.* pg 15–27.
[94] J. Habbi, *op. cit.* pg 116. A. van Roey "Les Études syriaques" pg 147 is thus incorrect when he speaks of Sulaqa succeeding: *"au patriarche Simon VII, décédé en 1551"*.
[95] Beltrami, *op. cit.* pg 2 and J. Habbi, *op. cit.* pg 203. Giamil, *op. cit.* pg 1–3.

Habbi has isolated three forms or stages in the drafting of Sulaqa's Profession of Faith and is able to illustrate the Roman adjustments to the Oriental original as Sulaqa was pressed for increasing doctrinal clarity.[96] In the sixteenth century and before Vatican II there was no thought that Eastern Christians might legitimately have seen or done things differently from Rome. Liturgical and Sacramental practice had to be conformed to Rome. It was in 1563 and before Pius IV that Antonin Zahara who accompanied Buttigeg made his report upon the Church he had been sent to visit. It was a highly critical evaluation of Nestorian failings.[97]

Before we return to Moses we may just summarise the situation under Julius III. The Curia had shown itself open to approaches from both Jacobites and Chaldaeans and most ready to accept their submission and Union. Conformity to Roman doctrine and practice was expected and Rome was prepared to send out missions to achieve this. The Cardinal Protector of the Vatican Library was aware of the desirability of a printed Syriac New Testament and prepared to pay for its production (though it is not clear whether he consciously had considered whether he was prepared albeit indirectly to pay Postel to print it). The technical problems however were inhibiting. Cervini also only had one man in Rome who could cope with Syriac and that was Masius. He was however now learning the language, as Teseo had done, from native speaking scholars. This was an obvious advantage, but not one which all producers of printed Syriac New Testaments would enjoy. Tremellius, by contrast, had no native teacher, and this single fact very much conditions the nature of his edition. We may be sure that Masius was working on Syriac biblical studies making notes from Syriac Gospel manuscripts and using Cervini's Library to do so.[98] But this in itself would not bring an edition any nearer.

---

[96] *Op. cit.* pg 206.

[97] Beltrami, *op. cit.* pg 17. For relations with the Chaldaean Church in the remaining years of the sixteenth century: Beltrami, Lemmans, *opera cit.*

[98] By the beginning of 1554 references are found in Masius's correspondence to annotations upon the Syriac gospels: *"illas ex evangelio Syro excerptas notatiunculas"* Lossen #130 pg 147. And: *"meas ex evangelio Syro excerptam annotatiunculas"* #133 pg 152. Masius clearly at this time was working on Syriac biblical studies. Levi della Vida, *Ricerche* pg 137–9 noted that an entry in Masius's Dictionary *Syrorum Peculium* (Printed in the Plantin Polyglot in Antwerp 1571) makes reference to Vat sir. 15 f. 168b s. v. *"RGLT* ` *'Torrens'*, χέιμαρρος, *Ioannes 18 Exemplar tamen Vaticanae habet praeposito Olaph 'RGLT* `*"*. This rare reading is found in Vat sir. 15.

Masius was able to do some useful translation of the Professions of Faith and other documents that the Eastern priests brought with them. It was probably also at this time he acquired a manuscript of the Anaphora (or Mass Liturgy) of St. Basil.[99] The manuscript itself has been lost, but Masius's translation survives.[100] This, at the time, was something of a challenge to translate and Masius needed a lot of help from Moses.[101] Nevertheless, this manuscript confirmed a growing interest in Eastern liturgical material amongst the scholars who worked on Syriac New Testaments. Their interest was not primarily concerned with the normalisation of the practices of heretical or schismatic churches. Rather they saw here historical material that might be used in confessional polemics against the Protestants.

Moses leaves Rome

Moses left Rome in April 1553. At this point we can follow his correspondence with Masius. In his first letter Moses tells Masius that after his departure a problem had arisen over Moses's priesthood. Some people had wanted to reconsecrate him as a Roman priest, so he says he has had to leave Rome taking with him some printing materials

---

[99] St. Basil's name has been connected with a text of the Eucharistic Liturgy since at least the fifth century. It exists in several versions—Byzantine Greek, Alexandrine Greek, Armenian, Coptic, Ethiopic and Syriac and in a long and short text form. See: W. E. Pitt "The Origin of the Anaphora of the Liturgy of St. Basil" Journal of Ecclesiastical History XII (1961) pg 1–13: Albert Houssiau "The Alexandrine Anaphora of St. Basil" in ed. L. Sheppard, *The New Liturgy* (DLT, London 1970) pg 228–243. B. Bobrinsky "Liturgie et Ecclésiologie trinitaire de Saint Basile" in *Eucharisties d' Orient et d'Occident II* (Éditions du Cerf, Paris, 1970) pg 197–240. A brief summary of the main issues here is found in Bryan D. Spinks, *The Sanctus in the Eucharistic Prayer* (CUP, Cambridge, 1991) pg 68–71.

[100] The translation was made before 7 November 1554 when Hubert Leodius, secretary of the Elector Palatine wrote to Masius saying: *"Missam divi Basili ex siro in latinum traductam si ad me misisses, non male fecisses"*. (Lossen, *op. cit.* pg 182). Masius seems to have translated the Anaphora for Julius Pflug, Bishop of Naumbourg, who was involved in discussions with Protestants. Masius made a visit to him September 1554 (Lossen, *op. cit.* pg 180). Further on Pflug: *Allgemeine Deutsche Biographie* XXV (Leipzig 1667) pg 688–690 (Brecker). A corrected version of the translation appeared in the *De Paradiso* of 1567 (pg 235–254). In the Preface Masius remarks on the reason for his revised version: *"... me in primis induxit quod meam illam rudem ... et deproperatum translationem ad multos lectores pridem emanasse meminissem"*.

[101] A large part of the 1555 correspondence is taken up with matters of translation: Jan Wim Wesselius, *op. cit.* pg 24–25.

and a manuscript of the New Testament in Syriac.[102] The mention of printing materials is interesting in the light of Cervini's investment, but we know no more about this. Moses asked Masius for some money and a letter of introduction to one of Masius's friends.[103]

Masius wrote to Johann Fugger[104] in Augsburg and advised Moses to go there.[105] After preparing the first draft of this letter Masius heard Moses had received money from Rome, so that his support did not seem so vital. Moses replied with a reproach from Venice where he was staying with Ludovico Beccadeli the Papal Nuncio. At this time Moses was once more in touch with Remalius (Giovanni Rignalmo) the agent of the Bomberg house.[106] The first exchange between Moses and Masius breaks off here.

In August 1553 Moses crossed the Alps in the company of his patron Reginald Pole who was on his way to Mary Tudor's England.[107] It may be that Moses was intent on visiting Fugger at Augsburg. However he met Johann Albrecht von Widmanstetter at Dillingen (which is near Augsburg) and subsequently accompanied him to Vienna. Moses's last letter of 23 November 1553 was addressed to Rignalmo and characteristically asked for money that Moses believed was owed him. The last letter also refers to his meeting Postel in Rignalmo's Company.

---

[102] One does not quite know what to make of this. Moses might have been regarded as heretical in some areas. Certainly the election of Paul IV in May 1555 Moses regarded as sufficiently disastrous as to prevent his return to Rome, and this might be evidence of different views within Rome which we shall shortly discuss. On the other hand Masius replied by saying he was sure it was just a misunderstanding.

[103] Letter of 8 June 1553.

[104] For contact between Masius and Fugger 1548–1551: J. Perles, *op. cit.* pg 222–223.

[105] Letter of 22 June 1553 sent on 26 June. The copy of this letter is interesting and is discussed by Wesselius, *op. cit.* pg 26–27, who comments on the fairly rudimentary nature of Masius's Syriac. It is also interesting to note that Masius drafted the letter in cursive Hebrew, no doubt with the intention of putting it later into Syriac characters. This demonstrates in a very concrete way that Masius thought of Syriac *in terms of Hebrew*. Often the words he uses are not in fact Syriac, though Masius was aware that he needed to collect specifically Syriac vocabulary and the *Peculium* was the result of his collecting. It would seem that all our scholars see Syriac in this way. This helps us to understand their treatment of Aramaic and Syriac as a mystical language like Hebrew.

[106] Letter of 3 July 1553.

[107] Widmanstetter's Preface f. 14v: "*in comitatu Rainaldi Poli...qui tum in Britanniam legatus profiscebatur*". They left the Benedictine House at Maguzzano near Garda 29 August 1553.

The Burning of the Talmud in 1553

In September 1553 by order of the Roman Inquisition the Talmud was burned outside the printers' shops in the Campo di Fiori. The decree was occasioned by the commercial competition between two Venetian printers, M Giustiniani and Alvise Bragadoni, both of whom had produced a *Mishneh Torah* in 1550.[108] Bragadoni's contained a commentary of R. Meir Katzenellenbogen of Padua, and Giustiniani appears to have suggested to the ecclesiastical authorities that they examine this. Both sides seem to have hired apostates to argue their respective cases and these exceeded their brief by attacking the Talmud itself as blasphemous. The Inquisition condemned the book to destruction and on 29 May 1554 Julius III in his bull *Cum sicut nuper* enforced the Inquisition's decree.

In an important interpretation of Julius III's policy, K. R. Stow has stressed the conversional intentions of *Cum sicut nuper*: the alleged blasphemies of the Talmud made it an obstacle to Jewish conversion to Christianity and it had therefore to be destroyed.[109] One recognises here the motives of the Cologne Dominicans who had opposed Reuchlin. Julius III however did permit the publication and study of Hebrew books other than the Talmud, though this was not the inclination of the Chief Inquisitor Cardinal Carafa who as Paul IV had the Inquisition (from the same conversionary motives[110]) prohibit Jews in 1557

---

[108] On the dispute, see: David Amram, *The Makers of Hebrew Books in Italy* (The Holland Press, London 1963) pg 252–276. For a summary of recent work on the Roman Inquisition from its reinstitution under Paul III in 1542; the influence of Carafa; and Cervini's relationship to all this see: W. V. Hudon, *Marcello Cervini* pg 116–144.

[109] K. R. Stow "The Burning of the Talmud in 1553 in the light of sixteenth-century Catholic attitudes to the Talmud" Bibliothèque d'Humanisme et Renaissance XXXIV (1972) pg 435–459. Previously: D. Kaufmann "Die Verbrennung Talmudischer Literatur" Jewish Quarterly Review (original series) XIII (1901) pg 533–538. Also the important: P. F. Grendler, *The Roman Inquisition and the Venetian Press 1540–1605* (Princeton UP, Princeton 1977) pg 89–92. Also his: "Destruction of Hebrew Books in Venice 1568" now conveniently in P. F. Grendler, *Culture and Censorship in Later Renaissance Italy and France* (Variorum, London 1981) pg 103–130. For a recent survey of scholarship on the thirteenth-century burning of the Talmud: ed. Gilbert Dahan, *Le Brûlement du Talmud à Paris 1242–1244* (Édition du Cerf, Paris, 1999) that reviews previous literature.

[110] Stow's subsequent *Catholic Thought and Papal Jewry Policy 1555–1593* (Jewish Theological Seminary, New York, 1977) considerably advanced our understanding of the turning point in relations between the Papacy and Jews marked by the newly elected Paul IV's bull *Cum nimis absurdum* of 17 July 1555 by placing it firmly within a conversionary and eschatological framework. He gives the bull on pg 291–8. Conversion of the Jews in the Last Days was of course anticipated long before these times,

from possessing any Hebrew book other than the Bible.[111] Thereafter
conversionary pressure was maintained upon the Jews, though books
other than the Bible were periodically tolerated. Such episodic laxness
however made little difference to Hebrew printing in Rome. This effectively ceased after 1553 until the early nineteenth century.

Stow's work illustrates how fluctuations in the status of non-biblical
Hebrew texts reflect the strength of different evaluations of their value
as conversionary tools. Voices in favour of the usefulness of Jewish
books for the conversion of Jews are few. The most extreme supporter
of their value as a conversionary tool and the most outspoken critic
of the policy of prohibition and destruction of non-biblical Hebrew
books was Masius. He may be seen as the spokesman for the group of
Orientalists, Hebrew and Syriac scholars, who found profound Christian
truth in the proscribed texts.

Masius wrote to Cardinal Pighino from Weingarten 24 December
1553.[112] (His anxieties were sharpened by worries about a copy of the
Talmud he had ordered and paid for but not yet received.)[113] Masius
is unwilling to concede that the Talmud contains blasphemies. He
cites Jerome's support of the importance of the Talmud for clinching
arguments with Jews. A long letter to Pighino of 25 February gives full
expression to his arguments.[114] These are particularly directed against
the Jesuit Franciscus de Torres and were influential in postponing
further burning.[115] Masius makes the point that the destruction of the

---

and Stow exposes these continuities. The Carafa Pope seems to have wished to hasten
events by his reform of Jewry policy.

[111] Stow "Burning" pg 443.

[112] Lossen, *op. cit.* #128 pg 144–145. Neither Pighino nor Cervini had voted for the
destruction of the Talmud (Amram, *op. cit.* pg 264). A good account of Masius's correspondence is found in J. Perles, *op. cit.* pg 219–231 which incidentally again illustrates
the breadth of Masius's Hebrew reading.

[113] A Letter of 19 February 1554 to Marcus Antonius de Mula, Venetian ambassador to the Imperial Court (Lossen, *op. cit.* #131 pg 147; J. Perles, *op. cit.* pg 226; Stow
"Burning" pg 448), shows Masius urging the Venetian Senate, inspite of the edict, not
to destroy a Babylonian and Jerusalem Talmud, Bomberg's *Biblia Magna* with commentaries, some Maimonides and Midrashim that he had bought but not yet collected:
"Nam metuo, ne mora capitale periculum adferat meis charissimis libris". A complete Talmud
was of course an expensive item.

[114] Lossen, *op. cit.* #134 pg 154–58.

[115] Stow "Burning" pg 440–441 gives an account of Francisco de Torres's *De Sola
lectione Legis, et Prophetarum Iudaeis cum Mosaico Ritu, et Cultu Permittenda, et de Iesu in Synagogis
Eorum ex Lege, ac Prophetis Ostendendo, et Annunciando. Ad Reverendiss. Inquisitores. Libri Duo*
(Rome 1555). The first part of the book deals with rabbinic literature, the second with
evangelising of the Jews from their own scriptures. Torres claims that it is necessary to

Talmud will destroy the access to a deeper knowledge of Hebrew.[116] He cites the practice of St. Jerome again and also of Nicolas of Lyra. In a most revealing passage Masius makes the strongest possible case by drawing alongside Pico della Mirandola. Masius is appealing here not merely to a different conversionary tactic, but is allying his interpretation with the kabbalistic traditions so characteristic of the sixteenth-century Syriac scholars.[117] Here then is the significance of the question of the Talmud for our interests: it was not only the Talmud but also the esoteric kabbalistic tradition which was threatened by the changes in Papal policy.[118] Rome in the second half of the sixteenth century was to increase her knowledge of the Eastern Churches and to enjoy something of a typographical Golden Age, but by that time there was no longer any significant interest in the kabbalistic notions which had been so characteristic of the Orientalism of the High Renaissance.

Stow observes plausibly that Julius III's decision to permit non-Talmudic post-biblical Hebrew texts was due to Cardinal Pighino having shown Masius's letter to the Pope that persuaded him into a compromise. But Masius's victory (if such it was) was short lived and expired with his patron Cervini, who as Marcellus II, after a Pontificate of twenty-one days, died on the night of 30 April 1555. The subsequent election of Paul IV brought to power a Pontiff quite out of sympathy with Masius's Hebrew and Jewish studies, and the man who had

---

remove from the Jews their traditional fables so that they may more easily understand the Gospel. These arguments were accepted and Paul IV's 1559 *Index* includes the Talmud and all its commentaries. Stow, *Catholic Thought* helpfully contrasts the missionary potential of the kabbalistic tradition (pg 204–207) with that of *De Sola Lectione* that he describes at some length (211–220).

[116] "*Atqui profecto Hebraeorum commentaria abolere nihil est aliud quam compendiossissimo modo sanctam Hebraeam linguam eradicare*". Subsequent correspondence also emphasises the usefulness of extra-biblical Hebrew books for explaining biblical details. A Letter of 25 February to P. Octavius Pantagathus from Weingarten explains Christ's remarks about Corban (Mark 7. 11) and Paul's reference to "forty strokes save one" (2 Cor 9. 24) from the Talmud to show: "*quid praestet linguae hebraeae cognitio... et quam temere sacras literas contrectent, qui eas nonnisi alienis oculis vident*". See: Lossen, *op. cit.* #132 pg 150.

[117] "*Nam nihil est in totis Bibliis prope, quod nostram fidem confirmet, quod non idem in Talmud congruenter ad nostrae ecclesiae sententiam de Christo interpretatur et in Cabala*"

[118] Stow "Burning" pg 449ff. is aware of the kabbalistic tradition and gives an interesting account of subsequent reactions to Galatinus's earlier defence of the utility of the Talmud for Christians. Stow however does not make the point one seeks to emphasise here, that it was such kabbalistic considerations that motivated Masius in the dispute and that his ultimate defeat saw the waning of the High Renaissance tradition in Rome. Those Catholics who published the Syriac New Testament elsewhere however belonged to that tradition.

insisted upon the burning of the Talmud. Such interests made Masius suspected of heterodoxy. Thereafter Pius IV, one of the most severe critics of Rabbinic Literature, placed Masius's *Joshua* of 1574 on the Index[119] and when the *Biblia Regia* was completed in Antwerp Masius's collaboration on the project jeopardised papal approbation.[120] Even Moses of Mardin regarded Paul IV's election with alarm, believing as we have seen that he would not be allowed back into Rome.

The change of atmosphere in Rome had considerable influence upon the future of the project to print a Syriac New Testament. The Hebrew printers, the obvious source of anything approaching the appropriate expertise, had been hard hit by *Cum nuper nos*. In Rome Hebrew printing was snuffed out. In Venice the ban on Hebrew typography seems to have lasted for a decade. It seems to have been lifted in 1563, though reimposed 8 December 1571 along with a prohibition upon employing Jews in printing presses.[121] It was, of course in Venice that Moses and Postel apparently intended to produce an *editio princeps*. We noticed above Moses's anxiety at the pontifical election. It is purely speculative to associate this with Moses's problems of his priesthood, or even his delay in making a Profession of Faith. Yet we have noticed Carafa's proposal to send Buttigeg and Zahara to Mosul. Maybe we should find here a contrast to the relaxed way Moses was initially received. Is it possible that some more rigorous prelates now wanted to press Moses harder? Whatever, the Oriental scholars and Moses left Rome. The Syriac New Testament would be produced in Vienna, Heidelberg, Antwerp and Paris. But not in Rome.

---

[119] J. Perles, *op. cit.* pg 229. The book was placed first on the Portugal 1581 and Spain 1583 indices before being placed on the Roman index of 1596. See J. M. De Bujanda et al., *Index des livres interdits* vol. IX, pg 459.

[120] On the subsequent suspicion with which Masius was viewed: J. H. Jonkees "Masius in moeilijkheden" De Gulden Passer XLI (1963) pg 161–168. The letter of Masius in 1572 to Cardinal Sirleto printed here pg 164–165 is important for Masius's defence of the Talmud in passages in his Grammar and *Peculium* printed in the Antwerp Polyglot. On this see Robert J. Wilkinson, *The Kabbalistic Scholars of the Antwerp Polyglot Bible* (E. J. Brill, Leiden 2007). From 1568 Cardinal Sirleto was the protector of the Domus Cathecumenorum and was empowered to supervise the enforcement of *Cum nimis* and the decrees against Jewish books. This is why Masius wrote to him.

[121] Amram, *op. cit.* pg 338ff.

CHAPTER FOUR

THE SCHOLARS OF THE *EDITIO PRINCEPS*: POSTEL

The two European scholars responsible for the *editio princeps* were J. A. Widmanstetter and Guillaume Postel. We have already met Postel. He is the single continuous thread between all our editions. We shall now consider his career up to 1553.[1] Thereafter we shall turn our attention to Widmanstetter.

It is generally agreed that Postel was born 25 March 1510 in the hamlet of Dolerie outside the village of Barenton in the diocese of Avranches, Normandy.[2] His parents died of plague when he was eight years old. He was evidently a most precocious child and began to teach in the village of Sagy (Seine-et-Oise) at thirteen, which earned him enough money to go to Paris. His first attempt to study in the capital was frustrated by a rogue who took his money and clothes. He fell ill with bleeding diarrhoea and remained in a Paris hospital for eighteen months during which time he nearly died. Thereafter he worked as a

---

[1] The bibliography on Postel is large. For this uncontroversial biographical sketch I have made extensive use of William J. Bouwsma, *The Career and Thought of Guillaume Postel (1510–1581)* (Harvard U.P., Cambridge, Mass. 1957); Marion L. Kuntz, *Guillaume Postel Prophet of the Restitution of All Things His Life and Thought* (Martin Nijhoff, The Hague 1981); F. Secret, *Bibliographie des Manuscrits de Guillaume Postel* (Droz, Geneva 1970) and the very many books, editions, articles and notices contributed by Secret which are noted in the appropriate place below; Claude Postel, *Les Écrits de Guillaume Postel publiés en France et leurs Éditeurs 1538–1579* (Droz, Geneva 1992); *Actes du Colloque International d'Avranches 5–9 septembre 1981 Guillaume Postel 1581–1981* (Guy Trédaniel, Éditions de La Maisnie, Paris 1985) which is an invaluable collection of papers, as is M. L. Kuntz (ed), *Postello, Venezia e il suo mondo* (Leo S. Olschki, Florence 1988). I have used F. Secret's French translation (which is effectively a new edition) of the original Latin text of Georges Weil, *Vie et Charactère de Guillaume Postel* (Archè, Milan 1987). A recent biographical sketch from an Orientalist's perspective is Hartmut Bobzin, *Der Koran im Zeitalter der Reformation* (Franz Steiner Verlag, Beirut 1995) pg 365–399 of which I have made extensive use. J. Kvačala "Wilhelm Postell. Seine Geistesart und Seine Reformgedanken" Archiv für Reformationsgeschichte IX (1911/12) pg 285–330; XI (1914) pg 200–227; XV (1918) 157–203 remains useful as does Père des Billons, *Nouveaux Éclaircissements sur la Vie et les Ouvrages de Guillaume Postel* (J. J. Tutot, Liège 1773). I have not given full supporting references for those aspects of Postel's life that are not disputed and are fully documented in the standard works. Yvonne Petry, *Gender and Kabbalah and the Reformation: The Mystical Theology of Guillaume Postel* (E. J. Brill, Leiden 2004) now deals with both Kabbalah and Postel's relationship with Mother Joanna.

[2] Bouwsma, *Career* pg 2–3; Kuntz, *Postel* pg 4–8.

farm hand at Beaunce near Chartres until once again he had enough money to return, fully-clothed, to the capital where he began his education at the Collège de Sainte-Barbe by entering into the service of the Spanish Aristotelean scholar Juan de Gelida (Gelidus).[3]

Postel was a natural linguist. He obtained from local Jews[4] an Alphabet, a Grammar,[5] and a Psalter in Hebrew and Latin[6] from which he taught himself Hebrew which he always regarded as the first and most important of languages.[7]

In the 1530s Sainte-Barbe was the centre of Geographical Studies in Paris and was frequented by Spanish and Portuguese scholars and students. It had been partially endowed by the Portuguese Crown for the training of missionaries. No doubt Postel's interest the voyages of discovery of the Spanish and Portuguese was stimulated at this time. Certainly he admired Columbus and shared his views of the providential significance of the discovery of the New World. Postel later wrote on Geography and himself undertook two voyages to the East.[8]

---

[3] J. Quicherat, *Histoire de Sainte-Barbe Collège, Communauté, Institution* (Paris, 1860–1864) vol. I pg 165–168 for Gelidus.

[4] Jews had of course supposedly been expelled from France at this time. See Kuntz, *Postel* pg 9 for other evidence of their presence. *De originibus* F iv indicates that Postel was also taught Hebrew by François Vatable (†1542).

[5] The possibilities include Reuchlin's *De Rudimentis Hebraicis libri tres* (Phorcae 1506) and François Tissard's *Grammatica Hebraica* (Paris 1508). See Secret, *Bibliographie* pg 60 for a copy of Reuchlin's *De accentibus et orthographia linguae hebraicae* (Hagenau 1518) with Postel's annotations. Reuchlin's book contains the rudiments of Hebrew and a pamphlet *De Judaeorum ritibus* (1508) see: Hermann Greive "Die hebräische Grammatik Johannes Reuchlin's *De rudimentis hebraicis*" Zeitschrift für die alttestamentlische Wissenschaft XC (1978) pg 395–409. Tissard who had studied in Ferrara claimed to have learned his Hebrew from a master learned in both Talmud and Kabbalah. Secret *Les Kabbalistes chrétiens* pg 151 considers this the first mention of Christian Kabbalah in France. His book was dedicated to François de Valois, the future King François I. For Paris Hebrew imprints in general, see Lyse Schwarzfuchs, *Le Livre hebreu à Paris au XVIe siècle* (Bibliothèque nationale, Paris 2004).

[6] Bobzin, *Der Koran* pg 374–375 suggests this Psalter was in fact a polyglot and may have been either Potken's 1518 *Psalterium in quatuor linguis Hebrea Graeca Chaldaea Latina* or Giustiniani's *Psalterium octaplum* (Genoa 1516). Postel's later possession of this book is shown by the text of *De originibus* E which Bobzin quotes and the text of a letter to Masius 24 August 1563 which is given in a corrected form in F. Secret "La lettre de Postel à Masius du 24 aout 1563" XXIII (1961) pg 534–540.

[7] *De originibus seu de Hebraicae linguae et gentis antiquitate* (Paris 1538) A iiii v and G iiiii.

[8] An incomplete listing includes: *Syriae descriptio* Paris 1540; *Descriptio Alcahirae Urbis quae Mizir et Mazar dicitur* 1547; *De Etruriae Regionis* Florence 1551; *De Universitate liber* Paris 1552; *Description et charte de la terre saincte* Paris 1553; *Des merveilles du monde, et principalement des admirables choses des Indes et du nouveau monde* Paris 1553; *De la République des turcs* Poitiers 1560; *Histoires orientales et principalement des Turcs* Paris 1575.

A later passage allows us to see how Postel subsequently came to view the providential significance of the Voyages of Discovery, yet in a way which contrived to point to the inherited maritime skills of the Etruscan sons of Noah.[9]

In February 1528 Ignatius Loyola came to the Collège de Montaigu and thence moved to Sante-Barbe in 1529 to study Theology with the Dominicans. It was here that he gathered around him the core of what was to be the later Societas Iesu: Simon Rodriguez, Pierre Lefèvre, François Xavier, Jacques Laynes, Alphonse Salmeron and Nicholas Alphonse. (The proposal that the Jesuits should go as missionaries to the Indias was in fact made by a Portuguese administrator of the college, James de Gouvea).[10] Postel was close to these men.[11] He shared their mystical and ascetic holiness, their urge for the reformation of the Church, for missions and for the necessary study of Oriental languages. Postel was just beginning to learn Arabic when he met Loyola, probably by copying out the text of Agostino Giustiniani's Psalter much as he had copied out his first Hebrew alphabet.[12] Later in Rome Postel would enter the Society.

Postel's First Oriental Journey

In 1536 Postel was chosen to accompany Jean de la Forêt to negotiate an alliance with the Turks against the Emperor.[13] This was to be

---

[9] Passage quoted by Kuntz, *Postel* pg 13 from British Library Sloane ms 1412 f. 114–114v. Kuntz gives further evidence of Postel's views and their similarity to those of Columbus. We may recall Giustiniani's similar interest in Columbus.

[10] A. Brou "Les Missions étrangères aux origines de la Compagnie de Jésus" Revue d'Histoire des Missions X (1928) 354–368.

[11] Kuntz, *Postel* pg 13–23 on Postel and the early Jesuits. An indication of the importance of the Jesuits to Postel was that he called the Fourth Age *'Jesuism'* or *'Restitution'* named for *"the Society which took on the name of Jesus and which had as its goal the restitution or true reformation of the whole world"* (pg 23). He understood their name as Hebrew for *'being saved'* and their mission as prophetic.

[12] *De originibus* (1538) E ii: *"In prima libri transcriptione quam triennio antequam adirem Constantinoplim Arabismum discendi gratia scripseram…"*. He had just referred to Giustiniani's Psalter.

[13] For the date of the trip see Bobzin, *Der Koran* pg 377 who follows E. G. Vogel "Über Wilh. Postel's Reise in der Orient" Serapeum XIV (1853) pg 49–58. Postel's account is found in a letter of 1562, one of two both biographical and apologetic, to the Emperor Ferdinand found in ms Sloane 1413 f. 84–89. The text is given in Jan Kvačala, *Postelliana* (C. Mattiesen, Jurjew 1915) pg 64–80. One may compare: F. Secret "Le Voyage en Orient de Pierre Duchastel Lecteur de François Ier" Bibliothèque d'Humanisme et Renaissance XXIII (1961) pg 121–126.

his first experience of Moslem society. Though we do not know his
itinerary, we know that he stopped at Tunis, saw Istanbul, Syria, and
Egypt. Postel himself had the special task of recovering the monies of a
citizen of Tours who had died in Algiers. Ibrahim Pasha, the Turkish
'Polemarch' or Grand-Vizier had been appointed executor and was to
receive 40,000 gold pieces for his trouble. Postel was to recover the rest
of the monies for the Frenchman's heirs from the reluctant Ibrahim. A
sudden summons from the palace and the subsequent swift execution for
unconnected reasons of Ibrahim effectively aborted Postel's mission. He
had nonetheless been asked to bring back books for François I and also
made use of his opportunities to perfect his Arabic and begin Turkish.[14]
Postel also made the acquaintance of a singular teacher.

This experience as Postel recalled it in 1562 when writing to King
Ferdinand I v. Hapsburg is of some significance for the way in which it
helped form Postel's Orientalism.[15] His teacher led him via the Koran
to discover an extraordinary number of crypto-Christians wanting nothing more than Arabic New Testaments! This belief in the social reality
of thousands of hidden Christians in addition to those in schismatic

---

[14] For Turkish words in Postel's work see Bobzin, *Der Koran* pg 379. His most important contribution to Turkish is found in the third edition of *De la République des Turcs*
printed by Jérôme de Marnef and Guillaume Cavellat (Paris 1575). This edition has a
new chapter entitled *"Instruction des motz de la langue turquesque les plus communs"*. It runs
to twenty pages and is dedicated: *"A Hault et Puissant Prince Monseigneur Monsieur Hercule
François de Valloys, Fils et Frere de Roy"*. The work contains a few grammatical notes,
declensions of nouns, personal pronouns and some verb forms that find themselves in
print for the first time here. The work also has a wordlist which is not Postel's work
but is taken from Bartholomaeus Georgievits *De Turcorum ritu et moribus* (Antwerp 1544).
A technical appraisal is found in Vladimir Drimba *"L'Instruction des mots de la langue
turquesque de Guillaume Postel (1575)"* in *Türk dili Araştırmaları Yıllığı Belleten* (Ankara,
1967) pg 77–126. There is now important comment in F. Tinguely, *L'Écriture du Levant
à la Renaissance* pg 225–260. For an overview of early modern European knowledge of
Turkish: Stéphane Yérasimos "Le Turc en Occident. La connaissance de la langue
Turque en Europe: XVᵉ–XVIIᵉ siècles" in ed. Michèle Duchet, *L'Inscription des Langues
dans les relations de Voyages (XVIᵉ–XVIIIᵉ siècles) Actes du Colloque de décembre 1988 à Fontenay
aux Roses* (ENS, Fontenay/St. Cloud 1992) pg 191–210.

[15] Ms Sloane 1413 continues: *"... sed de hac re omnino stupebam, quod singulis diebus ante
lectionem colligebat ex Alcorano locos illos communes qui in laudem Jesu Christi, Mariae Virginis,
Johannis Baptistae, Apostolorum, Evangelii tendunt aut in Articulorum nostrae fidei confirmationem
quovis modo concernunt, quae cum viderem coepi interrogare tamen per me et sine Turgimani praesentia ... loquendo, quid sibi vellet tanta Christi mensio in hoc Corano et in suo colloquio, tunc cum
lachrymis coepit, Ego mi frater sum Christianus nil aliud quaerens quam Evangelium si possem illud
in nostra lingua Grammatica quae est Arabica aut turchica habere, ut plusquam 300,000 hominum
sunt in hac urbe et in Aula , qui iam sunt una mecum conversi ex eo tempore, quo sub Selimo Patre
Domini nostri Suleimani licebat ut publice unusquisque suam legem praedicaret et non soli sumus sed
convertuntur quotidie multi in tot Regno. Haec audiens sane obstupui."*

Churches motivated Postel's missionary stance towards the East. It also reinforced and informed Postel's conviction of an essentially Christian substrate to Islam and other Eastern religions.[16]

Knowledge of the world through travel and languages became for Postel a fundamental integrating metaphor in both his religion and in his Orientalism. Kuntz provides an important account of the metaphysical underpinning of this notion.[17] Postel boasted of his own speed in picking up new languages and the communicative efficiency he had achieved by being able to speak without interpreter in almost any part of the World.[18] Postel however found a particular utility in knowledge of Arabic which is spoken by two thirds of the world's population and in which are written important medical, mathematical and philosophical texts.

Postel's first voyage to the East enabled him to bring back the alphabets of twelve scripts that as we shall see he was to publish together with

---

[16] This conviction that a Christian substrate may underlie Oriental religions is well illustrated in a later work *Des Merveilles du Monde* Paris 1552. (A full exposition of the mythological cosmology of the work which contextualises our remarks here is found in Frank Lestringant "Cosmographie pour une Restitution; note sur le Traite "Des Merveilles du Monde" de Guillaume Postel (1553)" in ed. M. Kuntz, *Postello, Venezia e il suo Mondo* pg 227–260. *Des Merveilles* contains a memoir of P. Nicolas Lancilotto sent from Cochin 12 December 1548 to Ignatius Loyola (the various editions of Lancilotto's memoir are given in Henri de Lubac, *La Rencontre du Bouddhisme et de l'Occident* (Aubier, Paris 1952) pg 54–57). The memoir gives details of Japanese religion that derive initially from Francis Xavier's informant Yagiro, a merchant from Cangoxima who knew a few words of Portuguese. Xavier met him in Malacca and took him with him to Goa. Yagiro entered the Jesuit College there and was subsequently baptised as Paul de Sainte-Foi. Paul's account of Japanese religion was sadly misleading. He gave an account of the history of Xaca, the cult and the lives of the monks: they believed in Heaven, Hell and Purgatory; they venerated Saints and Angels, but rendered them the same cult as Christians, reserving worship for God alone, but praying to the saints for intercession. They practised fasts, pilgrimages and confession. They meditated like Western monks and preached to the people once a fortnight warning them of the Devil and Hell. This material, carrying the double *imprimatur* of *"M. François Schabier, jesuite, homme très saint"* and M. Paul who he calls *"gouverneur du collège de sainte-Fois, aux Indes"*, was irresistible to Postel who expands upon it enthusiastically in his treatise.

[17] M. L. Kuntz "Journey as Restitution in the thought of Guillaume Postel" History of European Ideas I (no. 4) (1981) pg 315–329; "Voyages to the East and their Meaning in the Thought of Guillaume Postel" in eds. Jean Céard et Jean-Claude Margolis, *Voyager à la Renaissance (Actes du Colloque de Tours 1983)* (Maisonneuve et Larose, Paris 1987) pg 51–63. More generally: F. Secret "La Place de Postel dans la littérature de voyages" Bibliothèque d'Humanisme et Renaissance XXIII (1961) pg 362–366. The unpublished text is: *De Universitate* ms Sloane 1412 f. 38–39v.

[18] Postel tell us in *Linguarum duodecim* Dii and *Grammatica arabica* Diii that the Turks considered his abilities to learn languages daemonic. Thereafter he discusses the benefits of such a remarkably widespread language.

other linguistic material in Paris in 1538. From the specific diversity of
the scripts however was to be drawn a unified and unifying understanding arising from a grasp of their common origin. For recovery of the
Origin constituted Restitution, and this maxim in time was not only to
direct Postel's language studies but to become a structuring category
of all his thought.[19] All languages are united because of their common
origin in Hebrew.[20]

Discussions of Postel's first Voyage have passed lightly over the nature
of the Embassy of which Postel was a member, albeit in a subsidiary
role.[21] The embassy did however mark something of a diplomatic
innovation in that for the first time a Christian King, François I, was
seeking an alliance with the Moslem Suleiman against the Christian
Emperor Charles V. No treaty has been preserved but the instructions
given to de la Forest drawn up by Chancellor Du Prat and dated 11
February 1535 make it clear that Turkish cooperation during an attack
upon Genoa, anticipated for the following year, was solicited.[22] Whilst
treaties with the Infidel were not unknown, de la Forest's embassy was
singular in its attempt not merely to penetrate Turkey commercially,
but to introduce the Turks into the politics of Christendom and there
get them to play a limited and controlled role.[23] Of course François

---

[19] So in the later *De Originibus* by Oporinus 1553 pg 52.

[20] Ms Sloane 1411 f. 173. On the question of the world's original language (with an
interesting summary of the views of the Syriac Fathers): Milka Rubin "The Language
of Creation or the Primordial Language: a case of cultural polemics in Antiquity"
Journal of Jewish Studies XLIX (1998) pg 306–333.

[21] Bouwsma, *Career* pg 5; Kuntz, *Postel* pg 24–5; Bobzin *Der Koran* pg 377–380. Josée
Balagna Coustou, *Arabe et Humanisme dans la France des derniers Valois*. (Maisonneuve et
Larose, Paris 1989) discusses François's use of Postel for his own diplomatic ends pg
53–54, 63. For the Embassy I have used: E. de Charrière, *Négotiations de la France dans le
Levant Collection de Documents inédits sur l'histoire de France* (Paris 1848–1860); V. L. Bourilly
"L'Ambassade de la Forest et de Marillac à Constantinople" Revue historique LXXVI
(1901) pg 297–328; J. Ursu, *La Politique orientale de François I (1515–1547)* (Champion,
Paris 1908): Turkish and Arabic souces are cited in J. von Hammer "Memoire sur
les premières relations diplomatiques entre La France et la Porte" Journal Asiatique
X (1827) pg 19–45.

[22] On de la Forest: Bourilly "L'Ambassade" pg 301–303.

[23] There is a very large literature on the negative image of the Turk in the West:
S. H. Moore "The Turkish Menace in the Sixteenth Century" Modern Languages
Review XL (1945) pg 30–36; R. Pfister "Das Türkenbüchlein Theodor Biblianders"
Theologische Zeitschrift (Basle) IX (1953) pg 438–454; K. M. Setton "Lutheranism
and the Turkish Peril" Balkan Studies III (1962) pg 133–168: J. W. Bohnstadt, *The
Infidel Scourge of God The Turkish Menace as seen by German pamphleteers of the Reformation
Era* (American Philosophical Society, Philadelphia, 1968); Egil Grislis "Luther and the
Turks" Muslim World LXIV (1974) pg 275–291.

presented all this to the Emperor as the search for a peace which would serve the interests of all Christians without further bloodshed, but nobody was taken in.

It is interesting to contrast the rhetoric of universal peace with which de la Forest was to begin his embassy with that of a letter he wrote to Leo X. There Christendom was to be at peace, but only to fight the Turk:[24] here Christendom and the Turks are to be at peace, though with the necessity of both of them fighting the Emperor.[25] François sought a universal peace which would permit the Sultan: *"de joyr en repos de l'honneur et du fruict de ses grandes et memorables victories et conquests"* and: *"d'entre tenir toute la chrestienté en tranquilité sans la susciter contre luy à la guerre, dont les fortunes et hazards sont uncertains"*.

Postel has left us no comment on this aspect of the mission. It may appear merely fanciful to place alongside the duplicitous claims of princes Postel's own message of Reconciliation. On the other hand it may be that Postel took the negotiations of the King seriously and was able to integrate the Embassy into his own developing understanding of his Mission to the East. There is no doubt Postel subsequently sought to involve Western princes in eschatological undertakings in the East. It does not seem improbable that this first *rapprochement* opened the imaginative possibilities for the achievement of the Universal Tutelage that Postel would urge upon French Kings. These had been dreamed of before, but *Realpolitik* was now approximating to the inevitable diplomatic developments of the Last Days.

Postel left Constantinople to arrive in Venice in July 1537. He left Venice for Paris on 9 August 1537.[26] Back in Paris, Postel tells us that the King would have honoured him greatly but all he wished was to see Arabic taught in the West, and Arabic books printed so that the Gospel would be preached in the East.[27] Subsequently, however, Postel showed no hesitation in his efforts to recruit kings and princes to his related typographic and evangelical projects, as we shall see.

---

[24] François I to Leo X, Amboise, 15 November 1516. E. de Charrière, *Négotiations* Vol. I pg 17–18: *"Tu sais mon très heureux père...combien j'ai desire, qu'un fois terminés tous les conflicts entre les princes chrétiens et établie entre tous une paix commune par accord de tous les princes et de tous les peoples, la plus belle et honnête guerre soit déclarée aux Turcs et au reste des enemies de la foix chrétienne"*.

[25] E. de Charrière, *Négotiations* pg 255–256.

[26] For the date: F. Secret "Theseus Ambrosius et Postellus Ambolaeus Doctor Medicinae" Bibliothèque d'Humanisme et Renaissance XXIII (1961) pg 130–132.

[27] Kuntz, *Postel* pg 27.

During his very short stay in Venice in 1537 Postel met Bomberg who as we have seen was working with Elias Levita on Job and Daniel.[28] Bomberg we may be sure shared Postel's interest in a kabbalistic book he had brought back from Constantinople, and no doubt in the other books and treasures Postel had obtained for François I.[29] We may recall that it was also at this time that Postel had briefly shared his enthusiasm for 'mystical Armenian' with Teseo Ambrogio, and sought to obtain Teseo's types.[30]

Soon removed to Paris, Postel's linguistic knowledge quickly earned him a place in the prestigious group of scholars around the King.[31] Postel praised the King for his reformist attitudes (the King had wanted Erasmus as his confessor) and saw the group of the King's scholars as a bulwark against those from the Sorbonne who taught that the Pope alone had greater authority than Councils. Postel has left us an account of François I's establishment of the College of the Three Languages.[32] In 1530 or 1531 Postel was appointed *mathematicorum et peregrinarum Linguarum regius interpres* and in 1538 he was made one of the *lecteurs royals* in Greek, Arabic, and Hebrew. Postel enjoyed the patronage of Chancellor Guillaume Poyet through whom he received important favours. This

---

[28] G. Weil, *Élias Lévita* pg 127–128. In *Linguarum duodecim* Biii v Postel records meeting Levita when he cites him as an authority on Hebrew grammar: *"Ex Hebraeis diligenter tractavit Rabi Moses Kimhi in Michlol Sarraafin et compendio suo, Elias Germanus quo usus sum Venetiis in Sepher Habachur, pirze Sira, et Harcavah"*. In the same place Postel acknowledges his indebtedness to Reuchlin, Sante Pagnino, Campensis and Münster and acknowledges Franciscus Vatabilis, *lector regius*, as teacher.

[29] In *Linguarum duodecim* B iv Postel speaks of finding a kabbalistic book: *"Nil tamen usquam quicquam scriptum in his* (i.e. *characteribus hebraicis) reperi, praeter quondam Cabalam, cuius mihi copiam fecit Mose Almuli medicus Regius Iudaeus apud Constantinopolim"*. W. J. Bouwsma "Postel and the significance of Renaissance Cabalism" Journal of History of Ideas XV (1954) pg 218–232 at pg 220 dates the first traces of Postel's interest in Kabbalah to his stay in Rome 1544–1547. Bobzin, *Der Koran* pg 379 dates it to this Embassy and notes a proof of the Trinity in Book I of *De Orbis Terrae* of 1543 (Paris) and 1544 (Basle) pg 23ff: *"ex veteri Testamento & Cabala & Thalmud"*. F. Secret dates the interest to Postel's days in Paris, *Le Zohar* pg 8 & 26. Postel refers to a manuscript of Bomberg in a kabbalistic discussion of the Name of 72 letters: F. Secret, *Postelliana* (B. de Graaf, Nieuwkoop 1981) pg 71.

[30] A complimentary reference to Teseo is found in *Introductio* Bv: *"Vir ad rem Christianam ornandam natus, Frater Ambrosius Papiensis Ferrariae habet excussas formas. Fuit nescio quot annos apud summos pontifices conductis inde a Syria hominibus doctus versatus diligenter in hac"*.

[31] Kuntz, *Postel* for a discussion of Postel's appointments, and pg 30–31 on the question whether Postel was associated with the King's scholars before the Embassy of Jean de la Forest.

[32] For the College of the Three Languages see: ed. F. Secret, *Guillaume Postel, Paralipomènes de la vie de François Ier* (Archè, Milan 1989) pg 77–88. Previously F. Secret had published extracts of this text in Studi francesci IV (1958) pg 50–62.

was perhaps the happiest period of his life. When subsequently Poyet was disgraced through court intrigue, Postel loyally but perhaps rashly attempted to intercede for him with the King. As a consequence Postel lost his Readership in late 1542. It was, perhaps, "the first great disappointment of his life and its first great turning point".[33] His conversion from scholarly contemplation to missionary activity was complete. But before he gave up his readership in 1542 Postel published his first two books on language in 1538 and later his Arabic Grammar.

The early Parisian Language Books

These two books are plausibly said to have arisen from Postel's first Voyage to the East and to have been prepared during his short stay in Venice when Postel was in touch with both Bomberg and Teseo Ambrogio. The claim to 'autopsy', or new evidence that he was the first to see, that Postel made for these particular works may however be exaggerated.[34] The two works in question are: *Linguarum duodecim characteribus differentium Alphabetum* of March 1538, and the *De originibus seu de Hebraica Lingua* of the same month. Somewhat thereafter appeared the *Grammatica Arabica* (c.1538–1540). These books have been competently discussed by Bobzin and set in the context of Postel's emerging linguistic notions.[35] This enables us to forgo a full description here. The mere sight of a page of these books however impresses one with problems encountered in finding decent Oriental type. Postel's own remark that ligatures only exist in eastern languages *because they do not print* indicates his frustration.[36]

In the Preface to *Linguarum duodecim* Postel outlines his view of the genetic relationship of languages in a way that will not surprise us. Chaldaean—"*quae eadem praeter characteras, Hebraica est*"—and Samaritan find

---

[33] Bouwsma, *Career* pg 9. Kuntz, *Postel* pg 33, 41–42. However we shall see below that the end of Postel's academic career and his departure from the Royal circle should not be considered solely as a consequence of Poyet's disgrace. We must consider also the Sorbonne's handling of Postel's book *De orbis* and the prophetic encounter with the King in 1544.

[34] The claim is made in Michael Scutarius's Introduction to *De duodecim* Aiv. See further comments below.

[35] Bobzin, *Der Koran* pg 404–424, 425–430, 430–441 respectively. The *De Originibus* of 1538 is not the same work as the 1553 book produced by Oporinus with the same short title.

[36] *Grammatica arabica* Diiii.

themselves close to the original Hebrew, Samaritan being distinguished only by its script.[37] Then there comes *"Punica Arabicave"* and *"Indica"* (= Ge'ez),[38] and next *"Graeca"* which is divided into *"Georgiana"*[39] and *"Tzeruuiana, Poznianiave"*.[40] Thereafter there is *"Armenica"* and *"Illirica"*[41] and finally *"Latina"*.

Of particular interest to us are Postel's remarks about *lingua Chaldaica*. It is apparent that Postel deals promiscuously with (what we call) Syriac, the Jewish Aramaic of the Talmud, and the Aramaic of kabbalistic

---

[37] Postel's description of the Samaritans is of interest though this is a case where one may be suspicious of the claims of 'autopsy'. There is very little that need be more than hearsay and there are long quotations from St. Jerome and the Old Testament. He does however print a script. Postel had also obtained some Jewish coins from the Second Year of the First Revolt (66–73 A.D.). He noted the similarities between the script on the coins and Samaritan, though he erroneously dated them a millennium too early. Postel mentions the Samaritans again. A letter to Masius 10 June 1550 (Chaufpié III pg 216–217) recalls his visits to Samaritans in Damascus and Shechem on his second voyage. He found them observant and without idolatry, and honouring Torah as Scripture. James Fraser remarks that this record (in contrast to *De duodecim*) represents "The first informed account of any serious consequence by any Western Scholar after St. Jerome with respect to the Samaritans within their own environment". James G. Fraser "Guillaume Postel and Samaritan Studies" in ed. M. L. Kuntz, *Postello, Venezia e il suo Mondo a cura di Marion Leathers Kuntz* (Olschki, Florence 1988) pg 99–117, pg 112. A broader survey of encounters with Samaritans is found in Nathan Schur "The Samaritans as described in Christian Itineraries (14th to 18th Centuries)" Palestine Exploration Quarterly L (1986) pg 144–155. Ilana Zinguer "Tabourot des Accords et les charactères samaritains" in *Tabourot, Seigneur des Accords Actes du Colloque Dion 1988* (Dijon, 1990) discusses the Samaritan characters in Tabouroth's *Bigarrures* and gives bibliographical details of Moshe Basiola of Ancona's Samaritan alphabet brought back from Palestine in 1522 (pg 146–147). For a general introduction to the Samaritans themselves: J. A. Montgomery, *The Samaritans* (J. C. Winston, Philadelphia 1907) should be supplemented by John Macdonald, *The Theology of the Samaritans* (SCM, London 1964); R. J. Coggins, *Samaritans and Jews: the Origins of Samaritanism Reconsidered* (OUP, Oxford 1975); C.-A. Mayer, *Bibliography of the Samaritans* (E. J. Brill, Leiden 1964); S. Noja "Contribution à la bibliographie des Samaritains" Alon XXXIII (1973) pg 98–113. Postel also makes mention in his account of his second voyage (Chaufpié pg 216–217) of Karaites. These remarks may be placed in a broader context by Ilana Zinguer "Juifs et Karaites aux XVIᵉ et XVIIᵉ siècles" in ed. Ilana Zinguer, *Miroirs del'Altérité et Voyages au Proche-Orient* (Slatkine, Geneva 1991) pg 55–64. Also her "Exotisme au Philologie dans les récits de voyages juifs de la Renaissance" in ed. M. Duchet, *Inscription des Langues dans les Relations de Voyage (XVIᵉ–XVIIIᵉ siècles)* (ENS, Fontenay/St. Cloud 1992) pg 177–189.

[38] Postel (F, Fv) follows Teseo Ambrogio in his opposition to Johannes Potken's designation of Ethiopic as 'Chaldaean', making reference to a line from the Georgics (IV 293).

[39] Here Postel prints a Coptic alphabet that has of course some similarities to the Greek alphabet.

[40] South Slavic (Serbian/Bosnian). The script is a variant of Cyrillic.

[41] *"Vel Hieronymiana"*: Galgolithic Script. St. Jerome was born on the border of Dalmatia and Pannonia and says Postel *"suis conterraneis hos reperit characteres Hieronymus"*.

texts like the *Zohar*.[42] After his presentation of the Syriac alphabet (and Syriac text appears thereafter in Hebrew characters), Postel describes Syriac Grammar as no different to that in Münster's Grammar and proclaims Chaldaean useful for Targum Studies which in turn serve to elucidate the Prophecies to the confusion of Jews.

The general approach to Aramaic, as essentially one language without much internal distinction beyond the distinction in script, is character-istic of the sixteenth-century scholars of what we now call Syriac: they see the language as essentially one with primordial Hebrew, and also with the supposedly ancient tongue of the kabbalistic arcana. It is not that the developments and distinctions were not recognised: rather what we tend to see separately, they saw together. A consequence of this is that Syriac (in as much as it is Aramaic) is a language of primordial antiquity that can sustain mystical manipulation and also convey kab-balistic mysteries.

The beginning of Postel's work on the Syriac New Testament 1537

Postel's remarks on the *lingua Chaldaica* include a reference to Syriac Gospels that had been shown him recently (*nuper*: the date was 1538) by Bomberg. Where these came from we do not know, but the Maronite delegation at the Fifth Lateran Council (1513–1515) seems a likely guess. These Gospels seem to have been overlooked, indeed they are positively misidentified by Kuntz who misunderstands the passage in question to refer to a Hebrew text of Matthew's Gospel. Kuntz further claims to have discovered "the Gospel of Matthew about which Postel is speaking" in Mss Orientali no 216 (Ebraici 10) Collazione 82 in the Biblioteca Marciana in Venice. But as this really is a Hebrew Mat-thew, and Postel spoke merely of Bomberg considering printing Syriac Gospels in Hebrew letters, the texts simply have nothing to do with each other.[43] It is however most important for us to be able to place the

---

[42] On this Aramaic see: Gershom Scholem, *Major Trends in Jewish Mysticism* (Schocken, New York 1961) pg 163–168.

[43] I give the passage (Biiii) at length because of its importance and because it has been misunderstood: *"In hac autem de qua nunc agere decrevi, utrumque testamentum vidi. Quos-dam etiam ex libris meis Arabicis in margine diligenter hoc charactere notatos habeo. Magna spes est posse haberi ab illis genuinum Matthaei exemplar, cui rei diligenter invigilat Daniel Bombergus, cuius officio debemus Hebraicas litteras. Is mihi Venetiis nuper ostendebat Evangelia illorum characteribus descripta: putans futurum, ut fructus aliquis inde fieret, si characteribus Hebraeis illas emitteret. Vir ad rem Christianum ornandum natus, Frater Ambrosius Ferrariae habet excussas formas. Fuit nescio*

beginning of Postel's plans for the Syriac New Testament at this early date of 1537 or 1538. This is the third of our previously overlooked pieces of evidence that establish the priority of Postel's work in editing these Gospels and its unsuspected early date. We shall continue to refer to the significance of this.

De Originibus, *March 1538*[44]

The *De Originibus* treats of both the origins and consequent affinities of languages.[45] We are presented again with an account of the dispersion

---

quot annos apud summos pontifices conductis inde a Syria hominibus doctis versatus diligenter in hac". The passage refers to Syriac, Syriac annotations in Postel's Arabic manuscripts, the Syriac Gospels Bomberg (to whom we are indebted for Hebrew type) thought to put into Hebrew letters, and finally to Teseo who had Syriac type. Kuntz, *Postel* pg 26 has quite misunderstood all of this, possibly because Postel's promiscuous use of the word 'Chaldaean' enabled him to discuss a kabbalistic text (that of Mose Almuli, mentioned in a footnote above) immediately before our passage. By the courtesy of Dottoressa Susy Macon of the Marciana I have been able to examine the relevant Hebrew manuscript on microfilm. It has no title nor introductory material. The right-hand side of an opening has a pointed Hebrew text in square characters linked by identifying letters to cursive unvocalised Hebrew marginalia that are all quotations of supposedly relevant passages of the Hebrew Bible. There are occasional underlinings in the main text where corrections are made above the line in the cursive hand. All this material is repeated in Latin on the opposite left-hand page. There is an unannotated Mark. Kuntz identifies the hands as those of Postel and Guy Lefèvre de la Boderie. But as Guy Lefèvre de la Boderie was not born until 1541, knew Postel in Paris for at most a year before Postel's confinement in 1564, and made no known trip to Venice, the history to be imagined for the manuscripts by Kuntz will have to be quite complex. The sixteenth-century Hebrew Matthew was the work of Ibn Shaprut, a Jewish polemicist writing in thirteenth-century Spain, and was made more widely known by Münster in 1537. It is referred to in Teseo's *Introductio* (f. 132b): *"In Evangelio Matthaei nuper literis Hebraicis a Monstero in lucem edito"*. In 1555 Mercier published a Hebrew text of Matthew discovered by Jean du Tillet, Bishop of Brieu in Italy in 1553. This he claimed to be the original text, a claim resurrected by H. J. Schonfield, *An Old Hebrew Text of St Matthew's Gospel* (T & T Clark, Edinburgh 1927) who makes much of agreement with Old Syriac material that may perhaps be better accounted for by imagining an Old Latin original for the Hebrew text. See: G. Howard, *The Hebrew Gospel of Matthew* (second ed, Macon 1995) and his article in *Anchor Dictionary of the Bible* (Doubleday, New York 1992) vol. V pg 642–3. I have not seen Adolf Herbst, *Des Schemtob ben Schaphrut hebraeische Übersetzung des Evangeliums Matthaei* (Göttingen 1879). It should, of course, not be forgotten that Postel thought the original of Matthew was in *Syriac*. Dottoressa Susy Macon further supplied me with a photocopy of the Marciana's handwritten catalogue of Syriac manuscripts. Bomberg's Syriac Gospels are not there, the only Syriac biblical manuscript being a Psalter of 1571 (Codex LX).

[44] See: Jean Céard "Le 'De Originibus' de Postel et la Linguistic de son temps" in *Postello, Venezia e il suo Mondo* pg 19–43. Marie-Luce Launey "Le De Originibus de 1538: une rhétorique des origines" *Actes du Colloque* pg 307–316.

[45] For an important sketch of the linguistic myths of Postel and some of his con-

of the sons of Noah. The universal distribution of what are claimed as traces of their names are offered as corroboration of the account. The essential identity of Hebrew and Chaldaean is again stated: it was merely the separation of the eponymous Heber that gave rise to a distinction in terms.[46] The trauma of Babel—*mutatio et dispersio Linguarum*—is reflected in Greek mythology by the Gigantomachia. Thereafter the spread and degeneration of the original tongue has nevertheless left isoglosses, arising from shared origins, affinity, or linguistic exchange, which enable one

---

temporaries: Jean Céard "De Babel à la Pentecôte: La Transformation du Mythe de la Confusion des Langues au XVIe siècle" Bibliothèque d'Humanisme et Renaissance LXII (1980) pg 577–594. Postel's work contributed to the general linguistic orientation of many who followed him in addressing the diversity of language, and more specifically those who linked French to Greek. He develops comparative techniques in this short treatise—an awareness of phonetic change, structural similarity, and a notion of linguistic families—that arise from his lists of isoglosses. What however is more significant is the mythology of linguistic unity within which he makes sense of the diversity of languages. This myth is reinforced by Postel's conflation of language and culture, and of peoples and languages. General characterisations of Early Modern linguistic notions may be found in: M. K. Read "The Renaissance concept of Linguistic Change" Archivum Linguisticum VIII (n.s.) (1977) pg 60–69; G. Bonfante "Ideas on the Kinship of European languages" Cahiers d'Histoire mondiale I (1954) pg 679–699; Marian Rothstein "Etymology, Genealogy, and Immutability of Origins" Renaissance Quarterly XLIII (1990) pg 332–347; J.-C. Margolin "Science et nationalisme linguistiques, ou la bataille pour l'etymologie au XVIe siècle" in *The Fairest Flower The Emergence of Lingistic National Consciousness in Renaissance Europe* (Conference of Center for Medieval and Renaissance Studies, University of California, Los Angeles. 12–13 December 1983) (Presso L'Accademia, Florence 1985) pg 139–166. George J. Metcalf discusses Bibliander in "Theodor Bibliander (1504–1564) and the Languages of Japheth's Progeny" Historiographia Linguistica VII; 3 (1980) pg 323–333. Manfred Peters has an excellent edition of Konrad Gessner, *Mithridates. De Differentiis Linguarum tum Veterum tum quae hodie apud diversas nations in toto orbe terrarum in usu sunt* (Scientia Verlag Aalen, Darmstadt 1974). For an account of Babel within the kabbalistic interests which so characterise the scholars we are studying: Myriam Jacquemier "Le Mythe de Babel et La Kabbale chrétienne" Nouvelle Revue du Seizième Siècle X (1992) pg 51–67. For the notion of Indo-European in sixteenth century: George J. Metcalf "The Indo-European Hypothesis in the Sixteenth and Seventeenth Centuries" in ed D. H. Hymes, *Studies in the History of Linguistcs: Tradition and Paradigms* (Indiana University Press, Bloomington 1974) pg 233–257; Maurice Olender, *Les Langues du Paradis Aryens et Sémites: un couple providential* (Gallimard/Le Seuil, Paris 1989). M. J. Franklin, *Sir William Jones* (University of Wales Press, Cardiff 1995) and also his *Sir William Jones Selected Political and Prose Works* (University of Wales Press, Cardiff 1995) now provide an excellent introduction to the life of the scholar who did most to establish the notion of Indo-European. For an indication of how a modern scholar, not entirely without controversy, has treated some of the issues of language affiliation and distribution raised here: Colin Renfrew, *Archaeology and Language The Puzzle of Indo-European Origins* (Jonathan Cape, London 1987).

[46] (Aiv). Though Chaldaeans were strictly speaking the older race, Chaldaean was nonetheless the vernacular of Christ and it is necessary to understand the semitic words found in the New Testament (F). Chaldaean is also useful for Targum studies (Ev).

to see the essential etymological congruity between languages. Arabic lexica are shown to be the same as the Hebrew. Indic words similarly are on occasion found to be the same as Hebrew, Latin, and French words. Greek words show similar episodic identity. Some idiomatic expressions are common to Hebrew and Chaldaean, and Greek words may hide Semitic etymologies.[47] A list of French and Greek words that are the same is provided, and finally we find a list of ecclesiastical terms that French (really) has borrowed from Greek.[48] Postel summarises: *"Ita videmus quod proposueram, primos homines Chaldaeos Hebraeosve quadam vitae insigni innocentia ac beneficio divino, prima iusti aequique praecepta mundique genealogiam revera, atque primum usum literarum habuisse, a quibus ad Graecos demum, ut ad nos & in toto terrarum orbe transierint"* (G iiiii).

Bobzin's work has removed the need for a detailed discussion of the linguistic technicalities of Postel's Arabic in both the *Linguarum duodecim* and the *Grammatica arabica*. We may however draw attention here to the appeal Postel makes to the Council of Vienne in defence of the utility of Arabic (and Hebrew and Greek, though he omits Syriac!).[49] Postel here places his developing evangelical strategy towards the East in a larger perspective. The eleventh canon of the Council (1311–1312) to which he refers was in conception and scope quite remarkable for it required that teaching posts in Hebrew, Chaldaean, Arabic and Greek be set up at the Papal Court and also in Paris, Oxford, Bologna and

---

[47] Thus *'Hercules'* is not *'a Iunionis Gloria'* but from ערכל *"id est totus pelle tectus", "…ut qui insignis peregrinatur pelle quadam primorum hominum more tegeretur"*. Speculation about the transmission of the 'Chaldaean Discipline' to the Gauls by this same Gallic Hercules before writing follows. Bobzin, *Der Koran* pg 428–430 offers philological comment on Postel. The mythological content of his analysis should not conceal the generally sound knowledge of Hebrew, Aramaic, Arabic, and Ethiopic morphology that he displays.

[48] J. Céard "Le De Originibus" pg 39 notes the influence of contemporary theories about the relationship of Greek and French e.g. Henri Etienne, *Traicté de la conformité du langage François avec le Grec* (1565, 1569).

[49] For the influence of Raimund Lull upon the canon: B. Altener "Raymundus Lullus und der Sprachenkanen" Historische Jahrbuch der Gorres-Gesellschaft (München) LIII (1933) pg 191–219. In general: Ewald Müller, *Das Konzil von Vienne 1311–1312 Seine Quellen und Seine Geschicte.* (Verlag der Aschendorffischen Verlagsbuchhandlung, Münster in Westfalen 1934). For England specifically: Robert Weiss "England and the Decree of the Council of Vienne on the Teaching of Greek, Arabic, Hebrew, and Syriac" Bibliothèque d'Humanisme et Renaissance XIV (1952) pg 1–9. For the consequences of the canon in the Papal Court: B. Altaner "Die Durchfürung des Vienner Konzils-beschlusses über die Errichtung von Lehrstühlen für orientalische Sprachen" Zeitschrift für Kirchengeschichte (Stuttgart) LII (1933) pg 226–236. Notice that the canon speaks of *"lingua Chaldaea"* and not 'Syriac' though Jacobites, Nestorians and Maronites are specifically intended. B. Altaner "Raymundus Lullus" pg 218 & Bouwsma, *Career* pg 78–97 discuss the influence of Lull upon Postel.

Salamanca. Each place was to have two teachers to lecture and also produce Latin translations of texts in the languages of their speciality. The measure was prompted primarily by missionary enthusiasm for the conversion of the Infidel, but also with an eye to biblical exegesis. Though the canon gave legal force to these aspirations it was not a great success. Nevertheless the mediaeval antecedents of our sixteenth-century scholars are accurately evoked here by Postel.

Concordia

The period of 1540–1543 following the deposition of his patron was a troubled time for Postel. Nevertheless he wrote several books during the period, the most important of which was the *De orbis terrae Concordia*, a very large book written in only two months.[50] Postel waited several months for approval of his work from the Sorbonne. It was not forthcoming and the book was returned marked *"Ad facultatem non pertinens"*. The book was eventually published by Oporinus in Basle after the removal of material highly critical of Protestant "Evangelists" in Book IV.[51]

---

[50] The first book is entitled *"Verae religionis, id est Christianae, probatio, ex philosophia desumpta"* and is an apologia from Scripture and Jewish Sources for fundamental Christian belief directed at both Jews and Moslems. There is a *'probatio ex veteris Testamento & Cabale & Thalmud'* (pg 23–27). Page 24 has the interesting classification of Torah, Kabbalah and Talmud as respectively *'sacra, mixta, et humana'*. But they all serve nonetheless to prove the Trinity. He proceeds to find support from two Koranic suras: 5, 110 & 2, 253 & 84 (Bobzin, *Der Koran* pg 466). Book II treats of the life, upbringing, and way of Mohammed and of the Koran. Islam is presented as a punishment from God for the disunity of Christianity, and the Union of the Church will signify victory over Islam (pg 132f). The utility of learning Arabic for missionary purposes is stressed (pg 134) and the heretical origins of the religion are discovered (pg 145–147). The Koran is considered with respect to Old and New Testaments with a section on Doctrines of God, Eschatology, Angels and Daemons. Arabic sources in praise of Christ and the Gospel are quoted. Book III is entitled *"quid commune totus orbis tam iure humano quam divino habeat"* gives the theoretical ground for Book IV *"qua arte sine seditione falsae de Deo, diisve persuasions, ad veram pertrahi possint"*, that deals with the practical question of winning Moslems to Christianity. Bobzin, *Der Koran* pg 470f deals with translations of Koran texts in the *De orbis*.

[51] Postel published Book IV himself as *Alcorani seu legis Mahometi et evangelistarum concordiae liber* (Paris 1543). He calls the 'evangelists', that is the Protestants, *'cenevangelistae'* explaining the term from both *'vani'* and *'novi'*. They are the bastards of Mohammed as like him they do not believe in free-will, are literal-minded, inflexible and unforgiving. On the other hand Postel was on good terms with Plantin, Oporinus, Bibliander and several other Reformers and also with the Family of Love: see Kuntz, *Postel* pg 44–48. Oporinus had probably just published Bibliander's translation of the Koran. Bobzin,

The *De Orbis* is Postel's rational justification of Christianity, his refutation of the incompatible teachings of Judaism, Islam, and paganism, and yet his celebration of their deep hidden similarities.[52] It sets forth Postel's methodology of Conversion, and he wanted it translated into all languages. This universal mission handbook proclaims the unity of mankind as a basis for the *Respublica christiana*. One can recognise not only Raimond Lull but also Nicolas of Cusa as precursors, but now the Protestants as well as the Jews and Moslems had to be reintegrated into the Church.[53]

Shortly after the completion of the *De Orbis*, Postel had a vision that told him he must warn François I to reform his kingdom in preparation for his God-appointed role as the chosen royal initiator of Universal Restoration. Thereafter, Postel's prophetic self-consciousness, apparent in all his works, was to develop along quite distinctive lines that were in the end more easily handled by the authorities as insanity than in any other way. Yet Postel's vision of the role of the King of France would become a significant factor in the dynastic messianism and imperial aspirations of the Valois and Bourbons into the seventeenth century. These aspirations, when later articulated by a pupil of Postel, Guy Lefèvre de la Boderie, provide an essential context for the edition of the Syriac New Testament that was printed in Paris in 1584.

Prophecies concerning the King of France, and the association of the King with the Joachimite Angelic Pope, were not new and François I had been the object of such prophecies before. Postel went to Fontainebleau and spent an hour alone with the King. François was apparently disposed at first to be penitent, but then was persuaded by

---

Der Koran pg 464–465 notes that Postel's trenchant criticism of this work in *De Orbis* pg 136 did not stop Oporinus publishing Postel's book.

[52] Fillippo Mignini "I limiti della Concordia e il mito della ragione" in *G. Postel Actes du Colloque* pg 207–221 for an evaluation of coherence and tolerance in Postel's position. An earlier comment is Joseph Lecler, *Histoire de la Tolération au siècle de la Réforme* (Albin Michel, Paris 1996; First ed.1955) pg 423–429. An important new work of relevance to these issues is H. R. Guggisberg and B. Gordon, *Sebastian Castellio 1515–1563 Humanist and defender of Religious Toleration in a Confessional Age* (Ashgate, Aldershot 2003). Of course, one must not expect too much in this respect, even today. For the intransigence behind many of the banalities of modern Inter-Faith Dialogue, and also a useful schematisation of possible relationships: Rowan Williams, *On Christian Theology* (Blackwell, Oxford 2000) pg 93–106.

[53] For Lull generally at this time: Paolo Rossi "The legacy of Ramon Lull in sixteenth-century thought" Medieval & Renaissance Studies V (1961) pg 183–213. For Nicolas of Cusa and Islam: Ludwig Hageman, *Der Kur'an in Verständnis und Kritik bei Nikolaus von Kues* (Joesef Knecht, Frankfurt-am-M. 1976).

a "Dame of Poitiers" (in all probability Diane of Poitiers, who had calmed the king after previous similar warnings) to ignore him. Kuntz speculates that in this episode and Diane's management of it may lie the beginnings of the accusation of madness which were subsequently to dog Postel.[54]

Postel articulated his immediate warnings to the King within the context of an elaborated historical and prophetic myth about the destiny of the Gauls and their descendants the French. Postel's notions characteristically integrated theological and mystical considerations with an historical account that was able to promote French primacy within the legendary post-diluvian dispersal of Noah and his sons that we have already seen facilitated Viterbian and Papal pretensions. A similar mythology exploited with Postel's support by the Florentines under Cosimo I lies beyond the scope of this work.

The technique of linguistic research Postel characteristically employed in his forays into primordial history he called "emithology", a word that in itself nicely demonstrates the point. 'Emitholgy' is an etymology in which the constituent parts of a word themselves are symbols heavy with hidden truth: the first syllable of 'emithology' is from אמת 'truth'. For example: the primordial separation of the Earth from the Waters, Postel tells us, is designated in Hebrew by the word transcribed as *Galuyah*. (Thus *'Gaul'* is the name of the first land in the Universe.) This is also the origin of the word *'Gallois'* and the name *'Gallim'* means those 'saved from the waves'. This belongs by right of primogeniture to the senior descendants of Noah's family who are to rule the world. Gomer, the eldest son of Japhet, settled in Gaul. Emithology thus teaches us both the history and the destiny of France.[55]

Historically speaking, Postel had to adjust the Annian myth to accommodate French supremacy. We need not follow him in detail through this obstacle course. He shows how Julius Caesar derived his power from Gaul. This was not an isolated event but part of a long history of Gaulish intervention in Rome, which originated in the expulsion of the Gauls descended from Noah/Janus from the City by the followers of Romulus, the Romans. The Romans were essentially usurpers, and

---

[54] Kuntz, *Postel* pg 52–58.

[55] The essential characterisation of emithology is F. Secret "L'Emithologie de Guillaume Postel" in ed. E. Castelli, *Umanismo e Simbolismo* (CEDAM, Padova 1958) pg 381–437. The above is abbreviated from pg 406. We have seen above a similar etymology of *'Gallim'* from R. Samuel in Annius da Viterbo.

none more so than the Roman Pontiffs whose imperialistic belligerence
encroached upon the mission of the Kings of France. Caesar, like the
Gauls who sacked Rome in Livy's History, were merely reasserting
Gallic privilege. Postel dealt with the case of Charlemagne and the
Germanic pretensions to Empire in the same way as he had dealt with
Caesar. The two men represented the power of the Gauls, and Charlemagne's right of Empire derived solely from the fact that the Gauls
chose to make him Emperor. That, of course, put the long-running
opposition between François I and Charles V in its proper light.

Postel did not merely reinterpret Roman history. As always, the sheer
scope of his integrating rereading of pretty well everything compels
admiration. In this case he offers accounts of the Three Voyages of
the Gauls as far as Scythia, West to Italy and Germany, and finally to
Rome. He then offers an account of Gaulish religion to confirm the
election of this people, and finally astrological corroboration.[56]

With the Jesuits

From Fontainebleau where he had warned the King, Postel travelled
on foot during the Lent of 1544 to Rome to join Ignatius Loyola and
his followers and become a priest.[57] But his stay was short: by Decem-

---

[56] The fundamental work which obviates the need for further treatment here is
Claude-Gilbert Dubois, *Celtes et Gaulois au XVIe siècle* (J. Vrin, Paris 1972) which I have
used above. This work contains an edition of Postel's *De ce qui est premier pour reformer
le monde*. Dubois also has *Mythe et Langage au Seizième siècle* (Ducros, Paris 1970) and a
valuable collection of essays on this theme *La mythologie des origines chez Guillaume Postel: de
la naissance à la nation*. (Paradigme, Orléans 1994). Also his, "La Curiosité des origines."
In ed. J. Céard, La Curiosité à la Renaissance (Librairie Nizet, Paris 1986) pg 37–48
and his "Une Utopie politique de la renaissance" L'Information littéraire XX (1968)
pg 55–62. A broad treatment in English is R. E. Asher, *National Myths in Renaissance
France Francus, Samothes and the Druids* (Edinburgh University Press, Edinburgh 1993).
A modern account of the relationships between Celts and Romans is found in H. D.
Rankin, *Celts and the Classical World* (Croom Helm, London 1987).

[57] Kuntz, *Postel* pg 59–63; Bouwsma, *Career* pg 12–13. Henri Bernard—Maitre "Le
Passage de Guillaume Postel chez les premiers Jesuites de Rome" *Mélanges d'Histoire
littéraire de la Renaissance offerts à Henri Chamard* (Paris 1951) pg 227–243 remains the
fundamental study. Postel also describes his differences with the Jesuits in a letter to
Cardinal Cervino written probably in 1547. J. Schweizer "Ein Beitrag zu Wilhelm
Postels Leben und zur Geschichte des Trienter Konzils und der Inquisition" Römische
Quartalschrift für christliche Altertumskünde und für Kirchengeschichte XXIV (1910)
pg 105ff gives some of the text. Interestingly Postel was sending his *Candelabrum Mosis*
to Cervini whose role in the development of early Roman Orientalism we have already
discussed.

ber 1545 he had been separated from the Order. Postel had known Loyola and his companions in Paris and admired their discipline and their missionary spirit. But Postel had notions of his own which were hardly compatible with those of Ignatius and his friends. He certainly had no intention of giving absolute obedience to the Pope, and believed that supreme authority in the church belonged to General Councils. He believed that the world was to be regenerated through a Universal French Empire. More decisively he may have already begun to identify himself as the Angelic Pope, who would cooperate with the French King in the final stages of world history.[58]

Ignatius and the Jesuits remained sensible of Postel's good qualities—his learning and his piety—yet began to detect errors of judgment behind his more singular opinions and convictions. A passage quoted by Henri Bernard-Maitre suggests further unease at the influence of Rabbinic and Islamic learning upon Postel.[59] One should however guard against sweeping generalisations upon the attitude of the Jesuits (or any of the Orders) towards Kabbalah.[60]

Postel's departure from the Jesuits coincided with developments in the ecclesiastical world that did not please him. He disapproved of the divisions that developed from the hard line taken at Trent. He disapproved of the events that led to the moving of the Council from Trent to

---

[58] Postel's *Le Thresor des Propheties de l'Univers*, extant in two different versions of 1564–1565 and 1566, sheds considerable light on this period. It establishes both the vocation of Postel as the Angelic Pope, and that of the king of France as Universal Monarch. There is now an introduction and edition by F. Secret, *Guillaume Postel Le Thresor des Propheties de l'Univers* (M. Nijhoff, The Hague 1969). Pages 8–13 give an unedited manuscript account of this period by Postel, and pg 15–17 a short sketch of Rome at this period. F. Secret in "G. Postel et les courants prophétiques" Studi francesi III (1957) pg 377 & 392 considers this period in Rome the probable occasion of the crystallisation of Postel's identification with the Angelic Pope stimulated by Amadeus's *Apocalypsis Nova* which, we have seen, was, Amadeus claimed, dictated to him by the Angel Gabriel on the Janiculum. In *Histoires orientales* (1575 pg 15) Postel wrote: *"Noe dict Janus par l'invention du vin appelé Iain esleut sa sépulture à Rome au mont dict depuys Ianiculum iusques à ce que S. Pierre crucifié et ensevely sur le dict mont feist qu'on l'appelle Santo Pietro Montorio"*. Like Galatinus, Postel identified himself with the Angelic Pope. He had seen a picture *en toile* in the Monastery of S. Pietro in Montorio that Amadeus had founded on the Janiculum. The picture portrayed the revelation on that very special spot. In the picture Postel recognised himself (pg 378 & 392–393; *Thesor* f. 121v). We shall encounter below a similar pictorial recognition in Venice.

[59] *Op. cit.* pg 231.

[60] F. Secret "Les Jésuits et le Kabbalisme chrétien à la Renaissance" Bibliothèque d'Humanisme et Renaissance XV (1954) pg 139–144. Also his: "Les Dominicains et la Kabbale chrétienne à la Renaissance" Archivum Fratrum Praedicatorum XXVII (1957) pg 329–336.

Bologna, and he now considered François I responsible for urging Paul III to commit "the greatest sin in the world" in placing the authority of the Pope above that of the Council. It was an act that would only make the unity of Christendom more difficult. Postel had personally warned François on this matter at Fontainebleau. The Council that proclaimed the Pope's supreme authority convened at Bologna 12 March 1547. Ten days later François was dead. The divine inspiration of Postel's prophetic voice was thus decisively confirmed.[61]

Some significant Meetings: Widmanstetter and Masius

During his time in Rome Postel made several acquaintances and discoveries of significance for the future of Oriental studies in Rome and Syriac studies in particular. Postel met an Ethiopic priest who expounded the Book of Enoch to him.[62] It may be, though the evidence falls short of demonstration, that Postel came across some of the works of Egidio da Viterbo at this time. (Certainly he found and read Petrus Galatinus's unpublished works.)[63] Postel shares with Egidio, as Secret notes, an awareness of the arrival of the Last Times wherein the kabbalistic arcana are revealed and it behoves the Universal Monarch to

---

[61] Kuntz, *Postel* pg 63 for remarks here and the address to the Council *Pro scriptis*.

[62] *De Originibus* (1553 Basle) pg 10: *"Audivi etiam Romae librorum Enoch argumentum, et contextum mihi a sacerdote Aethiope (ut in Ecclesia reginae Sabba habetur pro canonico libro instar Moses) expositum: ita ut sit mihi varia supplex pro historiae varietate".* Postel had proposed to the Council that Enoch was a key to understanding Scripture: Joseph Schweizer "Ein Beitrag zu Wilhelm Postels Leben und zur Geschichte des Trienter Konzils und der Inquistion" Römische Quartalschrift für christliche Altertumskunde und für Kirchenge-schichte XXIV (1910) pg 100–101. He was similarly sympathetic to other Apocrypha as we shall see. On the meaning of the name Enoch for Postel: F. Secret "L'Emithologie" pg 441–413. A manuscript gloss about Enoch refers to Tasfa Sejon whom Postel had thus evidently met: F Secret, *Guillaume Postel et son Interprétation du Candélabre de Moyse* (B. De Graaf, Niewkoop 1966) pg 24. On page 29 of the same work is discussed the influence of Postel's Ethiopic knowledge upon his thought and his response to Damião de Goes, *Fides, religio moresque Aethiopum sub imperio precosi Iohannis degentium Damiano a Goes ac Paulo Iovio interpretibus* (Louvain 1540, Paris 1541) that was dedicated to Paul III. For knowledge of Enoch generally: Nathaniel Schmidt "Traces of early acquaintance in Europe with the Book of Enoch" Journal of the American Oriental Society XLII (1922) pg 44–52. The article discusses Pico, Reuchlin and Potken.

[63] In his *Retractatio* (ms Sloane 1412 f. 310v) of 1560 which he sent to Oporinus, Postel speaks of the influence upon him of Galatinus's unedited works which we have seen rely upon prophecy and Kabbalah to develop their theme of the Angelic Pope.

act.[64] We do know for certain however that Postel at this time met J. A. Widmanstetter who had been a friend of Egidio, and with whom he was also to develop a friendship. Together they would produce the 1555 *editio princeps* of the Syriac New Testament. In recalling this meeting Postel emphasises Widmanstetter's distinction in the knowledge of Kabbalah.[65] It seems that Widmanstetter at this point provided the stimulus for Postel to begin his own kabbalistic studies in earnest. Thereafter Postel synthesized his own distinctive notions and self-consciousness with his equally eccentric reading of the Kabbalah. The first-fruits of this distinctive *mélange* of Kabbalah, his own notions of Universal Concord, and his own "Eternal Gospel" he presented in a book he sent to Oporinus in Basle in February or March 1546 called *De Restitutione humanae naturae*. The book was intercepted which suggests that Postel was under some suspicion at the time.[66] Postel may at this time have been protected by his close personal friendship with the papal Vicar Filippo Archinto.[67] In 1547 he offered an *apologia* for the book.[68]

It was also at this moment that Postel met Masius in Rome, as we have seen, and began to teach him Arabic. We shall return subsequently to the relationships between these distinguished scholars and their contributions to the sixteenth-century editions of the Syriac New Testament.[69] At the time neither the stimulus of these new scholarly friendships, nor the patronage of men like Archinto and perhaps Pole, who admired his learning, could prevent the growing embarrassment felt by the Jesuits as Postel proclaimed both his ideas and his hostility

---

[64] F. Secret, *Le Zohar* pg 56.

[65] *Cosmographicae disciplinae compendium* (Basle 1561) *"Prefatio* a3:...*maxime autem ob secretioris inter Hebraeos doctrinae mysteria, quibus praeditus erat...".*

[66] So Postel's letter of 22 January 1547 to Masius from Venice (Chaufpié pg 319): *"Missum est Roma ad Oporinum opus restitutiae humanae naturae iam ante decem menses et interceptum est".* For Oporinus: M. Steinmann, *Johannes Oporinus, Ein Basler Buckdrucker um die Mitte des 16. Jahrhunderts* (Helbing & Lichtenhahn, Basle 1967).

[67] F. Secret "Filippo Archinto, Girolamo Cardano, et Guillaume Postel" Studi francesci XIII (n. 37) (1969) pg 73–76; Levi della Vida, *Ricerche* pg 321.

[68] *Guliemi Postelli sacerdotis apologia et postulatio pro iis quae ab eo scripta aut dicta sunt de restitutione omnium seu de naturae humanae absoluta instauratione* (Archivo di Stato, Florence, Carte Cervine 33 f. 34–36).

[69] F. Secret, *Candélabre* pg 9 & 12 also notes the presence of Alessandro da Foligno a convert from Judaism and protégé of the Jesuits who appears to have helped Postel to write, in Rome, against the Talmud. The work seems lost. Also, of course, in Venice Postel would have met *"Cornelium Adelkindum neophuton ex Judaismo"* (Postel 7 June 1555: Chaufpié III pg 228).

to Paul III.[70] Postel left Rome at the end of 1546 or the beginning of
1547 for Venice.[71]

Mother Joanna

Postel remained in Venice until sometime between 30 May and 21
August 1549 at which latter date he was in Jerusalem, as we know
from the letter he wrote from there to Masius.[72] It was in Venice that
Postel met Mother Joanna, the foundress of the Ospedaletto of Saints
John and Paul where Postel, like other followers of Ignatius, served as
a priest.[73] Mother Joanna was clearly a remarkable woman who had
devoted her life to the poor first in Padova and then in Venice where
she had convinced some wealthy Venetians to pay for a building near
the Monastery of SS Giovanni e Paolo where she might shelter and
care for the sick and indigent. Such charitable works were characteristic
of the Catholic Reformation at the time and perfectly congruent with
Postel's attitudes as proclaimed already in Rome. But Mother Joanna
was also a stigmatic and mystic.[74] Shortly after his arrival she asked
Postel to be her spiritual director and confessor. This relationship in
which Postel became her *"little son"* and deferred to his spiritual daughter as *"mia madre"* was to prove the consolidating experience of Postel's
life. Postel's broad notions of 'Restoration' were further secured, his
Orientalism and in particular his interest in Kabbalah reinforced, and
his personal consciousness of his mission became frankly messianic.
The experience released a flood of writings from Postel.[75]

---

[70] Pole seems to have offered some favour: *Cosmographicae disciplinae compendium Prefatio*
a3v.

[71] Postel wrote to Masius 22 January 1547 of his troubles in Rome and his resignation
to suffering (Chaufpié III pg 219). Postel had written in praise of the Venetian constitution in *De magistratibus Athenensium* that had been translated into Italian and published
in Venice in 1543. On this: M. L. Kuntz "Guillaume Postel e l'idea di Venezia come
La Magistratura più perfetta" in *Postello, Venezia e il suo Mondo* pg 163–178. Postel was
further to accommodate the city into his mythology of origins and eschatological roles
as a second Rome and, as we shall see, the home of Mother Joanna.

[72] Chaufpié III pg 216.

[73] Kuntz, *Postel* pg 69–92 on Mother Joanna, with bibliography on the Ospedaletto on pg 70. To this add: Giuseppe Ellero "G. Postel e l'Ospedale dei Derelitti
(1547–1549)" in ed. Kuntz, *Postello, Venezia e il suo Mondo* pg 137–161. Also Bouwsma,
Career pg 14–16.

[74] ms Sloane 1411 f. 109.

[75] Oporinus published Postel's *Panthenosia* in Basle in 1547. His *Candelabrum* appeared
in Venice in Hebrew and Latin in 1548. This work, the superb edition of which by

For Postel Venice had been graced—indeed preserved and made prosperous—by the presence of Mother Joanna, the "Venetian Virgin" into whose body the Spirit of God had descended and in whose person the Living Christ was present. There are few of his works after 1547 in which he does not refer to the "True Mother of the World". Mother Joanna became for Postel synonymous with the *Schekinah*, the Moon who reflects the Sun, the Revealer of the Mystery of Restoration to her little son whom God had chosen for her: all things were to be gathered into One Sheepfold; all religions and peoples were to be united in a general pardon and universal baptism; Postel himself was to be the Elijah of the Fourth Age and Mother Joanna its Angelic Pope.[76] This last surprising appointment—of a female Angelic Pope, to match Postel's male counterpart—inaugurated, inevitably, a new Papacy that from 1547 was to eclipse the old Papacy in Rome that characteristically did not allow women to teach (nor for that matter to be Pope). Postel's role was to preach universal restitution, universal penitence and universal

---

F. Secret we have already mentioned, may be seen as an anticipation of Postel's great kabbalistic translations to which we shall shortly turn. The text was produced in Hebrew, Latin, Italian and French to promote its dissemination (a practice one can find again with Postel at the time of 1566 Laon exorcisms that caused him to seek to promote the work that eventually became the Antwerp Polyglot). Postel sent a copy to Cervini (F. Secret's Edition p 26). Of the contents of the book, Secret (pg 15) remarks: *"Le Candélabre est en effet aussi, le miroir des délires qui le firent écarter de la Compagnie de Jésus, et qu'il a résumés dans Merveilles du Monde"*. The heart of the book is Mother Joanna though Postel also pursues his theme of Universal Concord and the role of France and the Angelic Pope. I shall not attempt to summarise its teaching further at this point, but quote a passage (pg 395) solely because it illustrates the possibility of Syriac letters carrying mystical meaning like the Hebrew: *"Et pour parler plus clairement comme tout cercle est mesuré par 22 septiesmes de son diamètre, ainsi par 22 est mise ceste mesure du monde rond. C'est par ce, les lettres de Adam. Moys, de Esdras, de Christ et les surienes et chaldéens descendues de la saincte, en laquelle est toute la doctrine du monde, ne sont plus que 22 combien qu'on peult adjouster beaucoup d'aultres prolations"*. The book was an inspiration to the next generation of Christian kabbalists. A French version was made by Jehan Boulaese. It is interesting to note that Guy Lefèvre de La Boderie intended to produce a translation. In his *Diction. Syro-chaldaicum* pg 8 Guy says: *"Ut videre est in Candelabro hebraice Venetiis impresso, quod et nos Deodante auctum et illustratum propediem in lucem emittemus"*. Blaise de Vigenère also took an interest in the work. See: F. Secret's edition pg 7.

[76] For Postel on all this, see *inter alia*: *Le Prima Nove del altro Mondo* (1555) on which: Enea Balmas "'Le prime nove dell'altro mondo' di Guglielmo Postel" Studi urbanati XXIX (1955) pg 334–377. Also: *Les très Merveilleuses Victoires des femmes* (1553) for which I have used the edition of Gustave Brunet (Slatkine Reprints, Geneva 1970). I avoid here a detailed exposition of Postel's teaching about Mother Joanna, their respective roles, the Kabbalah etc. For this see Kuntz, *Postel* pg 87–92. M. A. Screech "The Illusion of Postel's Feminism" in Journal of the Warburg and Courtauld Institute XVI (1953) pg 162–170 warns against too modern a (mis-) understanding of Postel's male/female imagery.

baptism. He was now entirely driven to a life of evangelical action, and yet one in which he would articulate his self-understanding through Jewish Kabbalah. Mother Joanna, untutored as she was in any ancient or Oriental tongue, had full understanding of the arcana of the *'prisci theologi'* and the ancient Hebrews. Indeed her role to a certain extent was to be the hermeneutic key that opened these secrets.[77]

It was in Venice at this time that Postel acquired his copy of the *Zohar*, a work which he was to be the first to print and which, read through Mother Joanna's distinctive interpretive lens, was to shape his development.[78] For it was Mother Joanna who was able to explain to him the difficult passages in spite of her apparent lack of any relevant knowledge of Aramaic. The acquisition of such an expensive book was, of course, as providential as his meeting with Mother Joanna.[79]

Postel began his translation in 1547.[80] As his work progressed he came to find the "Restitution of All Things" spoken of in other Jewish sources as well as in all the books of the Kabbalah. He translated the

---

[77] For the 'Key of David' in this sense: Kuntz, *Postel* pg 88. In *Le Prima nove* (Giii v) Postel complains that both Jews and Christians have ignored the Zohar's teaching about the Second Coming of Christ 'in the feminine person'.

[78] F. Secret "L'herméneutique de G. Postel" in *Archivio di Filosofia, Umanismo e Ermeneutica* (Padova 1963) pg 91–118.

[79] F. Secret, *Kabbalistes chrétiens* pg 185 quoting ms Theol 264 m f. 25 in the Library in Goettingen.

[80] On this translation see F. Secret, *Zohar* pg 51–78 and also pg 104–114 for the Latin text of Postel's introduction. The translation is replete with Postel's explanatory comments that show how he read his own Restitution by the Grace of Mother Joanna into the *Zohar*. Masius's later letter of 13 April 1554 (after Mother Joanna's death) that we cite below shows his anxiety for his friend. In 1553 Postel sent his translation of the Genesis section to Oporinus in Basle who had published the *De orbis terrae Concordia*. But Oporinus did not print it, probably because its annotations would have upset the censors (we shall see below that when Bibliander brought out the *Protoevangelium* he did so without the annotations) but nor did he return it. Joseph Perles, *op. cit.* pg 79 found a copy of this in Munich (though he wrongly thought it the autograph and misread the date which is 23 October 1553). (A manuscript note: *"Basilea acceptum totum volumen cum alii ejusdem Postelli"* is attributed by Perles (pg 78) to Masius). The original is in the British Library (Sloane 1410. 625 folios). Clearly Oporinus had allowed someone to make a copy. Postel asked Masius to try to get it back. See letters of 13 April 1554 from Masius and 25 November 1563 from Postel (Lossen, *op. cit.* #136 pg 160, Lossen, *op. cit.* pg 353, Chaufpié III pg 225). Unable to recover his book Postel started again and got to the end of the Exodus section (F. Secret, *Zohar*, pg 52). Postel entrusted this version in his will to Nicolas Lefèvre de la Boderie. Secret located this in Goettingen, some 350 pages in-folio, whence the translation given above. In the long title to his translation, Postel refers to the language of the *Zohar*, which he believed to have been compiled by Simeon ben Iochai as: *"Chaldaica sive vulgaris Syriaca"* (F. Secret, *Zohar* pg 57).

Bahir,[81] part of the commentary of Menachem of Recanti and part of *Bereshith Rabbah*.[82] At this period Postel also published *Or nerob hamenorah* in Hebrew and as its Latin translation *Candelabri typici in Mosis tabernaculo*. Mother Joanna was also responsible for obtaining for Postel a copy of the *Protoevangelium Jacobi Minoris*.[83] Postel was characteristically

---

[81] The translation of the *Bahir* was once considered lost (F. Secret, *Kabbalistes chrétiens* pg 174; *Bibliographie des Manuscrits de Guillaume Postel* (Droz, Geneva 1970) pg 40 & 46) but was found in 1969 in the Universitätsbibliothek at Basle (Shelfmark: A ix 99) F. Secret "Un Manuscrit retrouvé de G. Postel" Bibliothèque d'Humanisme et Renaissance XXXV 1973 pg 87–99. The manuscript is studied by Antonio Rotondo in "Guillaume Postel e Basilea" Critica Storica X/1 (1973) pg 114–159 at pg 131ff. Rotondo's appendix pg 146–155 gives extensive quotations from the text of the *Apologia* prefixed to the translation. (The article reappears in Rotondo's *Studi e Ricerche di Storia ereticale italiano del Cinquecento* (Edizione Giappichelli, Turin 1974) 117–159. Appendix pg 473–486). The text is also found in F. Secret, *Postelliana* (B. De Graaf, Nieuwkoop, 1981) pg 21–112 with a short introduction pg 8–11. Postel follows and translates the Hebrew text of *Bahir* inserting his own glosses in brackets. These of course concern the Mysteries of the Trinity and the Atonement. The revelation of Mother Joanna is prominent as is the contrast between male and female. The Thirty-two Ways of Wisdom are discussed. The text itself gives Postel plenty of opportunity to discuss the significance of Hebrew letters and the Sephirot. The kabbalistic significance of the signs of the Zodiac is also expounded. Postel makes reference to his own *Candelabrum* and to the misunderstanding of Kabbalah by Jews, Moslems and heretics.

[82] In *Il Libro della divina ordinatione* (Padua 1555 C iiii v), Postel speaks of his Hebrew sources for the 'Second Feminine Advent': *"Innumerabili luochi di questo secondo et feminile Auenimento sono, nelli secreti commentarii della scrittura sacra Hebraica, come nel libro Zohar, nel Bahir, nelli Raboth, Midras, Ialcuth, Tanchama, Ilanoth et commentarii sopra le diece Sefiroth s'arritrovano, secondo li sensi insegnati da Moseh al senato delli sua 72 auditori delli quali sono stati per successioni longhe, li Profeti, Tutta la Feminita della scrittura doue si parla senza male, o per, ouer del sesso Feminile, tende à figurar il figurato di questo secondo et Veneto auentimento".* Postel's translation of *Bereshit Rabbah* (the first twenty sections) is Sloane 1409 f. 1–150. His translation of Menahem of Recanti (up to the Noah section) is Sloane 1411 f. 1–151v. Postel's access to these books was no doubt facilitated by the request of the Nuncio Della Casa that he act as censor of the Hebrew books produced by Bomberg (F. Secret, *Kabbalistes chrétiens* pg 174; also his "Postel censeur des livres hébreux à Venice" Bibliothèque d'Humanisme et Renaissance XXII (1960) pg 384–5). Postel was quite unlike Egidio da Viterbo and Masius in that he did not apparently approve of the Talmud. He opposed the publication of the Basle Talmud corrected by Marco Marini and P Cevallerius (F. Secret, *Zohar* pg 54–55) and apparently wrote against the Talmud with Alessandro da Foligno (see note above). Postel nevertheless believed that the Talmud had been preserved solely because of the chapter *"Cadoss Hacadassim, hoc est Sanctus Sanctorum"* wherein one might read the word *'Iehochannai'* (i.e. *Zuana* or *Joanna*). Kuntz, *Postel* pg 81–82 discusses how just as Sarah, Abraham's first wife, was the mother of the Jews, Mother Joanna has become like Keturah, a second wife, though now of a 'greater Abraham', *"qui est Aeternus Pater"* and so is Mother of the Gentiles.

[83] Important here is Irena Backus "Guillaume Postel, Théodore Bibliander et le 'Protévangile de Jacques' Introduction historique, édition et traduction française du Ms Londres British Library, Sloane 1411 260r–267v" Apocrypha VI (1995) pg 7–65. Sloane 1411 contains both Postel's Latin translation of 1551 and his autograph copy of the Greek text of 1553. Backus corrrectly identifies the Greek text as one previously

always prepared to reach beyond the Canon of Scripture and the *Protoevangelium* with its emphasis on the Virgin Mary (who naturally prefigured the New Eve, Mother Joanna) and her Immaculate Conception was obviously attractive. He came to consider it the fundamental text upon which the Canonical Gospels' account of Christ's Birth was based and also as the missing beginning of the Gospel of Venice's patron, the Evangelist Mark. But this was not just a matter of New Testament criticism. Postel integrated his reading of the work into his own personal mythology, finding it fitted into the pattern prophesied by the Blessed Amadeus.[84]

Francisco Giorgio

At this point one may speculate about the influence upon Postel of Francisco Giorgio (1460–1540), one of the *confrères* of San Francesco della Vigna who had been Mother Joanna's Confessor before Postel came along. Francesco Giorgio's own subsequent relationship of confessor to the visionary Chiara Bugni probably illustrates the context of female spirituality and its management in which we should place the

---

considered independent of Postel's *Vorlage*. She displays Postel's translation with the subsequent emendations made by Bibliander (though he had no Greek text!), who discarded Postel's glosses. The Protestant Bibliander was, of course, not in the slightest interested in Postel's cult of the Virgin, Venetian or otherwise, nor in questions of the feminine role in the Restoration of All Things. He did however share Postel's conviction that Hebrew was the *Ursprache* and also entertained ideas of Universal Concord brought about by the peaceful conversion of Jews and Moslems which lie behind his edition of the Koran in 1543. See: R. Pfister "Das Türkenbüchlein Theodor Biblianders" Theologische Zeitschrift (Basel) IX (1953) pg 438–454. For his comparative linguistics: G. J. Metcalf "Theodor Bibliander and the Languages of Japhet's Progeny" Historiographia Linguistica VII: 3 (1986) pg 323–333. For relations between the thought of Postel and that of Bibliander, Wolf Peter Klein, *Am Anfang war das Wort. Theorie und Wissenschaftsgeschichtliche Elemente frühneuzeitlichen Sprachbewusstseins* (Berlin 1992) pg 230–260. Bibliander's interest in the *Protevangelium* concerned its canonical status and the (consequential) credibility of the miracles in the text. The publication was nonetheless controversial. (ed. H. Aubert, H. Meylan, A. Dufour, *Correspondence de Th. de Bèze* I (Droz, Geneva 1960) pg 103: Beza to Bullinger 24 July 1553: "*Protevangelium illud a D. T. Bibliandro editum multos hic pios et doctos homines valde offendit, cuius rei poteris illum admonere*"). For the totality of Postel's relations with Oporinus and the Basle publishing world we have: A. Rotondò, *Studi e Ricerche di Storia ereticale italiana del Cinquecento* (Giappichelli, Turin 1974) pg 117–159 (The chapter 'Guillaume Postel e Basilea'); Peter G. Bietenholz, *Basle and France in the Sixteenth Century. The Basle Humanists and Printers in their contacts with Francophone Culture* (Droz, Geneva 1971) pg 137–144; F. Secret, *Bibliographie* Appendix pg 147–151.

[84] So Sloane 1411 f. 200.

beginnings of Postel's relationship with Mother Joanna.[85] Georgio was a Kabbalist. He wrote his *De harmonia Mundi* in 1525 and his *Problemata* in 1536. The latter quotes extensively from the *Zohar*. He also wrote the *Elegante poema*. A recent essay upon Giorgio with an up-to-date bibliography by Giulio Busi removes the need for a representation of that material here.[86] Giorgio is important for the aristocratic Franciscan piety and mystical speculation he exemplifies, and for his search for the Jewish roots of the Christian faith in Kabbalah. He was familiar with Pico's *Conclusiones cabalisticae*, and dependent upon Reuchlin, yet it was Busi's concern to show the extent of Giorgio's own Hebrew reading. Reflections upon Hebrew words and possible combinations of them and play with the letters of the alphabet are his familiar techniques. One cannot speak with certainty of Giorgio's relationship to Postel, though one may perhaps conjecture plausibly that Mother Joanna had absorbed a little of kabbalistic notions from her previous confessor. We do know however that Postel's pupil Guy Lefèvre de La Boderie who produced the Syriac New Testaments of Antwerp and Paris translated Giorgio's *De Harmonia Mundi* into French in 1578.

We may finally turn to a work of Postel written in Venice in 1549, *Dall' Apologia premessa all'Interpretazione del Bahir*.[87] Postel wrote of the

---

[85] Cesare Vasoli "Un 'precedente' della 'Virgine Veneziana': Francesco Giorgio Veneto e la clarissa Chiar Bugni" ed. Kuntz, *Postello, Venezia, e il suo Mondo* pg 203–225.

[86] Giulio Busi "Francesco Zorzi, a methodical dreamer" in ed. J. Dan, *The Christian Kabbalah Jewish Mystical Books and their Christian Interpreters* (Harvard College Library, Cambridge Mass. 1997) pg 97–126. In addition to which I have used C. Wirszubski "Franceso Giorgio's commentary on Giovanni Pico's kabbalistic theses" Journal of the Warburg and Courtauld Institutes XXXVII (1974) pg 145–156; C. Vasoli, *Profezia e Ragione* (Naples 1974) pg 129–403; also his "Da Marsilio Ficino a Francesco Giorgio Veneto" in his *Filosofia e Religione nella Cultura de Rinascimento* (Guida Editori, 1988) pg 233–256.(This is chapter seven of a book paginated only within individual chapters); F. A. Yates, *The Occult Philosophy in the Elizabethan Age* (Routledge, London 1979) pg 29–36. There is also J.-F. Maillard "Sous l'Invocation de Dante et de Pic de la Mirandole: les manuscrits inédits de Georges de Venise (Francesco Zorzi)" Bibliothèque d'Humanisme et Renaissance XXXVI (1974) pg 47–61. Also his critical edition *Francesco Giorgio Veneto, L'elegante poema & Commento sopra il Poema* (Arche, Milan 1991). Finally, there is now also C. Vasoli "Hermeticism, in Venice. From Francesco Giogio to Agostino Steucho" in eds. Carlos Gilly and Cis van Heertum, *Magic, Alchemy and Science 15th–18th Centuries: The Influence of Hermes Trismegistus* (Centro Di, 2002) pg 50–67. Giorgio was consulted by Richard Croke travelling in disguise as 'Giovanni di Fiandra' on the matter of Henry VIII's divorce. See Vasoli, *Profezia e Ragione* pg 181–212.

[87] The text is conveniently printed in A. Rotondò, *Studi e Ricerche di Storia ereticale italiana del Cinquecento* pg 473–490. He discusses the passage I cite on pg 141. I quote the passage extensively as its significance for the story of Syriac New Testaments has

purpose of this and his other work: *"Haec omnia ad hoc sunt comparata, ut orbis Christianus sibi ipsi consentiat antequam de pace cum caeteris agat"*. This was to be preparatory to his great evangelical campaign *"ut possint externae nationes lumine evangelico perfundi"*. But, said Postel, in the realisation of this plan he had met nothing but obstacles. The Pope, the Emperor and *"omnes Italiae potentiae"* had remained indifferent to his plans to carry Christianity to the East not with armies but with editions of the New Testament in Syriac and Arabic. Syriac New Testaments in Hebrew characters, we note particularly, he intends for Jewish missionary work, though Christians will benefit from access to the mysterious etymologies of New Testament names which will be apparent when transcribed from Syriac script into Hebrew script. The help Postel had received from Bomberg in this respect was providential but the Papal Legate was working against him. It remained therefore for Postel to turn to France and Germany invoking their common origins: *"Una Germania et Gallia tanquam filius et pater, tanquam Gomeritarum et Askenaziorum genus superest"*.

This passage is of considerable interest as it shows Postel's state of mind as he departed on his Second Voyage. In particular it indicates from where at that time he thought he would, and would not, receive support for his mission. It shows us again his willingness to look around for different political patrons for the final *dénouement*. It was always

---

not previously been realised: *"Haec omnia ad hoc sunt comparata ut orbis Christianus sibi ipsi consentiat antequam de pace cum caeteris agat. Ut autem possint exterenae nationes lumine evangelico perfundi sategimus suis facultatibus iuvante Daniele Bombergo, ut in lingua Syriaca, qua usus est Christus apud populum et in qua hactenus sacra remanserunt apud Syrianos Christianos ad fines usque mediae [...], in ea inquam transcripta in characteres Hebraeos et sanctos [?] et sibi uni restituta lingua patefaciat Iudaeis evangelium, et nobis nominum Novi Testamenti dubiam interpretation, ex qua lux rerum pendet, certiam faciat eaque quae alioqui salvari non possent vera ostendat. Pridem autem insudo si quomodo etiam Arabice prodeat Evangelium ut toti Asiae, Africae et tertiae Europae parti lumen ab Ismaelitis Alcorano utentibus perditum reddat. In hoc unus inter Christianos, quod sciam, sum a Christo lingua mediocriter donatus. Iam vero omnes Italiae potentias et cum ills, per suos legatos, Caesarem et pontificem summum rogavi ut vellent in opus tam pium impendere, et non reperii hactenus qui vel trecentos aureos in rem tanti momenti proferret, praeter unam ducem [...] foeminam suo loco dignissimam, quae tamen a tanto opere impeditur ob praepeditam a legato pontificio senatus licentiam. Non vult enim permittere ut edatu, licet qui alioqui fide habear dignissimus in examinandis doctrinis Hebraicis et Chaldaicis ut possint excudi, [...] vetustissimorum exemplarium et a me una cum Syris, Chaldaice et Arabice doctis excussorum ac cum Latinis Graecisque emendatissimis collatorum faciam. Sic est illis pro ratione voluntas. Nec intrant nec intrare sinunt. Sed iudicet Christus calcati sanguinis [causa]. Ea una de [re] valefeci regiae liberalitati et spei alioqui ab huius mundi amatoribus non post habendae. Ea de re sacerdotia, tanquam quae facta sunt, reliqui, ut in hanc unam curam edendi Arabice evangelii, quod totus doctorum Oriens et Auster magis quam ipsum Alcoranum desiderat, totus ferrer. Una Germania et Gallia tanquam filius et pater, tanquam Gomeritarum et Askenaziorum genus superest."*

possible to fit them in somewhere into his comprehensive but flexible scheme of History and Eschatology. We shall not detail his pursuit of Cosimo I, but shall see how he was to turn to the Emperor Ferdinand I at the time of the *editio princeps*. After that it was Philip II to whom he turned to sponsor what became the Antwerp Polyglot, though Guy Lefèvre de la Boderie thereafter returned in the preface to his 1584 Paris edition to court the French Henri III.

Most significant for us is what Postel says about his work on a Syriac New Testament. We recall his meeting with Bomberg in 1537 and his collaboration with Teseo that resulted in the *Linguarum duodecim characteribus* of 1538. In that work Postel tells us Bomberg had shown him in 1537 Syriac Gospels that he was considering printing in Hebrew characters. Postel's letter to Masius of January 1547, some ten years later, that we have mentioned above also spoke of Postel's preparations of a text for printing. The text we are currently considering (*Dall'Apologia premessa all' Interpretazione del Bahir* 1549) confirms Postel's early engagement upon the Syriac New Testament with Bomberg back before the Second Voyage in 1549. These previously overlooked pieces of evidence support each other and show us just how early Postel was working on the Syriac New Testament. There is a real but previously unnoticed continuity here between the time of Teseo and the *editio princeps* and it lies with Postel. Postel with his singular projects was behind every Catholic printing of the Syriac New Testament, for after the failed ambitions of Teseo Ambrogio, it was Postel who first took the matter in hand.

Postel's Second Voyage

Postel remained under suspicion in Venice and so did Mother Joanna. We know that she informed the Venetian Senate that Abbot Joachim's mysterious carvings over the North Door of the Church of St. Mark represented her with her son Postel.[88] The atmosphere at the Ospedale appears not to have been entirely supportive of the considerable claims now being made by its founder and her confessor. Nevertheless when Postel left Venice to go to Jerusalem in 1549 he was forever caught in his mythology of Mother Joanna, who was transformed into a symbol of mediation, an embodiment of the Maternal Principle, and who had

---

[88] F. Secret, *Kabbalistes chrétiens* pg 174–175; ed. Secret, *Le Thresor* pg 248 where an illustration of the carvings is found on pg 49.

promised to give him the Garment of the Immortal Corporeal Substance of Corporeal Immortality.[89]

The Embassy of d'Aramon

Seven scholarly travellers, Pierre Belon, Jean Chesneau, Jacques Gassot, Pierre Gilles, Nicolas de Nicolay, Andre Thevet and Postel took part at various times and to different degrees in the Embassy of Gabriel d'Aramon (1546–1553) in the pursuit once more of a *rapprochement* with the Sultan as a geo-strategic counter to Charles V. The Emperor had made peace with the Sultan in 1547, but d'Aramon's Embassy was not just a political response to this. It appears to have been a diplomatic success in re-establishing the prestige of France in Turkish eyes particularly as the Franco-Imperial Treaty of Crépy-en-Laonnois of September 1544 had been considered a betrayal by the Turks. It was an opportunity for magnificence which François I was not going to pass up, and in the Ambassador's entourage were gentlemen and scholars eager to travel and likely to appeal to the Sultan's taste for letters and science. From 2 May 1548 to 28 January 1550 the Frenchmen under the protection of the Sultan travelled through Anatolia, Armenia, Persia, Syria, Palestine and Egypt. The length of the trip, the richness of the itinerary and official protection made this trip a uniquely privileged opportunity for the western scholars to study the East.

Frédéric Tinguely has recently offered an inter-textual examination of the *corpus* of these several scholars to establish the modalities of their 'Oriental discourse'.[90] The 'New World' of the Near East was not, of course, quite as new as the New World in the Americas, though it did however excite considerable interest in the sixteenth century.[91] It was known from scripture and hagiography, from Classical authors like Strabo, Pomponius Mela, Pliny and Solinus, and from the Crusades and pilgrimage. These were rich traditions and authoritative ones that established the fundamental approach of these scholar-travellers to what they saw. The tendency to reproduce this accumulated wisdom

---

[89] Kuntz, *Postel* pg 92.

[90] Frédéric Tinguely, *L'Écriture du Levant à la Renaissance Enquête sur les Voyageurs français dans l'Empire de Soliman le Magnifique* (Droz, Geneva 2000).

[91] Geoffroy Atkinson, *Les Nouveaux Horizons de la Renaissance français* (Droz, Paris 1935) pg 10 remarked that between 1480 and 1609 there were about twice as many books printed in France on Turkish subjects than upon the two Americas.

is scarcely avoided in their works. Tradition, authorities, standardised *topoi* and mere psittacism make up an inherited lumber that is never quite escaped. Where there is autopsy and things are seen for the first time it is through (though perhaps in spite of) the lens of the past, and there is a great reluctance to chose between what had been learned previously in the library and what was seen on the ground, even when they seemed irreconcilable. One may sympathise: Autopsy without Tradition lacks focus, goal and system and tends to a mere collection of similarities. Fundamentally these scholars' apprehension of the Near East was conditioned by the past in spite of the present relevance of the Turkish armies and their future threat.

Postel is the only scholar amongst those who produced the Syriac New Testaments to have travelled to the East. He moreover stands out in certain respects from his scholarly travelling companions whom Tinguely has described. We have seen the importance for Postel of the deep metaphor of life as Journey. *Peregrinatio* and *Restitutio* appear similarly as structuring notions and entail that the past condition the future. Yet Postel is critical of the commonplace value judgments of his companions as he seeks to further his own ambitious project for religious and political unity under the King of France (though, as we have said, we shall see such a Universal Tutelage subsequently offered to the Emperor Ferdinand and Philip II). Postel's vision—that of a common denominator implicit in the revealed religions, and visibly close to Catholic doctrines—had been seen before in Nicolas of Cusa. Nevertheless it is striking to meet this aspiration in an age of consolidating national and confessional identities. In contrast with the surrounding religious and political competition, the utopian and ahistoric features of Postel's vision stand out in relief. It is, I would argue, almost paradoxically true that Postel's diplomatic experiences merely consolidated his idealistic programme. We must not overstate the case though: despite Postel's real and unusual disposition to make concessions, his Universal Concord is not, we have indicated above, all that we mean by religious tolerance.

Like the Jesuits to whom he was so close, Postel's approach to the Near Eastern 'Other' was by way of as deep as possible an understanding of their customs and beliefs. The paradox of the missionary stance that demands the sharpest possible apprehension of the singularities of the target people as a means to their neutralisation and effacement by conversion does not escape Tinguely. Nonetheless Postel's ethnographic writing—for example the *Republique de Turcs* (1560) and *Histories orientales* (1575)—distinguish themselves within sixteenth-century 'Orientalist' production by their richness and the desire for impartiality in description. At the very beginning of *Republique de Turcs*, Postel seeks to distinguish himself from those of his precursors writing about Ottoman society who spoke only of its demerits: *"des choses odieuses, et des vices, sans aucune memoire de vertu, ce qui nul people universellement, tant barbare soit il, ne peut ester".* Indeed, the universal theological *'disputatio'* that was to inaugurate Universal Concord would require a certain climate of confidence in the Moslem interlocutors. Postel sets out the grounds for such confidence in the Turkish sense of Justice.[92]

Part of Postel's missionary virtuosity is his perception of similarities between Faiths and he twice drew up lists of axioms and dogmas common to both Christianity and Islam. Postel discovered in the Koranic account of the Annunciation the apocryphal legend of the Child Jesus making clay birds fly. For him the thaumaturgy was material sufficient to support the claim of the Divinity of Christ. Indeed, Postel was encouraged to find that Moslems accepted many things that Jews did not. But in spite of these deep structures (and here we are reminded that we are dealing with the sixteenth century), the superstructure built upon them is a *"foy et loy bastarde"* based upon a book cobbled up by a madman who was also a liar. More positively, it does really seem a step forward in imagining other peoples' religions when Postel distinguished between dogma and piety and he also found ritual similarities in festivals and fasts. We have here a strategy of both exclusion and assimilation. There are below the surface real deep analogies between Christianity

---

[92] For Postel's work in the context of other French travellers and giving a detailed comparison of their response to many aspects of Moslem cult: Yvelise Bernard, *L'Orient du XVI siècle à travers les récits des Voyages français: Regards portés sur la Société musulmane* (Editions L'Harmattan, Paris 1988) especially pg 320–371. Also for a wider survey of French voyages: Jacques Paviot "D'un énnemi l'autre: des Mamelouts aux Ottomans. Voyages de renseignement à Levant XIIIᵉ–XVIIᵉ siècle" in *D'un Orient l'autre* (Editions de CNRS, Paris 1991) Vol. 1 pg 317–328. Also M.-C. Gonez-Gerand "L'Empire turc au XVᵉ siècle ou L'Empire des apparences: regards des voyageurs français et flamands" in ed. Ilana Zinguer, *Miroirs de l'Altérité. Colloque internationale del'Institute d'Histoire et de Civilisation françaises de l'Université de Haïfa 1987* (Slatkine, Geneva 1991) pg 73–82. Essential is F. Lestringant "Guillaume Postel et l'obsession turque" in ed. Kuntz, *Postello Venezia e il suo Mondo* pg 265–297. Also his "Alterities critiques: du bon usage du Turc à la Renaissance" in *D'un Orient l'autre* pg 86–105. F. Secret in "Postel et l'origine des Turcs" in ed. Kuntz, *Postello, Venezia e il suo Mondo* pg 301–306 uses manuscript evidence to present an exposition of Postel's *tour de force* linking the Turks, their Scythian origin, the Ten Lost Tribes of Israel and the Samaritans. Postel describes how the Ten Tribes became Moslems (pg 303).

and Islam, yet the very existence of Islam testifies to a fracture of the spiritual world that the missionary seeks to heal.[93] The fresh gaze of autopsy provides for a less prejudiced apprehension of the 'Other', but only to return them to their place prescribed in the oldest of texts.

Finally it is no surprise to find that Postel uniquely distinguishes himself amongst his fellow travellers by his interest in languages: he does actually learn to speak and read them. Yet here again there is a paradox. Behind the new language he has learned Postel with his uncommon philological acuity will perceive the pattern of the old and ultimately through the instrumentality of his emithology the words of the 'Other', even in their own language, will testify to the loss of the original linguistic harmony when all were once one.

Postel's Itinerary

Postel himself tells us that he left Venice for Jerusalem to look for New Testament books in Arabic to publish not only for Moslems but also for Arabic-speaking Christians in the East and to perfect his Hebrew.[94] He gave an account of his journey in a letter of 10 June 1550 to Masius from Constantinople that I follow here.[95]

We also have a letter written by Postel to Cardinal Grevelle 21 August 1549. In the letter Postel develops his theme of Restitution by stressing the role of language in the restoration of human reason and in allowing men to participate in the *Instauration* in which there will be but One Shepherd and One Sheepfold. Grevelle was to use his influence with Charles V for the training of learned men in knowledge of Hebrew, Chaldean, Syriac and Arabic in order to enable true religion to become available to all.[96] The importance of knowledge of languages as a means of accomplishing world unity is of course a theme of Postel: it is found once more for example in *De phoenicum literis, seu de prisco latinae*

---

[93] Jacques Bailbe "Postel conteur dans 'La Republique des Turcs'" in ed. Kuntz, *Postello, Venezia e il suo Mondo* pg 45–63 draws attention to Postel's discursive rhetoric in these works that he wrote in French: *"a celle fin de donner facultaté à tous les Gaulois generalement de se préparer pour reconcilier le people d'Ismael avec celuy d'Isaac"*.

[94] Ms Sloane 1413 f. 87.

[95] The letter is found in Chaufpié III pg 216–217.

[96] We shall see shortly that Widmanstetter had proposed a similar scheme to Clement VII († 25 September 1534), though the Pontiff's death prevented anything being done.

et graecae linguae charactere ejiusque antiquissima origine et usu (Paris 1552).[97] Postel ends with a request for money. He can get his hands on Syriac and Arabic books if he can pay for them.[98]

On the day he wrote this letter, 21 August 1549, he also wrote to Masius from Mount Zion.[99] Postel was visiting the Holy Places, and pressing on with his languages in the interests of Universal Concord. He had found Syriac New Testament manuscripts that completed the (Syriac) canon, which seems to confirm that whatever he previously had (that is, whatever he was working on with Bomberg in 1547) was only the Four Gospels.[100] Lack of funds had also prevented him acquiring books in Cairo and Damascus.[101]

The Death of Mother Joanna

Sadly for Postel, he returned to Venice to discover that Mother Joanna had died—probably 29 August 1550. He did not therefore return to the Ospedale but went back to Paris. Postel's reputation was apparently more acceptable there than it had been seven years earlier, perhaps because of the Eastern trip. Henri II (1547–1559) was now King. Postel enjoyed good relations with him and offered him some heavy flattery,

---

[97] M. L. Kuntz "A New Link in the Correspondence of Guillaume Postel" Bibliothèque d'Humanisme et Renaissance XLI (1979) pg 575–581 where Kuntz has some interesting remarks. Postel did not know Grevelle when he wrote. Grevelle however was later to be the friend and protector of Plantin. As Bishop of Malines and an advisor to Philip II he was to be involved in the Antwerp Polyglot. Kuntz suggests this correspondence may be further evidence, not merely of the complexities of relationships in sixteenth-century Europe, but also of links between churchmen within the Hierarchy and those we see as less obviously conformist.

[98] *Loc. cit.* pg 581.

[99] Chaufpié III pg 216. The letter is an important account of Postel's journey through Syria to Constantinople and on to Jerusalem, where he located his supposedly Samaritan coins in the ruins (*De Phoenicum Literis* Paris 1552 Bii). Postel discusses the Samaritans, the Druze, and the Karaites (Bomberg had produced the first printed Karaite book when he brought out his liturgy of 1528–1529). He discusses the Maronites. He also mentions Arabic books he has come by including: *"varia Evangelii & Novi Testamenti Exemplaria"*. Kuntz, *Postel* pg 97 n. 313 discusses Postel's Arabic manuscripts that entered the Jesuit Collège de Clermont.

[100] *"Post illa nostra IV Evangelia repperi iam reliquum Novi Testamenti…"*. Sebastian Brock raises privately the possibility that Postel had seen a Harklean manuscript with Apocalypse and Minor Catholic Epistles.

[101] See here again, M. Kuntz "A New Link in the correspondence of Guillaume Postel" Bibliothèque d'Humanisme et Renaissance XLI (1979) pg 578–581 for a letter written to Cardinal Grevelle on the same day as the letter to Masius offering Syriac and Arabic books if funds could be made available.

possibly with the intention of being reinstated as Royal Lector. Postel dedicated *Les Très Merveilleuses* to the King's sister, Margaret.[102] This was an exceptionally productive period for Postel, and between 1551 and 1552 he produced some fifteen books. Of particular interest to us, in 1552 he published in Paris his *Abrahami Patriarchae Liber Iezirah* from a text he had brought back from the East.[103]

6 January 1552 marks a decisive date in Postel's own spiritual journey: it is the date of his *'Immutation'*. This experience, whatever it was, hereafter defined Postel's own identity and he returns to it repeatedly in his later work. Mother Joanna returned to Postel in a spiritual experience that left his body burning as the Spirit of the Mother of

---

[102] Printed January 1553 by J. Gueullart and later that year again by Jehan Ruelle. The latter is the basis of the Slatkine reprint but is not in Secret, *Bibliographie*. For Postel at this time, Kuntz, *Postel* pg 100.

[103] There is now a facsimile reprint with an excellent introduction to which we may make reference here: Wolf Peter Klein, *Sefer Jezirah ubersetzt und kommentiert von Guillaume Postel* (Frommann-Holzboog, Stuttgart—Bad Cannstatt 1994). This includes the text of *Liber Rationis Rationum* that was printed in the 1552 edition, and reference should be had to Klein for an excellent exposition of Postel's theology and reading of this text with its arcane teaching on Creation, the Godhead, and Letter Mysticism. Postel's text comprises a dedication, his translation (pg 71–79, Klein's pagination), the Commentary (pg 80–140) and a Postface (pg 141). The first chapter of the commentary sets out fundamental assumptions and informs the reader of the intellectual antecedents of the book. These include the *prisci theologi* and not surprisingly the tradition from Abraham to the 72 Auditors of Moses. More unusual are the Indian Brahmins who are named *'(A) Bramini'* from *'Abraham'* (pg 80–81): *"Illi autem sunt Abrahami filii ex Ketura qui quum Isaaco non voluissent obtemperare, sunt ab ipso in orientis partes destinati, ubi ad hanc usque diem sub Brahminorum nomine servant sacrae doctrinae praecepta, in quibus eadem praescripta habent quae & Moses coelitus accepit"* (Bv. r). The same tradition is followed down to the Celtic Druids and the Pythagoreans, indicating once again the essential philosophic and theological identity of traditional material throughout the East and West. Chapter Two gives an exposition of Postel's understanding of Creation and the Trinity. The three aspects of the Triune Creator God, *Potentia, Sapientia, and Benevolentia* and associated with distinct types of creation—*Creatio, Formatio and Factio*. The Second Person *'Sapientia'* receives a particular emphasis. Chapter Three offers an ideal rather than corporeal understanding of Creation with particular reference to the combination of letters and numbers and the force of analogy. Chapter Four relates the themes explored to Postel's own prophetic consciousness and his mission of Restoration. Postel refers (Fiii) to the book as a *"versio ex lingua sancta Adami Mosis & Christi…"* thereby again illustrating the 'inclusive' nature of his category of Aramaic. The first Hebrew printing was ten years later in 1562 in Mantua. There is of course a huge bibliography of the Hebrew text and its role in Jewish mysticism which I must omit here. For the text I have used: Ithamar Gruenwald "A preliminary Critical edition of Sefer Yezira" Israel Oriental Studies I (1971) pg 132–177; Nicolas Sed "Le Sefer Yesira. L'Edition critique, Le Texte primitif La Grammaire et La Métaphysique" Revue des Etudes juives CXXXIII (1973) pg 513–528; Eveline Goodman-Tau & Christoph Schilte, *Das Buch Jezira* ספר יעירה (with Afterwords by Moshe Idel & W. Schmidt-Biggermann) (Aka-demie Verlag, Berlin 1993).

the World purified his old body and infused her own spiritual presence into his very bones. He became a New Man, his reason restored to that of Adam before the Fall. He felt himself covered with a spiritual body as with a white garment. Another similar garment was given to him, this time red, that repaired his *animus* and his *anima*—the male and female aspects of his reason. Postel's personal Restoration drove him to a frenzy of evangelism: he had obtained the Power of Christ within himself; he had the Soul of the Mother of the World dwelling in him by a metempsychosis that was, in fact, the indwelling of the *Shechinah* or the Feminine Spirit of Christ; he was the Firstborn of the Fourth Age. He was the Son born of the New Adam (Christ) and the New Eve (Mother Joanna), begotten by Mother Joanna's descent into him on the momentous day in 1552 when he was clothed in his new garments.[104]

Postel threw himself into preaching, though it does appear that Henri II soon put a stop to his public evangelisation. Postel left Paris for Basle where he arrived in June 1553. He was there for only two months but enjoyed the hospitality of Oporinus and the friendship of Bibliander. It may have been the climate of affairs in Geneva where Servetus was to be burned on 27 October that made Postel eager to leave: certainly he was no happier with Calvinistic tyranny than he was with Papal pretensions. Nevertheless, he established some important friendships: Sebastian Castellio, David Joris, and his future correspondents Theodore Zwinger[105] and Caspar Schwenchfeld.[106] By August 1553 Postel was back in Venice and turned his attention to preaching about his Immutation, and the Syriac Gospels. It was at this point that he first came in touch with Moses of Mardin, a meeting of the

---

[104] Kuntz, *Postel* pg 101ff. See pg 106–107 on the language and notion of Postel's *immutatio*, and also on the importance of the *Zohar* for his personal unravelling of the great mysteries he felt had been entrusted to him.

[105] Postel allowed Zwinger, who was Oporinus's nephew, to keep his translation of the Zohar that had not been published at Oporinus's death (Secret, *Zohar* pg 52–53). In a letter to Zwinger 23 May 1579 he refers to a copy of his Latin translation of the Zohar that he kept with him and the safekeeping of which he asked for in his last will (BN. Fonds franc. 2115 f. 118). The letter (Sloane 1413 f. 108) is interesting in its terminology. Postel speaks of: *"Zohar apud me est ex Suriana lingua Latinus"*. Here Postel is clearly refering to Zoharic Aramaic as *'Syriac'*. The Kabbalistic significance of the *'Suriana lingua'* is thus made evident.

[106] Kuntz, *Postel* pg 108–110 for this paragraph, with discussion of Postel's defence of Servetus and similarities to Castellio's tolerance. For Basle, see the bibliography mentioned above.

utmost significance for the development of the printing of the Syriac New Testament.

Back in Venice: Moses of Mardin

Postel returned from the East in 1550 or 1551, as we have seen, with ancient and accurate Arabic New Testament manuscripts. He left some of his manuscripts in the Bomberg house in Venice and departed for Paris and afterwards Basle. By August 1553 he was back in Venice and at work on the Syriac New Testament. He discussed with the late Bomberg's editor, Iohannes Renialnus, the question of the Syriac version which he had brought back with Bomberg's money. It was at this time that Postel met Moses of Mardin and (as he presented matters to the Emperor Ferdinand after Widmanstetter's death) was able to collate Moses's ancient copies with his own text. The two texts in which Postel discusses this indicate that Postel had brought a Syriac manuscript back with him.[107]

In 1987 Marion Leathers Kuntz suggested that Postel's manuscript that he brought back to Venice was to be identified with ms 3. 1. 300. Aug. fol. in the Herzog August Bibliothek Wolfenbüttel, a seventh century codex that was once in the possession of the Jesuit polymath Athanasius Kircher.[108] Kircher's dedicatory letter to the Duke claims that the text agrees with that in the Antwerp Polyglot: *"Porro textus Evangelicus ubique conformis est ei, qui in Bibliis Regiis Plantinianus Syriace impressis exhibetur"*. Kuntz suggested that in fact it *was* the manuscript used by Postel, Masius and Guy Lefèvre de la Boderie to establish that text. Kuntz presents two arguments: first the claimed identity of

---

[107] Sloane 1413 f. 87 and *Cosmographicae disciplinae compendium* (Basle 1561, also dedicated to the Emperor Ferdinand) a3 both quoted above. Kuntz, *Postel* pg 98–99 suggests after the letter to Masius 10 June 1550 that Postel brought back a thirteenth-century Hebrew bible. F. Secret, *Guillaume Postel (1510–1581) et son Interprétation du Candélabre de Moyse* (B. De Graaf, Niewkoop 1966) pg 26 n. 36 emends this out of existence to find reference to a Sephirotic Tree.

[108] M. L. Kuntz "Guillaume Postel and the Syriac Gospels of Athanasius Kircher" Renaissance Quarterly XL (1987) pg 465–484. Of particular interest is an extract from a letter from Kircher to Duke August (Rome, 19 March 1666) attached to the manuscript Kircher tells us that Syriac can be quickly learned by those knowing Hebrew: *"maxime si in Lingua Chaldaea, quam Chargumicam vocant, excitatus fuerit: cum haec ab illa non nisi charactere differat"*. The reader is supplied with a practice alphabet: *"in Charaxtere Estrangehelico, qui a Syriaco vix differt"* to help. (The manuscript in question is no. 5 in J. Assfalg's *Syr. HSS* (1963) and dated to 633 AD).

the texts; and secondly that the editor of the manuscript was Abbot S. Saba *'whose dwelling is in Bethali near Damascus'* and Postel's manuscript also came from Damascus. Kuntz correctly follows Levi della Vida who clearly distinguishes the text of Postel in question here from the other text he brought back, Vat. sir. 16, that Tremellius used in the Palatine Library in Heidelberg.[109] Kuntz concedes moreover that Guy Lefèvre de la Boderie described Postel's manuscript as *"iam ab anno 1500 regni Alexandri, a quo Syri annos suos numerant…"*.[110] Furthermore Postel's codex was a complete New Testament and Kircher's merely the Gospels.

I find it very difficult to consider that Kuntz has really made a case.[111] Whilst we shall see that our scholars are quite capable of collating manuscripts, not a great deal can hang upon Postel's claim that the texts were identical, and not merely because Kuntz herself has not chosen to check the collation. Postel in a text quoted by Kuntz made exactly the same claim for the relationship between his manuscript and an'older one' brought by Moses of Mardin with which he collated his manuscript.[112] We do not know Postel's standards of carefulness in these matters, though we shall have reason to question this claim below, but we do know—as they, of course, did not—that the Peshitta tradition is very well preserved and that manuscripts do not show great variations.[113] Frankly one would be surprised and very interested to discover that they found great discrepancy. It is possible to believe they found none, but one would wish to know the editor's notions of precision and the extent of the text collated. There is very little in Kuntz's claim that both came from Damascus, where there were, of course, Syriac scholars and scribes to produce them. Her arguments here may I think be safely forgotten, but her case is most decisively refuted by the fact that we do know the manuscript used for the Syriac New Testament

---

[109] *Ricerche* pg 303–306: Tremellius's ms: "si trovava nella Biblioteca Palatina di Heidelberg fin dal 1555, quando il Fabricio non aveva che quattro anni…". Hence: "…il codice usato dal Fabricio dev'essere stato diverso dal Vat. Sir. 16" (pg 305).

[110] *Ricerche* pg 305.

[111] Bobzin, *Der Koran* pg 315 n. 229 is not convinced.

[112] Bibliothèque nationale, fonds lat. 3402 f. 91.

[113] On pg 482 Kuntz writes: "Even if the Wolfenbüttel codex is not the Postel codex, the two codices must have had a common ancestor, since, according to Lachmann's rule, their readings are "in agreement everywhere". Given that Kuntz is arguing for the identity of *a codex*, the discovery of a common ancestor for the *texts* seems quite bizarrely beside the point. In view of the homogenous nature of the Peshitta tradition, the application of Lachmann's rule seems unlikely to be the most useful way of describing the relationship between manuscripts or texts.

in the Antwerp Polyglot, Louvain ms Cod 1198. Unfortunately Kuntz appears not to be aware of the existence of this manuscript.

Kuntz does however draw our attention to a contemporary work of Postel, a broadsheet probably printed in Basle 1552–1553, *Omnium Linguarum quibus ad hanc usque diem mundus est usus, origo....*[114] In it Postel presents a Syriac alphabet and writes of Syriac. He states his conviction that the original version of Matthew's Gospel and the Epistle to the Hebrews, if they exist anywhere, will be in Syriac. He then tells us that the mysteries which are hidden in the etymologies of New Testament names can only be found through the Syriac version, in the very vernacular of Jesus. Once again we see that one of the interests of the Syriac version lies in the particular semitic form of its proper names which are suitable for mystical manipulations *and may only be known in Syriac.*[115] He then refers to his transcription of the four Gospels in Syriac into Hebrew characters for Bomberg. This is his transcription of Bomberg's Syriac Gospels that Postel first saw in 1537 and worked on thereafter and mentioned in 1547.[116] The recovery of this early work of Postel is of the first significance for the history of the study of the Syriac New Testament.

Postel's Orientalism

Postel constructed his prophetic mission around the search for the universal religious and political Harmony which he believed was to characterise the Last Days. We may recognise within the quite extraordinary richness of his imagination features of the eschatological

---

[114] Kuntz, *op. cit.* pg 472. A facsimile of *Omnium Linguarum* is found in Maurice de Gandillac "Le Thème de la concorde universelle" in *Guillaume Postel Actes du Colloque* pg 192–197.

[115] *"Si usquam gentium genuinum Matthaei exemplar extat, cum epistola ad Hebraeos, in hac lingua est. Ideo ex his literis curavi Danieli Bombergo, ut vetustissimum exemplar quatuor Euangeliorum in characterem priscum Hebraeorum transcriberetur ut liceat excudere, et fideliter etymologiam venari nominum novi Testamenti, in quibus sunt adita singularia mysteria, quae non nisi ab hac lingua, in qua cum plebe locutus est Iesus, peti possunt".*

[116] This passage is very similar to the passage in *Linguarum duodecim* of 1537 (Biiii) that Kuntz wrongly understood to refer to a Hebrew Matthew and identified with a manuscript in the Marciana, and further evidence that that passage should be understood of a Syriac Gospel text. The several infelicities of Kuntz's translation of the 1552–1553 text on pg 472 of her article conceal the fact that Syriac is transcribed into Hebrew, even though there one assumes she considers Postel to believe that the original Matthew was in Syriac.

expectations of those other scholars we have already discussed. Yet
Postel's mission gives a distinct scope and coherence to his Orientalism. Postel travelled to the East to learn the languages and customs of
those he sought to evangelise, to obtain their books and to penetrate
their faith, to find through fieldwork the common substrate of universal
truth—substantially Catholic dogma—upon which the eschatological
consensus would be built. I have suggested above that the diplomatic
context of Postel's voyages that has not previously been emphasised
gave an air of immediate credibility in Postel's own eyes at least to
the projected Universal Sovereignty of the King of France. Postel
had assisted at the beginnings of an understanding between the Most
Christian King and the Sultan. His books sought to set out the basis
on which Concord would be reached with real contemporary Turks
and Moslems and with the estranged Christians of the East.[117] There
is a clear sense in which Postel *actively worked for* the establishment of
universal political and religious Harmony through the proposed conversion of the East and political lobbying of sovereigns. Postel wanted a
real political initiative in the East and he worked to persuade princes
of its necessity. The references to Eastern sway in his dedications to
princes are not empty flattery, they are an increasingly desperate call to
action as the End approaches. His projects to produce Oriental bibles,
including the Syriac New Testaments, cannot be properly understood
outside this perspective. These projects we have seen can be traced
back before 1547.

A complementary strand to Postel's Orientalism is his recovery of
the ancient East, the "Aramaean" legacy, as the historic substrate of
Western European history, culture and religion.[118] Postel's linguistic
studies, his emithological philology, his studies of the *prisci theologi* and
the Aramaic arcana, display the same fundamental truths. *And on the
basis of this too*, princes are urged to alliances in anticipation of the final
Harmony. The East is thus both out there and to be recovered back
here: it is the universal substrate of Catholic Truth that will unite all
mankind.

---

[117] Note the remarks about Postel in Victor Sègesvary, *L'Islam et la Réforme Etude sur
l'attitude des Réformateurs zurichois envers l'Islam 1510–1550* (Editions L'Age d'Homme,
Montreux 1977) pg 244 & 257.

[118] Considerations of space have led to the omission of a detailed consideration
of Postel's work on the Aramaean origins of Etruria and particularly Florence that
develops the Annian tradition and also reflects his attempts to interest Cosimo I in
preparing the way for Universal Restoration.

Postel discovered the Truth of the arcane Kabbalah through the guidance of Mother Joanna. Together they seemed to have reimagined some fairly fundamental features of Catholic Orthodoxy as progressively they came to terms with their own eschatological roles. Postel's self-awareness would reach its final messianic status only after the death of Mother Joanna. Thereafter his mission would be hampered, but not stopped, by his confinement as a madman.

CHAPTER FIVE

THE SCHOLARS OF THE *EDITIO PRINCEPS*:
WIDMANSTETTER

Before we turn to consider the 1555 *editio princeps* of the printed Syriac New Testament, we need finally to consider the Western scholar who is generally known as its editor. Johann Albrecht Widmanstetter was born in 1506 in Nellingen near Ulm which belonged at that time to the Grafschaft Helfenstein.[1] He tells us that his first teacher was the local priest Gregor Bauler.[2] As a young man he knew of Reuchlin.[3] He learned Jurisprudence from the celebrated humanist Bonifacius Amerbach in Basle and Hebrew from Jakob Jonas[4] and also from Sebastian Münster.[5]

---

[1] Fundamental is Max Müller, *Johann Albrecht v. Widmanstetter 1506–1557 Sein Leben und Wirken* (Handels-Druckerei, Bamberg 1907). This supersedes all previous accounts especially S v. Riezler's article "Johann Albrecht Widmanstetter" in *Allgem. Deutsch. Biographie* Vol. XLII pg 357–361, which needs to be corrected throughout from Müller. Müller pg v–viii conveniently lists all the major primary sources. Widmanstetter refers in the *Conclusio* at the end of the *Prima Elementa* to an autobiography he had written, evidently in more than one book: "... *(quemadmodum primo de Vita mea libro narratum est)...*", but this has been lost. In the mid-eighteenth century A. F. von Oefele took considerable interest in the Widmanstetter books and papers in the Staatsbibliothek in Munich. Apart from manuscripts which still today carry his name in their shelf-mark, he himself made a collection of *Widmanstadiana* which he gleaned from notices in others' books, marginal comments in Widmanstetter's own books etc. This is preserved today as Oefleana 245. It has 133 folios and comprises 190 notices, and is an interesting collection for anyone interested in the reception of Widmanstetter's work. H. Bobzin, *Der Koran* pg 277–363 summarises previous biographical work and adds a valuable assessment of Widmanstetter as an Arabist. For the correct form of Widmanstetter's name, Müller, *Johann Albrecht v. Widmanstetter* pg 9f and for his *alias* 'Lucretius' pg 19.

[2] In the *Conclusio ad Widmanstadios suos* at the end of the *Prima... Elementa* G iii. On Bauler: Müller, *op. cit.* pg 12 n. 8.

[3] At *Dedicatio* f. 6v (I shall use *Dedicatio* consistently below to mean the *Dedicatio* to the *editio princeps*) Widmanstetter speaks of his "*superioris aetatis curriculum in quod Capnionis virtus, doctrina, atque industria incidit*", but Müller, *Johann Albrecht v. Widmanstetter* (pg 12–13) points out "*damit will er wohl nur sagen, dass seine früheste Jugendzeit noch mit Wirken des berühmten Gelehrten zusammenfällt*".

[4] *Dedicatio* f. 6v. See L. Geiger, *Das Studium der hebräischen Sprache in Deutschland vom Ende des XV. bis zur Mitte des XVI. Jahrhunderts* (H. Skutsch, Breslau 1870) pg 105f. Also on Jonas, Joseph Ritter von Aschbach, *Die Wiener Universität und ihre Gelehrten 1520 bis 1565* (Hölder, Vienna 1888) pg 57, 180. He became Councillor and *Hofvizekanzler* in Vienna.

[5] Professor of Hebrew at Heidelberg 1524–1527, Münster had previously taught

Widmanstetter in Italy

In 1527 Widmanstetter went to Italy[6] and fought the French for the Emperor.[7] He lectured in Turin in spite of his youth and there he perfected his Greek. He attended the coronation of Charles V by Clement VIII in Bologna 24 February 1530. On his way to Bologna in 1529 Widmanstetter stayed in Reggio near Modena in the House of the Augustinians. It was there that he had his fateful meeting with Teseo Ambrosio to which we have already alluded and to which we shall return again. He made his first acquaintance with Arabic there in the house of the Bishop of Burgos, Innicus López de Mendoza y Zúniga, where he met Diego López Zúniga (the Stunica who had edited the Greek Text of the Complutensian Polyglot and the opponent of Erasmus) who taught him.[8] Later in the year he was in Spanish Naples where, although only about twenty-five years old, he was appointed to the Chair of Greek as the successor of Constantine Lascaris.[9] Particularly outstanding were his lectures on the Iliad. But Widmanstetter was also able to further his semitic studies and frequented the house of Don Samuel Abarbanel, the head of the small Jewish colony that settled in Naples after the expulsion of the Jews from Spain and Portugal. It was about this time that he met Pico della Mirandola's teacher of Kabbalah, Rabbi Dattilus, and it was here that Widmanstetter's kabbalistic education began.[10]

---

in the city 1521–1523 for the Franciscans. We have discussed him in a previous chapter.

[6] BSB ms Cod. lat. M. 27 081 f. 12 (Widmanstetter's *Verteidigungsschrift* explaining his feud with Gumppenberg that we shall mention below): *"Fateor me... anno huius saeculis XXVII in Italiam profectum esse"*.

[7] In Widmanstetter's patent of nobility in 1548 we learn that he fought on foot against the Florentines under Garzia Manriquez.

[8] See Bobzin, *Der Koran* pg 302–303.

[9] Carlo de Frede, *I Lettori di Umanità nello Studio di Napoli durante il Renascimento (L'Arte Tipographia, Naples 1968)* Ch. 3 pg 81–140 'Constantine Lascaris e l'insegnamento del Greco' especially pg 102–108. For his lectures on the Iliad: Müller *Johann Albrecht v. Widmanstetter* pg 17, 74ff.

[10] Widmanstetter refers to Dattilus several times: The first reference is the *Theologia... Mahometis* Annotation XXXIII that we shall discuss below. The second is *Dedicatio* f. 6v: *"Mar. Datyli Hebraei quem ego arcanos de divino Libros Taurini in summa eius senectute subtilissime interpretantem"*, and the third Cod lat M 27 081 f. 12: *"Eodem tempore audivi R. Dattilum magnis illi Pici Mirandoli praeceptorem"*. See also: J. Perles, *Beiträge zur Geschichte der hebräischen und aramäischen Studien*, pg 185–188, 192 and Bobzin, *Der Koran* pg 298. We shall have cause to return to this meeting later. Widmanstetter's note on his copy of the Spanish Josef Jachia's Commentary on the Five Megillot (Munich 2° A heb

Another important friendship from his period was that made with Hieronymus Seripandus then preaching in Naples, but later to be the man who succeeded Egidio da Viterbo as the General of the Augustinians and also Bishop of Salerno.[11]

In the summer of 1531 Widmanstetter had hoped to visit Africa to hear *"Leo Eliberitanus"* from Granada. This was, of course, none other than the Leo Africanus who had taught Egidio da Viterbo.[12] The trip did not come off: but the Augustinian connection held: Egidio on the recommendation of Seripando invited Widmanstetter to Rome to further his Arabic and kabbalistic studies. Widmanstetter accepted in Hebrew.[13]

Egidio was to die 13 November 1532 and the two men cannot have known each other for long, but Widmanstetter was later to call Egidio his teacher.[14] Seripando, however, was able to give Widmanstetter several manuscripts from Egidio's library; these are the codices marked *'ex Bibliotheca Aegidiana'* that passed after Widmanstetter's death into the Staatsbibliothek in Munich.[15]

Widmanstetter was also able to take advantage of the late Cardinal's scholarly contacts. He studied with Zematus (Michael b. Shabtai Zemat) one of the Cardinal's Jewish collaborators and also learned Talmud with Benjamin Arignanus. He was introduced to Pope Paul III's personal physician, Jacob b. Samuel Mantino with whom he was able to

---

97. Bologna 1538) tells us that he used to go to hear him lecture in Abarbanel's house. (Widmanstetter's note transposes the name of father and son.) The text of the note is given in J. Perles, *Beiträge* pg 180f. On Abrabanel see: Ben Zion Netanyahu, *Don Isaac Abravanel—Statesman and Philosopher* (Jewish Publication Society of America, Philadelphia 1953).

[11] The standard work is Hubert Jedin, *Girolamo Seripando. Sein Leben und Denken im Geisteskampf des 16 Jhds* (Würzburg 1937).

[12] On Leo see above and Bobzin, *Der Koran* pg 85f. Widmanstetter refers to this in *Dedicatio* 12v. In the same place Widmanstetter speaks of Egidio's almost unique Arabic: *"ut Aegidius...Arabicarum literarum dignitatem inter Christianos prope solus tueretur".*

[13] The Letter is published in J. Perles, *Beiträge* pg 177, but he is wrong to suggest it was never sent. See: Müller, *Johann Albrecht v. Widmanstetter* pg 21 n. 56.

[14] Oefeleana 245. 51 records the name written inside a now lost book: *"J. Egi. Viterb"* to which Widmanstetter had added: *"Jo Alb. Widmanstadius emit a Romae a Zena librario in Campo Florae a 1543 mense Feb. Fuit Cardinalis Aegidii Viterbiensis praeceptoris mei"*, Müller, *Johann Albrecht v. Widmanstetter* pg 22.

[15] *Dedicatio* f.a*** 3v–a***4v is the whole relevant passage. There Widmanstetter speaks of Egidio's death cutting short his patronage: *"quod [sc. me adiuuare] etsi praestare, ob vitae brevitate nequiverit".* For the importance of Seripando's friendship: H. Striedl, "Der Humanist Johann Albrecht Widmanstetter (1506–1557) als klassischer Philologe" in *Festgabe der Bayer. Staatsbibliothek für E. Gratzl* (Otto Harrassowitz, Wesbaden 1953) pg 96–120 and pg 101–102.

further his interest in Kabbalah and also to R. Ahron de Scazzocchio from whose library Widmanstetter was able to obtain several volumes in 1544.[16] Already in 1532 we know he was pursuing his kabbalistic studies with Baruch Benedictus (of Beneventum) who through the patronage of Egidio had spread the knowledge of the Zohar among Christians.

The Syriac Gospels in Siena

In 1533 it appears Widmanstetter was in Siena for, four years after his meeting with Teseo, he discovered in the Library of the learned Sienese Lactantius Ptolemaeus[17] the four Gospels in Syriac and several small works of Ephrem and of the *'Syrian Jacob'*.[18] The identity and precise provenance of this remarkable find remains quite unknown, which is a great pity for Widmanstetter's transcripts of these Gospels were to be at hand in Vienna when the *editio princeps* was prepared.[19] In addition this is, I believe, the first Western appearance of a Syriac

---

[16] Important for Widmanstetter's Jewish contacts and teachers are H. Striedl, "Der Humanist Johann Albrecht Widmanstetter (1506–1557) als klassischer Philologe" pg 101–102; H Striedl "Geschichte der Hebraica-Sammlung der Bayerischen Staatsbibliothek" in (ed.) H. Franke, *Orientalisches aus Münchener Bibliotheken und Sammlungen* (Franz Steiner, Wiesbaden 1957) pg 1–37, pg 5–6 and Bobzin, *Der Koran* pg 298–299. On Zematus: J. Perles, *Beiträge* 186 n. 1. On Ariganus *ibid.* pg 190. For the books from R. Ahron (BSB Hebrew codices 77 and 265) see H. Striedl "Geschichte der Hebraica-Sammlung der Bayerischen Staatsbibliothek" pg 4. On Baruch: *Dedicatio "Eodem tempore* [1532] *audivi Baruch beneventanum optimum Cabalistam, qui primus libros Zoharis per aegidium Viterbiensem Cardinalem in Christianos vulgavit"*. We have mentioned Baruch in our discussion of Egidio above.

[17] Widmanstter writes of the family in the *Dedicatio*: *"In Italia inventa est Ptolemaeorum Senensium nobilis familia, in qua Lactantius pater, Johannes Lälius et Aemylius Filli sacrarum linguarum omnium perita insignes existere"*. Widmanstetter makes a further reference to Lactantius in the Annotations of his *Mahometis... Theologi* where he recalls explaining to him a kabbalistic interpretation of the 14 × 3 ancestors of Christ in Matthew.

[18] *Dedicatio* f. 11v. Müller pg 24 notes that Widmanstetter added in his own copy of the *editio princeps* the marginal note *"Symeon episcopus Libani praeceptor meus"* at 11v of the *Dedicatio*. In the *Conclusio* to the *Prima Elementa* Widmanstetter refers to finding a miscatalogued (*librariorum errore*) Ptolemy in the same Library.

[19] We do, however, know that the books were of Maronite origin. J. Perles, *Beiträge* pg 183 discovered a reference to these texts in a work of the baptised Jew Geraldus Veltvyk from Ravenstein, שבילי תהו *Itinera Deserti* printed in 1539 in Venice by Bomberg with a view to converting Jews. Veltvyk identifies them as being of Maronite origin (14 iii):

ואני מעאהי תרנום טוב וישר אשר בידי שר לקטנטוש תלמדי אי״נ
מהלל בדורו בכל חכמות ולשנוה ויתנן קרטיו נדמנ איש חכם ויודעו הוא
תרנום קהל הקדש בהר לבנון אשר לא יהרם את המקרא כי ההורסים.

(Lucretius is an *alias* of Widmanstetter. "The Holy Congregation on Mount Lebanon" identifies the Maronites.)

text of St. Ephrem (or at least one bearing his name, for there is a lot attributed to Ephrem that is not his) who was not otherwise known until considerably later. Though scarcely competent in the language, Widmanstetter copied the texts and retained them (together with Teseo's Gospels) until he could be instructed in Syriac by the Maronite Bishop Symeon, who was apparently resident in Rome. Symeon remains a certain source of Syriac instruction, and a possible source of Syriac manuscripts, though I am not aware of any manuscript that may be certainly traced to him.

Diplomat and Scholar

In 1533 Widmanstetter began his diplomatic career when he became Secretary to Pope Clement VII.[20] In the second part of the year he presented a commissioned lecture on the Copernican System in the Vatican Gardens. Clement VII (the same Pope who had commissioned Egidio's *Scechina*) rewarded him with a Greek manuscript, an expensive parchment codex with gold initial letters and miniatures containing various philosophical texts.[21]

Widmanstetter sought to interest Clement VII in plans to introduce both Syriac and Arabic into Christian Schools.[22] In this he received the support of Nicolaus Schonberg, and we might expect Clement VII to have been sympathetic. But after the death of the Pontiff on 25 September 1534, Widmanstetter's plans came to naught.[23] This

---

[20] Müller, *Johann Albrecht v. Widmanstetter* pg 25.

[21] Munich BSB Ms. Cod. graec. 151. Widmanstetter wrote on the back of the end paper: "*Clemens VII pont. max. hunc Codicem mihi d.dd. anno MDXXXIII Romae, postquam ei presentibus Joh. Salviuto cardd. Joh. Petro Episcopo Viterbien. et Mathaeo Curtio Medico physico in hortis Vaticanis Copernicianam de motu terrae sententiam explicavi.*" Bobzin, *Der Koran* pg 290 suggests Widmanstetter had learned his Copernicanism from Alexander Scultetus in Rome, following Ernst Zinner, *Die Geschichte der Sternkunde* (Berlin 1931) pg 461 and the same author's *Entstehung und Ausbreitung der copernicanischen Lehre* (Erlangen 1943) pg 228, which I do not know. Copernicanism was perfectly compatible with the mystical convictions of many of our authors. Guy Lefèvre de la Boderie put into French a Latin poem of the celebrated doctor and astrologer Cornelius Gemma (1535–1577) from the Netherlands as '*Sur la Sphere des Revolutions de Nicolas Copernic*'. This can be found in ed. Rosanna Gorris, *Guy Lefèvre de la Boderie Diverses Meslanges Poetiques* (Droz, Geneva 1993) pg 287 with notes.

[22] Dedicatio 12b. One wonders who, other than himself, he thought the teachers would be.

[23] We have seen above however that they were aired again in a letter from Postel to Cardinal Grevelle 21 August 1549.

period in Rome was, however, in other respects more productive for
Widmanstetter and brought him into contact with several important
scholars. Outstanding amongst these were Agostino Steucho,[24] Girolamo
Aleandro[25] and Marcello Cervini, later to be Pope Marcellus II but at
the time the intimate adviser of Paul III. We have already considered
Cervini's contacts with Postel and his support of Moses of Mardin in
the late 1550s.

Biblical Scholarship

One of Widmanstetter's teachers, Nicolaus von Schonberg O.P., Archbishop of Capua, who became a Cardinal in 1535 was much concerned
with the exposition of New Testament books and several of his Latin
Paraphrases that were once in Widmanstetter's library are to be found
in the Staatsbibliothek in Munich.[26] In support of Nicolaus's work,
Widmanstetter prepared new translations in Latin from the Greek text
of the New Testament. Amongst the Oefleana of the Staatsbibliothek
we have Widmanstetter's version of the Letter to the Ephesians and the
First Epistle of John (Oef. 248) and John's Gospel (Oef. 247).[27] These
display philological learning, and both a knowledge Hebrew and an
ability to draw linguistic parallels from Classical Greek usages. Widmanstetter shows a preference for older manuscripts over the Vulgate
and Erasmus's 1527 Edition. In contrast to Erasmus, Widmanstetter
reserves the same Latin translation for each occurrence of a Greek
expression, and expresses sharply his dissent from Erasmus's practice
of varying translations for the same Greek. Widmanstetter's version

---

[24] (1497–1548), later Bishop and Vatican Librarian.

[25] Jérome Aléandre (1480–1542) who taught Greek in both Paris and Orléans.

[26] In Munich SB Cod. lat. M 27 081 f. 12v Widmanstetter speaks of his teachers von
Schonberg and Cardinal Thomas de Vio (Cajetanus). See Müller, *op. cit.* pg 23–24 for
Widmanstetter's relations with Cajetan before his death in 1534. On Von Schonberg
almost the only thing is: A. Walz "Zur Lebensgeschichte des Kardinals Nikolaus von
Schonberg" in *Mélanges Mandonnet Études d'histoire littéraire et doctrinale du Moyen Age* (J. Vrin,
Paris 1930) Vol. II pg 371–387.

[27] I have consulted the originals (Oefeleana 255–259) in Munich but an accurate
account with an excellent tabulation of variants from the Vulgate is found in H. Striedl
"Der Humanist Johann Albrecht Widmanstetter (1506–1557) als klassischer Philologe"
pg 114–118. Also his "Die Bücherei des Orientalisten Johann Albrecht Widmanstetter"
in ed. H. J. Kisslig and A. Schmaus, *Serta Monacensia Franz Babinger zum 15. Januar 1951
als Festgruss dargebracht* (E. J. Brill, Leiden 1952) pg 200–244, pg 217ff; 224ff.

often differs noticeably from the Vulgate. He also clearly considered the *Pericope Adulteriae* as a later addition.[28]

Considerable interest here attaches to the philological and textual scholarship of the future editor of the *editio princeps*, particularly in respect to the authority of the Vulgate.[29] Nicolaus, who in places incorporated Widmanstetter's translations into his Paraphrases, sent his Paraphrase of 1 John to Archbishop Federico Fregoso for criticism.[30] His reply is preserved.[31] In response Nicolaus removed several striking departures from the Vulgate. In the Forward to a second draft he remarked that he had no wish to impugn the authority of the Vulgate, but merely to illuminate its difficulties.[32]

Nicolaus appeared both eager to avoid the scandal of a too widely divergent version, and yet also to distinguish between the public liturgical and doctrinal place of the Vulgate and his attempts as a private scholar to clarify its difficulties and corruptions by reference to the Greek. It may be that Widmanstetter would have given a similar reply. Certainly such a view had been held by Cardinal Ximenes in producing his great Complutensian Polyglot.

Return to Germany

After Nicolaus's death Widmanstetter became in 1538 *'Geheimrat der Deutschen am apostolischen Stuhe in Rom'*.[33] The following year he returned

---

[28] BSM. Oef. 247 f. 15v.

[29] Widmanstetter's annotations to his work (to be found described in H. Striedl, "Der Humanist Johann Albrecht Widmanstetter (1506–1557) als klassischer Philologe") are all philological and concerned to produce an accurate translation of the Greek informed by a knowledge of both Greek and Hebrew usage. He does not concern himself with theological or doctrinal matters.

[30] Archbishop of Salerno (1507), Administrator of Gubbio (1539), died in Gubbio 1541. See: H. Striedl "Die Bücherei des Orientalisten Johann Albrecht Widmanstetter" pg 225.

[31] H. Striedl "Die Bücherei des Orientalisten Johann Albrecht Widmanstetter" pg 224; Oef. 261.5.

[32] *"Nec propterea existimare quenquam velim, ipsam vulgatam minoris apud me auctoritatis fuisse. Absit hoc, cum ea per omnes ecclesias atque inter divinas res celebretur; verum quod graecam noramque sequor, est quidem studiose magis, quam curiose lucubrationis meae, si forte assequi possem, ut vulgate saepe loca difficiliora, et interdum mendosa ac corrupta, non minus huius nove verbis, paraphrasi insertis, quam aliorum aut meis declarem"* H. Striedl "Die Bücherei des Orientalisten Johann Albrecht Widmanstetter" pg 118, especially note 132 for full details. The first version is Clm 298; the second version is Oef. 258.

[33] See Müller, *Johann Albrecht v. Widmanstetter* pg 29 for the description. The same year Widmanstetter recorded in his own copy of Conrad Gesner's *Bibliotheca Universalis*

from his twelve year sojourn in Italy to Germany where he entered
the service of Prince Ludwig X of Bayern-Landshut.[34] He returned
to Rome several times thereafter, particularly during the period of his
longstanding and bitter quarrel with his erstwhile friend Ambrosius von
Gumppenberg.[35] Widmanstetter was in Rome on Easter Day 1541 when
the Pope himself made Widmanstetter a Deacon so that he could sing
the Gospel in Greek: a faculty of contracting a subsequent marriage
was given at the same time.[36]

In 1541 Widmanstetter accompanied the Prince to the Reichstag in
Regensburg, though nothing is known of his political activities. The
Regensburg Reichstag brought together perhaps the most conciliatory
of the Catholics eager to reconcile the Protestants and possessed of
a theology close enough to that of the moderate Protestants to make
agreement seem possible: Julius Pflug (1499–1564), Georg Witzel, a
lapsed Protestant (1501–1573), Johann Gropper of Cologne (1503–1559)
and Albert Pighius from the Netherlands (1491–1542). The Pope was
represented by Gasparo Contarini. The Protestants were represented
by Melanchthon, Bucer and Johannes Pistorius. Over April and May
agreement was reached even on Justification. Both the Curia and
Luther rejected this compromise and discredit subsequently fell upon
the conciliatory group and their aspirations for a negotiated resolution
to the developing schism. Within this generous and cooperative context, however, scholarly exchanges—both Classical and Oriental—were
possible. The diary that the Theologian and reformer Martin Frecht
(1494–1556) from Ulm kept during the Reichstag gives us a glimpse

---

(Tiguri 1545: BSM Cod. Oef. 31 n. 84) a reference to Elias Levita, noting a meeting
in Venice in 1538. J. Perles, *Beiträge* pg 158 published with translation a letter of 1543
about Hebrew books from Levita to Widmanstetter found in Oef. 249 no 6. A French
translation appears in Weil, *Elias Lévita* pg 244ff.

[34] In Rome in 1539 the Jewish scholar Jacob Mantino published his *Averrois Paraph-
rasis super libros de republica Platonis nunc primum latinitate donata Jacob Mantino Medico hebraeo
interprete*. Widmanstetter had given some support to this scholar. J. Perles, *Beiträge* pg 161
n. 1 gives evidence of criticism of Widmanstetter for his association with Jews. J. Perles
pg 164–5 also prints the text of a letter of *apologia* from Widmanstetter to a Polish Jew
Menachem Pfefferkorn with whom he had apparently had some differences. In this same
year the Armenian Archbishop Martyrus Murad wrote a small book in Armenian for
Widmanstetter. This is MSB Cod. arm Mon 5 in 12° in which Widmanstetter wrote:
*"Rev. Martyrus Murad archiepiscopus Armeniae h.e. locorum Carahamidh (*margin: *Cara civitas)
et Mardin scribebat Joanni Alberto Widmanstadio cog'to Lucretio Romae XXVI Oct. MDXXXIX"*.
(i.e. Amid (Diyarbakir) = Kara Amid or 'Black Amid').

[35] For the Quarrel: Müller, *Johann Albrecht v. Widmanstetter* pg 33–46.

[36] Müller, *Johann Albrecht v. Widmanstetter* pg 47.

of Widmanstetter's scholarly activities. He was displaying Greek and Hebrew manuscripts and imprints, coins and seals, and a Latin translation of the Koran.[37]

The reference to a translation of the Koran here is intriguing. It was not published and has been lost. Bobzin notes that Bucer who was playing a prominent part in the Reichstag had also at this time seen this version.[38] We shall have cause to return to Widmanstetter and his koranic studies shortly, as the work he did publish on Islam contains some very important observations about Kabbalah. It was also at Regensburg that Widmanstetter met Masius before another short visit to Italy.[39]

15 January 1542 Widmanstetter married Anna von Leonsberg, the natural daughter of Prince Ludwig, who brought with her a dowry of 6000 florins. Anna's mother was later married to Jakob Jonas, Widmanstetter's Hebrew teacher at Tübingen. After a short trip to Rome, Widmanstetter returned to Landshut where at the beginning of the next year 1543 he completed the dedicatory epistles to his first printed book the *Mahometis... Theologia*.

Oriental Studies

Widmanstetter was at this time much involved in his Oriental Studies as a letter to Elias Levita indicates. In October 1543 he was in Rome

---

[37] *"Cum Musculo* (Wolfgang Musculus) *adii D. Naellingensem, qui codices Graecos ac hebraeos venerandae antiquitatis scriptos et nonnullos excusos ostendit, cum numismatiibus et imaginibus aereis adfabre fusis Bacchii et Fauni, Arabice scriptum Alcoranum et ab eo Latine redditum vidi, de abusibus Ecclesiae et curiae Romanae aliqua, item vitem Constantini a quodam Episcopo et Palatino Bibliothecaro adfabre descriptam et Carlo Caesari dedicatam ostendit."* The life of Constantine here mentioned had been commissioned by Steucho: Müller, *Johann Albrecht v. Widmanstetter* pg 48.

[38] Bobzin, *Der Koran* pg 291, 189 n. 209 quotes a letter from Bucer to Bonifacius Amerbach 27 November 1541: *"At quae in Ratisponae in Alcorano ab Alberto Widmanstadio ex Arabica verso in Latinum legi, tam foeda, tam monstrosa, tam horrende fanatica ac dura sunt..."*. A later letter of 14 September 1542 has: *"ut domino Alberto Widenstadio viro πολυγλωττάτωι, in comitiis Ratisponensibus auctor fuerim, ut Alcoranum, quod ipse ex Arabico vertit, purum ederet, quo nostri homines certo muniri contra Turcarum impietatem possent..."*. Widmanstetter himself refers to his translation in his note to his printer placed at the beginning of the *Mahometis... Theologia* aiii v: *"Alcoranus vero ex libris quatuor bene longis, quos Latinos a me factos edendos tibi propediem dabo,..."*

[39] As is apparent from Masius's Hebrew letter to Widmanstetter of 1541; see J. Perles, *Beiträge* pg 206 and our discussion in a previous chapter.

again to deal with the litigious quarrel with Gumppenberg.[40] On the trip
he was able to meet Levita twice and answer his letter in person.[41]

Widmanstetter's dispute with Gumppenberg seems at this point to
have affected his scholarly contacts. Such was Widmanstetter's status
with the Curia as an Orientalist that Cervini, who was at this time the
Papal Legate at Trent, sent the deacon Petrus Ghalinus from Damascus[42] to Germany to assist Widmanstetter with his Arabic.[43] Sadly their
collaboration was brought to naught, or so Widmanstetter alleges, by
the machinations of his enemies, though the episode remains another
clear example of Cervini's patronage of the Catholic Orientalists. It
was an attempt to arrange one of those one-to-one scholarly contacts
between Eastern churchmen and European scholars that we have
already seen were so important for the growth of Western knowledge
of Eastern languages: the later meeting of Widmanstetter and Moses
was, of course, to be another similar collaboration.[44]

Ennoblement and Father Joseph

Herzog Ludwig died 22 April 1545 and Widmanstetter passed into
the service of his brother Archbishop Ernst von Salzburg. The next
year 1546, upon the outbreak of the Schmalkaldic War, Widmanstetter

---

[40] Müller, *Johann Albrecht v. Widmanstetter*, pg 53f. On 5 December he bought from
the bookseller Zena in the Campo di Fiori a Latin ms of Nicolas of Lyra's *De dif-
ferentia translationis nostrae ab Hebraica* that is now BSB Cod. lat 307. On the first sheet
under Widmanstetter's name is: *"Emptus Romae in Campo Floro a Zena V Xbris MDXLIII"*.
Widmanstetter's continuing interest in Biblical versions is evident. On 18 February
1544 he purchased a Hebrew manuscript from Abraham Scacciotius (BSB Heb Cod
Mon 315). See: J. Perles, *Beiträge* pg 156–157.

[41] Müller, *Johann Albrecht v. Widmanstetter* pg 53 n. 122 and J. Perles, *Beiträge* pg 158,
160.

[42] Little is known about Petrus Ghalinus other than that he stole an Arabic manuscript
(*Kitab ar-Rawabi' li-Aflatun*) from the Vatican Library (Bobzin, *Der Koran* pg 293). It is
now in Munich (Cod arab 649) and bears a note in Widmanstetter's hand expressing
his intention of returning it (Levi della Vida, *Ricerche* pg 79f): *"Bibliotheca Vaticanae
quem Ghalinus Damascenus commodato acceptum in Germaniam clam secum attulit, Joannes Alb.
Widmestatius restitui curavit"*. Oefele 245 pg 23 remarks pointedly: *"Widmanstetter restituit,
quomodo ergo hic est?"* Letters extant from this year suggest that Widmanstetter was not
good at returning books borrowed from monastic libraries either: Müller, *Johann Albrecht
v. Widmanstetter* pg 36 and texts at pg 90–91.

[43] *Dedicatio* a ˣˣˣˣ 1. See Müller, *Johann Albrecht v. Widmanstetter* pg 54f.

[44] Cod. Oef. 245 pg 23 mentions a Hebrew letter from Widmanstetter to Paulus
Fagius of 15 September 1544 about 'Petrus Damascenus' but the letter is no longer
extant.

led a Spanish Regiment through Salzburg's territory to the Bavarian border.[45]

In the same year he became Chancellor and Archivist of the Bishop of Augsburg, Cardinal Otto Truchsess von Waldburg (1514–1573). Widmanstetter served the Cardinal for six years. He was at the 1547 Augsburg Reichstag on the Cardinal's behalf.[46] In the next year,[47] 2 March 1548 the Emperor found time to ennoble Widmanstetter and his brothers Sebastian, and Jacob Philipp.[48] Widmanstetter was subsequently in Rome for the Papal Election of Julius III 7 February 1550; though he was back in Augsburg for the summer as on 23 July 1550 he met, evidently more happily than in the case of Petrus Ghalinus, a monk, Father Joseph, from Mount Lebanon. In return for a letter

---

[45] Müller, *Johann Albrecht v. Widmanstetter* pg 55–57.

[46] When the Reichstag met 1 September 1547 the Pope had moved the Council of Trent to Bologna in the Papal States and was conducting its business without regard to Charles V's diplomatic needs. Charles had then to try to impose an 'Interim' Settlement (essentially a moderate Catholic Reformation after the fashion of Pflug and Gropper) upon the Reich. The failure of Protestant and Catholic princes to agree upon any draft of this threatened to turn Charles V's victory over the Protestant League into 'administrative and political chaos'. Charles published the Imperial Clarification of Religion ("The Interim") 15 May 1548 as a creed for Protestants and also as a separate reform Edict for Catholics. E. Cameron, *The European Reformation* (OUP, Oxford 1991) pg 347.

[47] Correspondence with Sebastian Münster 30 June 1548 to whom Widmanstetter sent *"Salisburgensium episcoporum historiam ex vetustissimis exemplaribus descriptam"* appears in Münster's *Cosmographia*. See Müller, *Johann Albrecht v. Widmanstetter* pg 53.

[48] Widmanstetter was given the freedom of the City of Rome in 1551. This honour coming after his ennoblement indicates the esteem in which he was held as a diplomat and scholar. Considerable interest attaches to the ennobled Widmanstetter's arms. The curious appearance of an elephant is explained by the fact that his family had the name *Helphensteiner*. The lower legend (Psalm 122.7: "May peace be within thy walls and prosperity within thy palaces") is given in Hebrew, Syriac and Latin. The upper legend has I Samuel 16.12 in Hebrew thus: וישלח ויביאה והוא אדמוני איק. *"(Jesse) sent (David) and brought him in. Now he was ruddy (admoni)...".* Why this verse? Probably because the word אדמוני ('admoni') is an anagram of וידמאן ('Widman'). The three letters that follow, איק ('IQ), seem to be the initials of 'Albertus Iohannes Iuris Consultus', though this should have two yods and a caph not a qof. But as it is, the numerical value of איק is exactly that of both אדמוני (admoni) and וידמאן (Widman) that is to say 111. Below this appears "VIDManstaDIorVM/Insignia". The two groups of the same letters VIDM and DIVM have a numerical value of 1506, probably the year of Widmanstetter's birth. On this see I. Loeb "Les Armes de Widmanstadt" Revue des Études juives I (1875) pg 298–301 with more observations, and Müller, *Johann Albrecht v. Widmanstetter* pg 7 with additional evidence of Widmanstetter's taste for these 'kabbalistic' games. Other similar *notarika* may be found in H. Striedl "Die Bücherei des Orientalisten Johann Albrecht Widmanstadt" pg 243. Documents relating to the ennoblement are in Müller, *Johann Albrecht v. Widmanstetter* pg 92–97.

of introduction to the Bishop and the inevitable financial subvention
Widmanstetter received a Syriac missal.[49]

---

[49] The manuscript is BSB Cod. syr. Mon 5 of 139 folios in quarto written in a large
Jacobite (Maronite) script and dated f. 111v to the Greek year 1859 which is 1547/8
A.D. The manuscript is described in the *Verzeichnis der Orientalischen Handschriften der
K. Hof- und Stadtsbibliothek in München* 1875 (Reprinted Otto Harrassovitz, Wiesbaden
1970) pg 114. On f. 1r: *"Est Johannis Alberti Widmanstadii. dono dedit frater Joseph ex Mon-
asterio S. Antonii in monte Libano die XXIII Julii MDL. Augustae, quem ego vicissim et litteris
Rev et III Cardinalis Augustiani nomime scriptis et viatico juvi dedique ipsi dono fl. vii"*. The first
folios 1v–2r have been labelled by Widmanstetter: '*Symbolum Apostolicum Nicenum*'. The
Creed states that Christ rose on the third day 'as he wished' (so the Syriac) to which
Widmanstetter has added: *"Nōn Jacobitas, Cophitas, Abasinos et Armenios Symbolum Apos-
tolicum profiteri circa articulum resurrectionis haec verba: et surrexit tertia die sicut voluit"*. At the
Procession of the Spirit from the Son, Widmanstetter noted: *"Non profitentur spiritum
S. procedere a Patro, Graeci, Jacobitae, Cophtitae, Abasini, Armeni et Nestoriani"*. The missal
proper with its liturgical material and anaphoras comprises f. 2–139. The composers
are given as (f. 48r) St. Xystus, Bishop of Rome; St. John The Evangelist (f 66v); Peter
Chief of the Apostles (f. 79r); The Twelve Apostles (f. 88v); Matthew the Shepherd
(f. 96r); Dionysus Bishop of Amid with the nickname Barsalibi, Expositor of the Holy
Scripture (f. 103r); and Peter the Apostle (f. 112r). The manuscript is of interest as a
probable indication of Widmanstetter's reading ability in Syriac at this time, though
admittedly the annotation of the Creed may have been done later, and we know that
this material could be difficult for the early scholars: translating the Anaphora of St.
Basil caused problems for Masius that he was able to overcome only by repeated reference to Moses of Mardin. However, far greater interest for us may lie in a fragment in
another hand gummed into the end of the manuscript (*"Am Schlusse der Handschrift steht
von anderer Hand auf einem eingeklebten Zettel" op. cit.* pg 114). This declares: *"Hoc Sanctorum
Johannis Evangelistae etc … Missale una cum Calendario Sirijs usitato concinnavit, collegit ac ad finem
deduxit Moses Antiochenus Sacerdos regnante Rom. etc Rege Ferdinando A. Chr. MDLV Mense vero
decembri"*. The importance of this is not only in the statement that Moses of Mardin
completed the Missal given to Widmanstetter by Father Joseph, but more especially
in his production of a *Calendari[um] Sirijs usitat[um]* in 1555. It has not previously been
noticed that this is in all probability a reference to Moses's work in preparation for the
list of Festivals for the Liturgical Year placed at the end of the *editio princeps*. The missal
at f. 111v carries the date 1547/8. It would be interesting to examine the original again
to see if f. 112r and following had been added in another (Moses's?) hand. The date of
1547/8 may suggest that Father Joseph had copied the Missal for his own use before
coming west. It is not clear in what sense a Missal ending at f. 112r would have been
'incomplete'. Perhaps the meaning is merely that Moses brought to a conclusion what
had inevitably become a larger collection. Moses did not in all probability describe
himself as '*Antiochenus Sacerdos*' though Widmanstetter uses this adjective of the Patriarch in the *Dedicatio*. The date of December would indicate that the whole work was
finished after the appearance of the *editio princeps* between February and September.
In this respect one may notice the manuscript of Moses that persuaded Nestle that
the type of the *editio princeps* was based on Moses's hand (E. Nestle "Zur Geschichte
der syrischen Typen" Zeitschrift der Deutschen Morgenländischen Gesellschaft LXXV
(1903) pg 16–17). This was Cod. or 278 that he saw in the Staatsbibliothek in Hamburg.
The manuscript has: *"Hunc librum rituum ecclesiastorum, qui Thesaurus inscribitur … Domini
Ferdinandi … iussu ex antiquissimo codice descripsit Moyses Meridinaeus Syrus presbyter catholicus,
Viennae Austriacae, mense Januario, Anno MDLVI"*. The can be little doubt of the importance placed upon this liturgical material by Widmanstetter.

If the Syrian Symeon who taught Widmanstetter to read the treasures he had received from Teseo, and his transcripts from Siena, was the Maronite Bishop in Rome greeted by Sulaqa in 1553, he may have been instrumental in sending Joseph to Widmanstetter, though we have no evidence of this. But clearly it was nothing unusual when, three years later, Moses sought out Widmanstetter 'in Suavia' though, as we shall see, Widmanstetter had already had to flee from there.

It was at this time that Widmanstetter sought to devote himself entirely to his studies and requested of the Bishop leave to withdraw to his estates: to remain *"in praediis meis ad amoenissimam Danubii ripam sitis".*[50] However in early 1552 the troops of the anti-Imperial coalition around Moritz von Sachsen entered Swabia[51] and Widmanstetter, his expectant wife and their family had to flee their plundered home.[52] During the subsequent negotiations at Passau 2 June 1552[53] King Ferdinand I took Widmanstetter whom he met there into his service and in 1553 named him Chancellor of Eastern Austria.[54]

Final Years

Two major projects filled the last years of Widmanstetter's life. By decree 17 January 1554 Ferdinand I appointed Widmanstetter Superintendent of the University in order to promote its reform.[55] The second project

---

[50] *Dedicatio* f. 13v: Widmanstetter on 9 June 1555 writes: *"Annis abhinc quatuor..."*

[51] The Princes' War (Fürstenkrieg) set the Protestant Elector, Moritz of Sachsen, Wilhem of Hesse, and Albrecht Alcibiades of Brandenburg-Kulmbach against the Hapsburgs. In March 1552 Moritz had driven Charles V from Innsbruck into Carinthia but then became bogged down in long discussions with King Ferdinand at Passau (which was where Ferdinand met Widmanstetter). The Peace Treaty 10 August 1552 postponed the religious issue to the next Reichstag. This was that of 1555 that was, as it turned out, to be left by Charles entirely to Ferdinand. At its end (25 September 1555) it left Princes free to choose either the Augsburg Confession or Catholicism for themselves and their subjects. See: E. Cameron, *The European Reformation* (OUP, Oxford 1991) pg 348.

[52] *Dedicatio* f. 14v.

[53] Also in 1552 we know that Widmanstetter published a small booklet, 62 pages in 16°, of prayers and devotions for a Knight, Müller, *Johann Albrecht v. Widmanstetter* pg 61–62. He also received the dedication of Sebastian Meyer's *"Rechnung der 70 Wochen Danielis"* (*ibid.* pg 62). Widmanstetter's interest in this prophecy is apparent in his *Dedicatio* as we shall see below.

[54] *Dedicatio ibid.*

[55] See Müller, *Johann Albrecht v. Widmanstetter* pg 64 on the state of the University. In 1530 there were no more than thirty students in all Faculties and the Faculties of Law and Theology were moribund. Ferdinand had already attempted reform in 1533 and

was the *editio princeps* of the Syriac New Testament that is our main interest.

Widmanstetter's appointment as Superintendent brought him into contact with the Jesuits who had been invited to Vienna shortly before by the King. They had lodged initially with the Dominicans, but Superintendent Widmanstetter was involved with Urban Textor Bishop of Laibach (†1558) in the selection of a site for a Jesuit College and in 1554 chose the Old Cloister of the Carmelites. In return for the Jesuits teaching at the University, Ferdinand instructed Widmanstetter to set aside monies for books and for other needs of the College. It was at this point that Widmanstetter's warm friendship with Peter Canisius began.[56] It is worth realising the closeness of Widmanstetter's links with the Jesuits,[57] both to set their alleged opposition to Postel in perspective,

---

1537. His reforms of 1 January 1554 were known as the *Reformatio Nova* and formed the constitution of the University until the mid-eighteenth century. The reforms were intended to promote the formation of students fitted for State service and it was the role of the Superintendent to ensure they did. On the Superintendent's duties J. v. Aschbach, *Die Wiener Universität und ihre Gelehrten 1320–1565* which is Volume III of his *Geschichte der Wiener Universität* (Alfred Hölder, Vienna 1888) pg 30ff. The biographical remarks about Widmanstetter on pg 299f should be ignored as based only on printed material and now long superseded by Müller.

[56] See Müller, *Johann Albrecht v. Widmanstetter* pg 65, 71 and a letter from Widmanstetter to Canisius on pg 105. Canisius was the first Provincial for Southern Germany, Apostolic Nuncio, and confidant of Ferdinand I.

[57] Widmanstetter sent his younger brother Jacob Philipp to the Jesuit School in 1552 and 5 March 1556, at the age of seventeen, he was elected to the Order. He became Rector of the Braunsberg Jesuit College in 1576 and died in that post in 1586. Five months after his reception into the Order there appeared over the name of the seventeen-year-old *De Societatis Jesu initiis, progressis, rebusque gestis nonnullis Philippi Jacobi Widmanstadii Academii Viennensis, ad Johannem Albertum Widmanstadium fratris filium epistula. Ingolstadii Anno MDLVI Cal. Oct.* The work is eight folios in quarto. I have examined the copy in Munich. It is in the form of a letter and is dedicated to the son of Widmanstetter's elder brother. This nephew was also Johann Albert and is distinguished from his uncle in the work as 'junior'. A letter from Canisius to the Vicar General and Ignatius's successor, Jacob Lainius (Diego Laínez), makes it clear that he was aware that the author of the work was really our Widmanstetter not his younger brother (Müller, *Johann Albrecht v. Widmanstetter* pg 65). The 'letter' links an unexpected family death with that recently announced of Ignatius Loyola. A brief biography of the latter follows, and a defence of the Society's name against the charge of presumption. A catena of New Testament passages is applied to the Society's work in the name of Jesus. (This includes Mark 16, upon which: *"...in nomine Jesu secundum eius promissionem Apostolis factam novis linguis etiamnum, apud Arabes, Aethiopes Brasilios & Indos loquuntur"* links the Society's sense of mission with its knowledge of exotic languages.) The Society is shown to be no threat to the Church and its achievements are recalled. Ignatius's physical state on death was so reduced that his continuing existence up until the final moment was said to be almost miraculous. The division of the Society into provinces is mentioned. Finally a greeting is sent to the daughters of the author, J. A. Widmanstetter ('senior'): Maria

and also lest Widmanstetter be claimed for a Viennese eirenicism in a schema that too starkly paints the Jesuits as the opposition.[58]

In spite of his heavy administrative duties, Widmanstetter persisted with his studies in both Arabic and Syriac, nor was deflected from his long-standing ambition to bring these languages into the service of the Church.[59] He enjoyed at this time the company of Georg Gienger and his old teacher Jakob Jonas, who had married Anne Widmanstetter's mother, and was now Vice-Chancellor and Councillor to the King. He was to salute these two friends at the end of the *editio princeps* in a dedicatory letter explaining the presence and significance of the Syriac liturgical lections found in his edition.

The Arrival of Moses

At the end of 1553 Cardinal Reginald Pole, Julius III's Apostolic Legate to England left Italy and crossed the Alps into Germany. In Dillingen the Cardinal met the Emperor Charles V to discuss the proposed marriage of his son Philip to Pole's cousin Mary Tudor. Widmanstetter was

---

Jacobe, Virginia Cassandra and Hilaria Justina, *"Vidmanstadias nostras Latinarum literarum studiosas"*. (We shall meet these learned ladies in poverty shortly.) The piece is claimed by Müller as the first biography of Ignatius, the first apology for the Order, and indeed the oldest publication about the Order. Whilst there is little new to be learned from it, it is sober and well informed and important in indicating the positive relationships enjoyed between Widmanstetter and his family and the Jesuits. There is a similar positive reference to Loyola's Ten Men and their mission in the *Dedicatio* a****i.

[58] Howard Louthan, *The Quest for Compromise Peacemakers in Counter-Reformation Vienna* (CUP, Cambridge 1997) offers a suggestive account of religious compromise and moderation in the Viennese Court of Maximilian II (1564–1576). His mention of Widmanstetter (pg 164), admittedly as an omission deserving of more study, is nonetheless unfortunate. Louthan describes him as 'a Swabian Bishop' (!) driven from Vienna by the Jesuits (!). This is all nonsense, and Louthan's notes indicate he has overlooked the considerable modern bibliography on Widmanstetter. The Jesuits may well have been wary of Postel (Louthan indicates Canisius's reservations on pg 130): we know the history of their relationship. But to link Widmanstetter to Postel as an object of their persecution is fantastic. One suspects that Louthan is looking to draw clear party lines in a situation where personal, academic and confessional relationships may have been considerably more complex than he supposes.

[59] Bobzin, *Der Koran* comments authoritatively on Widmanstetter's progress in Arabic pg 302–312. His remark pg 313 that we know no details of Widmanstetter's Syriac studies between 1533 and 1553 is true, though we do know about Father Joseph in 1550. He tells us in the *editio princeps* that he had prepared a text of the Syriac New Testament in Hebrew characters and though we cannot know precisely when he did this, we may assume it was before he realised he was going to be able to print in Syriac characters.

staying at Dillingen on the return journey from the *"heilbronner Tage"* and there met Moses of Mardin whom he took back to Vienna with him, to undertake the printing of the *editio princeps* of the Syriac New Testament.

Widmanstetter in his *Dedicatio* deliberately emphasies (*"ex improviso"*) the chance *of the immediate circumstances* of their meeting at Dillingen. Moses, he says, had been coming to see him anyway, but expected him to be in Swabia, not knowing about his flight. Moses had been provided not only with a Pontifical Diplomat to travel with but also *"literisque amicorum ipsi ad me datis"* which seems to indicate that the letters were written to, not merely given to Widmanstetter. It would not be unusual (as we have seen) for Moses to have been sent as an eastern monk from Rome to Widmanstetter.

On the other hand however it is possible that Moses was on his way to see Fugger in Augsburg as Masius had suggested and to whom he had written on Moses's behalf. Upon leaving Masius in Rome, Moses had gone to Venice where he had been with Postel. Postel later would claim that it had been *he* who sent Moses to Widmanstetter.[60] It does though seem a little unlikely that Postel would have had the necessary clout to get Moses into Pole's party. Cervini seems the obvious person to have done so, but it is possible that Ludovico Beccadeli the Papal Nuncio in Venice with whom Moses was staying may have had a hand in things. We do not know. It is, however, apparent that Widmanstetter soon set Moses to work on Syriac projects.[61]

---

[60] Kuntz, *Postel* pg 116 with references, including *De Cosmographia* f. A4r/v. Kuntz discusses Postel's relations with Pole pg 67, 69 and 116.

[61] We have mentioned above Moses's 'completion' of the Missal of Father Joseph and his preparatory work on the festal lectionary. BSB Cod. Syr 1 comes from Widmanstetter's Library and contains at f. 1–32r The Grammar of Barhebraeus with Latin and Italian glosses in Widmanstetter's hand, followed by a work of the same author on synonyms. At the end of this work f. 51v we read: "The Grammar has been copied completely and to its end by a poor sinner, Moses, from the East, from region of the town of Mardin in the Province of Sor, from the blessed place Khelok, son of the priest Isaac. I write it for Herr Johannes Lucretius (i.e. Widmanstetter), Chancellor, and State Superintendent of the King of the Romans. In the year of the Greeks 1864 and 1553 A.D. in the month of November in Vienna, the city strong in God, where the King of the Romans lives. [In fact November 1553 should be A.G. 1865!] The Lord give him long life and good days to ask of Him that he might be blessed of Him and bless others by the prayer of the Mother of Christ our God, Lady Mary and all the Saints. Yea and Amen". The date indicates that this must have been copied directly on Moses's arrival. Folios 53–88 are a partially vocalised Ezekiel. Folios 89–329 are a Syriac lexicon that Widmanstetter evidently had Moses write. Widmanstetter's Latin title is *Dictionarium syriacae linguae cum interpretatione Arabica et latina, atque ubi opus est, etiam*

Postel's Arrival

However seriously we take Postel's presentation of his own role in sending Moses to Vienna, he himself arrived in the city at the end of 1553.[62]
He was appointed to the University, no doubt with Widmanstetter's
connivance, as Regius Professor of Foreign Languages and Mathematics.
He appears also to have had responsibility for Greek. He received a
noticeably large salary that doubtless represented his scholarly reputation
and the extent to which his presence would enhance the reputation of
Ferdinand's newly reformed University.[63] The proximity of the Turks to
Vienna made the cultivation of Oriental languages, especially Arabic
and Turkish, of some diplomatic importance to the King.[64] Ferdinand's
generous sponsorship of the *editio princeps* may be seen in the same light:
beyond the prestige of the edition itself (the first book with oriental
type to be printed in Vienna and in a language and characters that
even Ximenes at Alcalà had not managed), the printing can be seen as
having a certain strategic significance as a gesture of support to Eastern
Christians living under Turkish rule.[65] Once persuaded to the venture

---

Graeca. The Latin translation is provided by Widmanstetter, the Arabic by Moses. The
colophon tells us that it was written by Moses in Vienna and that it took him until
March 1555 to finish it. He reports that he had to compose the lexicon himself as he
did not have one to copy from, and this had entailed a lot of work in a short time.
There is one more manuscript of Moses in the BSB, Cod. Syr. 6, a Syriac Psalter
with an Italian translation of the first verse of every Psalm placed in the margin. The
Colophon says Moses copied it for Bishop Lodovigus of Bologna in the land of Italy
1553 A.D. A subsequent dedication from M. Erhardus Weinmann (*'Ecclesiastes aulicius'*)
to Herzog Johan Friedrich von Wirtemberg (Tübingen 1623) suggests that the manuscript had a more circuitous route to Munich than merely being amongst the books
Moses gave to Widmanstetter. I do not know why Moses made his dedication. These
manuscripts are all described in *Verzeichniss der orientalischen Handschriften der K. Hof- und
Staatsbibliothek in München* Vol. I Part 4 1875 (New Edition: O. Harrassowitz, Wiesbaden
1970) pg 109, 110 & 114.
[62] We know this from a letter to Masius 13 April 1554 Von Lossen #136 pg 160.
The letter is discussed below.
[63] He received an annual salary of 200 gulden, whereas the normal pay for a
Professor was 80: J. v. Aschbach, *Die Wiener Universität und ihre Gelehrten 1320–1565*
pg 246 and *De Cosmographia* f. A 5v; *"quod ubi vix tuae Universitatis summis professoribus ex
prisco studiorum usu 80 aureos nummos in annum salarium curares, mihi statim ab ipso ingressu
200 repraesentari statuisti."*
[64] Paula S. Fichtner, *Ferdinand I of Austria: the Politics of Dynasticism in the Age of the
Reformation* (Columbia University Press, New York 1982) pg 70 observes that as Suleiman approached Vienna in 1529, Ferdinand had nobody who could read the Sultan's
letters.
[65] Fichtner, *Ferdinand I of Austria* pg 7 is of the opinion that Ferdinand wished to use
Postel's attempts to spread Christianity in the Ottoman Empire as a way to undermine

of the edition, the desirability of Postel's presence was unavoidable. Moses would of course be able to tell Widmanstetter of the advanced state of Postel's preparations for an edition. Moreover he was, after Teseo's decease, the only European who had cut Syriac letters. Other than Masius, Postel was the only other competent European. More than that, he was the expert.

---

it. Peter Canisius was far from impressed by Postel's proposals, as we have seen Howard Louthan noted. Canisius discussed Postel in a letter to Ioanni de Polanco S.J. 5 January 1554 in ed. Otto Braunsberger, *Beati Petri Canisii Societatis Jesu, Epistolae et Acta* 8 vols. (Herder, Freiburg i.B. 1896–1923) I pg 449–450: " I cannot see the point of Arabic, for in this world it does not seem that there are people who would want to go to the Turk and convert them through the use of this language". Ferdinand was exhorted to consider the Eastern Christians and help overthrow the Mohammedans and the Nestorians in the Latin dedication to the manuscript of the Syriac Gospels Moses copied for him in 1554. The manuscript is now in the Nationalbibliothek in Vienna, shelf-marked Cod. Vindob. Syr. 1. It comprises 160 parchment pages in serto containing the Four Gospels. The Latin *Dedicatio* f. I–III is dated 10 August 1554 and the same date is given in a Latin colophon. J. Adler, *De Versione Simplici* pg 59 summarises it as follows: *"In epistola dedicatoria ad Ferdinem Imperatorem latine codice praemissa, conqueritur adversam suam fortunam, quod Syriacis typis destitutus, consilium de imprimendo novo Testamento syriaco reiicere coactum fuerit, Caesaremque exhortatur, ut sua munificentia editionem adiuvare velit"*. A decorated first page has a cruciform design with the legend in Syriac: "In Thy name we destroy our enemies, in Thy name we triumph over those who hate us" that also appears in a plate in the *editio princeps*. Folio 1v has in Syriac: "In the strength of our Lord Jesus Christ we begin to write the books of the Holy Gospel. At the beginning stands the Gospel of Matthew which he preached in Aramaic in the land of Palestine". It is interesting to see again a Syriac affirmation of the Aramaic origin of Matthew that our European scholars also considered likely. We saw a similar claim in Elias's manuscript Vat sir. 15 of 9 December 1529. Subsequent Syriac legends at the beginnings of the Gospels tell us Mark was written in Rome, Luke in Alexandria and John in Ephesus. Folio 160v concludes: *"Hic sanctorum quatour* (sic) *Evangeliorum liber scriptus est per Moysen Syrum et ad finem perductus anno MDLIIII regnante divo Ferdinando Romanorum, Hungeriae, Bohemiaeque rege. Laus Deo. Amen"*. This manuscript has no obvious connection with the production of the *editio princeps*, and is probably best seen as an instance of the practice now familiar to us of scribes copying manuscripts for important patrons. It is certainly in Moses's hand, and it is this hand that lies behind the beautiful type of the *editio princeps*. It is also in all probability a copy of the text of the manuscript he brought from the Patriarch. A. Ricardo Jones, *Textus Sacrorum Evangeliorum Versioni Simplicis Syriacae* (Clarendon, Oxford 1805) considered that this manuscript had been used to print the *editio princeps* stating: *"Adservatur quidam Viennae in Bibliotheca Caesarea exemplum authenticum e quo haec edito... sed recens est, a Mose Syro, patriarchatu Antiocheno, patria Meredidnensi exaratum, quo tempore Editionem meditaretur"*. There is, however, no reason to believe that this manuscript marks any stage in the production of the *editio princeps*. It is not in anyway marked in preparation for printing; the vocalisation is not original but added later (I rely on the catalogue as this is not clear from my microfilm); the manuscript has stitchwords which the *editio princeps* lacks; and it does not have the lectionary material that characterises the *editio princeps*. The manuscript is described in P. Severinus Grill, *Vergleichende Religionsgeschichte und Kirchenväter Beigabe: Die syrischen Handschriften der Nationalbibliothek in Wien* (Ferdinand Berger Horn, N.Ö.) pg 54.

Postel's Inaugural Lecture

During his stay in Vienna Postel wrote his *De Linguae Phoenicis sive Hebrai-cae Excellentia.*[66] The work articulates what Postel (at least) thought he was about in the production of the *editio princeps*. It is dated February 1554, printed by Michael Zimmermann, the printer of the *editio princeps* and dedicated to Jacob Jonas and Georg Gienger, the two dedicatees of the explanation of the Syrian lectionary Calendar at the back of the *editio princeps*.[67]

The work is effectively Postel's Inaugural Lecture composed with an awareness of his new appointment. It seeks to defend the utility of the study of oriental languages and, of course, the anticipated edition of the Syriac New Testament. He takes as his theme language that makes us social, intellectual and spiritual animals. He speaks particularly of the King's interest in the study of languages as a power for human reconciliation; of the importance of Syriac in bringing the whole East back to Orthodoxy, and of his own providentially guided career. Rather than call Ferdinand *Rex Romanorum*, Postel calls him *Antipolitanus Rex* evoking the name of the city Antipolis founded on the future site of Rome by Noah/Ianus, thirteen hundred years before Romulus. Postel here recalls the glorious Noahian heritage of Rome we have seen celebrated by Annius and Egidio to insert Ferdinand into the greater scheme of things. Ferdinand's role as the present incumbent, so to speak, is to promote saving Concord and Peace within Christendom and the whole world by sponsoring the *editio princeps*. The Council of Vienne had long ago deemed necessary what the Antipolitan King was only then being the first to do.

The anticipated appearance of the *editio princeps* and the concomitant spread of knowledge of languages heralds the establishment of Postel's long announced Concordia. It is in this light that Postel's presence had

---

[66] From this period we also have *Clarissima et ex Aristotelis...* (Oef. 262 in Munich) dedicated to Widmanstetter. See: F. Secret, *Bibliographie* pg 141 for summary.

[67] The title page has Arabic characters but not in moveable type. They have some resemblance to those Postel cut for his *Linguarum duodecim* in 1538. The text is Psalm 32.1 from Giustiniani's 1516 Genoa Polyglot Psalter with an omission. There are also the same Arabic characters in the colophon. Nevertheless Postel claims in the *De Cosmographia* A 5v that Kaspar Kraft, who produced the Syriac type for the *editio princeps*, also produced an Arabic: "... *statim apud Gasparum sculptorem curavi rem ipsam pro utriusque linguae apparatu (characteres enim Arabicos minisculos etiam ibi exculpi curavi, nedum Christianos fundi suis legibus feci)*".

been solicited by Widmanstetter in the King's name to teach Arabic and *"Typographiae eius instituendae praeesse"*. The force of the final verb is surely unmistakable. Postel is here claiming to have been in charge of setting up the press for the *editio princeps*.

A letter from Masius

Postel wrote to Masius from Vienna at the end of 1553 and Masius replied from Waldsassen 13 April 1554. He greeted both Widmanstetter and Moses. He was most eager for the edition and hoped Moses would be persuaded to print the Syriac New Testament, *"quod habet vetustissimum et accuratissime scriptum"*.[68] Masius had seen a Syriac New Testament, and in both Gospels and Epistles he believed the Syriac illuminates the Greek and Latin. He believed it was probably independent of both.[69] He further suggested that Moses's vernacular fluency in Syriac might help Postel in the area of *Hebrew* lexicography.[70] In response to Postel's demand for Arabic books, Masius describes his

---

[68] Concern for the antiquity of the manuscript is characteristic of our scholars who did not have our appreciation of the broad homogeneity of the Peshitta text. The concern is most evident in the case of Tremellius, see Robert J. Wilkinson "Emmanuel Tremellius' 1569 Edition of the Syriac New Testament" Journal of Ecclesiastical History 58/1 January 2007 pg. 9–25.

[69] Lossen pg 160–165 #136: *"ego vero optarim Mosen illum Syrum quoque persuaderi posse, ut non prius vos desereret, quam Novum Testamentum Syrum, quod habet vetustissimum et accuratissime scriptum, typis evulgatum esset. Nam ex 4 evangeliorum studiosa collatione atque ex inspectis hic illic aliquot epistolarum locis persuasus sum magnam ex illa editione in latinam ac graecam lumen transfundi posse, videorque mihi compertum habere Syrum illud neque ex graeco neque ex Latino translatum esse, aut si translatum sit, id in ipso statim initio vel ab ipsis auctoribus factum esse, qui, ut est verisimile, suis gentilibus primum gratificari eosque ad viam veritatis adducere studuerunt"*. Masius's careful collation here must be a comparison of Syriac, Latin and Greek readings. He would not suggest Moses printed the most ancient manuscript if he had himself collated Syriac manuscripts (and thereby effectively created an edition). Nor would such a collation lead him to suggest that light could shine on the Greek and Latin versions from the Syriac, but only a comparison of those versions could indicate that. Masius was wrong to consider the Peshitta independent of the Greek, though it is, of course, independent of the Vulgate. His alternative hypothesis of a very early (Apostolic) translation from Greek to form the Peshitta is similar to the text-historical scenario that underpins Tremellius's work (See my article referred to in the previous note which also expands upon references made in the main text above to Tremellius), and is proposed by Guy Lefèvre de la Boderie in the Antwerp Polyglot. A tantalising detail of Masius's comparisons is preserved when he notes that Jerome: *"in quadam questione in hebraeo evangelio sui temporis scriptum fuisse dicit, pro 'velo templi scisso', 'superliminare magnum corruisse', id quoque in hoc Syro haberi videtur. Nam pro 'velo templi' habet... [Lacuna!]"*.

[70] A point Masius makes again in the *Syrorum Peculium*.

own insufficiency in the language: he says he can scarcely compare an Arabic Gospel with the Latin.[71]

The letter contains important references to codices Postel had brought back from Syria but which he now feared he must return as he was unable to pay for them. Pfalzgraf Ottheinrich von Neuburg was offering to buy them for the Library he was about to found. The books were indeed bought by Ottheinrich and became part of the Bibliotheca Palatina at Heidelberg. There they supported a distinctive school of Orientalists, and there Tremellius was to make use of one particular manuscript in the production of his Syriac New Testament.

What is most noticeable in Masius's letter is his nervousness, indeed stupefaction, upon hearing about Mother Joanna and her interpretations of the Zohar from Postel. Masius recognised Postel as his old teacher *"veterem meum praeceptorem"*, and confessed his own interest in the Hebrew Mysteries *"Hebraeorum penetralibus"*, yet he hoped Postel was rightly 'trying the spirits'. Concern and a lack of comprehension mark his reception of Postel's doctrine of Male and Female roles in Cosmic Redemption and (suspecting Postel of no malice) there is an evident fear of Postel passing beyond the received doctrines of the Church. The letter is an interesting indication of the growing problem Postel's notions could pose even for his friends who shared his arcane interests and respected both his learning and his piety.

Others were less sympathetic. Postel had come to Vienna to take charge of the printing in this all-important project that he had worked on since 1537 when he had seen the Gospels in Venice—that he had discussed with Bomberg before he died, and that he and Moses had collaborated upon in Venice. However, at the beginning of May 1554, before the printing began, he fled Vienna and returned to Venice. Widman-stetter and Moses alone would see the *editio princeps* through the press. Both men offered accounts of this sudden departure: Widmanstetter in the *Dedicatio* of the *editio princeps* (he evidently did not feel that this embarrassing departure could be passed over completely in silence), and Postel himself in subsequent letters of *apologia* to Ferdinand. Widmanstetter spoke of the activities of *"perversi quidam homines"* which is no doubt deliberately not illuminating. Postel said that he left because

---

[71] Masius mentions Postel's plans for an Arabic lexicon and his own desperate need for one.

his books were to be put on the Index in Venice and he wanted to stop this happening. We shall consider both accounts later.

The Death of Widmanstetter

Widmanstetter increasingly found the demands of his office heavy, in addition to the labour of bringing out the *editio princeps*. Already in the *Dedicatio* he had asked to retire. His wife Anna died aged only 30 on 18 May 1556 and was buried in Regensburg. Thereafter on 24 February 1557, on the recommendation of both Ferdinand and the Herzog Albrecht V von Bayern, Widmanstetter was received into the priesthood in Regensburg. He died on 28 March 1557 and was laid to rest in the Cathedral there. He appears to have left his daughters, living in Landshut with their guardians, in difficult straits. Georg Airnschmalz, Doctor in Law, writing to Herzog Albrecht V 2 February 1561 mentions that the girls *"zu irem standt wenig genug haben"*.

The poverty of the girls led them to consider the sale of their father's library. It seemed at first likely to pass to Vice-Chancellor Seld, but Herzog Albrecht V was in need of a library to enhance his princely standing and took an interest. So did the Jesuit College in Ingolstadt. The collection eventually formed the basis of Albrecht's Hofbibliothek and thus it is in Munich today that the remains of Widmanstetter's library are to be found.[72]

Müller had supposed that Albrecht had sought to claim the type and the matrices from the *editio princeps* for himself, basing his conviction upon the letter of Georg Airnschmalz mentioned above that announced not only the girls' poverty but also the finding of the type.[73] Hartig was able to correct this account and to show that Albrecht was merely negotiating at the request of Ferdinand I between the printer Michael Zimmerman in Vienna and Widmanstetter's orphans for the return of the type. Hartig's account is based upon an archive of letters of which Müller had used only one. The whole collection is still extant

---

[72] The essential work is Otto Hartig, *Die Gründung der Münchener Hofbibliothek durch Albrecht V und Johann Jakob Fugger* (Verlag der Königlich Bayerischen Akademie der Wissenschaften, Munich 1917) pg 9–19. This work supersedes Müller in the matters it touches upon and especially with respect to the question of the fate of Widmanstetter's type.

[73] Müller, *Johann Albrecht v. Widmanstetter* pg 71–73. The letter is on pg 111.

in Munich and comprises an exchange of letters between the end of 1560 and the beginning of 1562.[74]

In spite of this little archive, however, the fate of the type, matrices and punches (just as was the case with Teseo's Syriac) remains unknown. What does however emerge from this sadly frustrating correspondence is the importance attached by Ferdinand I to securing them. The search became a matter of insistent diplomatic correspondence. Just as Albrecht had sought the prestige of possessing Widmanstetter's library, so the King sought to preserve his considerable investment in the prestigious printing of the *editio princeps*. Without the type (at least) no more Syriac could be printed in Vienna. Without the matrices and the punches there would be no more type. Ferdinand had been deprived of Postel through flight, Widmanstetter through death, and Moses had returned home: he sought to salvage what he could. But, alas, Vienna was not to become the prestigious home of Oriental printing that Postel had

---

[74] Bayerische Hauptstaatsarchiv, Oefeleana 18/2. I owe my copy of this archive to the generosity of Dr. Trevor Johnson, who was patient enough also to initiate me into the *Schrift*. A summary of the correspondence is given in Hartig, *Die Gründung der Münchener Hofbibliothek* pg 18–19. The sequence is a little complicated. Michael Zimmermann, the printer, had already in October 1560 received from Albrecht an order for 200 copies of a 'Polish Confession' and sent them in November with 15 copies of the Psalter and the *Quaestiones* of Doctor Gienger (Zimmermann to Albrecht 6 Nov 1560: Bundle #1, item 3). About the same time he addressed himself to Vice-Chancellor Seld on Albrecht's behalf about the type and the matrices of the *editio princeps* (Bundle #1, item 1) that the Herzog wished to buy at a reasonable price. Seld, who did not have the type, in turn commended Zimmermann to the Herzog as a good man and printer (Bundle #1, item 2). On 20 January 1561 Zimmermann wrote about the matter to Erasmus Fendt, the Court Secretary (Bundle #2) and on 28 February 1561 to Albrecht himself (Bundle # 3). A letter of Albrecht to Ferdinand, I April 1561, refers to the printer. We learn that Ferdinand himself wanted the type and that Albrecht had not been able to get them for him: they were in the hands of Widmanstetter's heirs. Printed copies of the Syriac bible were to be handed over to Zimmermann. (This may not be unconnected with the '1562 edition' of the *editio princeps*. See below.) A letter of Ferdinand to Albrecht from Vienna (Bundle # 4) 7 May 1561 indicates that Zimmermann was to be sounded out in Munich where Albrecht had just taken possession of the Library. Zimmermann himself wrote to Fendt 10 May 1561 saying in self-justification that he had not known that Widmanstetter's books were to go anywhere other than to his daughters. Fendt sent Zimmermann an answer 29 June 1561. Albrecht was writing to help Ferdinand acquire the type. He had been in contact with the Trustees and would help Zimmermann to obtain the type at a reasonable price. At this point Dr. Georg Airnschmalz from Landshut wrote 2 December 1561 (this is the letter Müller knew) mentioning the location of the type (but not the matrices and the punches) and Widmanstetter's daughters' poverty. On 30 January 1562 Zimmermann acknowledged a letter of Fendt of 16 November 1561 and reported on his exertions. A final letter of Ferdinand 29 March 1562 to Albrecht indicates that, even in the absence of the punches and matrices, Ferdinand wished through Albrecht's good offices to acquire the type.

anticipated in his Inaugural Lecture, though the glory of the *editio princeps* would not fade.

Widmanstetter as a Scholar

The existence of several substantial treatments of Widmanstetter's broad and considerable scholarly achievements will allow us to pass them in quick review here. We shall then seek to establish a more balanced judgment than heretofore upon his interest in Kabbalah.

Helmut Bobzin has recently reviewed the literature and characterises Widmanstetter generally as a moderate Catholic reformer whose language skills are to be understood within the context of Church Apologetics and Missionary strategy—an evaluation that will not surprise us.[75] He thus places Widmanstetter in the tradition of the Dominicans, the Franciscans at the time of the Council of Vienne, and the missionary linguists of the thirteenth and fourteenth centuries like Raimond Lull and Raymand Martin. Hans Striedl has dealt with Widmanstetter as a Classical Philologist and has given an excellent account of Widmanstetter's oriental books.[76] It is Bobzin's account that is now the most authoritative treatment of Widmanstetter's Arabic.

When we turn to consider Widmanstetter as an Hebraist, impressionistic characterisations can add nothing to the solid evidence of the inventory of his library provided in the detailed descriptions of

---

[75] Bobzin, *Der Koran* pg 295–363: pg 298–302 on Hebrew and pg 303–312 on Arabic.

[76] Hans Striedl "Der Humanist Johann Albrecht Widmanstetter 1506–1557 als klassischer Philologe" in *Festgabe der Bayerischen Staatsbibliothek Emil Gratzl zum 75 Geburtstag* (Harrassowitz, Wiesbaden 1953) pg 96–120. Also his "Die Bücherei des Orientalisten Johann Albrecht Widmanstetter" in ed. H. J. Kissling & A Schmaus, *Serta Monacensia Franz Babinger als Festgruss dargebracht* (Brill, Leiden 1952) pg 200–244 which deals especially with the works that were never published. Again important is his later "Geschichte der Hebraica-Sammlung der Bayerischen Staatsbibliothek" in ed. H. Franke, *Orientalisches aus Münchener Bibliotheken und Sammlungen* (Franz Steiner, Wiesbaden 1957) pg 1–39, which discusses Widmanstetter's Hebrew books on pg 6ff. The basic work on the Munich Hebrew collection is Moritz Steinschneider, "Die heb. Hss. der K. Hof- u. Staatsbibl. in München Ein Beitrag zur Geschichte dieser Bibliothek" in *Sb. BAW phil-hist K* (1875) pg 169–206. Steinschneider also wrote the catalogue, *Die Hebr Hss. der K. Hof- u. Stattsbibl. in München beschrieben* (2nd ed. Munich 1895) (= *Cat.codd. mss. Bibl. Reg. Mon.* Vol. I: 1). The Syriac manuscripts in Munich are found in *Cat. codd. mss. Bibl. Reg. Mon.* Vol. I: 4 pg 109–119 and were described by J. Schönfelder. The place of Widmanstetter's books in the foundation holding of the Library is described by Otto Hartig, *Die Gründung der Münchener Hofbibliothek* pg 9–19 with an inventory on pg 173–193. The list of Hebrew books on pg 191–192 is of particular importance for us.

Steinschneider's Catalogue. Marking continuity with Egidio da Viterbo, we can find there manuscripts copied from the Cardinal's library and volumes themselves that Egidio once owned, as well as Hebrew incunabula. Widmanstetter obtained many kabbalistic texts from Egidio, but it is worth attempting to appreciate his own enthusiasm for Kabbalah from the extent of his own personal collection.[77] This is important in the light of Steinschneider's own characterisation of Widmanstetter as an Hebraist: he saw him as a distinguished collector, but a mediocre scholar.[78]

Streidl has properly sought to reverse this evaluation, but by using the master's own judgment.[79] Cod. heb. 124 gives excellent evidence of Widmanstetter's wide and easy linguistic and learned competence, but was not at the time identified by Steinschneider as Widmanstetter's. He described it in his catalogue as a work of native Jewish scholarship, which must make Widmanstetter more than a mere collector.[80]

---

[77] Stiedl "Sammlung" pg 6–8 offers an indication of Widmanstetter's Hebraica in broad categories: 17 Biblical manuscripts; 10 Midrashim; 18 Talmud and Exegesis; Kabbalah 27; Philosophy and Polemic 36; Belles Lettres 13; Philology 4; Science 24; Medicine 28. He lists eight Hebrew Incunabula on pg 8. Manuscripts copied from Egidio's books include Codd. Heb. 81; 96; 103; 217; 218; 219; 285 initio. Manuscripts themselves obtained from Egidio's library include Codd. heb. 74; 92; 215 (these are two Kabbalistic collections). Amongst printed volumes from the Cardinal's library are a *Tractate Sanhedrin* (Salonika 1498. A. heb 280), and Reuchlin's *Rudimenta* (Phorcae 1506), both with the Cardinal's marginalia. From Steinschneider's catalogue we can gauge the size of Widmanstetter's kabbalistic collection. Anthologies of kabbalistic writings are represented by manuscripts Codd. heb. 92; 112; 221; 285. Kabbalistic manuscripts are 76; 81; 96; 103; 115; 119; 129; 215; 240; 246; 248; 305; 311; 325. Thus, for example, 76 offers Menachem Zivni on the ten Sephiroth and their relationship to the Ten Commandments; 81 contains a collection of mystical writings by Eleasar of Worms and others copied (and edited?) by Elias Levita for Egidio (Widmanstetter had this copied from Egidio's library. He added an amusing note in 1555: *"Moses scriba meus, qui mihi tribuit titulos Magisterii ord. S. Augustini, ignarus quid scriberet"*); 92 is again a kabbalistic collection with Egidio's marginalia including commentaries upon *Jezira*: 103 has Abulafia and Menachem Recanti; 215 offers 219 folios with Egidio's annotations dealing with the Sephiroth, and the Name of God with 72 letters: 285 is another great collection at the end of which Widmanstetter wrote: *"Ex codice Zoharis quem habet Jac. Mantinus Hebr. Romae A 1537. franc. Parnassus scribit"*. It also contains Egidio's glosses.

[78] *"Der Verdienst eines eifrigen Sammlers muss man Widmanstad in vollen Maase zuerkennen: bis zum Kenner der neuhebraischen Sprache und Literatur hat er es nicht gebracht, auch wenn wir einen, für Zeit und Verhöltnisse verkleinerten mastab anlegen, obwohl er in Rom das Hebräische von Juden zu erlernen suchte und wohl auch bei seinen Notizen deren Hilfe in Ausspruch nahm"*. Sb. BAW (cited above) pg 175.

[79] Striedl "Sammlung" pg 9–10.

[80] *"Adversarien eines christlichen, wohl in Judentum geboren Gelehrten"*.

Widmanstetter did not merely collect Hebrew manuscripts, he read them. He understood Kabbalah much as Pico and Egidio had. He found evidence of an ancient tradition bearing testimony to the profound Christian truths of the Trinity and the Incarnation that had been fundamentally misunderstood by Judaism. Thus Steidl remarks that no book of Widmanstetter has been worked through by him with the same intensity as his edition of the large printed Talmud (2° A heb 258) and his Hebrew manuscript of the *Zohar* (Cod heb 217–219) where all the margins bear annotations in his clear and distinctive hand.[81] The same doctrinal reading is found in his annotations to his copy of Abarbanel's *Mashmi'a Jeshu'a* (2° A heb 3), Bachja b. Ascher's Pentateuchal Commentary (2° A heb 31) and of the mystical Torah commentary of Menachem de Recanti (4° A heb 225).

Nor was Widmanstetter himself above verbal manipulations in the kabbalistic manner. His Coat of Arms, as we have seen, gives evidence of cryptic and numerical correspondences which may not have been entirely playful. He also left signatures in his books in numerical alphabetical code.[82]

Widmanstetter as a Kabbalist

If Widmanstetter's reputation as an Hebraist has suffered from Steinschneider's dismissive judgment, his attitudes to Kabbalah have not been entirely redeemed by Striedl, primarily because of the weight of an assessment made by Gershom Scholem in a pioneering 1954 article that first offered a reliable framework for the study of Renaissance Christians interested in Kabbalah.[83] A reconsideration of Scholem's evaluation

---

[81] Striedl "Sammlung" pg 9.

[82] See remarks and references above. Striedl "Bucherei" pg 243 gives a fascinating account of the identification by means of these bizarre 'kabbalisic' signatures of Vat. ar. 23, 118 and 177 as having belonged to Widmanstetter before passing to Heidelberg and thence to Rome with the Bibliotheca Palatina in 1623. Even Levi della Vida had missed this!

[83] Gershom Scholem, 'Zur Geschichte der Anfänge der christlichen Kabbala' in *Essays presented to Leo Baeck* (East and West Library, London 1954) pg 158–193. A French version by Paul Kessler appeared in *Kabbalistes chrétiens* Cahiers de l'Hermétisme (Albin Michel, Paris 1979) pg 19–46. I have quoted from Debra Prager's English Version in ed. Joseph Dan *The Christian Kabbalah* (Harvard College Library, Cambridge Mass. 1997) pg 17–51. Subsequently Scholem wrote of Widmanstetter's religious and philosophical interest in Kabbalah for its own sake in *Kabbalah*. (Keter, Jerusalem 1974) pg 199. The 1954 article however still determines Widmanstetter's reputation.

will enable us to obtain a more balanced estimate of Widmanstetter's attitude to Kabbalah.

Scholem acknowledged Widmanstetter's uncommon learning and his role in gathering the kabbalistic manuscripts now in the Staatsbibliothek in Munich, yet he cited Widmanstetter primarily to illustrate the "profound distrust" with which Jewish Esotericism came to be regarded in some informed Christian circles in contrast to the earlier enthusiasm of Pico della Mirandola. He based this judgment on a passage from the 1543 work of Widmanstetter against Islam, *Mahometis Abdallae Filii Theologia Dialogo Explicata...* that was in fact his first printed book.[84] This book contains two Latin texts that Widmanstetter did not write but merely reprinted: an epitome of Robert of Ketton's Latin translation of the Koran[85] and the *Masa'il 'Abdallah b. Salam*, an Islamic theological dialogue between the Prophet and Jewish scholars *Hermano Nellingaunense interprete.*[86] To these Widmanstetter added a very brief life of the Prophet by himself, and importantly for us, his own Annotations upon the two Latin texts he printed. There is also a dedicatory epistle and a letter to his bookseller, Johann Otto of Nuremberg.

Scholem evidently knew of the passage in question (which is the thirty-third Annotation to Robert of Ketton's *Epitome*) from its quotation

---

[84] *Mahometis Abdallae filii theologia dialogo explicata Hermanno Nellingaunense interprete....* As none is mentioned on the title page, the place of printing is deduced from Widmanstetter's letter to the Nuremburg bookseller Johann Otto included in the volume. This is corroborated by Widmanstetter's handwritten note on the title page of his own *Handexemplar.* I have used this copy which is preserved in the Staatsbibliothek in Munich, shelfmark A.or.1590. An account of the book and a short bibliography is given in ed. Francine de Nave, *Philologia Arabica, Arabische stüdien en drukken in de Nederlanden in de 16de en 17de eeuw.* (Museum Plantin—Moretus, Antwerp 1986) pg 94–96.

[85] Robert of Ketton was Archdeacon of Pamplona and completed his version with the aid of a Saracen, Mohammad, in 1143. See: James Kritzeck, "Robert of Ketton's translation of the Qur'an" Islamic Quarterly 2 (1955) pg 309–312. For the issues that arose around Koran translations: Harry Clark "The Publication of the Koran in Latin: a Reformation Dilemma" Sixteenth Century Journal XV (1984) pg 3–12. That the arcane mysteries may be found in Islamic texts is also innovative, but not unique. On the other hand, the worthlessness of the Islamic *superstitio* in this respect, contrasted with what can be extracted from the Hebrew tradition is asserted by Flavius Mithridates: C. Wirszubski, *Flavius Mithridates Sermo de Passione Domini* pg 90.

[86] For this, see: Bobzin, *Der Koran* pg 50, 335, 355. The work is the *Masa'il Abi-al-Harith 'Abdallah ibn Salam.* It was translated by F. Pijper, *Het boek der duizend vragen.* (Leiden, 1924) which I have not seen. For a discussion of the work, J. Horovitz, "Abd Allah ibn Salam", *Encyclopaedia of Islam* (New Edition) I. I. (1954) pg 52. Also C. G. F. Burnett "Arabic into Latin in Twelfth Century Spain: the works of Hermann of Carinthia" Mittellatein Jahrbuch XIII (1978) pg 100–134.

by Joseph Perles in 1884.[87] Perles was interested in the passage because in it Widmanstetter records hearing one of Pico della Mirandola's kabbalistic teachers, Dattylus (who is still not identified), and describes his teaching. Perles hoped that Widmanstetter's description of the teaching would eventually facilitate the identification of Dattylus. Scholem, however, was able to point out that the doctrine mentioned, that of the *'Transformation of All Things' (din bne chalof)* was first developed by Joseph ben Shalom Ashkenazi in Barcelona in the first quarter of the fourteenth century and that Dattylus, whoever he was, might himself have encountered the doctrine in any number of manuscripts.[88]

It was Widmanstetter's comment upon the doctrine of the *'Transformation of All Things'* from the simplest life-form to the highest level of the Sephiroth that formed the basis of Scholem's judgment, particularly his final words that Kabbalah had become a Trojan Horse threatening the Church.[89]

It was Scholem who identified the doctrine here and handled the whole passage with both precision and circumspection. Furthermore he acknowledged that Widmanstetter's reaction attached to "this particular point". (This particular point is, of course, one to which it would be practically impossible for any orthodox Christian scholar publicly to subscribe.) Nevertheless the structure of Scholem's rightly influential article is such that Widmanstetter, on the basis of this passage alone, is made to illustrate informed Christian scholars profoundly mistrustful of Kabbalah. An otherwise excellent recent book on the Zohar casually betrays this natural understanding of Scholem's article: Widmanstetter there appears as the polar opposite of Pico.[90]

---

[87] J. Perles, *Beiträge zur Geschichte der hebräischen und aramäischen Studien* pg 186. Widmanstetter recalls Dattylus again in the *Dedicatio* to the *editio princeps* where he calls Pico: "*Mar. Dattyli Hebraei, quem ego arcanos de divino auditu libros Taurini in summa eius senectute subtilissime interpretantem audivi, Illustris discipulus*". This reference does not seem at all critical. J. Perles, *op. cit.* pg 191 suggested implausibly identification with Yohanan Alemanno. On whom, see his "Les Savants juifs à Florence à l'époque de Laurent de Médicis" Revue des Études juives XII (1886) pg 245–256.

[88] G. Scholem "The Beginnings of the Christian Kabbalah" pg 20. On this doctrine one may consult further Scholem's *Encyclopedia Judaica* article 'Gilgul' which reappears in *Kabbalah* (Keter, Jerusalem 1974) pg 344ff and the learned note of F. Secret "Une texte mal connu de Simon Luzzato sur la Kabbale" Revue des Études juives CXVIII (1959/60) pg 121–128 at pg 127.

[89] "*Haec idcirco commoravi, ut indicarem, ex hac Iudaeorum Caballa infinita opinionum portenta, veluti ex equo Troiano educta, impetum in Christi ecclesiam fecisse*".

[90] Maurice-Ruben Hayoun, *Le Zohar. Aux Origines de la Mystique juive* (Noêsis, Paris 1999) pg 392.

In fact, Widmanstetter's attitude was far more nuanced than may be appreciated from the thirty-third Annotation alone. An examination of the whole body of Annotations that makes up the bulk of Widmanstetter's original contribution to the book enables one to see that whilst Widmanstetter might, not altogether surprisingly, baulk at the doctrine of *din bne chalof*, he had a most positive appreciation of other aspects of Kabbalah. Widmanstetter's book is exceedingly rare.[91] Secret had formed a correct evaluation of his meaning: otherwise Bobzin alone seems to give evidence of having read the Annotations in pursuit of his own interests and has noted, as any reader must, their kabbalistic content. This however does not lead him to readjust the received view of Widmanstetter's attitude to Kabbalah, which is what I wish now to argue is necessary.

The Annotations

The Annotations are linked to the two Latin texts, the *Dialogus* (D) and the *Epitome* (E), by lemmata that appear at the beginning of each numbered Annotation. In the text itself a number appears in the margin which is that of the relevant Annotation to that place.

The Annotations purport to display the alleged inconsistency of the Prophet and of the Koran. They also indicate alleged borrowings by the Prophet from both Judaism and Christianity.[92] Not surprisingly, the Prophet is said to have misunderstood the fundamental mystery of the Holy Trinity,[93] the nature of the Incarnation,[94] and the import of the philosophical debate over the eternity of the World.[95]

What has not previously been generally observed, however, is the extent to which Widmanstetter describes and accounts for the teachings of the Prophet as distortions of kabbalistic doctrine, specifically of Sephirotic doctrine.[96] It is here that the centre of our argument lies.

---

[91] I know only the copy in Munich which is what Bobzin read. He discusses the work at some length *Der Koran* pg 325ff, mentioning the Annotations at pg 335.

[92] For example: E60.

[93] E26.

[94] E36.

[95] D47.

[96] Thus the lemma: *Hierusalem terrae medium* gives rise to a characteristically Sephirotic gloss: *"Hoc Iudaei referunt ad septem numerationem, quam Hierusalem divinam, & coelestam adpellant".* Equally freely E21: *"Bos sustinet terram Cabalistae hoc figmentum ad quadrigas septimae numeratione suppositas referri arbitrantur".* D18 introduces the *"quinque numerationes mundi*

There is nothing in the two texts upon which he comments to give
rise to thoughts of the Sephirot. In that sense the introduction of the
Sephirot is entirely gratuitous. It arises from Widmanstetter's own interests, indeed from his beliefs, rather than from the texts. Widmanstetter
assumes the relevance of the Sephirotic doctrine because he not only
believes that it is of sufficient antiquity to have been misunderstood
by the Prophet, but because more fundamentally he believes that the
ancient and venerable traditions of the Kabbalah offer an authentic
and authoritative basis for understanding of the Christian mysteries.[97]
For Widmanstetter Sephirotic doctrine is true and is how the Incarnation is to be understood. Some Jews, and certainly the Prophet, have
misunderstood or perverted the tradition, but it is no less authoritative.
In this respect then Widmanstetter may be seen to share the views of
Egidio and of Postel upon the antiquity and authority of Kabbalah.

There is a noticeable but not entirely consistent tendency in the Annotations to distinguish between 'Jews' and 'Kabbalists'. The former tend
to be spoken of abusively, especially when their opposition to Christian
doctrine is in question: the latter are far better received, though again
not when clearly opposed to the teaching of the Church, and such is
the case with the doctrine of the *'Transformation of All Things'* which
gave rise to the outburst about the Trojan Horse. There are occasions
when the 'Jews' failed to understand what Kabbalah taught, and they
passed their misunderstanding on to the Prophet.[98] Sometimes passages
were understood only superficially by *'Thalmudistae'* where Kabbalists
are able better to expound a *'mysterium magis reconditum'*.[99] (This passage is of particular interest because it preserves a *bon mot* of Egidio
da Viterbo favourable to a Jewish kabbalist.) Sometimes kabbalistic

---

archetypi inferiores, quibus omnes omnium rerum proprietates & actiones exprimuntur". D24 also:
"de mundo archetypo". Embedded in a complicated exegesis we find the origins of the
souls located in the appropriate Sephirot in D45: *"Efflabit ex ea Animarum radices primas
esse in quinque numerationibus, deinde sub septima eas produci ad huius vitae theatrum Cabalistae
docuerunt"*. All these remarks gratuitously introduce Sephirotic doctrines.

[97] Kabbalah is also written in the original language of mankind which gives it a
particularly efficient access to truth. D3.

[98] D9.

[99] E37. *"Infra piscis] De huius piscis epulo suaviter sibi blandiuntur Thalmudistae. Cabalistae
mysterium magis reconditum hoc loco enuntiant. Aegidius Card. Viterbiensis per iocum saepe M
Žemato praeceptori nostro dicere solebat, Christum post Resurrectionem suam, Apostolis hoc epulum
exhibuisse. Cui Zematus, Vides igitur, inquit, Messiam vestrum, discipulos suos convivii huius
expectatione plenos omnino fallere noluisse"*. The reference is to Leviathan. On Zematus, see
J. Perles *op. cit.* pg 186 note.

teaching is found *"non…omnino absurda"*, because it finds parallels in Gospel texts—in contrast to the extraordinary *'portentosum'* exegesis of the Talmudists and the Prophet.[100] Widmanstetter may also distinguish between *'Cabalistae obtusiores'* who speak of numberless worlds and their inhabitants created and destroyed before our own, and the *'acutiores'* who understand such speculation more acceptably as statements about the Divine Imagination.[101] Kabbalists have had the misfortune to be misunderstood not only by their co-religionists but also by Christian heretics. Those heretics who have followed kabbalists in teaching Universal Salvation, even of daemons, have in fact misunderstood the Kabbalah which speaks *"de reversione quadam, non de salute"*.[102] In this instance it is interesting, remembering Widmanstetter's outburst over the *'Transformation of All Things'*, to see just what he is prepared to find a positive gloss for here.

Annotation D4 may be taken as a text to illustrate the range of Widmanstetter's distinctions and how he deploys them in his notes. Widmanstetter alleges that the lemma shows that the Prophet confused the Sephirot (*numerationes*) of *'Pulchrido'* and of *'Pietas'*.[103] Of course whilst the text of the *Dialogue* mentioned the Latin word *'Pulchritudo'* it was not intending to name the Sephirah, and there is no kabbalistic content in the *Vorlage* at all. Nonetheless this is what Widmanstetter finds here. The Prophet was misled, he says, by the bad faith of Jewish imposters *"a Iudaeis impostoribus pessima fide"*, but he was not the only one. Formerly they, the *"prava et perversa gens Hebraeorum"*, had similarly stimulated heresy within the Church. He mentions Saturninus, Basilides, Cerinthus, Hebion, Valentinus, Sabellius, Manes, Arius, Nestorius et *"alii fere innumeri.…"* This passage manages to attack the Jews, the Prophet and the heretics, but leaves the Kabbalah unscathed. Indeed, what they have in common is misunderstanding it.[104] As Widmanstetter similarly remarked in Annotation D28 *"Hoc loco depravatum est admirabile mysterium septem numerationum"*. Which is an admirable summary of his views. Of course the real issue here is the deity of Christ, but our

---

[100] D28.

[101] E18. This illustrates how even the most apparently intractable doctrines might be understood in another way and thus become acceptable to Orthodoxy.

[102] E3.

[103] Similarly E12.

[104] Similarly D14. In D17 Arius is guilty of confusing the *"supremam Sapientiam"* and the *"Sapientiam inferiorem"*.

argument is that that is precisely what Widmanstetter believed was taught by Sephirotic Doctrine.

Annotation E22 may be taken as a final demonstration of Widmanstetter's belief that the very core of the Christian faith was to be found in the Kabbalah. The lemma from Robert of Ketton's Epitome is again *"Christi pulchritudo"* and again there is no Kabbalistic content in the text. Yet Widmanstetter here finds Christian Truth breaking through in spite the Prophet: because the Kabbalists place the seat of the Messiah in the Sephirah Beauty (which is part of the Godhead) they show the Messiah to be Son of God.[105]

Widmanstetter was clearly able to find the Mysteries of the Christian Faith in Kabbalah. He was not alone in this, as we know. My argument is that there is simply no basis for the current estimate of Widmanstetter as a representative sceptic in these areas. It was only if the misunderstandings of 'Jews', infidels and heretics were received into Church doctrine that Kabbalah became 'a Wooden Horse'. Like Egidio and Postel, Widmanstetter was also prepared to offer a 'history of religions' approach to misunderstandings of the kabbalistic tradition. It will come as no surprise to discover that Widmanstetter not only believed that the kabbalistic Tradition was old enough to have been distorted by the Prophet, but also that the Ancients were beneficiaries thereof. It was from Kabbalah that Thales learnt that Water was the primary material, though his insights were attacked by the uncomprehending Aristotle.[106] But it was the Greek poets who tended most to corrupt the tradition *"ad voluptatem"*.[107] This again we can recognise as a commonplace amongst Christians interested in Kabbalah, and the theme of Hellenic corruption of an earlier Semitic tradition we have found in Annius da Viterbo, Egidio and Postel. But Widmanstetter here goes further: he exploited his knowledge of the arcane tradition to give an account not merely of Jewish, pagan and heretical misunderstandings, but also to offer a conceptually systematic critique of Islam as a misprision of Sephirotic doctrine. This interesting view is also found

---

[105] *"Christi pulchritudo] Imprudente, & invito Mahomete, veritas manifestatur. Nam et Cabalistae Messiae sedem in pulchritudis numeratione, quae ipsa est divinitas secundum eos, constituerunt. Quapropter Messiam filum Dei esse hoc loco diserte confitetur".*

[106] E16.

[107] See E72 and E9. D6 is characteristic as is also D42 The Mount Olympus of Classical mythology arises from a similar distortion. D22.

in Postel.[108] In this respect Widmanstetter's work may be seen as an interesting complement to Postel's writings on Islam.

The Conclusion to the Annotations

At the conclusion of the Annotations on the Epitome, Widmanstetter apologises for his excessive use of Kabbalah, but it was the only way to refute these three groups, Jews, Moslems and heretics: what they have in common is their deviation from true Sephirotic Doctrine.

We have established that the Annotation E33 upon which Scholem based his characterisation of Widmanstetter's beliefs about Kabbalah is quite misleading when taken without reference to the work of which it forms a part. We have examined that work with a view to exposing the use made therein of kabbalistic notions and have shown that Widmanstetter considered (as did our other similarly inclined Christian scholars) that Sephirotic Doctrines contained true though often misrepresented teaching of the Mysteries of the Christian Godhead and the Incarnation. Certainly Widmanstetter was not a man who believed *tout court* that Kabbalah entered the Church as a Trojan Horse.

Having establishing this more accurate perspective, we are now better placed to interpret the kabbalistic material in the *editio princeps*.

---

[108] See the translation of *Sefer ha-Bahir* in F. Secret, *Postelliana* (B. De Graaf, Niewkoop 1981) pg 21–111 at pg 82; "... *(ab hac parte Cabalae male intellecta Muhamedes dux et pseudo Messias decem tribuum Israel coepit introducere Alfurcani doctrinam in mundum agens de unitate Dei contra idololatras et contra Christianos...)*".

CHAPTER SIX

THE *EDITIO PRINCEPS*[1]

The *editio princeps* of the printed Syriac New Testament was, as we have said, the product of an extraordinary cooperation between a scribe sent by the Patriarch of Antioch, and two Western scholars working under the patronage of Ferdinand I who was looking to enhance the reputation of his newly reformed University and perhaps also (in the light of his confrontation with the Turks) taking an interest in Eastern Christians and the evangelisation of Moslems.[2] The Patriarch wanted

---

[1] *Liber Sacrosancti Evangelii De Iesu Christo Domino & Deo nostro. Reliqua hoc Codice comprehensa pagina proxima indicabit. Div. Ferdinandi rom. imperatoris designati iussu & liberalitate, characteribus & lingua Syra, Iesu Christo vernacula, Divino ipsius ore cōsecrata, et a Ioh. Euāgelista Hebraica dicta, Scriptorio Prelo diligēter Expressa...* A description of the Bible is given in T. H. Darlow and H. F. Moule, *Historical catalogue of the printed editions of Holy Scripture in the library of the British and Foreign Bible Society* (2 vols in 4) (BFBS, London 1903, reprinted New York, 1963) Vol. IV pg 1528–1529. Technically there appear to be two versions of the book, A & B, which have minor but unmistakable differences. These are described by Darlow and Moule, *loc. cit.* They conjecture there that type A are early circulation copies perhaps for presentation or those dispersed by Moses who we shall see sold his stock. The bulk of the copies (Version B), they believe, were published in 1562 and bear that date. I do not believe that anyone has previously connected the second edition with the information given in Bayerische Hauptstatarchiv Oefeleana 18/2 which we have described above and is summarised in O. Hartig, *Die Gründung der Münchener Hofbibliothek* pg 18–9. A letter there to Ferdinand from Albrecht 1 April 1561 indicates that Zimmermann was to be allowed all the remaining printed copies of the *editio princeps*, though not, of course, the type. It is not stated but one assumes that he was able to buy them from Widmanstetter's orphans. Surely the second edition then is the result of Zimmermann coming into possession of these remaining copies in 1561 and putting them on the market with a new title, border, date etc. in 1562.

[2] The type of the *editio princeps* is of a particular distinction and delicacy. There is no reason to doubt Postel's claim that it was he who supervised its production. We know of no one with comparable expertise. He was the only person from whom Plantin ever asked advice on cutting type, and he sent him directions on how Granjon should proceed. (See the letter of Postel to Plantin on Syriac ligatures 28 July 1569 in M. van Durme, *Supplement à la Correspondance de Christophe Plantin* (De Nederlandsche Boekhandel, Antwerp 1955) pg 111–112.) The letters were clearly based upon Moses's hand (E. Nestle "Zur Geschichte der syrischen Typen" Zeitschrift der Deutschen Morgenländischen Gesellschaft LXXV (1903) pg 16–17 for the first recognition of this). The steel punches for striking the matrices were engraved by Kaspar Kraft, a Swabian artist from Ellwangen: *"characteres syros ex Norici ferri acie sculptebat"* it says at the end of the book. The printer was Michael Zimmermann (Cymbermannus). After both working for the printer Aegidius Aquila (Adler) who is reported to have been interested in Oriental languages,

printed Syriac Gospel-books and New Testaments for use amongst his flock as scribal production in the East had never satisfied pastoral needs. It is evident that for his purposes the *editio princeps* had to be serviceable as a recognisably Eastern book with the necessary liturgical material and also printed to an acceptable standard of accuracy. Less straightforward are the motivations of the Western scholars. Much of our discussion so far has been dedicated to exposing and making intelligible the interests of Postel and Widmanstetter in the printing of the Syriac New Testament. We shall turn now to examine the *editio princeps* more closely to isolate in turn the features characteristic of East and West in this remarkable collaborative production.

The Eastern Book

The intended liturgical and pastoral use of the *editio princeps* by the Patriarch necessitated a book that retained essential features of a Syriac manuscript. The canon, order of books, and the Peshitta text[3]

---

these two had a distinguished partnership that from 1553 produced books in German, Italian, Spanish, Latin as well as Hebrew and Arabic. Theirs was the first Arabic in Germany and preceded that produced in Heidelberg by 27 years. Zimmermann died in 1565. Kraft also worked with the printer Raphael Hofhalter until he fled Vienna for Hungary in 1565. After this we lose all trace of Kraft. The two are discussed in Georg Fritz, *Geschichte der Wiener Schriftgiessereien* (H. Berthold Messinglinienfabrik, Vienna 1924) pg 20–24. Postel left Vienna in May 1554 before printing actually began, though he had evidently done what was necessary for the felicitous engraving of the punches. Matthew was completed (as is evident from the colophons) on 14 February 1555 and all Four Gospels on 18 May. The Pauline Epistles were printed by 18 July and Acts (which follows the Epistles in the order of the books) by 14 August. The final colophon is dated 27 September. Sebastian Brock has drawn attention to what appears to be a delightful competition for praise for the lion's share of the work conducted by Moses and Widmanstetter in the successively appearing colophons: "The Development of Syriac Studies" in ed. K. J. Cathcart, *The Edward Hincks Bicentenary Lectures* (Univ. Coll. Dublin, Dublin 1994) pg 94–113 on pg 96–97.

[3] The text of the Gospels was printed from two manuscripts that Widmanstetter in the *Dedicatio* calls *"vetustissima"* and in the Colophon *"Singularis fidei exemplaria"*. Of the text of the Pauline Epistles, Acts and the Catholic Epistles nothing specific is said other than the following which follows the title of the Three Epistles: *"Reliquae S.S.S. Petri, Johannis, et Judae Epistolae una cum Apocalypsi, etsi extant apud Syros, tamen in exemplaribus quae sequuti sumus defuerunt"*. For the Gospels Widmanstetter had whatever he had received from Teseo, his Sienese transcripts from the Ptolemean Library and Moses's manuscript that Masius said in the Dedication to his *Grammatica Linguae Syriacae* (Pg 4) had been copied at Mosul: *"...ille librarius, qui in urbe Mozal ad flumen Tigrim exemplar illud Novi Testamneti scripsit; de quo id optimi & benignissimi Caesaris Ferdinandi liberalitate & Mosis Mardeni industria typis est expressum..."*. (This remark is made in regret that the manuscript did not have a *massorah* and is discussed further below). It may be that the manuscript Gospels

are Syriac.[4] The text runs from right to left, and, to Western eyes, the book opens from the back. The textual divisions are naturally those of the Syriac-speaking Church. Thus characteristically a page from the body of this bible has no Western language except for supplementary Latin pagination at the top of the page and foliation at the bottom. The titles of the books are in Syriac, as are sub-headings and lectionary markings. Titles of books and subscriptions are printed in an older character known as Estrangela.[5] The appended list of feasts tabulates

---

dedicated to Ferdinand by Moses and now in Vienna give the text of his manuscript. Teseo in his *Introductio* quotes Mat 6. 9–13; 22. 1–14; Luke 1. 46–55; John 1. 16 and 17 and presumably used his own manuscript for these. However, in Matthew 6. 5 he has a unique and surprising liturgical reading from the Lord's Prayer: "our debts and our sins" which is certainly not in the *editio princeps*. Gwilliam thought that the manuscript that Postel had brought from Damascus and whose readings were employed in the Antwerp Polyglot and collected by Raphelengius differed so markedly from the *editio princeps* that it was not employed in its text: [G. H. Gwilliam] "The Ammonian Sections, Eusebian Canons and the Harmonizing Tables in the Syriac Tetraevangelium" in ed. S. R. Driver et al., *Studia Biblica et Ecclesiastica* (Clarendon, Oxford 1890) Vol. 2 pg 241–272, pg 267–268. Postel, however, tells us that he had collated his manuscript with that of Moses and they were identical: Bibliothèque nationale, fonds lat. 3402 f. 91: *"Dolet quidem vehementer quod exemplaria illa Syriaca quae attuli tibi non sint data sicut et promissa. Sed sis omnino certissimus ne Iodo quidem uno differe ab eo exemplari Mosis Mesopotamii, quo usi sumus ad emittendum typis. Nam una cum eo contuleram meum, eo quod antiquius videbatur suum esse, et ne litera quidem una differre comperi, licet meum exemplar Damasci sim nactus, suum autem Meredinii sit scriptum, in media Mesopotamia"*. I think we must conclude that for the Gospels at least Postel was being inaccurate. The remainder of the New Testament came from Moses's manuscript but the second manuscript hinted at in the title of the Three Epistles (*"in exemplaribus"*) must be the Damascus manuscript of Postel unless there were other texts of which we are totally ignorant. J. Adler, *De Versione Simplici* pg 32–41 had argued for similarities between the *editio princeps* and Nestorian manuscripts but these were dismissed by Gwilliam, *op. cit.* pg 268. The *editio princeps* does not have the famous Nestorian reading at Hebrews 2. 9 (χωρις Θεου), on which: S. P. Brock "Hebrews 2. 9B in Syriac Tradition" Novum Testamentum XXVII 3 (1983) pg 236–244, and the characters and vocalisation are Western or Maronite.

[4] This is not the place for a discussion of the Syriac text of the New Testament. A good introduction to the Syriac versions is Bruce M. Metzger, *The Early Versions of the New Testament their Origin, Transmission and Limitations* (OUP, Oxford 1977) which may be updated by articles and bibliography to be found in ed. B. D. Ehrman & M. W. Holmes, *The Text of the New Testament in Contemporary Research Essays on the Status Quaestionis* (Eerdmans, Grand Rapids 1995). On the morphology of the word 'Peshitta': E. Nestle "Zum Namen der syrischen Bibelübersetzung Peschitta." in Zeitschrift der Deutschen Morgenländischen Gesellschaft XLVII (1893) pg 157–159 and the article by E. König with the same title in the same volume at pg 316–319. The word is a past participle of the verb PŠṬ 'stretched out'. The sense may be either 'simple', or 'widespread' in the sense of *'Vulgate'*.

[5] This is a rather square script, and a calligraphic 14 pt type has been used. A more recent script called in Syriac *'Serta'* is used for the main text of the *editio princeps*. This is generally 12 pt but with some larger 16 pt on the errata sheet. (16 pt also appears in the *Linguae Syriacae... Prima Elementa.*). It is also called 'Maronite' or 'Jacobite'.

the lections for the whole of the liturgical year. There are no Western verse-divisions (which we owe to Robert Estienne) in the text although discreet marginal Arabic numerals mark the Western chapter-breaks. The book with its clear and confident type could have been read immediately and serviceably as a Syriac Bible by literate members of the Patriarch's flock. They would not have been distracted by extraneous and incomprehensible Latin intrusions. Comparison with the early Syriac manuscripts made for Western scholars that we have previously examined is here instructive. Whereas an early page of a Psalter like Vat. sir 9 which Elias copied in 1518 with Latin Psalm headings and numbers offers considerable guidance and orientation to the Western novice following the text, a page of the *editio princeps*, except in those minor particulars just mentioned, does not. It is a *Syriac* book.

Book headings are traditional and colophons preserve a characteristic feature of the manuscript book. We have seen that they mark the chronology of the printing of the book. They may also indicate (they would certainly facilitate) an intention of separate binding and distribution of the New Testament books in the East where a manuscript would not necessarily be expected to contain all the books of the New Testament canon. This consideration also allows us to imagine the possible circulation in the East of the essential textual matter of the Syriac Scriptural books without the encumbrance of the Latin prefatory material.

Such a consideration however should not obscure the fact that page-layout and foliation indicate that the completed book was designed to combine inseparably the features of the Syriac manuscript book, now produced by moveable type, and the more familiar features of a Western humanist book. There is a judicious bi-lingualism in book-headings and colophons and in the list of feasts (where Syriac and Latin appear on opposite sheets of the openings) but the East is spared much of the dedicatory and prefatory material that appears only in the Latin. The title page combines a splendid printed evocation of a Syriac manuscript hand with a Latin title. The motto is given in both Syriac and Latin. The prophylactic verses given in Syriac on all the illustrative plates (except the Sephirotic Tree!) allow a customary pious Eastern reading of the images, even where the 'Austrian' imagery conveys different messages to Western eyes and must in Eastern circumstances have remained mute.[6]

---

[6] The plates cleverly blend Syriac and Hapsburg *motifs* and some occur several times

On the other hand the beginning of the book with its Privilege and Dedication would fall quite naturally on sixteenth-century humanist eyes—once it was realised that the book had to be read backwards.[7] The Dedication, which is given the alternative title *"De illustribus signis Christianae Religionis brevi tempore universo terrarum Orbi propagandae"* is however no mere predictable nicety, but one of the most significant texts of Renaissance scholarly awareness. It provides not only the basis for our knowledge of Widmanstetter's own Oriental learning, but has been the source for much of what we know of the whole history of Oriental Studies in the sixteenth century. In this connection we have already frequently cited it. More specifically the *Dedicatio* presents Widmanstetter's view of the significance of his bible. Our preparatory considerations of the context and nature of early Syriac studies will enable us fully to appreciate the place of this remarkable bible in the mystical and eschatological ideology of its time. They will also allow us to detect the remarkable tendentiousness of Widmanstetter's *Dedicatio*.

---

with variations. A Cross with Syriac trellis work with a Hapsburg eagle and shield appears three times with prophylactic Syriac texts. A wooden cross in Chi form with three crowns, hearts and ΒΑΣΙΛΕΥΣ running from centre several times has the text: *"Cor Regis in manu Domini"* but there are no Syriac features. A Cross with Hapburg insignia, Lion and Dragon, has the Syriac and Latin text: *"In hoc signo vinces & conculcabis Leonem & Draconem"*. This plate with its text that was generally understood to speak of the victory over heresy occurs three times. There is a pièta at the foot of the Cross with the Instruments of Christ's Torture, townscape, Hapsburg crown and shield and Syriac text. Moses was, no doubt, responsible for these Syriac features and the *ensemble* of the plates make an interesting mixture of Eastern and Western features.

[7] The Privilege was for three years within Ferdinand's realms, preserving the characters from *sculptorio fusoriove opere imitari*—i.e. from being copied in woodcut or cast. (The search for the type documented by Oefleana 18/2 appears to have begun in 1560 when the Privilege had expired.) The text itself is preserved from reproduction in Hebrew type: *"aut etiam Hebraeorum usitatis formulis denuo exprimere"*. Tremellius had publication of his Syriac New Testament in this form imposed upon him because of his lack of Syriac type. However it was clearly felt to be a desirable form of publication, mainly for the evangelisation of Jews, by Guy Lefèvre de la Boderie and others. In this case Widmanstetter indicates in his introductory remarks to the Calendar of Festal Readings (KK3) that at the time he himself intended to produce such an edition: *"Hosce Novi Testamenti libros Hebraeorum literarum usitatis formis (dummodo vos consilii huius mei aeque ac laboris iam exantlati approbatores habeam) exscriptos, propediem edi atque pervulgari curabo"*. The novelty of reading the book backwards is marked by an appropriately placed poem to Philipp Gundelius *"Cur hic liber fine a Latinis diverso claudatur. Carmen J. A. W."* and a short reply. The learned conceits of the poem require the gloss: *"Ianus pro Noacho"*.

The Dedicatio

The *Dedicatio*[8] begins with a commonplace we recognise from Egidio
and Giustiniani and Postel (though no less important for its currency)
drawing a parallel between two contemporary wonders: the geographical
discovery over the previous sixty years that had carried at least a superficial knowledge of the Gospel all over the globe; and the concomitant
and equally providential growth in knowledge of the semitic languages
to the extent that no University or scholar worthy of the name was
complete without Hebrew to supplement their Latin and Greek. Current
geographical knowledge, especially since the crossing of the Ocean by
Magellan in 1522 had not been paralleled in the thirty-nine centuries
since Noah (or Janus). Similarly the new knowledge of semitic languages
went some way to undoing the curse of Babel, for never in the history
of the Church had there been so many in Europe skilled not only in
Latin, but also in Greek, Hebrew and Chaldaean.

As if to reinforce his point Widmanstetter was able to list very quickly
those of the Patristic period or Middle Ages who had pretensions and
sometimes expertise in these areas. He reviewed the great Byzantine
scholars who brought their Greek scholarship to the West, and those
who had pioneered the teaching of Hebrew: Reuchlin in Germany;
Aelius Antonius Nebrensis in Spain, together with Stunica who also
read Arabic. Not to forget the Italians, he subsequently mentioned
the Siennese family of Lactantius Ptolemaeus and his sons. (It was,
we recall in Ptolemaeus's Library that he had discovered his Syriac
manuscripts). He recalled his own teacher and colleague in Vienna,
Jakob Jonas. This contemporary note allowed Widmanstetter (still within
a providential perspective) to pass to the history of his own semitic
studies from their beginnings, by way of his initiation into kabbalistic
arcana and his association with Egidio da Viterbo. As a precursor of
this Europe-wide scholarly movement, Widmanstetter recalls the require-
ments of the Council of Vienne for instruction in Semitic languages
in the same way as we have seen Postel do. He mentions the Spanish
glories of the Complutensian Polyglot, but concedes that Paris, Oxford,
London and Louvain have all played their part. The breadth of the

---

[8] I shall not give page references in the description of this short text. For a helpful
general discussion of the importance of dedications to sixteenth-century authors L. Voet,
The Golden Compasses... (P. Vangeendt & Co, Amsterdam 1972) Vol. II pg 283–290.

movement is truly European. Nor is this any accident, Providence has contrived that all Provinces of the Latin Church shall take part in this great linguistic movement.

Widmanstetter then consolidated his presentation of the significance of semitic language study with a numerical-prophetic calculation that illustrates the very precise nature of eschatological calculations that lie behind Widmanstetter's more general phrases. Like Egidio and Postel, Widmanstetter worked within a repeatedly (re-)calculated eschatological framework within which Oriental Studies played a 'salvation-historical' role.[9] As with the other prophetic expositions in the *Dedicatio*, this was not a conceit but serious and learned exposition of prophecies currently coming to pass.

The foundations of Syriac and Arabic study (the pairing is now familiar to us) were laid by Leo X at the Lateran Council when Teseo Ambrogio was taught Syriac. Immediately after this *démarche*, Widmanstetter was able to introduce himself into the story. In a quite memorable passage enlivened by the pen picture of the venerable old scholar, and the very words of the commission, Widmanstetter told how in 1529 he met the old Teseo who had devoted fifteen years to his Syriac studies and was looking for someone to take over the sacred task.[10]

Widmanstetter accepted the charge. He received a few hours tuition and was given the Gospels in Syriac. The history of Syriac studies becomes at this point Widmanstetter's own intellectual history: he tells of his discovery in Siena four years later of four Syriac Gospel books *"una cum Ephremi & Iacobi Syrorum opusculis nonnullis"* and also of his meeting with Simeon from the Lebanon. Widmanstetter, however,

---

[9] Widmanstetter noted that at the beginning of the century that saw these two wonders (geographical exploration, and increased linguistic knowledge) fell the beginning of the thirty-first jubilee of the Christian Church (i.e. $50 \times 30 = 1500$). This is to be interpreted typologically by referring the age of Christ at the time of key events in his life to current events in the life of his mystical body, the Church. Now Christ was baptised at thirty, which by the calculation above gives us the year 1500. After his baptism, Christ was tempted by Satan. Widmanstetter finds that the period of 38 years between Magellan in 1522 and the end of the Jubilee in 1550 represents Satan's attempt to tempt the Church. The Church however will thwart his plans by preaching in the newly recovered languages. In the current year, which has seen the completion of the thirty-first Jubilee and has progressed a tenth of the way through the thirty-second (i.e. $50 \times 31 = 1550 + (50 \div 10 = 5) = 1555$), Widmanstetter seems to anticipate a preaching of Eternal Salvation for two years.

[10] *"utinam obveniat mihi aliquando prompto paratoque ingenio vir, qui sermonem hunc Iesu Christi sanctissimis labris consecratum, posteris tamquam per manus tradendum, nam aestas mihi prope iam exacta est, a me accipere velit"*.

does not lose sight of the complementary study of Arabic. After mention of Leo Eliberitanus and Egidio, he tells us of Seripando and his generosity in allowing him access to Egidio's books. He speaks also of his attempt to have Syriac and Arabic taught under Clement VII and of the support he received in this from Nicolaus Schonberg. The story is, of course, the story of Widmanstetter.

Widmanstetter then gives an account of his diplomatic career and mentions his strife with Gumppenberg. He desired no more than to be able to get on with his studies. Turning to the present Widmanstetter wrote of his providential (*"divinities"*) meeting with Moses who had been sent to him and of Ferdinand's commission of the *editio princeps*. Addressing Ferdinand, he describes the purpose of the edition: to provide Gospel books for the many dispersed Syriac speaking Christians whose lack of these has almost extinguished their religion.[11]

At this point Postel appears *'intervenit Guilemus Postellus'* whom Widmanstetter praises. He notes his abilities in Syriac and Arabic and says that he was of no small assistance to him. These generous though imprecise few lines are followed by a page devoted to an account of *'what happened to Postel'*. Evidently Widmanstetter felt some explanation for Postel's departure and flight to Venice was necessary, though Ferdinand can hardly have cherished the memory. It cannot be claimed that Widmanstetter here is not well-motivated: he had no doubt been embarrassed and claimed that the whole business had caused him inconvenience. He may well not have been eager to emphasise the now controversial Postel's role in the production of his edition.

On the other hand it cannot be overlooked that Postel had received no notice earlier in the *Dedicatio*, and (like Masius) was given no part to play in Widmanstetter's account of the tradition of Oriental scholarship begun by Leo X at the Vatican Council. Postel's early association with Teseo, his printed works, his Syriac manuscripts, and his work with these are all ignored. Postel's prior collaboration with Moses in preparation of a Syriac edition is not mentioned nor Postel's possible role in sending Moses to Widmanstetter. One consequence of all this is that we are in fact altogether ignorant of Postel's contribution to the preparation and printing of the *editio princeps*, though particularly in the latter respect

---

[11] *"...ut Asiaticis Christianis, qui vetere Syrorum lingua partim vulgo, partim in sacris tantum utuntur, eorumque incredibilis multitudo, ut Syri ipsi affirmant, ad finem usque Orbis illius dispersa ob Evangelicorum librorum indigentiam, praeter Baptismum, vix ulla religionis vestigia retinent, immortale hoc beneficium tribuere posses".*

it is difficult to believe it was negligible. Postel later complained about this. Another consequence is that all Postel's work on the Syriac New Testament since 1537 that we have traced above has previously gone unrecognised. Widmanstetter was a competitive Renaissance scholar as well as possessed of a notion of his own providential significance. He has succeeded in imposing his version of the story upon the history of the *editio princeps*, principally through this *Dedicatio*. It is only our cumulative and in part newly-recovered knowledge of Postel's previous and subsequent contributions to the production of Syriac Bibles that allows us detect Widmanstetter's tendentiousness.

Widmanstetter presents the *Dedicatio* as the conclusion of a project conceived forty years previously by the highest authority of the Church at the Vatican Council. The work had been taken up and laid aside many times because of the vicissitudes of Widmanstetter's life, but was now *"Divini Spiritus vi peculari"* offered to Ferdinand. The struggle had been Widmanstetter's, and, a few unavoidable compliments notwithstanding, he the providential tool that had executed Teseo's commission. Thus it fell to Ferdinand, as King of the Romans, and thus legitimate protector of the Latin Church, to renew knowledge of the Gospels in the East. This book was to supply the Syrians' need. Widmanstetter then hinted that Ferdinand might also finance an Arabic New Testament and praised the missionary work of the Society of Jesus.

The Festal Lections

The Eastern and Western elements of the *editio princeps* are brought together in the parallel pages in Syriac and Latin of the list of the festivals and their lections at the end of the book.[12] Widmanstetter wrote an explanatory essay to introduce these to the Western reader. He began by summarising the significance of his edition: the new Bible was suitable for the conversion of the Jews; it allowed the Latin Church to experience the language of Christ for the first time; it would promote Catholic concord; and it would bring the peoples of the East back to the bosom of the Church. Looking to the future he hoped Moses would

---

[12] It should perhaps be mentioned that the *editio princeps* shows no sign of the Ammonian Sections nor the Eusebian canons: [G. H. G. William] "The Ammonian sections, Eusebian Canons and the Harmonizing Tables in the Syriac Tetraevangelium" in ed. S. R. Driver *et al. Studia Biblica et Ecclesiastica* (Clarendon, Oxford 1890) Vol. 2 pg 241–272, pg 242.

return to the East to bring back the 'missing books' of the Western
canon and a Targum and the Decrees of the Ancient Church Councils
that would promote Church unity.

Similar in intention to this proposed recovery of ancient Eastern
copies of Conciliar Decrees, was Widmanstetter's presentation in Latin
of all the Feasts in the lectionary. He is not particularly interested in
the lections. He does however offer a factual description of the feasts
of the whole of the liturgical year in addition to the list itself.[13] This
was to prove the antiquity and universality precisely of such liturgical
practices that were being assailed by the Protestants. We have seen
an interest in Eastern liturgy on Masius's part and Guy Lefèvre de la
Boderie was also to edit some Syriac liturgical material. Both of these
were conscious of the polemical possibilities of ancient or Eastern
liturgical evidence, whatever other interests they may have entertained.
This lectionary material here will reappear in the Antwerp Polyglot and
in the 1584 Paris edition of the Syriac New Testament. But the full
force of the polemic was to break about Tremellius's head when he
produced a Syriac New Testament that omitted the lectionary material
Widmanstetter had so prominently displayed.[14]

A kabbalist's bible?

We have stressed not only the serious and non-trivial interest in Kabbalah shown by the early scholars—Egidio, Masius, Postel and Widmanstetter—but also the suitability of the Syriac as well as the Hebrew
script for the carrying of such arcana. It remains for us now to consider
the part played by kabbalistic interests in the production of the Bible

---

[13] The fundamental work is A. Baumstark, *Festbrevier und Kirchenjahr der syrischen Jakobiten*
(F. Schöningh, Paderborn 1910). Codex Phillips 1388 acquired in 1865 by the Royal
Library in Berlin has a lectionary system discussed by Arthur Allgeier, "Cod. syr. Phil-
lipps 1388 und seine ältesten Perikopenvermerke" Oriens Christianus (N. S.) VI (1916)
pg 147–152 and also his "Cod. syr. Phillipps 1388 in Berlin und seine Bedeutung für
die Geschichte der Peshitta" Oriens Christianus (3rd series) VII (1932) pg 1–15. Hs.
Sach 349 also in Berlin has its lectionary material discussed in O. Heiming, *Syrische
'Eniane und Griechische Kanones* (Verlag der Aschendorffschen Verlagsbuchhandlung,
Münster in Westf. 1932).

[14] This is discussed extensively in Robert J. Wilkinson "Emmanuel Tremellius'
1569 Edition of the Syriac New Testament" Journal of Ecclesiastical History 58/1
January 2007 pg 9–25.

itself. There is no hint of Kabbalah at all in Syriac tradition, so any kabbalistic material detected is a product of the Western scholars.

We may begin with a note placed by Widmanstetter at the beginning of the book in the *Authoris Editionis huius Obtestatio ad Lectorem*. This comprises four notes that assert Widmanstetter's orthodoxy, appeal to Jerome's authority for the semitic origin of Matthew, apologise for typographic errors and the absence of the *Historiam Adulterae apud Iohannem*, and also warn against reading Syriac in ignorance of Targumic Aramaic as if it was Hebrew to the detriment of Catholic understanding.[15] The third note deserves to be considered in detail because it specifically discourages ignorant kabbalistic manipulation of the text.[16] Clearly Widmanstetter was able to imagine precisely this sort of manipulation of the text. The presence of the warning—nothing more than a *"ne existimanto"*—in a series of observations specifically designed to deflect criticism from Widmanstetter need not be taken too seriously as an indication of his rejection of the techniques. One might consider the note almost an incitement to the practices it counsels against. Yet the note does make distinctions characteristic of Widmanstetter and need not be cynical. Popular Jewish ignorance is set against *"admirabilis de Divino auditu Scientiae"*. This is precisely the teaching Widmanstetter in the *Dedicatio* recalled hearing when he had sat at the feet of the aged Dattylus.[17] The contrast between the value of the tradition and vulgar distortion is of course the distinction he drew in the Annotations of the *Mahometis…Dialogo*. Whether or not Widmanstetter approved of *notarikon* etc. as tools of New Testament exposition, he was committed to the deep mysteries of the kabbalistic tradition.

---

[15] *"Interpretes in Grammaticis Hebraeorum praeceptionibus etymisque tantum versati, atque Syrothargumicae proprietatis imperiti rudesque, a temeraria distortaque Syriacarum vocum explicatione, catholicaeque intelligentiae deprevatione abstinento"*.

[16] *"Calculatores Notariique Cabalistae, admirabilis de Divino auditu Scientiae ignari, spinosis & exilibus literarum subductionibus, syllabarum aut verborum collocationibus variis, numeris concisis, ieiunisque ratiocinationibus idem heic sibi licere, quod in Testamenti Veteris libris, anceps incertumque de Salute sua Iudaeorum vulgus Sapientibus suis attribuit, ne existimanto"*.

[17] *"Mar. Datyli Hebraei, quem ego arcanos de Divino auditu libros Taurini in summa eius senectute subtilissime interpretantem audivi"*. This positive evaluation of the tradition should of course be set in the balance when Widmanstetter's criticism of this same Dattylus's teaching as constituting a Trojan Horse is evaluated.

The Crucifix and the Sephirotic Tree

Nothing can make this point more forcefully than the plate of the Crucifix and the Sephirotic Tree that appears in John's Gospel. The course of our review of early Syriac studies to this point has had as one of its motivations the necessity of explaining the presence of this remarkable image in a Syriac Bible.

Though the plate is as far as I know unique, a partial parallel may be found in a *Liber cabalisticus* described in Pal. lat. 1950 f. 1–59v *Catalogus Voluminum hebraeorum Bibliothecae Palatinae*.[18] That diagram that shows the head and arms of a cross, marked with the first three Sephirot.[19]

The Plate in the *editio princeps* is preceded by an explanatory Latin text at the beginning of the Gospel of John f. 101: John was asked by the bishops of Asia Minor to write of Christ's divine origin. He went up into a mountain near Ephesus with Prochorus [20] and there heard a voice declaring "In the beginning was the Word etc." which was to begin his Gospel. John had been present at the crucifixion and thus appreciated the connection between the sacrament of the wounds of Christ and the Sephirot.[21]

---

[18] The *Catalogus* is in Cassuto, *I Manoscritti Palatini Ebraici delle Bibliotheca Apostolica Vaticana e loro Storia* (BAV, Vatican City 1935) pg 130–155. The diagram is on pg 135.

[19] The *Catalogus* has: "*Der Autor sagt, has tres numerationes, vel virtutues divinitatis, esse aprentes reliquarum numerationum divinitatis. Et addit:* כתר *Kether, Corona, est caput;* הכמה*, Chochma, Sapientia, et* בינה*, Intellegentia, sunt bracchia. Fortasse hac forma Christus crucifixus est, ut bracchia et corpus ita composita sanctam Trinitatem Deitatis significarint*".

[20] Prochoros was considered by the fifth century *Acta Johannis* to have written down the Gospel at John's dictation: eds E Junod et J.-D. Kaestli, *Acta Iohannis* (Corpus Christianorum, Brepols 1983) Vol 2 pg 743–744. Elsewhere Papias is said to have done this: J. H. Bernard, *International Critical Commentary St. John* (T & T Clark, Edinburgh 1928) vol. 2 pg lviii–lix. In the plate we are considering, the evangelist himself is apparently writing down the revelation.

[21] "*Iohannes Iesu Christi Apostolus et Evangelista, Haereticis Ecclesiam turbantibus ab Asiae Episcopis rogatus, ad Divinam ipsius generationem scribendam animum adpulit: solennique ieiunio indicto, atque adhibito Prochoro socio, montem Epheso propinquum, aetate confecto iam corpore, ascendit: ibique vocem tonitruum & fulgurium fragore elisam, atque In Principio erat Verbum & Verbum erat apud Deum, & Deus erat Verbum resonantem, auribus castissimis excepit & Evangelicae historiae reliqua deinceps est prosequutus. Nam cum ex omnibus Apostolis solus ad crucem constitisset, Christumque peregrino supplicii genere, praeterque morem legitimum Hebraicae gentis, manibus pedibusque transverbatis in ea distractum eiusque sanctissimum pectus vulnere saucium attente spectasset, Omnia altissima & Crucis, & praeter caetera innumerabilia, quinque insignium vulnerum sacramenta: videlicit, Individuam in redimito spinis capite Trinitatem, in manu dextra Bonitatis, in sinistra Severitatis, in utraque pede utriusque subalternum symbolum, ac demum in aperto latre Pulchritudinis divinae Calicem Lunarem ad se attrahentis, atque sanguine & aqua manantis Notam & universe in toto adflicti corporis habitu, Dextra Sinistraque Dei, eorumque Emanationes*

The plate thus displays the revelation to the Evangelist John of the Mystery of the Incarnation that stands at the head of his Gospel through the Five Wounds that he alone of the Apostles had observed at Calvary.[22]

The Plate itself carries the words of the beginning of John's Gospel, and also *"Qui expansis in cruce manibus traxisti omnia ad te Secula"*,[23] that are not identified. I owe to Dr Sebastian Brock the observation of their similarity to Apostolic Tradition §4 *"extendit manus suas cum pateretur, ut patientes liberaret qui in te speraverunt."*[24] The Titulus of the Cross carries יצמה which is the Hebrew equivalent of the Latin acronym I. N. R. I.

The designer of the plate is unknown. Whilst we have been at pains to argue that Widmanstetter under whose direction the *editio princeps* passed through the press would have been sympathetic and understanding of such a plate, there is I think a probability that it was designed by Postel. This is not only because one may easily document Postel's

---

oculis animaque diligentissime potuit contemplari. Quapropter Iohanni virgini, pectoris Divini alumno, tantorumque mysteriorum spectatori, explicandae Christi Iesu divinitatis cura necessaria, a tribus Evangelicae historiae providentia fuit transmissa".

[22] The devotion to the Wounds of Christ goes back to the twelfth and thirteenth centuries. Medieval missals contained a special Mass called the Golden Mass in honour of Christ's Wounds that was believed to have been composed by John the Evangelist and revealed to Boniface II. The five large beads of the Dominican Rosary and the associated Paternosters are intended to honour the Five Wounds. The feast in honour of the Wounds was celebrated in Vienna by the fifteenth century. See further: *The Catholic Encyclopaedia* (Encyclopaedia Press, 1913) s.v.

[23] "Thou, who spreading out thy hands upon the Cross, drew all the ages to Thyself"

[24] R. H. Connolly, *The So-Called Egyptian Church Order and Derived Documents* (CUP, Cambridge 1916) gives an account of this complex text. The Latin text appears pg 174–194. Dr Brock generously pointed out the appearance of the motif of the outstretched hands in several Patristic texts: Irenaeus *Dem.* 46 ("Jesus, who delivered Israel from Amalek by the extension of his arms leads and raises us to the Kingdom of his Father"); Athanasius *de Inc.* 25. 3 (PG 25. 140) ("With one hand he will draw the Ancient People, with the other those of the Gentiles, and will join both in himself"); Cyril of Jerusalem *Cat.* 13. 28 (PG 33 805b) ("...in order to embrace the extremities of the World"): *Acts of Andrew* A 14 ("...in order to gather the World into One"). He also drew my attention to the Syrian Orthodox Good Friday Service: "He stretched out his hands on the honoured Cross and took hold of the four quarters of the World" in ed. Mar Athanasius Y Samuel, *The Book of the Church Festivals* (Lodi, NJ 1984) pg 216–7 (Cp 222–223, 224–225, 232–233). The Sephirotic tree here is recalled by Postel's pupil Guy Lefèvre de la Boderie in the *Ad Sacrarum Linguarum Studiosum Lectorem...Praefatio* to the Syriac New Testament in the Antwerp Polyglot. Noting that the direction and *ductus* of the Syriac script leads scribes to make the Sign of the Cross, he quotes the legend from this plate: *"Imitati Syri in depingendis suarum litterarum notis, sacrosanctam cruces mysticam figuram compleverunt, in memoriam illius qui sublatus in eo, manibus expansis, universa ad se traxit saecula".*

familiarity and interest in this Sephirotic material. The translation of *Bahir* of 1547 with its interpolated exposition of the mysteries of Christian Doctrine illustrates these clearly: the later part of the book deals with the Sephirot and, moreover, refers the reader to Postel's other great exposition of the matters in the *Candelabrum*. There is in addition a text that I believe has hitherto been overlooked as a claim that it was Postel who conceived the plate. In *De Magia orientali* f. 107v Postel writes mentioning the editio princeps and its Sephirotic Tree as his work.[25]

We need not delay over the fascinating story of the exiled Englishman and his enthusiasm for kabbalistic diagrams,[26] nor even Postel's pressing eschatological calculations[27] which make this passage so fascinating. What is apparent is an unmistakable claim that Postel got the plate prepared *(curaverat)* and a clear description of what it is.

The plate relates the Crucifix and the wounds of Christ to the Sephirotic Tree, taking advantage of the fact that the Sephirot often symbolise parts of the body.[28] This latter symbolism is clearly dominant in the link between the Sephirotic Tree and the genitals. The highest three Sephirot, below the orb of the *Ein-Soph* are understood as the Trinity and surmounted by a Cross. They are linked as the introduc-

---

[25] "*...nostrae et vere ultimae foelicitatis ideam post illam quam Guil. Postellus Regiorum Parisiis lectorum decanus et Venetiis iam pridem in Candelabro Mosaico hebraice Venetiis seu Romae novae, et Viennae Austriae in impressione Novi Testamenti in syriaca Iesu Christi lingua pridem ante curaverat cum 10 divinorum nominum virtutibus unde 10 coeli et decalogi coeterarumque sacrarum virtus ordo et dispositio pendent Thomas Copleus vir vere Ecclesiae catholicae Miles Britannicus Berithanus etiam in aere procudi in suo exilio curavit in universi huius mundi inferioris subsidium, ut simus omnes parati in isto Babylonici mundi fine cuius finis iam a 1565 salutis anno ad 1584 per 19 annorum intervallum parasceve multe facte sunt divinitus, sed nil potentius ad asserendam victoriosam rationis humanae potentiam demonstrandam quam est essentiae substantiae ipsius Regis totum genus humanum judicantis praesentia*". The text is F. lat 3402 in the Bibliothèque nationale. See: F. Secret, *Bibliographie* pg 90–93. Folio 107 gives the date as 1580. The text may be found in F. Secret, *Postelliana* (B. De Graaf, Niewkoop 1981) pg 240–272 at pg 271–272. The last page of the *editio princeps* carries, quite appropriately for the last page of a New Testament, the motto *Finis Praecepti Charitas*. Postel's correspondence with Plantin about David Joris and the Family of Love (CPI 80–81; 82–84; 154–155) suggests that this may have been a favourite motto of Postel and thus another mark of his influence on the *editio princeps*.

[26] Sir Thomas Copley (1514–1584) was one of the Elizabethan Catholic exiles: *Dict. Nat. Biog* s. v. *Berithanus* is Postel's emithological concoction linking *Britannica* with ברת.

[27] We may compare the interest in Hunt Add. E. D. (Roll), a copy of a Sephirotic Tree in a manuscript of Egidio given to Bodley in 1608 and discussed above in connection with Egidio's books.

[28] For Sephirot and parts of the body in Postel: Kuntz, *Postel* pg 90.

tory text describes to the head. The third Sephirah, *Bonitas*, is joined to both of the hands to symbolise both the Goodness and Severity of God (taken from Romans 11.22). The Sephirot also symbolise the Patriarchs, and Abraham's interrupted sacrifice of Isaac (Genesis 22) is represented as a typological anticipation of the Passion. Below that is Jacob's dream at Bethel of the ladder ascending to Heaven (Genesis 28) used typologically of Christ in John's Gospel (1.51). Thus the mechanism of the Passion and the opening of the Kingdom of Heaven are included in the Sephirot. The Sun and the Moon are joined to Christ's wounded side as the introductory text suggests and structure the lower Sephirot. The pillars are perhaps those of Solomon's Temple, and the penultimate Sephirah may either show Christ creating and supporting the world or carrying its sins. Certainly the Chalice of the Mass marks the point of contact between upper and lower worlds. The lower world is clearly represented by the orb and the Zodiac band and set in front of it is the Menorah that Postel expounded at length. At the foot of the Cross is a sacrifice, representing perhaps the ram provided by the Lord to replace Isaac in Abraham's sacrifice. The Evangelist's symbol, the eagle, is present wearing a Hapsburg shield on its breast.

We may also, at the risk of overstating our case consider the title page of the *editio princeps* which carries the motto (first in Syriac in red and then in Latin typographically so:) *PRINCIPIUM sapientiae timor Domini.* This quotation, from Proverbs 9.10, may perhaps be a reference to the Sephirah *Sapientia* and for that reason be typographically emphasised.[29]

The Syriacae Linguae... Principia Elementa

In 1556 Widmanstetter published a small quarto Syriac alphabet of 28 leaves that is often found bound with the New Testament.[30] Again the

---

[29] I refer the reader to the several quotations from Postel's work cited above and below, and also generally to: Marie Thérèse d'Alverney "Quelque Aspects du Symbolisme de la 'Sapientia' chez les Humanists" in *Archivio di Filosofia Umanismo et Esoterismo* (Padua 1960) pg 321–333 who discusses Postel on pg 321–322.

[30] *Syriacae Linguae Iesu Christo, eiusque Matri Virgini atque Iudaeis omnibus, Christianae redemptionis Euangelicaeque praedicationis tempore, Vernaculae & popularis, ideoque a Novi Testamenti Scriptoribus quibusdam Hebraicae dictae Prima Elementa. Quibus adiectae sunt Christianae Religionis solennes, quotidianaeque Precationes. Viennae Austricae Anno MDLV XXI Novemb.* But for the date see next note. The text is badly reproduced in Werner Strothmann, *Die Anfänge der syrischen Studien in Europa* (O. Harrassowitz, Wiesbaden 1971 pg 63–113. It is

skill in cutting the characters was that of Kaspar Kraft who used a 16 pt serto with an occasional 12 pt and Estrangelo for running titles and chapter headings.[31] There is also a 12 pt *ashkenazi* Hebrew.

The first pages are taken up with an alphabet and a syllabary. The main purpose of the booklet is to teach one to read the script. What one notices here, compared to the previous work of Teseo Ambrogio or Postel, is Widmanstetter's detail in describing the articulation of the sounds: *"Gomal: g durum & tenue; Teth: t intra fauces; Coph: k & ch palatale; Koph: k imi gutteris etc"*. He is aware of the different pronunciation of (o) as (a) but unsurprisingly gives West Syrian vocalisation. He has had the advantage of a native teacher and remarks *"Harum literarum recta pronuntiatio viva potius voce, quam magistris mutis percipi potest"*. Widmanstetter also displays the three main Syriac scripts. He notes vocalisation points and the five 'Greek' vowels. His syllabary sets out combinations of both consonants and vowels.[32]

Widmanstetter gives a list of Syriac names for God with Latin meaning, and Latin and Hebrew transliteration. We saw a similar list in Teseo whence he no doubt took it. There follow fifteen pages of prayers again with Latin meaning and transcription into Latin and Hebrew: A Trisagion; Nicean Creed; Paternoster; Ave; Magnificat; Oratio pro Defunctis; Precatio super Mensa ante et post comestionem etc. There is thus no attempt to describe Morphology or Syntax.[33]

---

discussed in ed. F. de Nave, *Philologia Arabica* pg 88: Rijk Smitskamp, *Philologia Orientalis* pg 102–103; and by Bobzin, *Der Koran* pg 319–323.

[31] The last page has: *Div. Ferdinando Rom. Regnum administrante. In urbe Vienna Austriae orient. metropoli, Casparo Craphto ingeniosas operas praebente: excusa sunt haec Christianae Linguae Prima Elementa, In Officia Michaelis Cymbermanni, Mens Februar. MDLVI*. Notice the praise of Kraft's *ingeniosas operas* and the date.

[32] It is not unusual to teach people to read or write a script, especially one with ligatures by getting them to read out or write out combinations of letters. This was the practice in Roman schools, and I myself remember a children's Hebrew book that worked on the same principle. One is nonetheless struck by the similarities between the combinations of letters, set out exhaustively, in this grammar and the similar presentation of Hebrew combinations in the *Sepher Yesirah*. Indeed the presentation of all the alphabetic material in Widmanstetter bears considerable resemblance to this kabbalistic work that is itself set out as a grammar. The presentation and treatment of the letters seems almost inevitable to us today, but is not found to my knowledge in quite the same way before the Sepher Yesirah. I hesitate to draw any conclusion from this: but the temptation is strong.

[33] The work was reprinted by Guy Lefèvre de la Boderie with Plantin in Antwerp in 1572. Bobzin, *loc. cit.* sees this as a sign that the text was valued as useful ("Daß das Werk durchaus geschätzt wurde..."). No doubt; but it seems also worth noting that it was reprinted without Widmanstetter's name on the title page. The 1572 version is the second part of Guy Lefèvre de la Boderie's *D. Severi Alexandri...* in the preface to

Finally the author adds a *Conclusio ad Widmanstadios suos* that touches upon his education, circumstances and hopes for the evangelical success of Syriac, but which at this stage will teach us nothing new.

The Reception of the editio princeps

The preface 'The Translators to the Reader' in King James's English Bible of 1611 says that: "The *Syrian* translation of the New Testament is in most learned men's Libraries, of *Widminstadius* his setting forth", and well indicates the ubiquity and reputation of this great Bible. The edition had consisted of a thousand copies. Five hundred were retained for use in Europe and, as I have suggested in a footnote above, those that fell to Widmanstetter may, after his death have constituted the 1562 edition. Five hundred were entrusted to Moses who offered his stock to Masius and then sold them elsewhere. Three hundred were intended for the Patriarch, though I am not aware that anyone knows about the whereabouts of any of these.[34]

In the West, all subsequent editions make much of their own merits in contrast with the *editio princeps*. It is not difficult to grant that they have their own distinctive characteristics and excellences, but none quite match the beauty of the first edition. It is the requirement that it be both an Eastern Scripture and a Western scholarly text (though this of course is to be understood within a pressing eschatological timetable) that establishes the tension within which its particular excellence arises.

We have mentioned the collection of A. F. Oefele (Oef. 245). It gives an interesting survey of Widmanstetter's reputation through a selection of notices in subsequent authors. Those notices relating to the Syriac New Testament are helpful in considering the influence of this edition on subsequent Syriac new Testaments.

---

which it is expressly mentioned. It omits the syllabary and adds four more prayers. See Rijk Smitskamp, *Philologia Orientalis* pg 106–7 for the 1572 version. Guy's Dictionary did not escape accusations of plagiarism either.

[34] Sebastian Brock "The Development of Syriac Studies" in ed. K. J. Cathcart, *The Edward Hincks Bicentenary Lectures* (Univ. Coll. Dublin, Dublin 1994) pg 94–113 on pg 110–111 refers to a notice of Y. Dawlabani writing in Syriac in 1929 who specifically says that "copies are preserved to this day in the Library of Mar Hnanya (i.e. Dayr ez Za'faran, outside Mardin) and elsewhere". Anton Baumstark brought a copy from a Jacobite priest in Jerusalem at the beginning of the last century: *Festbrevier und Kirchenjahr der syrischen Jakobiten* (F. Schöningh, Paderborn 1910) pg 38.

An interesting single copy of the 1562 reissue was described many years ago by Burkitt.[35] This handsome book had a series of slips pasted in the cover facing the title page. From the friendly messages on these slips we can conclude that the owner of the book was one Michael Hortin who apparently was a student at Heidelberg about 1562 under Olevianus and Tremellius. The slips are evidently testimonials and messages of encouragement from his teachers. Two of the slips are in Tremellius's hand, one of which offers Proverbs 1.10 in Hebrew and the other a Hebrew alphabet followed by Psalm 13.5 and 6. Caspar Olevianus, the leader of the Calvinists in Heidelberg and Professor of Dogmatics from 1560–1577 offers 2 Timothy 3.12 to Hortin as a text from which he had in the past gained much encouragement in persecution. Petrus Colonius, a Calvinist refugee from Metz, offered a text in French and Greek that is almost 1 Timothy 6.6. There is also a greeting from no less than Peter Martyr Vermigli offering 2 Timothy 3. 16 and 17. This delightful volume thus shows us a Heidelberg scholar treasuring in his *editio princeps* of the Syriac New Testament the good wishes of his teachers. Some five years after copying the verses into Michael's *editio princeps*, Tremellius had produced his own, very different edition, but one which showed no continuity with the work of the Catholic kabbalistic orientalists that we have been studying.[36]

---

[35] F. C. Burkitt "A Note on some Heidelberg Autographs" Proceedings of the Cambridge Antiquarian Society XI (1906) pg 265–268.

[36] I offer for the first time a technical description of Tremellius's achievement in his edition and an introduction to the controversy it provoked from previously unused sources in J. E. H. 58/1 January 2007 pg 9–25.

CHAPTER SEVEN

CONCLUSION

The second half of the sixteenth century saw an increasing number of contacts between Rome and the Eastern Churches. These contacts brought native Syriac speakers to Rome and led to the establishment there of an oriental scholarship based upon a profound knowledge of the language and its literature, and quite removed from the kabbalistic fantasies of the High Renaissance.

The Maronite College

Of particular importance were two missions to the Maronites between 1578 and 1580 undertaken by the Jesuit Giambattista Eliano the Younger, Roman nephew and disciple of Elias Levita who was baptised in Venice 21 September 1551.[1] Eliano had entered the Company of Jesus in 1552,[2] had undertaken a dangerous mission to the Copts 1561–1563 (and was to make another 1582–1585) and had taught

---

[1] Levi della Vida, *Ricerche* pg 257; G. Weil, *Elie Lévita* pg 163–164 (His mother was Elias's daughter). The fundamental documents appear in Antoine Rabbath S. J., *Documents inédits pour servir à l'Histoire du Christianisme en Orient* I (Paris 1905–07) pg 305ff. (A posthumous second volume has the name of P. Tournebize S. J.). This is supplemented by J. C. Sola "El P. Juan Bautista Eliano un documento autobiográfico inédito" Archivum Historicum Societatis Iesu IV (1935) pg 291–321. Matti Moosa, *The Maronites in History* (Syracuse University Press, New York 1986) discusses this mission on pg 245–255. GERSL (Groupe d'Etudes et Recherches souterraines du Liban), *Momies du Liban Rapport préliminaire sur la découverte archéologique de 'Asi-l-Hadat (XIII siècle)* (Edifra, Beirut 1994) pg 114 & 161–162 has interesting evidence of Eliano as a book-burner and destroyer of literature he found unacceptable.

[2] See Kuntz, *Postel* pg 16 for the early Jesuits' positive attitudes to newly converted Jews. The Order however later introduced a racial standard for office-holders and then membership. The 'Aryan Clause' was dropped in 1946. See Jerome Freidman "Jewish Conversion, the Spanish Pure Blood Laws and the Reformation: A Revisionist View of Racial and Religious Antisemitism" The Sixteenth Century Journal XVIII/1 (Spring 1987) pg 3–29 at pg 23 with reference there to the work in this area of J. Rieters and J. P. Donnelly. For a general survey of the Jesuits in the Near East: Bernard Vincent "Les Jésuites et l'Islam méditerranéen" in ed. B. Bennassar & R. Sauzet *Chrétiens et Musulmans à la Renaissance (Actes du 37e Colloque du CESR 1994)* (Champion, Paris 1998).

Hebrew and Arabic at the Collegium Romanum.[3] As a result of his missionary efforts on his visit to the Maronites 1578–1582 there was founded the Maronite College at Rome by Gregory XIII under Jesuit direction.[4] Two young Maronites who were sent to Rome by Eliano in 1579 were housed initially in the Collegio dei Neofiti and attended lectures at the Collegium Romanum. In 1580 Elias sent four more students from the Lebanon. A third group of ten—some so young as eight—arrived in 1583. They were allowed to celebrate their own liturgy and 12 May 1584 they were given their own College. The College grew and was in time the home of great Syriac scholars like Gabriel Sionita and Abraham Ecchellensis[5] in the sixteenth and seventeenth century and the Assemanis of the eighteenth century. Many books from the Lebanon passed through the College and eventually ended up in the Vatican Library where they now remain.[6] The College thus came to be the focus of a new school of Syriac studies in Rome in the second part of the century.

By contrast the resources of Western scholars in the first half of the century, with whom we have been concerned, were meagre indeed. The major stimulus was those few monks who came to Rome for the Fifth Lateran Council and the manuscripts they brought with them or copied. A native teacher was a rare prize, a manuscript a treasure. The Catholic scholars who until 1553 enjoyed the support of the Curia commanded all the accumulated linguistic knowledge built up under Egidio da Viterbo, and in the person of Postel all the available expertise in Syriac printing.

---

[3] Francesco Pericoli-Ridolfini "La Missione pontificia presso il Patriarca copto di Alessandria Gabriele VII nel 1561–1563" Revista degli Studi Orientali XXXI (1956) pg 129–167. Mario Scaduto "La Missione di Cristoforo Rodriguez al Cairo (1561–1563)" Archivum Historicum Societatis Jesu XVII (1958) pg 233–278. The mission may be seen in the broader context of relationships between the Copts and Rome at this time in Vincenzo Buri "L'Unione della Chiesa copta con Roma sotto Clemente VIII" Orientalia Christiana XXIII. 2 (1931) pg 106–171. Giorgio Levi della Vida, *Documenti intorno alle Relazioni delle Chiese orientali con La S. Sede durante il Pontificato di Gregorio XIII* (Studi e Testi 143: Biblioteca Apostoilica Vaticana, Vatican City 1948) pg 114–171 adds text and discussion of a letter to Gregory XIII from the Coptic Patriarch John XCVI.

[4] Pierre Raphael, *Le Rôle du Collège Maronite romain dans L'Orientalisme aux XVIIe et XVIIIe siècles* (Université Saint Joseph de Beyrouth, Beirut 1950) discusses the early history of the College pg 11–69.

[5] On Ecchellensis, recently: Peter Rietbergen, Power and Religion in Baroque Rome: Barberini Cultural Politics (E. J. Brill, Leiden 2006) pg 296–335.

[6] Levi della Vida, *Ricerche* pg 185–191.

The main finding of the present work has been the identification and reconstruction of the Christian kabbalistic *milieu* out of which the *editio princeps* arose. We have sought to explain both the production of the edition and specific features of the printed book in terms of the heady combination of language mysticism, historical mythology, prophetic self-awareness and eschatological time-tables that characterised the small group of Catholic scholars who worked on Syriac in the first half of the century. The evidence both of their kabbalistic scholarship and their scholarly contacts has been set out for the first time in full detail. The first cannot be dismissed as marginal in their work, nor can the cumulative evidence of their inter-relationships allow one to minimise their significance as a small, but identifiable and influential group. In the course of this presentation we have shown that the current estimate of Widmanstetter's attitude to Kabbalah needs revision, and have provided an accurate description of his position.

The significance of this Catholic kabbalistic world-view we have illustrated by supporting accounts of the initial studies of other oriental languages in the early sixteenth century. This has enabled us to offer a broad characterisation at least of Postel's orientalism as something discernibly distinct from its mediaeval predecessors.

The fortunes of this Catholic kabbalistic orientalism we have been able to trace from a period of papal patronage to subsequent hostility on the part of the Curia. We have proposed the burning of the Talmud in Rome in 1553 as a particularly significant turning point in papal attitudes. Throughout emphasis has been placed on the interest in and support of these scholars by princes and prelates. Their eschatological and prophetic programmes met with a sympathetic reception and a competitive awareness of the prestige their work might bring a ruler. These scholars and their fantasies were not without political relevance or influence.

Two further Catholic editions of the Syriac New Testament in the sixteenth century belong in this newly identified intellectual context. The critical role of Postel in the conception of the Antwerp Polyglot has not yet been clearly stated, nor the kabbalistic material in that great bible systematically inventoried. Work now published seeks to show the essential continuities between the *editio princeps* and this rather different project. Similarly the 1584 Paris edition which, in the person of Guy Lefèvre de la Boderie, enjoyed the same editor as the Syriac text in the Antwerp Polyglot is properly to be understood only in the light of the kabbalistic orientalism described fully here for the first time.[7] The story thus has not yet been fully told, but the appearance of the companion volume to this will complete the tale.

Previous accounts of the *editio princeps* itself have suffered from a naïve reliance upon Widmanstetter's narrative in his *Dedicatio*. The tendentiousness of this document has not previously been exposed. Consequently the true significance of Postel's early work on Syriac New Testament manuscripts from 1537 has been obscured. Egregious misunderstanding of several of his comments and of the nature of the Marciana's Hebrew Matthew has further muddied the waters. The present work has restored Postel to his rightful role in the production of sixteenth-century Catholic editions of the Syriac New Testament. Similarly, though less centrally, Cervini's support for printing the Syriac New Testament has now been fully established.

On a more detailed level, the present work has been able to find manuscript evidence of Moses's work in preparation of the festal lections of the *editio princeps* in BSB Cod. Syr Mon 5. We have also been able to use the evidence of Oefeleana 18/2 not only to shed (alas! only some) light on the fate of the type and illustrate the interest in Syriac typography shown by Ferdinand I and Herzog Albrecht V, but also to provide an historical context for the '1562 edition' of the *editio princeps*.

Finally, the present work has sought to give a full and convincing explanation of the significance of the remarkable plate of the Apostle John's vision of the Sephirotic Tree that appears in the *editio princeps*. In pursuit of its meaning we have been led to consider not only the demand of the Eastern Churches for printed bibles and the mission of Moses of Mardin, but also to reconstruct the thought-world and motivation of the western scholars who contributed to its production. The result has been the discovery of a quite unexpected history of early Syriac studies, presented here for the first time.

---

[7] I address both of these editions in the light of the kabbalistic tradition in Robert J. Wilkinson, *The Kabbalistic Scholars of the Antwerp Polyglot Bible* (E.J. Brill, Leiden 2007).

BIBLIOGRAPHY

Principal Manuscript Sources

Biblioteca Apostolica Vaticana

Vat sir 9
Vat sir 15
Vat sir 16
Vat sir 265

Vat et 5
Vat et 20
Vat et 25
Vat et 68

Biblioteca Marciana Venice

Mss Orientali no 216 (Ebraici 10)

Staatsbibliothek Munich

Ms heb 74, 81, 92, 103, 215, 217, 218, 219, 285
Oefeleana 245, 247, 255–259, 262
Cod lat M 27 081 f.12

Cod syr 1
Cod syr 5
Cod syr 6

Cod arab 920/2 (Cod Or 100)

Bayerische Hauptstaatsarchiv Munich

Oefeleana 18/2

Nationalbibliothek Vienna

Cod Vindob. Syr 1

Principal Printed Sources before c. 1800

Abel, Léon: Une mission religieuse en Orient au seizième siècle. Relation adressé à Sixte-Quint par l'évêque de Sidon Translated by A. d'Avril (Benjamin Duprat) Challamel, Paris 1866).
Adler, J. G. Chr: Novi Testamenti Versiones Syriacae. Hafniae 1789.
Aethiops, Petrus: Testamentum Novum cum epistola Pauli ad Hebreos tantum, cum concordantiis evangelistarum Eusebii et numeratione omnium verborum eorundem, Missale cum benedictione incensi cerae, Alphabetum in lingua gheez, id est libera, quia a nulla alia originem duxit et vulgo dicitur Chaldaea. Quae omnia Fr Petrus Aethipos auxilio piorum sedente Paulo III Pont. Max. et Claudio illius regni Imperatore imprimi curavit. Romae 1548.

Ambrogio Degli Albonesi, Teseo: Teseo Ambrogio Introductio in Chaldaicam linguam, Syriacam, atque Armenicam, et decem alias linguas. Characterum differentium Alphabeta, circiter quadraginta, et eorundem invicem conformatio, Mystica et Cabalistica quamplurima scitu digna. Et descriptio ac simulachrum Phagoti Afranii. Theseo Ambrosio ex Comitibus Albonesii I.V. Doct. Papieň. Canonico Regulari Lateranensi, ac Sancti Petri in Coelo Aureo Papiae Praeposito, Authore MDXXXIX. Linguarum vero, & Alphabetorum nomina sequens pagella demonstrabit. Pavia excudebat J. M. Simoneta, sumptibus & typis auctoris libri.

Annius Viterbiensis: Commentaria fratris Joannis Annii Viterbiensis super opera diversorum auctorum de antiquitatibus loquentium. Rome: Eucharius Silber 1498.

Assemani, J. S.: Bibliothecae Orientalis Clementino-Vaticanae Tomus Primus de Scriptoribus Syris Orthodoxis. Rome 1719.

Assemani, S.: Catologo dei Codici manoscritti orientali della Biblioteca Naniana, compilato dall' abate Simone Assemani. 2 vols., Padova, 1789/93.

Assemani, Steph Ev: Bibliothecae Mediceae Laurentianae et Palatinae codicum mss orientalium catalogues…Steph. Evodius Assemanus archiep. Apameae recensuit, digessit notis illustravit, Ant.Franc. Gorio curante. Florentiae, 1742.

Billan, François des: Nouveaux Éclaircissements sur la vie et les ouvrages de Guillaume Postel. Liège: J. J. Tutot 1773 (Slatkine Reprint: Geneva 1970).

Caninius, A.: Institutiones Linguae Syriacae, Assyriacae atque Thalmudicae una cum Aethiopicae atque Arabice collatione….Paris, Apud Carolum Sephanum 1554.

Chaufepié, Jacques George de: Nouveau Dictionnaire historique et critique pour servir de Supplement ou de continuation au Dictionnaire Historique et Critique de M. Pierre Bayle. Amsterdam/The Hague/Leiden, 1750–1756.

Christmann, Jakob: Alphabetum Arabicum cum isagoge scribendi legendique arabice auctore M. Jacobo Christmanno Iohannisbergensi Neapoli Nemetum (Neustadt) 1582.

Da Rieti, Mariano Vittori: Chaldeae seu Aethiopicae linguae institutiones, numquam antea a Latinis visae, opus utile aceruditum. Item omnium Aethiopiae regum qui ab inundato terrarum orbe usque ad nostra tempora imperarunt Libellus hactenus tam Graecis quam Latinis ignoratus, nuper ex aethiopica translatus lingua. Rome 1552.

Galatinus, Petrus: Opus toti christianae Reipublicae maxime utile de arcanis catholicae veritatis, contra obstinatissimam judaeorum nostrae tempestatis perfidiam: ex Talmud, aliisque hebraiicis libris nuper excerptum: & quadruplici linguarum genere eleganter congestum, Orthona maris impressum per Hieronymum Suncinum 1518.

Gesner, Conrad: Mithridates De differentiis linguarum Zurich 1555. Edition by Manfred Peters Scientia Verlag: Aalen 1974.

Giustiniani, Agostino: Psalterium Hebraeum, graecum Arabicum, & Chaldaeum, cum tribus latinis interpretationibus & glossis, Genuae P. P. Porro 1516.

Jones, A. Ricardo: Textus Sacrorum Evangeliorum Versioni Simplicis Syriacae (Clarendon, Oxford 1805).

Leo Africanus: De Viris 1527 in J. A. Fabricius, *Bibliotheca Graeca* XIII (Hamburg 1726) pg 259–294.

——: Descrittione dell'Africa in J. B. Ramusios *Naviagazioni e viaggi* Venice 1550. Subsequently the collection appeared in Latin (1556), French (1556), English (1600) and Dutch (1665). The English is: A History and Description of Africa tr. John Pory 1600 (3 Vols., Hakluyt Society, London 1896).

Masius, Andreas: Briefe von Andreas und seinen Freunden 1538–1573, ed. M. Lossen Leipzig 1886 (Publication der Gesellschaft f. Rheinische Geschichtskunde, II).

——: De Paradisio commentarius, scriptus ante annos prope septingenos a Mose Bar-Cepha Syro, episcopo in Beth-Raman et Beth-Ceno ac curatore rerum sacrarum in Mozal, hoc est Seleucia Parthorum. Invenies, lector, in hoc commentario, praeter alia multa lectu et digna et iucunda, plurimos etiam peregrinos scriptores citatos.

Adiecta est etiam divi Basili Caesariensis episcopi λειτουργία sive ᾽αναφορά ex vetustissimo codice syrica lingua scripto. Praeterea professiones fidei duae, altera Mosis Mardenis Iacobitae, legati patriarchae Antiocheni, altera Sulacae sive Siud Nestoriani, designati patriarchae Nestorianorum. Ad haec duae epistolae populi Nestoriani ad Pontificem Romanum, quarum altera ex Seleucia Parthorum, altera ex Ierusalem scripta est. Omnia ex syrica lingua nuper translata per andream Masium Bruxellanum. Antverpiae, ex officina Christophori Plantini 1569.

——: Josuae Imperatoris Historia, illustrata atque explicata...Antwerp: Plantin 1574.

Minuccius, M.: De Aethiopia 1598 in Alberto Marani ed. *Minuccio Minucci Storia inedita dell Ettiopica (De Aethiopia)* (Il Mamiani, Rome 1968).

Mithridates, Flavius: Sermo de passione Domini ed. Ch Wirszubski (Publications of the Israel Academy of Sciences and Humanities, Jerusalem 1963).

Müller, A.: Symbolae syriacae, sive I Epistolae duae amoebeae...(Berolini s. a.) II Dissertationes duae de rebus itidem Syriacis. Coloniae Brandeburgiciae, 1673.

Münster, Sebastian: Chaldaica Grammatica. Basle 1527.

——: Accentuum Hebraicorum liber unus. Basle 1539.

Postel, Guillaume: Linguarum duodecim characteribus differentium alphabetum, introductio, ac legendi modus longe facillimus. Paris: P. Vodovaeus Vernoliensis 1538.

——: De originibus seu de hebraicae linguae et gentis antiquitate. Paris: P. Vodovaeus Vernoliensis 1538.

——: Grammatica Arabica. Paris: Petrus Gromorsus (c. 1539–40).

——: Syriae descriptio. s. l. (Paris) Hieronymus Gormontius 1540.

——: De magistratibus Atheniensium liber singularis. Paris M. Vascosanus 1541.

——: Alcorani seu legis Mahometi et Evangelistarum concordiae Liber, in quo de calamitatibus orbi christiano imminentibus tractatur. Additus est libellus de universalis conversionis, iudiciive tempore & intra quot annos sit expectandum, conjectatio, ex divinis ducta authoribus, veroque proxima. Paris: Petrus Gromorsus 1543.

——: De oribis terrae concordiae Libri Quatuor, multiiuga eruditione ac pietate referti, quibus nihil hoc tam perturbato rerum statu vel utilius, vel accomodatius poyuissein publicum edi, quivis aequus lector iudicabit. Adiectae sunt quoque Annotationes in margine a pio atque erudito quodam viro, ne delicatioris palati, aut iniquioris etiam iudicii aliquis, ut sunt fere hodiequamplurimi, offenderetur. Proinde ut pectore candido accipere, quae in Ecclesiae misere adeo afflictae utilitatem scribuntur, Lector velis, per Christum & animae tuae salutem obtestatum te volumus. (s.l. s.d. Basel: Oporinus 1544).

——: Descriptio Alcahirae Urbis quae Mizir et Mazar dicitur. 1547.

——: Candelabrum...Venice 1548. F. Secret, ed. *Guillaume Postel et son Interprétation du Candélabre de Moyse* (B. De Graaf, Niewkoop 1966).

——: De Etruriae Regionibus. Florence 1551. G. Cipriani ed. *De Etruriae Regionibus* (Consiglio Nazionale delle Ricerche, Florence 1984).

——: De Foenicum Literis, seu de prisco Latine & Graece lingue charactere, eiusque antiquissima origine & usu. Paris: Vivantius Gaultherot 1552.

——: Abrahami Patriarchae Liber Iezirah. Paris 1552. Edition by Wolf Peter Klein, *Sefer Jezirah ubersetzt und kommentiert von Guillaume Postel* (Frommann-Holzboog, Stuttgart-Bad Cannstatt 1994). This includes the text of Liber Rationis Rationum that was printed in the 1552 edition, Omnium Linguarum quibus ad hanc usque diem mundus est usus, origio....

——: De originibus seu, de varia et potissimum orbi Latino ad hanc diem incognita, aut inconsyderata historia. Basle: Oporinus 1553.

——: Omnium linguarum quibus ad hanc usque diem mundius est usus, Origio. (s.l. s.d.). Facsimile in C. Gilly "Guillaume Postel et Bâle. Quelques additions à la *Bibliographie des Manuscrits de Guillaume Postel*" in *Actes du Colloque International d'Avranches 5–9 septembre 1981 Guillaume Postel 1581–1981* (Guy Trédaniel, Éditions de La Maisnie, Paris 1985) pg 41–77.

——: Les très merveilleuses victoires des femmes du nouveau monde. Paris: Jehan Ruelle 1553. Edition by Gustave Brunet (Slatkine Reprints, Geneva 1970).

——: De Linguae Phoenicis sive Hebraicae excellentia. Vienna: M. Cimmerman 1554.

——: La Prima Nove del altro Mondo. 1555. Enea Balmas "'Le prime nove dell'altro mondo' di Guglielmo Postel" Studi Urbanati XXIX (1955) pg 334–377.

——: De la Republique des Turcs & là ou l'occasion s'offera, des meurs & loy de tous Muhamedistes. Poitiers: Engilbert de Marnef 1560.

——: Des Histoires orientales et principalement des Turcs ou Turchikes et Schitiques ou Tartaresques et autres qui en sont descendues. Paris: H. de Marnef et G. Cavellat 1575.

——: De Cosmographia Diciplina: Leiden J. Maire 1636.

Potken, Johannes: Psalterium et canticum canticorum et alia cantica biblica, aethiopice; et sullabarium seu legendi ratione, Romae Marc. Silber alias Franck 1513.

——: Psalterium in quatuor linguis Hebraea Graeca Chaldaea Latina, Coloniae, Johannes Soter) 1518.

Reuchlin, Johannes: De Verbo Mirifico 1494. Facsimile Friedrich Frommann Verlag, Stuttgart-Bad Cannstadt 1964.

——: De Rudimentis Hebraicis libri tres: Phorcae 1506.

——: Augenspiegel 1511.

——: De Arte Cabalistica 1517. Edition by M. & S. Goodman (Bison Books, University of Nebraska Press, Nebraska 1993).

——: E. Ed L.Geiger, *Reuchlins Briefswechsel* (Tübingen 1875).

Schnurrer, C. F. de: Biblioteca Arabica. Auctam nunc atque integram edidit....Halae ad Salam 1811 (Reprint Amsterdam 1968).

Torres, Francisco de: De Sola lectione Legis, et Prophetarum Iudaeis cum Mosaico Ritu, et Cultu Permittenda, et de Iesu in Synagogis Eorum ex Lege, ac Prophetis Ostendendo, et Annunciando. Ad Reverendidd. Inquisitores. Libri Duo. Rome 1555.

Venetus, Gregorius Georgius: Septem horae canonicae, a laicis hominibus recitandae, iuxta ritum Alexandrinorum seu Jacobitarum Alexandrino Patriarchae subditorum Arabicae, editae a Gregorio Georgio Veneto, sub auspiciis Leonis X Pontificis Maximi in urbe Fano. 1514.

Widmanstetter, Johann Albert: A. Mahometis Abdallae filii theologia dialogo explicata Hermanno Nellingaunense interprete. Alconani epitome, Roberto Ketenense Anglo interprete. Iohannis Alberti Vuidmestadij Iurisconsulti Notationes falsarum impiarumque opinionum Mahumetis, quae in hisce libris occurrunt. Iohannis Alberti Vuidmestadij Jurisc. ad Ludovicum Alberti F. Paltij Rhenani Comitem, Bavariae utriusque Principem Illustriss. optimumque Dicatio. MDXLIII. (no place: Nuremberg?) 1543.

——: B. Liber sacrosancti Evangelii de Jesu Christo Domino et Deo nostro etc. characteribus et langua syra, Viennae Austriacae: Mich. Cymbermann 1555.

——: C. Syriacae linguae…prima elementa, Viennae Austriacae: Mich. Cymbermann 1555 [1556]. Reprint in W. Strothmann, *Die Anfänge der syrischen Studien in Europa* (Otto Harrassowitz, Wiesbaden 1971) pg 63–114.

——: D. Syriacae linguae…prima elementa, Antwerpiae: Chr. Plantinus 1572.

Widmanstetter, Philipp Jacob: De Societatis Jesu initiis, progressis, rebusque gestis nonnullis Philippi Jacobi Widmanstadii Academii Viennenis, ad Johannem Albertum Widmanstadium fratris filium epistula. Ingolstadii Anno MDLVI Cal. Oct.

William of Tyre: Historia Rerum in Partibus Transmarinis Gesta (Migne PL 201).

Ximenez de Cisneros, D. F. F.: Biblia sacra, hebraice, chaldaice et graece cum tribus interpretationibus latinis: de mandato ac sumptibus Cardinalis D. F. Francisci

Ximenez de Cisneros. Alcalà 1514–1517. Reimpression by the Fundación Biblica Española y Universidad Complutense de Madrid (1984).

Books and articles after 1800

Aboussouan, C. [ed.], *Le livre et le Liban jusqu'a 1900* (UNESCO/AGECOOP, Paris 1982).
Adler, E. N. [ed.], *Jewish Travellers* (Routledge, London 1938).
Alberigo, G. [ed.], *Christian Unity The Council of Ferrara-Florence 1438/9–1989* (Leuven University Press, Leuven 1991).
Allen, D. C., *The Legend of Noah; Renaissance Rationalism in Art Science and Letters* (University of Illinois Press, Illinois 1949).
Allgeier, A., "Cod. syr. Phillipps 1388 und siene ältesten Perikopenvermerke" Oriens Christianus (n. s.) VI (1916) pg 147–152.
——, "Cod. syr. Phillipps 1388 in Berlin und seine Bedeutung für die Geschichte der Peshitta" Oriens Christianus (3rd series) VII (1932) pg 1–15.
Altaner, B., "Die Durchfürung des Vienner Konzilsbeschlusses über die Errichtung von Lehrstühlen für orientalische Sprachen" Zeitschrift für Kirchengeschichte (Stuttgart) LII (1933) pg 226–236.
——, "Raymundus Lullus und der Sprachenkanen (can. 11) des Konzils von Vienne 1312" Historisches Jahrbuch der Gorres-Gesellschaft München LIII (1933) pg 191–219.
Amran, D. W., *The Makers of Hebrew Books in Italy* (1909. Reprint Holland Press Ltd., London 1963).
Anaissi, T., *Bullarum Maronitarum* (Max Bretschneider, Rome 1911).
Anon, "The Printed editions of the Syriac New Testament" Church Quarterly Review XXVI 1888 pg 257–294.
Apel, K.-O., "The Transcendental Conception of Language-Communication and the Idea of a First Philosophy" in [ed.] H. Parret, *History of Linguistic Thought and Contemporary Linguistics* (New York, 1976) pg 32–62.
Aschbach, J. R. von, *Die Wiener Universität und ihre Gelehrte* (Dritte Band 1520 bis 1565) (Alfred Hölder, Vienna 1888).
Asher, R. E., *National Myths in Renaissance France* (Edinburgh University Press, Edinburgh 1993).
Assfalg, J., *Syrische Handschriften (in Verzeichnis der Orientalischen Handschriften in Deutschland V)* (Franz Steiner Verlag, Wiesbaden 1962).
Astruc, C., & Monfrin, J., "Livres latin et hébreux du Cardinal Gilles de Viterbo" Bibliothèque de Humanisme et Renaissance XXIII (1961) pg 551–554.
Atkinson, G., *Les Nouveaux Horizons de la Renaissance français* (Droz, Paris 1935).
Austin, Kenneth, From Judaism to Calvinism: the Life and Writings of Immanuel Tremellius. Unpublished Doctoral Thesis. St. Andrews University 2003.
Baarda, T., "The Syriac Versions of the New Testament" in [ed.] B. D. Ehrman and M. W. Holmes, *The Text of the New Testament in Contemporary Research Essays on the Status Quaestionis* (Eerdmans, Grand Rapids, 1995) pg 97–112.
Babinger, F., "Ein vergessner maronitischer Psalterdruck auf der Nürnberger Stadtbücherei" Zeitschrift für alttestamentliche Wissenschaft (1925) pg 275.
Backus, I., "Guillaume Postel, Théodore Bibliander et le 'Protévangile de Jacques' Introduction historique, édition et traduction française du Ms. Londres British Library, Sloane 1411 260r–267v" Apocrypha VI (1995) pg 7–65.
Bailbe, J., "Postel conteur dans 'La Republique des Turcs'" in [ed.] M. L. Kuntz, *Postello, Venezia e il suo Mondo* pg 45–63.
Balagna Coustou, J., *Arabe et Humanisme dans la France des derniers Valois* (Maisonneuve et Larose, Paris 1989).
Balagna, J., *L'Imprimerie arabe en Occident (XVIᵉ, XVIIᵉ et XVIIIᵉ siècles)* (Maisonneuve and Larose, Paris 1984).

Balmas, E., "*Le prime Nove dell'altro Mondo* di Guglielmo Postel" Studi Urbinati XXIX/2 (1955) pg 334–377.

Bar-Ilan, M., "Prester John: Fiction and History" History of European Ideas XX/1–3 (1995) pg 291–298.

Baroni, V., *La Contre-Réforme devant La Bible La Question biblique* (Imprimerie de la Concorde, Lausanne 1943).

Basetti-Sani, G., "L'unione della chiesa copta Alessandrina alla chiese Romana nel Concilio di Firenze" in Alberigo Giusseppe [ed.], *Christian Unity The Council of Ferrara-Florence 1438/9–1989* (Leuven University Press, Leuven 1991) pg 623–644.

Bauch, G., "Flavius Wilhelmus Raimundus Mithridates" Archiv für Kulturgeschichte III (1905) pg 15–27.

Baumstark, A., *Festbrevier und Kirchenjahr der syrischen Jakobiten* (F. Schöningh, Paderborn 1910).

——, *Geschichte der syrischen Literatur mit Ausschluss der christlich-palästinischen Texte* (Bonn, 1922: reprint 1968).

Beltrami, G., *La Chiesa caldea nel Secolo dell'Unione* (Orientalia Christiana Analecta, Rome 1933).

Bernard, J. H., *International Critical Commentary St John* (T&T Clark, Edinburgh 1928).

Bernard, Y., *L'Orient du XVIe siècle à travers les récits des Voyages français: Regards portés sur la Société musulmane* (Editions L'Harmattan, Paris 1988).

Bernard-Maître, H., "Le passage de G. Postel chez les premiers Jésuites" *Mélanges offerts à Henri Chamard* (Librairie Nizet, Paris 1951) pg 223–243.

Bietenholz, P. G., *Basle and France in Sixteenth Century. The Basle Humanists and Printers in their contacts with Francophone Culture* (Librairie Droz, Geneva 1971).

Biggemann, Wilhelm Schmidt, "Political Theology in Renaissance Christian Kabbalah: Petrus Galatinus and Guillaume Postel" Hebraic Political Studies 1/3 2006 pg 286–309.

Biondi, A., "Annio da Viterbo e un aspetto dell' orientalismo di Guillaume Postel" Bolletino della Società di studi Valdesi XCIII (1972) pg 46–67.

Blau, J. L., *The Christian Interpretation of the Cabala in the Renaissance* (New York, 1944).

Bobrinsky, B., "Liturgie et Ecclésiologie trinitaire de sainte Basile" in *Eucharisties d'Orient et Occident II* (Édition du Cerf, Paris 1970) pg 197–240.

Bobzin, H., Der *Koran in Zeitalter der Reformation* (Franz Steiner Verlag, Beirut 1995)

——, "Agostino Giustiniani (1470–1536) und seine Bedeutung für die Geschichte der Arabistik" in eds. Werner Diem & Aboli Arad Falaturi, *XXIV Deutscher Orientalistentag (Köln 1988)* (Stuttgart 1990) pg 131–139.

Bohnstadt, J. W., *The Infidel Scourge of God The Turkish Menace as seen by German Pamphleteers of the Reformation Era* (American Philosophical Society, Philadelphia 1968).

Bonfante, G., "Ideas on the Kinship of European Languages" Cahiers d'Histoire mondiale I. (1954) pg 679–699.

Bourilly, V. L., "L'Ambassade de la Forest et de Marillac à Constantinople 1535–1538" Revue historique LXXVI (1961) pg 297–328.

Bouwsma, W. J., "Postel and the significance of Renaissance Cabalism" Journal of History of Ideas XV (1954) pg 218–232.

——, *The Career and Thought of Guillaume Postel (1510–1581)* (Harvard UP, Cambridge, Mass. 1957).

Brecker, B., "Pflug" *Allgemeine Deutsche Biographie* XXV (Leipzig 1667) pg 688–690.

Brock, S. P., "Proper Names" in [ed.] B. M. Metzger, *The Early Versions of the New Testament* (OUP, Oxford 1977) pg 85–89.

——, "Aspects of Translation Technique in Antiquity" Greek, Roman and Byzantine Studies XX (1979) pg 69–87 reprinted in [ed.] Sebastian Brock *Syriac Perspectives on Late Antiquity* (Variorum, London 1984) ch 3.

——, "Towards a history of Syriac Translation Technique" in *IV Symposium Syriacum* (OCA 221) (Pont. Institutum Studiorum Orientalium, Rome 1983) pg 1–14.

Reprinted in [ed.] Sebastian Brock *Studies in Syriac Christianity* (Variorum, Aldershot 1984) ch 4.

———, "Hebrew 2:9B in Syriac Tradition" Novum Testamentum XXVII (1985) pg 236–244.

———, "The Development of Syriac Studies" in [ed.] K. J. Cathcart, *The Edward Hincks Bicentenary Lectures* (Univ. Coll. Dublin, Dublin 1994) pg 94–113.

———, "The Use of the Syriac Fathers for New Testament Textual Criticism" (pg 224–236) that appear in [ed.] B. D. Ehrman and M. W. Holmes, *The Text of the New Testament in Contemporary Research Essays on the Status Quaestionis* (Eerdmans, Grand Rapids, 1995).

Brod, M., *Johannes Reuchlin und sein Kampf. Eine historische Monographie* (Fourier, Wiesbaden 1988).

Brou, A., "Les Missions étrangères aux origins de la Compagnie de Jésus" Revue d'Histoire des Missions X (1928) 354–368.

Brown, H. M., "A Cook's Tour of Ferrara in 1529" Rivista Italiana da Musicologia X (1975) pg 216–41.

Bujanda, J. M. de, *Index des Livres interdits* (Nine volumes: Droz, Geneva 1985–1996).

Buri, V., "L'Unione della Chiesa copta con Roma sotto Clemente VIII" Orientalia Christiana XXIII. 2 (1931) pg 106–171.

———, *L'unione della Chiesa copta con Roma sotto Clemente VIII* (Orientalia Christiana XXIII, Rome 1931).

Burkitt, F. C., "A Note on some Heidelberg Autographs" Proceedings of the Cambridge Antiquarian Society XI (1906) pg 265–268.

———, "The Syriac forms of New Testament Proper Names" Proceedings of the British Academy V (1911–1912) pg 377–408.

Burmeister, K. H., *Sebastian Münster: Versuch eines biographischen Gesamtbildes* (Basel und Stuttgart, 1963).

Burnett, C. G. F., "Arabic into Latin in twelfth century Spain: The Works of Hermann of Carinthia" Mittellatein Jahrbuch XIII (1978) pg 100–134.

Burnett, S. G., *From Christian Hebraism to Jewish Studies Johannes Buxtorf 1564–1629 and Hebrew Learning in the Seventeenth Century* (E. J. Brill, Leiden 1996).

———, "A Dialogue of the Deaf: Hebrew Pedagogy and anti-Jewish Polemic in Sebastian Münster's *Messiahs of the Christians and the Jews* (1529/39)" Archiv für Reformationsgeschichte XCI (2000) pg 168–190.

Busi, G., "Francesco Zorzi, a methodical dreamer" in ed. J. Dan, *The Christian Kabbalah Jewish Mystical Books and their Christian Interpreters* (Harvard College Library, Cambridge Mass. 1997) pg 97–126.

Cameron, E., *The European Reformation* (OUP, Oxford 1991).

Carini, I., "Guglielmo Raimondo Moncada" Archivio storico Siciliano XXII (1897) pg 485–492.

Cassuto, U., *I Manoscritti Palatini Ebraici delle Bibliotheca Apostolica Vaticana e loro Storia* (BAV, Vatican City 1935)

———, "Wer was der Orientalist Mithridates?" Zeitschrift für die Geschichte des Judentums in Deutschland V. (1935) pg 230–236.

Céard, J., "De Babel à la Pentecôte: la transformation du mythe de la confusion des langues au XVI siècle" Bibliothèque de Humanisme et Renaissance XLII (1980) pg 577–594.

———, "Le 'De Originibus' de Postel et la Linguistic de son temps" in [ed.] M. L. Kuntz *Postello, Venezia e il suo Mondo* (Leo S. Olschki, Florence 1988) pg 19–43.

Centi, T. M., "L'attività letteraria di Sancti Pagnini (1570 *sic*–1536) nel campo delle scienze bibliche" Archivum Fratrum Praedicatorum XV (1945) pg 5–51.

Chaine, M., "Un monastère éthiopien à Rome aux XV et XVI siècles, San Stephano dei Mari" Mélanges de l'Université Saint Joseph V (1911) pg 1–36.

Charrière, E. de, *Négotiations de la France dans le Levant Collection de Documents inédits sur l'histoire de France* (Paris, 1848–1860).

Chaze M., "Review of Chaim Wirszubski *Trois chapitres sur l'Histoire de la Kabbale chrétienne* (Bialik, Jerusalem 1975)" Revue des Études juives CXXXIV (1975) pg 137–140.

Christ, K., *Die Bibliothek Reuchlins in Pforzhein* (Otto Harrassowitz, Leipzig 1924).

Cioni, A., "Daniel Bomberg" *Dizionario Biografico degli Italiani* (G. Ernest and S. Foa, Rome) vol. X, pg 382–387.

Clark, H., "The Publication of the Koran in Latin: a Reformation Dilemma" Sixteenth Century Journal XV (1984) pg 3–12.

Cocks, W. A., "The Phagotum: an attempt at reconstruction" The Galpin Society Journal XII (1959) pg 57–9 (with Plate III).

Codazzi, A., "Il Trattato dell'arte metrica di Giovanni Leone Africano" *Studi orientalistici in onore di Giorgio Levi della Vida* Vol. I, (1956) pg 180–198.

Coggins, R. J., *Samaritans and Jews: the Origins of Samaritanism Reconsidered* (OUP, Oxford 1975).

Combero, C., 'Colonna Pietro' in *Dizionario Biografico degli Italiani* (G. Ernest and S. Foa, Rome) vol. XXVII pg 402–404.

Comparetti, D., *Vergil in the Middle Ages* (Swan Sonnenschein, London 1908).

Connolly, R. H., *The So-Called Egyptian Church Order and Derived Documents* (C.U.P., Cambridge 1916).

Contini, R. "Gli studi siriaci" in *Giorgio Levi della Vida nel centenaria della nascita 1886–1967* (Rome 1988) pg 25–40.

——, "Gli Inizi della Linguistica Siriaca nell'Europa rinascimentale" Rivista Studi Orientali LXVIII (1994) pg 15–30.

Crawford, R. W., "William of Tyre and the Maronites" Speculum XXX 1955 pg 222–8.

D'Alverny, M. T., "Quelques Aspects du Symbolisme de la *Sapientia* chez les Humanistes" in ed. E. Castelli, *Umanismo e Esoterico* (Padua, 1960) pg 321–333.

Dahan, G. [ed.], *Le Brûlement du Talmud à Paris 1242–1244* (Édition du Cerf, Paris 1999).

Dan, J. [ed.], *The Christian Kabbalah. Jewish Mystical Books and their Christian Interpreters* (HUP, Harvard 1997).

——, "The Kabbalah of Johannes Reuchlin and its historical significance" in [ed.] Joseph Dan, *The Christian Kabbalah Jewish Mystical Books and their Christian Interpreters* (Harvard College Library, Cambridge Mass. 1997) pg 55–96.

Danielsson, O. A., "Annius von Viterbo über die Gründungsgeschichte Roms" *Corolla Archaeologica Principi Hereditario Regni Sueciae Gustavo Adolpho Dedicata*, (Humphrey Milford, London 1932) pg 1–16.

Dannenfeldt, K. H., "The Renaissance Humanists and knowledge of Arabic" *Studies in the Renaissance II* (1955) pg 96–117.

Darlow, H. & Moule, H. F., *Historical Catalogue of the printed editions of Holy Scripture in the Library of the British and Foreign Bible Society* (2 vols. in 4) (BFBS, London 1903, reprinted New York, 1963).

Delaruelle, L., "La Séjour à Paris d'Agostino Giustiniani" Revue du Seizième Siècle XII (1925) pg 322–337.

Dell'Acqua, G. & Munster, L., "I Rapporti di Giovanni Pico della Mirandola con alcuni Filosofi ebrei" *L'Opera e il Penserio di Giovanni Pico della Mirandola nella Storia dell' Umanismo* Vol. II (Instituto Nationale di Studi sul Rinascimento, Florence, 1965) pg 149–167.

Demonet, Marie-Luce, *Les voix du signe: nature et origine du langage à la Renaissance. 1480–1580* (Librairie Honoré Champion, Paris 1992).

Derenbourg, H., "Léon l'Africain et Jacob Mantino" Revue des Etudes juives VII (1883) pg 283–285.

Di Segni, R., "La Qabbalah nella comunità ebraica romana" in ed. Fabio Troncarelli, *La Città dei Segreti. Magia Astrologia e Cultura Esoterica a Roma (XV–XVIII)* (Franco Angeli, Milan 1985) pg 119–126.

Dib, P., *Histoire de l'Eglise maronite* (2 volumes, Beirut 1962).

Diez Macho, A., *Neofiti I Targum palestinense Ms. de la Biblioteca Vaticana I Génesis*, 1968, *II Exodo*, 1970, *III Levitico*, 1971, *IV Numeros* 1974, *V Deuteronomio* 1978, *VI Apendices* 1979 (Madrid-Barcelona).

Dorez, L., "Le Cardinal Marcello Cervini et l'Imprimerie à Rome 1539–1550" Mélanges d'Archaeologie et d'Histoire XII 1892 pg 289–313.

——, "Le Registre des dépenses de la Bibliothèque Vaticane" *Fasiculus Ioanni Willis Clark Dicatus* (CUP, Cambridge 1909) pg 142–185.

Drimba, V., "*L'Instruction des mots de la langue turquesque de Guillaume Postel (1575)*" in *Türk dili Araştırmaları Yıllığı Belleten* (Ankara, 1967) pg 77–126.

Dubois, C.-G., "Une Utopie politique de la Renaissance française Rêverie de G. Postel" L'Information Littéraire XX (1968) pg 55–62.

——, *Mythe et Langage au XVIe siècle* (Ducros, Bordeaux 1970).

——, *Celtes et Gaulois au XVIe siècle: Le Développement littéraraire d'un Mythe nationalistic* (J. Vrin, Paris 1972).

——, "La curiosité des origines. Spéculations de Guillaume Postel autour de Cequi est premier" in [ed.] J. Céard, *La Curiosité à la Renaissance Actes de la Sociètè français des Seizièmistes* (Paris 1986) pg 37–48.

——, *La mythologie des origines chez Guillaume Postel: de la naissance à la nation* (Paradigue, Orléans 1994).

Duchet, M. [ed.], *Inscription des Langues dans les Relations de Voyage (XVIe–XVIIIe siècles)* (ENS, Fontenay/St. Cloud 1992).

Durand, A., "Les Editions imprimées du Nouveau Testament syriaque" Recherches de Science religieuse (Paris) XI (1921) pg 385–409.

Ehrman B. D. & M. W. Holmes, M. W., [eds.] *The Text of the New Testament in Contemporary Research* (Eerdmans, Michigan 1995).

Ellero, G., "G. Postel e l'Ospedale dei Derelitti (1547–1549)" in [ed.] Kuntz, *Postello, Venezia e il suo Mondo* pg 137–161.

Engberding, H., *Das eucharistische Hochgebet der Basileosliturgie* (Theologie des christlichen Orients 1) (Aschendorff, Munster 1931).

Euringer, S., "Das Epitaphium des Tasfa Sejon" Oriens Christianus (3rd series) I (1926–1927) pg 49–66.

——, "San Stephano dei Mori (Vatikanstadt) in seinen Bedeutung für die abbessinische Sprachwissenschaft und Missionsgeschichte" Oriens Christianus (3rd series) X (1935) pg 38–59.

Fenlan, Dermont, *Heresy and Obedience in Tridentine Italy. Cardinal Pole and the Counter-Reformation* (OUP, Oxford 1972).

Fitchtner, P. S., *Ferdinand I of Austria. The Politics of Dynasticism in the Age of the Reformation* (East European Monographs, Boulder) (Columbia University Press, New York 1982).

Franklin, M. J., *Sir William Jones* (University of Wales Press, Cardiff 1995).

——, *Sir William Jones Selected Poltical and Prose Works* (University of Wales Press, Cardiff 1995).

Fraser, J. G., "Guillaume Postel and Samaritan Studies" in [ed.] M. L. Kuntz, *Postello, Venezia e il suo Mondo a cura di Marion Leathers Kuntz* (Olschki, Florence 1988) pg 99–117.

Frazee, C., "The Maronite Middle Ages" Eastern Churches Review X (1978) pg 88–100.

Frede, C. de, *I Lettori di Umanità nello Studio di Napoli durante il Rinascimento* (L'Arte Tipografica, Naples 1960).

Freudenberger, T., *Augustinus Steuchus aus Gubbio, Augustiner Chorherr und päpstlicher Bibliothekar (1497–1548) und sein literarisches Lebenswerk* (Münster, 1935).

Friedman, J., *The Most Ancient Testimony. Sixteenth Century Christian-Hebraica in the Age of Renaissance Nostalgia* (Ohio University Press, Athens/Ohio 1983).

——, "Jewish Conversion, the Spanish Pure Blood Laws and the Reformation: a Revisionist View of racial and religious Anti-semitism" Sixteenth Century Journal XVIII/1 (1987) pg 3–29.

Fritz, G., *Geschickte den Wiener Schriftgiesserein*. (H. Berthold Messinglinienfabrik und Schriftgiesseres Gen. M. G. B. H., Vienna 1924).

Fücks, J., *Die arabischen Studies in Europa bis in der Anfang des 20 Jahrhunderts* (Leipzig, 1955).

Fumagalli, E., "Aneddoti della Vita di Annio da Viterbo O P." Archivum Fratrum Predicatorum L. (1980) pg 167–199.

——, "Un falso tardo-quattrocentesco: Lo Pseudo–Catone di Annio da Viterbo" in ed Rino Avesani, *Vestigia: Studi in onore di Giuseppe Billanovich* (Rome, 1984) pg 337–383.

Galbiati, G., "La Prima stampa in Arabo" *Miscellanea Giovanni Mercati Vol. VI* (Studi e Testi Vol. CXXVI) (Rome, 1946) pg 409–413.

Galpin, F .W., "The Romance of the Phagotum" Proceedings of the Musical Association LXVII (1941–1942) pg 57–72.

——, and Oldham, G., "The Phagotum" in ed. Stanley Sadie, *The New Grove Dictionary of Music and Musicians* (Macmillan, London 1986) Vol. XIV pg 616–17.

Gandillac, M. de, "Le Thème de la concorde universelle" in *Guillaume Postel Actes du Colloque* pg 192–197.

Gaskell, P., *A New Introduction to Bibliography* (OUP, Oxford 1972).

Geiger, L., *Das Studium der Hebräische Sprache in Deutschland vom Ende des 15 bis zur Mitte des 16 Jahrhunderts* (Schletter'sche Buchhandlung/H. Skutsch, Breslau 1870).

GERSL (Groupe d'Etudes et Recherches souterraines du Liban), *Momies du Liban Rapport préliminaire sur la découverte archéologique de 'Asi-l-Hadat (XIII siècle)* (Edifra, Beirut 1994).

Giacone, F. & Bedouelle, G., "Une Lettre de Gilles de Viterbe 1469–1532 à Jacques Lefèvres d'Etaples c. 1460–1536 au sujet de l'Affaire Reuchlin" Bibliothèque de Humanisme et Renaissance XXXVI (1974) pg 335–345.

Giamil, S., *Genuinae relationes inter Sedem apostolicam et Assyriorum Orientalium seu Chaldaeorum Ecclesiam nunc maiori ex parte primum editae* (Ermano Loescher & Co, Rome 1902).

Gill, J., *The Council of Florence* (CUP, Cambridge 1959).

Ginsburg, C. D., [ed. & trans.] *E. Levita Massoreth ha- Massoreth* (London, 1867).

Goeje, M. J. de, *Catalogus Codicum Orientalium Bibliothecae Academiae Lugduno-Batavae* (E. J. Brill, Louvain 1873).

Gomez-Géraud, M.-C., "L'Empire turc au XVI siècle ou L'Empire des apparences: regards des voyageurs français et flamands" in [ed.] I. Zinguer, *Miroirs de l'altérité et voyages au Proche-Orient. Colloque international de l'Institut d'Histoire et de Civilisation Françaises de l'Université de Haïfa 1987* (Slatkine, Geneva 1991) pg 73–82.

Goodman-Tau, E. & Schilte, C., *Das Buch Jezira* יצירה ספר (with Afterwords by Moshe Idel & W. Schmidt-Biggermann) (Akademie Verlag, Berlin 1993).

Gorny, L., *La Kabbale. Kabbale Juives et Cabale Chrétienne* (Pierre Belfond, Paris 1977).

Gottfarstein, J., [trans.] *Le Bahir Livre de la clarté* (Verdier, Paris 1983).

Graf, G., *Geschichte der christlichen arabischen Literatur* (Vatican City, 1947).

Grafton, A., *Forgers and Critics: Creativity and Duplicity in Western Scholarship* (Princeton UP, Princeton 1990).

Greive, H., "Die christlische Kabbala des Giovanni Pico della Mirandola" Archiv für Kulturgeschichte LVII (1975) pg 141–161.

——,"Die hebräische Grammatik Johannes Reuchlins" Zeitschrift für die alttestamentischen Wissenschaft XC (1978) pg 395–409.

Grendler, P. F., "The Roman Inquisition and the Venetian Press 1540–1605" Journal of Modern History LXVII (1975) pg 48–65.

——, *The Roman Inquisition and the Venetian Press 1540–1605* (Princetown UP, Princetown 1977).

——, "Destruction of Hebrew Books in Venice 1568" in P. F. Grendler, *Culture and Censorship in Later Renaissance Italy and France* (Variorum, London 1981) pg 103–130.

Gribomont, J., "Gilles de Viterbe, le Moine Elie et l'influence de la litterature maronite sur la Rome érudite" Oriens Christianus LIV (1970) pg 125–129. Gribomont, J., "Documents sur les Origines de l'Eglise maronite" Parole de L'Orient V (1974) pg 95–132.

Griffiths, R. [ed.], *The Bible in the Renaissance* (Ashgate, Aldershot 2001).

Grill, S., *Die Syrischen Handschriftenden National Bibliothek in Wien* (Vergleichende Religionsgesschichte de Kirchenväter). (Beigabe der Nationalbibliothek in Wein, Vienna 1959).

——, "Eine unbekannte syrische Handschrift in Innsbruck (cod 401 Bibl. Univ.)" Oriens Christianus LII (1968) pg 151–155.

Griño, R., "Importancia del *Meturgeman* de Elias Levita y del MS Angelica 6–6 para el estudio del mismo" Revista da Sefarad XXXI (1971) pg 353–61.

——, "Un nuevo manuscrito del *Meturgeman* de Elias Levita" in *Homenaja a Juan Prado* (Cosejo Superior de Investigaciones cientificas, Instituto Benito Arias, Madrid 1975) pg 571–583.

——, "El *Meturgeman* y *Neofiti(I)*" Biblica LVIII (1977) pg 153–188.

Grislis, E., "Luther and the Turks" Muslim World LXIV (1974) pg 275–291.

Gruenwald, I., "A Preliminary Critical Edition of Sefer Yezira" Israel Oriental Studies I (1971) pg 132–177.

Guggisberg, H. and Gordon, B.: *Sebastian Castellio 1515–1563. Humanist and defender of Religious Toleration in a Confessional Age* (Ashgate, Aldershot 2003).

Guidi, I., "La prima stampa del Nuovo Testamento in etiopico fatta in Roma nel 1548–1549" Archivo della R. Società Romana di Storia di Patria IX 1886 pg 273–278.

Gulik, W. van, "Die Konistorialakten über die Begründung des uniert-chaldäischen Patriarchates von Mosul unter Papst Julius III" Oriens Christianus IV (1904) pg 261–277.

Gutierrez, D., "De Antiquis Ordinis Eremitorum Sancti Augustini Bibliothecis Annotationes Praeviae" Analecta Augustiniana XXIII (1954) pg 164–174.

Gwilliam, G. H., "An Account of a Syriac Biblical Manuscript of the Fifth Century with special reference to its bearing on the text of the Syriac Version of the Gospels" in [eds.] S. R. Driver et al. *Studia Biblica I* (Clarendon, Oxford 1886) pg 151–174.

——, "The Ammonian Sections, Eusebian Canons and the Harmonising Tables in the Syriac Tetraevangelium" in [eds.] S. R. Driver et al. *Studia Biblica II* (Clarendon, Oxford 1890) pg 241–272.

——, "The Materials for the Criticism of the Peshitto New Testament, with Specimens of the Syriac Massorah" in [eds.] S. R. Driver, T. K. Cheyne, W. Sanday, *Studia Biblica et Ecclesiastica* (Clarendon, Oxford 1891) Vol. III pg 47–104.

Haag, E. & E., "Junius" *La France protestante ou vies des Protestants français* (J. Cherbuliez, Paris 1846–1859) Vol. IV pg 382–390.

Habbi, J., "Signification de l'Union chaldéenne de Mar Sulaqa avec Rome en 1553" L'Orient Syrien XI (1966) pg 99–132; 199–230.

Hachett, M. B., "A 'Lost' Work of Giles of Viterbo" in *Egidio da Viterbo e il suo tempo Egidio da Viterbo O.S.A. e il suo tempo. Atti del V Convegna dell' Instituto Storico Agostiniano, Roma—Viterbo 20–23 ottobre 1982.* (Analecta Augustiniana, Rome 1983) pg 117–127.

Hagemann, L., *Der Kur'an in Verständnis und Kitik bei Nikolaus von Kues* (Josef Kneckt, Frankfurt-a-M 1976).

Hamilton, A., "Eastern Churches and Western Scholarship" in [ed.] A. Grafton, *Rome Reborn The Vatican Library and Renaissance Culture* (Library of Congress, Washington 1993) pg 225–250.

Hammer, J. von, "Mémoires sur les premières relations diplomatique entre la France et la Porte" Journal Asiatique X (1827) pg 19–45.

Hammerstein, N., "The University of Heidelberg in the Early Modern Period" in *History of the Universities* Vol. VI (OUP, Oxford 1986–1987) pg 105–133.

Hartig, O., *Die Gründung der Münchener Hofbibliothek durch Albrecht V und Johann Jakob Fugger*. (Abhandl.der Bayerischen Adademie der Wiss. XXVIII 3: Munich 1917).

Hassens, I. M., "Un ancien Catalogue d'Anaphores syriennes" Ephemerides Liturgicae XLVI (1932) pg 439–447.

Hayek, M., *Liturgie Maronite* (Maison Mame, Paris 1963).

Hayoun, M.-R., *Le Zohar. Aux origines de la mystique juive* (Editions Noésis, Paris 1999).

Heiming, P. O., *Syriche 'Eniane und Greichische Kanones. Die Ms Sach 349 den Staatsbibliothek zu Berlin*. (Verlag der Aschendorffschen Verlagsbuchhandlung, Münster in Westf. 1932).

Henkel, Willi, "The Polyglot Printing Office of the Congregation: The press apostolate as an important means for communicating the Faith" in [ed.] J. Metzler, *Sacrae Congregationis de Propaganda Fide Memoria Rerum* Vol. 1/1 1622–1972 (Herder, Rome, 1971) pg 335–350.

Hirsch, S. A., *A Book of Essays. Jewish Historical Society of England* (MacMillan, London 1905).

Hirst, D., "The Bodleian Scroll: Hunt Add. E.R. (Roll): The European Background to Clement Edmondes' Gift to Sir Thomas Bodley for his new library of a large illustrated scroll of the Kabbalah" in [eds.] G. Sorelius and M. Srigley, *Cultural Exchange between European Nations during the Renaissance* (Almquist & Wiksell International, Stockholm 1994).

Hitzel, F. [ed.], *Livres et Lecture dans le Monde ottoman* (Revue des Mondes musulmans et de la Méditerranée, Edisud, Aix-en-Provence 1999).

Holmes, G. [ed.], *Art and Politics in Renaissance Italy* (British Academy/OUP, London, 1993).

Hossiau, A., "The Alexandrine Anaphora of St. Basil" in [ed.] L. Sheppard, *The New Liturgy* (D. L. T., London 1970) pg 228–243.

Howard, G., "The Hebrew Gospel of Matthew" in *Anchor Dictionary of the Bible* (Doubleday, New York 1992) vol. V pg 642–3.

——, *The Hebrew Gospel of Matthew* (2nd ed., Macon 1995).

Hudon, W. V., *Marcello Cervini and Ecclesiastical Government in Tridentine Italy* (Northern Illinois University Press, 1992)

Hudon, W., "Marcellus II, Girolamo Seripando and the Image of the Angelic Pope" in [ed.] M. Reeves, *Prophetic Rome in the High Renaissance Period* (Clarendon, Oxford 1992) pg 373–387.

Idel, M., "The Throne and the Seven-branched Candlestick: Pico della Mirandola's Hebrew Source" Journal of the Warburg and Courtauld Institute XL (1977) pg 291.

——, "The Magical and Neoplatonic Interpretation of the Kabbalah in the Renaissance" in [ed.] B. D. Cooperman, *Jewish Thought in the Sixteenth Century* (Harvard U. P., Cambridge Mass. 1983) pg 186–242.

——, *Kabbalah, New Perspectives* (Yale U.P., New Haven 1988).

——, "The Anthropology of Yohanan Alemanno: Sources and Influences" Annali di Storia dell' Esegesi (Bologna) VII /1 (1990) pg 93–112.

Jacquemier, M., "Le Mythe de Babel et la Kabbale chrétienne au XVI siècle" Nouvelle Revue du Seizième Siècle X (1992) pg 51–67.

Javary, G., *Recherches sur l'utilisation du thème de la Sekina dans l'apologétique chrétienne du quinzième au dix-huitième siècle* (Champion, Paris 1977).

——, "A propos du thème de la Sekina: variations sur le nom de Dieu" in *Kabbalistes chrétiens* (Albin Michel, Paris 1979) pg 281–306.

Jedin, H., *Girolamo Seripando. Sein Leben und Denken im Geisteskampf des 16 Jhds* (Würzburg 1937).

Jongkees, J. H., "Masius in moeilijkheden" De Gulden Passer XLI (1963) pg 161–168.

Kantenbach, F. W., "Die Vertreibung der Lutheraner aus Heidelberg 1583/4 nach dem Stammbuch Jacob Schoppers" Blätter für Pfalzische Kirchengeschichte und Religiöse Volkskunde XLII 1975 pg 118–121.

Kaufhold, H., Review of Helga Anschütz, *Die syrischen Christen von Tur 'Abdin* Oriens Christianus LXX (1986) pg 205–211.

Kaufmann, D., "Die Verbrennung Talmudischer Literatur" Jewish Quarterly Review (original series) XIII (1901) pg 533–538.

——, "Elia Menachem Chaftan: Jews teaching Hebrew to non-Jews" Jewish Quarterly Review IX (1896) pg 500ff.

Kévorkian, R. H., *Catalogue des 'Incunables' arméniens (1511/1695) ou Chronique de L'Imprimerie arménienne* (Crainer, Geneva 1986).

Kieszkowski, B., "Les Rapports entre Elie de Medigo et Pic de la Mirandole (D'après le ms. Lat 6508 de la Bibliothèque nationale) Rinascimento IV (1964) pg 58–91.

Klein, M., "Elias Lévita and Ms. Neofiti I" Biiblica LVI (1975) pg 242–246.

Klein, W. P., *Am Anfang war das Wort. Theorie und Wissenschaftsgeschichtliche Elemente früh-neuzeitlichen Sprachbewusstseins* (Berlin, 1992).

——, [ed.], *Sefer Jesirah. Übersetzt und kommertiert von Guillaume Postel. Neudruck der Ausgabe, Paris 1552. Herausgegeben, eingeleitet, und erläutert von WPK* (Frommann-Holzberg, Bad Connstatt/Stuttgart 1994).

Kleinhaus, A., "De vita et operibus Petri Galatini" Antonianum I (1926) pg 145–179; 327–356.

Knefelkamp, U., *Die Suche nach dem Reich des Priesterkönigs Johannes* (Verlag Andreas Müller, Gelsenkirchen 1986).

König, E., "Zum namen der syrischen Bibelubersetzung Peschitta" Zeitschrift der Deutschen Morganlandischen Gesellschaft" XLVII (1893) pg 316–319.

Kristeller, P. O., "G. Postel lettore di Marsilio Ficino" in [ed.] M. L. Kuntz, *Postello, Venezia e il suo Mondo* pg 1–18.

Kritzeck, J., "Robert of Ketton's translation of the Qur'an" Islamic Quarterly II (1955) pg 309–312.

Kuntz, M. L., "A New Link in the Correspondence of Guillaume Postel" Bibliothèque de Humanisme et Renaissance XLI (1979) pg 575–581.

——, *Guillaume Postel. Prophet of the Restitution of All Things. His Life and Thought* (Martinus Nijhoff, The Hague 1981).

——, "Journey as restitution in the Thought of Guillaume Postel" History of European Ideas I/4 (1981) pg 315–329.

——, "Voyages to the East and their meaning in the thought of Guillaume Postel" in [eds.] J. Céard & J.-C. Margolin, *Voyager à la Renaissance Actes du Colloque de Tours 1983* (Maisonneuve & Larose, Paris 1987) pg 51–63.

——, "Guillaume Postel and the Syriac Gospels of Athanasius Kircher" Renaissance Quarterly XL (1987) pg 465–484.

——, [a cura di], *Postello, Venizia e il suo mondo* (Leo S Olschki, Firenze 1988).

——, "Guillaume Postel e l'idea di Venezia come La Magistratura più perfetta" in [ed.] Kuntz, *Postello, Venezia e il suo Mondo* pg 163–178.

Kvačala, J., "Wilhelm Postell Seine Geistesart und Seine Reformgedanken" Archiv für Reformationsgeschichte IX (1911–1912) pg 285–330; XI (1914) pg 200–227; XV (1918) pg 157–203.

Launey, M.-L., "Le De Originibus de 1538: une rhétorique des origins" in *Actes du Colloque International d'Avranches 5–9 septembre 1981 Guillaume Postel 1581–1981* (Guy Trédaniel, Éditions de La Maisnie, Paris 1985) pg 307–316.

Le Déaut, R., "Jalons pour une Histoire d'un manuscrit du Targum palestinien (Neofiti I)" Biblica XLVIII (1967) pg 509–533.

Lecler, J., *Histoire de la Tolérance au siècle de la Réforme* (Albin Michel, Paris 1994. First edition 1955, Editions Montaigne).

Lefevre, R., "Su un codice etiopico della 'Vaticana'" La Bibliofilia XLII (1940) pg 97–102.

———, "L'Etiopica nella Politica orientale di Gregorio XIII" Annali Lateranensi XI (1947) pg 295–312.

———, "Documenti e Notizie su Tasfa Seyon e la sua attivita Romana nel sec. XVI". Rassegna di Studi Etiopici (Rome) XXIV (1969–1970) pg 74–133.

Lefranc, A., *Histoire du Collège de France* (Hachette, Paris 1893).

Leftley, Sharon A., Millenarian Thought in Renaissance Rome with special reference to Pietro Galatino c. 1464–c. 1540 and Egidio da Viterbo c. 1469–1532. Unpublished Doctoral Thesis. Bristol University 1995.

Lemmens, L., "Notae criticae ad initia unionis Chaldaeorum" Antonianum I (1926) pg 205–218.

———, "Relationes Nationem Chaldaeorum inter et Custodiam Terrae Sanctae 1551–1629" Archivum Franciscanum Historicum XIX (1926) pg 17–28.

Leroy, J., *Moines et Monastères du Proche-Orient* (Horizons de France, Paris 1958).

———, *Les Manuscrits syriaque à peintures* (Paul Geuthner, Paris 1964).

———, "Une Copie syriaque du Missale Romanum de Paul III et son Arrière-plan historique" Mélanges de l'Université de St. Joseph, XLVI (fasc. 23) (1979) pg 355–382.

Lestringant, F., "Guillaume Postel et l'obsession turque" in [ed.] M. L. Kuntz, *Postello Venezia e il suo Mondo* pg 265–297.

———, "Cosmographie pour une Restitution; note sur le Traite 'Des Merveilles du Monde' de Guillaume Postel (1553)" in [ed.] M. L. Kuntz, *Postello, Venezia e il suo Mondo* pg 227–260.

———, "Alterities critiques: du bon usage du Turc à la renaissance" in *D'un Orient l'autre* pg 86–105.

Levi della Vida, G., *Ricerche sulle Formazione del piu antico fondo dei manoscritti orientali della Biblioteca Vaticana. Studi e Testi 92* (Biblioteca Apostolica Vaticana, Città del Vaticano 1939).

———, *Documenti intorno alle Relazioni delle Chiese orientali con La S. Sede durante il Pontificato di Gregorio XIII* (Studi e Testi 143: Biblioteca Apostolica Vaticana, Vatican City 1948).

———, "Teseo Ambrogio" in *Dizionario Biografico degli Italiani* (G. Ernest and S. Foa, Rome 1993) vol. II pg 39–42.

Loeb, I., "Les Armes de Widmanstadt" Revue des Études juives I (1875) pg 298–301.

Londi, A., "Prophecy at the Time of the Council of Pisa (1511–1513)" in [ed.] M. Reeves, *Prophetic Rome in the High Renaissance Period* (Clarendon, Oxford 1992) pg 53–61.

Lossen, M., "Masius" in the *Allgemeine Deutsche Biographie* (Leipzig, 1884) Vol. XX pg 559–562.

———, *Briefe von Andreas Masius und Seinen Freunden 1538 bis 1573* (Verlag von Alphons Düre, Leipzig 1886).

Loutham, H., *The Quest for Compromise. Peacemakers in Counter-Reformation Vienna* (C.U. P., Cambridge 1997).

Lubac, H. du, *La Rencontre du Bouddhisme et de L'Occident* (Aubier, Paris 1952).

Macdonald, J., *The Theology of the Samaritans* (SCM, London 1964).

Maillard, J.-F., "Sous l'Invocation de Dante et de Pic de la Mirandole: les manuscrits inédits de Georges de Venise (Francesco Zorzi)" Bibliothèque d'Humanisme et Renaissance XXXVI (1974) pg 47–61.

Malton, S. [ed.], *Documents oubliés sur l'Alchemie, la Kabbale et Guillaume Postel* (Droz, Geneva 2001).

Mann, J., "Glanures de La Gueniza" Revue des Etudes juives LXXIV (1954) pg 148–159.

Margolin, J.-C., "Science et nationalisme linguistiques, ou la bataille pour l'etymologie au XVIᵉ siècle" in *The Fairest Flower The Emergence of Linguistic National Consciousness in Renaissance Europe* (Conference of Center for Medieval and Renaissance Studies, University of California, Los Angeles. 12–13 December 1983) (Presso L'Accademia, Florence 1985) pg 139–166.

——, "Sur quelques ouvrages de la bibliothèque de Postel annotés de sa main" in *Guillaume Postel 1581–1981* pg 112–117.

Martin, F. X., *Friar, Reformer and Renaissance Scholar: the life and work of Giles of Viterbo 1469–1532* (Augustinian Press, Rome 1992).

——, "The problem of Giles of Viterbo: A historiographical survey" Augustiniana IX (1959) pg 357–379: X (1960) pg 43–60.

——, "The Palaeological Character of Codex Neofiti I" Textus III (1963) pg 1–35.

Massa, E., "Egidio da Viterbo e la Metodologia del sapere nel Cinquecento" in *Pensée humaniste et Tradition chrétienne au XVᵉ et XVIᵉ siècles* (CRNS, Paris 1950) pg 185–239.

Mayer, C.-A., *Bibliography of the Samaritans* (E. J. Brill, Leiden 1964).

Mayer, T. F., *Reginald Pole, Prince and Prophet* (C. U. P., Cambridge 2000).

Mercati, G., "Ambrogio Teseo primo traduttore e raccoglitore di liturgie orientali" Rassenga Gregoriana V (1906) pg 551–557.

Messina G., *Notizia du un Diatessaran Persiano Tradolto dal Siriaco* (Pontificio Instituto Biblico, Roma 1943).

Metcalf, G. J., "The Indo-European Hypothesis in the Sixteenth and Seventeenth Centuries" in [ed.] D. H. Hymes, *Studies in the History of Linguistics: Tradition and Paradigms* (Indiana University Press, Bloomington 1974) pg 233–257.

——, "Theodor Bibliander and the Languages of Japhet's Progeny" Historiographia Linguistica VII: 3 (1986) pg 323–333.

Metzger, B. M., *The Early Versions of the New Testament* (OUP, Oxford 1977).

Meyendorff, J., Papadakin, A, *L'orient chrétien et l'essor de la papauté* (Cerf: Paris 2001 [English: *The Christian East and the Rise of the Papacy* (St Vladimir's Press, New York 1994)].

Meyer, J. F. (tr), *Das Buch Jezira* [Original edition Leipzig 1830]. New edition by Eveline Goodman (Thom. & Christophe Schulte, Berlin 1993).

Mignini, F., "I limiti della Concordia e il mito della ragione" in *Actes du Colloque International d'Avranches 5–9 septembre 1981 Guillaume Postel 1581–1981* (Guy Trédaniel, Éditions de La Maisnie, Paris 1985) pg 207–221.

Minnich, N. H., "The Concept of reform proposed at the Fifth Lateran Council" Archivum Historiae Pontificae VII (1969) pg 163–251.

——, "The Participants at the Fifth Lateran Council" Archivum Historiae Pontificae XII (1974) pg 157–206.

——, "Prophecy and the Fifth Lateran Council 1512–1517" in [ed.] M. Reeves, *Prophetic Rome in the High Renaissance Period* (Clarendon, Oxford 1992) pg 63–88.

——, "The role of Prophecy in the Career of the Enigmatic Bernadino López de Caravajal" in [ed.] M. Reeves, *Prophetic Rome in the High Renaissance Period* (Clarendon, Oxford 1992) pg 111–120.

Moeller, B., "Scripture tradition and Sacrament in the Middle Ages and Luther" [eds.] F. F. Bruce & E. G. Rupp, *Holy Book and Holy Tradition* (MUP, Manchester 1988) pg 113–135.

Monfasani, J., "Sermons of Giles of Viterbo as Bishop" in *Egidio da Viterbo e il suo tempo Egidio da Viterbo e il suo tempo Egidio da Viterbo O.S.A. e il suo tempo. Atti del V Convegna dell' Instituto Storico Agostiniano, Roma—Viterbo 20–23 ottobre 1982.* (Analecta Augustiniana, Rome 1983) pg 137–189. Monfasani, J., "Hermes Trismegistus, Rome and the myth of Europa: an unknown text of Giles of Viterbo" Viator XXII (1991) pg 311–342.

Montgomery, J. A., *The Samaritans* (J. C. Winston, Philadelphia 1907).

Moore, S. H., "The Turkish Menace in the sixteenth century" Modern Languages Review XL (1945) pg 30–36.

Moosa, M., *The Maronites in History* (Syracuse U.P., New York 1986).

Morisi, A., *Apocalypsis Nova: Ricerche sull' origine e la formazione del testo dello Pseudo-Amadeo* (Studi storici 77, Rome 1970).

——, "Galatino et La Kabbale chrétienne" in *Kabbalistes chrétiens* (Cahiers de Humanisme, Albin Michel, Paris 1979) pg 213–31.

Morisi-Guerra, A., "The Apocalypsis Nova: a Plan for Reform" in [ed.] M. Reeves, *Prophetic Rome in the High Renaissance Period* (Clarendon, Oxford 1992), pg 27–50.

Moss, C., *Catalogue of Syriac printed books and related literature in the British Museum* (BM, London 1982).

Muller J., Róth E., *Aussereuropäische Druckereien in 16 Jahrhundert. Bibliographie der Drucke* (Verlag Librairie Heitz GMBH, Baden-Baden 1969).

Müller, E., *Das Konzil Von Vienne 1311–1312 Seine Quellen und Seine Geschichte* (Verlag der Aschendorffschen Verlagibuckhandlung, Münster in Westfalen 1934).

Müller, M., *Johann Albrecht Widmanstetter 1506 bis 1557 Sein Leben und Wirken* (Bamberg, 1908).

Muller, R. A. & Thompson, J. L. [eds.], *Biblical Interpretation in the Era of the Reformation* (Eerdmans, Grand Rapids 1996).

Narducci, E., *Catalogus codicum mss praeter orientales qui in Bibliotheca Alexandrina Romae asservantur* (Rome, 1877).

Nasrallah, J., *L'Imprimerie en Liban* (Harissa, 1949).

Nau, F., "Martyrologies et Ménologies orientaux, I–XIII: Un martyrologie et douze ménologies syriaques" Patrologia Orientalis X (1915) pg 131.

Nave, F. de, *Het Museum Plantin-Moretus Te Antwerpen. I: De Bibliothoek* (Publikaties MPM/PK, Antwerpen 1985).

——, *Het Museum Plantin-Moretus Te Antwerpen. II: De Archieven* (Publikaties MPM/PK 2, Antwerp 1985).

——, *Philologia Arabica. Arabische studiën en drukken in de Nederlanden in de 16de en 17de eeuw* (Publikaties MPM/PK 3: Antwerp 1986).

Nestle, E., "Zum Namen der syrischen Bibelübersetzung Peschitta." in Zeitschrift der Deutschen Morgenländischen Gesellschaft XLVII (1893) pg 157–159.

——, *Syriac Grammar with Bibliography, Chrestomathy and Glossary* (Reuther, Berlin 1889).

——, *Syriac Grammar with Bibliography, Chrestomathy and Glossary*. Eng translation from Second German edition, by R. S. Kennedy (Berlin, 1889).

——, "Zur Geschichte der syrischen Typen" Zeitschrift der Deutschen Morgenländischen Gesellschaft LXXV (1903) pg 16–17.

——, "Aus einem sprachwissenschaftlichen Werk von 1539" Monatschrift der Deutschen Morganlandischer Gesellschaft (Wiesbaden) LVIII (1904) pg 601–616.

Netanyahu, B. Z., *Don Isaac Abravaniel* (Philadelphia, 1953).

Neubaner, A., *Mediaeval Jewish Chronicles II* (OUP, Oxford 1895).

Niccoli, O., *Prophecy and People in Renaissance Italy* (Princetown UP, Princetown 1987).

——, "High and Low in Prophetic Culture in Rome at the beginning of the 16th Century" in [ed.] M. Reeves, *Prophetic Rome in the High Renaissance Period* (Clarendon, Oxford 1992) pg 203–222.

Noja, S., "Contribution à la Bibliographie des Samaritains" Alon XXXIII (1973) pg 98–113.

Nuovo, A., "Il Corano arabo ritrovato" La Bibliofilia LXXXIX (1987) pg 237–271.

O'Malley, J. W., "Giles of Viterbo: A Sixteenth Century Text on Doctrinal Development". Traditio XXII (1966) pg 445–450.

——, "Giles of Viterbo: a Reformer's Thought on Renaissance Rome". Renaissance Quarterly XX (1967) pg 1–11.

——, "Historical Thought and the Reform Crisis of the Early Sixteenth Century" Theological Studies XXVIII (1967) pg 531–548.

——, *Giles of Viterbo on Church and Reform. A Study in Renaissance Thought* (E. J. Brill, Leiden 1968).

——, "Fulfilment of the Christian Golden Age under Pope Julius II: Text of a discourse of Giles of Viterbo 1507" Traditio XXV (1969) pg 265–338.

——, "Man's Dignity, God's Love and the Destiny of Rome: A text of Giles of Viterbo" Viator III (1972) pg 389–416.

——, *Egidio da Viterbo and Renaissance Rome. Egidio da Viterbo OSA, e il suo tempo: Atti del V Convegio dell'Instituto Storico Agostino, Roma—Viterbo 20–23 ottobre 1882 (Studia Augustia Historica 9)* (Analecta Augustina, Rome 1983).

O'Reilly, C., "Maximus Caesar et Pontifex Maximus: Giles of Viterbo proclaims the Alliance between the Emperor Maximillian I and Pope Julius II" Augustiniana XXII (1972) pg 80–117.

——, " 'Without Councils we cannot be saved...' Giles of Viterbo addresses the Fifth Lateran Council". Augustiniana XXVII (1977) pg 184–204.

Olender, M., *Les langues de Paradis. Aryens et Semites: un couple providential* (Gallimond/Le Seuil, Paris 1989).

Overfield, J. H., *Humanism and Scholasticm in Late Mediaeval Germany* (Princeton University Press, New Jersey 1984).

Palandjian, H. & Tonoyan A. et al., *Festschrift Prof. Dr. Dora Sakayan zum 65 Geburtstag* (Diocese of the Armenian Church of Canada, Montreal 1996).

Parente, F., "La Chiesa e il Talmud" in [ed.] C. Vivanti, *Storia d'Italia Annali II: Gli Ebrei in Italia* (Turin, 1996) pg 521–643.

Paviot, J., "D'un énnemi l'autre: des Mamelouts aux Ottomans. Voyages de renseignement à Levant XIIIᵉ–XVIIᵉ siècle" in *D'un Orient l'autre* (Editions de CNRS, Paris 1991) Vol. 1 pg 317–328.

Pélisser, L.-G., "Manuscrits de Gilles de Viterbe à La Bibliothèque Angélique (Rome)". Revue des Bibliothèques (1892) pg 228–240.

——, "Pour la biographie du Cardinal Gilles de Viterbe" in *Miscellanea di studi critici edita in honore di Arturo Graf* (Bergamo, 1903) pg 789–815.

Pentry, Yvonne, *Gender and Kabbalah and the Reformation: The Mystical Theology of Guillaume Postel (1510–1581)* (E. J. Brill, Leiden 2004).

Percival, W. K., "The Reception of Hebrew in Sixteenth-Century Europe: the impact of the Cabala" Historiographa Linguistica XI 1/2 (1984) pg 21–38.

Perles, J., *Beiträge zur Geschichte der hebräischen und aramaischen Studien* (Theodore Achermann, München 1884).

——, "Les Savants juifs à Florence à l'époque de Laurent de Médicis" Revue des Études juives XII (1886) pg 245–256.

Perrone, B., "Il '*De Republica Christiana*' nel pensiero filosofico e politico di P. Galatino." *Studi Pugliese in Onore di G. Chiarelli II* (Galatina, 1973) pg 449–633.

Pfister, R. "Das Türkenbüchlein Theodor Biblianders" Theologische Zeitschrift (Basel) IX (1953) pg 438–454.

Pflaum, H., "Leone Ebreo und Pico della Mirandola" Monatschrift für Geschichte und Wissenschaft des Judentums LXXII (1928) pg 344–350.

Pitt, W. E., "The Origin of the Anaphora of the Liturgy of St. Basil" Journal of Ecclesiastical History XII (1961) pg 1–13.

Postel, C., *Les Écrits de Guillaume Postel publiés en France et leurs Éditeurs 1538–1579* (Droz, Geneva 1992).

Quicherat, J., *Histoire de Sainte-Barbe Collège, Communauté, Institution* (Paris, 1860–1864).

Rabbath, A., *Documents inédits pour servir à l'Histoire du Christianisme en Orient I* (Paris 1905–1907) (A posthumous second volume has the name of P. Tournebize S. J.).

Raes, A., *Anaphorae Syriacae* (Pont. Inst. Or. Stud, Rome 1939).

Rahlfs, A., "Die aethiopische Bibelübersetzung" in idem *Septuaginta Studien* (2nd ed. Gottingen 1965).

Rankin, H. D., *Celts and the Classical World* (Croom Helm, London 1987).
Raphael, P. Pierre, *Le Rôle de Collège Maronite Romain dans l'orientalism aux XVIIe et XVIIIe Siècles*, (Université Saint Joseph de Beyrouth, Beirut 1950).
Raubenheimer, M., *Paul Fagius aus Rheinzaben. Sein Leben und Wirken als Reformator und Gelehrter* (Emil Sommer, Grünstadt (Pfalz) 1957).
Read, M. K., "The Renaissance concept of Linguistic Change" Archivum Linguisticum VIII (n.s.) (1977) pg 60–69.
Reeves, M. *The Influence of Prophesy in the Late Middle Ages: A Study in Joachism* (OUP, Oxford, 1969)
——, [ed.], *Prophetic Rome in the High Renaissance Period* (Clarendon Press, Oxford 1992).
——, *Joachim of Fiore and the Prophetic Future* (London, 1976).
——, "The Medieval Heritage" in [ed.] M. Reeves, *Prophetic Rome in the High Renaissance Period* (Clarendon, Oxford 1992) pg 3–21.
Reichert, K., "Pico della Mirandola and the Beginnings of Christian Kabbalah" in [eds.] K. E. Grözinger & J. Dan, *Mysticism, Magic and Kabbalah in Ashkenazi Judaism (Symposium at Frankfurt-a-M. 1991)* (Walter de Gruyter, Berlin 1995) pg 195–207.
Renfrew, C., *Archaeology and Language The Puzzle of Indo-European Origins* (Jonathan Cape, London 1987).
Rietbergen, Peter, *Power and Religion in Baroque Rome: Barberini Cultural Politics* (E. J. Brill, Leiden 2006).
Riezler, S. v. "Johann Albrecht Widmanstetter" in *Allgem. Deutsch. Biographie* Vol. XLII pg 357–361.
Roey, A. van, "Les début des Études syriaques et André Masius" in [ed.] René Lavenant, *V Symposium Syriacum 1988* (Orientalia Christiana Analecta CCXXXVI) (Pont. Institutum Studiorum Orientalium, Rome 1990) pg 9–11.
——, "Les Études syriaque d'Andreas Masius" Orientalia Louvansia Periodica IX (1978) pg 141–158.
Rooden, P. T. van, and Wesselius, J. W., "J. S. Rittangel in Amsterdam" Nederlands Archief voor Kerkgeschiedenis LXV (1985) pg 131–152.
——, "Two early cases of publication by subscription in Holland and Germany: Jacob Abendana's *Mikhal Yophi* (1661) and David Cohen de Lara's *Keter Kehunna* (1668)" Quaerendo XVI 2 (1986) pg 110–130.
Rooses, M., *Correspondance de Christophe Plantin* (Antwerp 1883; Kraus Reprint: Nendeln-Liechtenstein, 1968)
Rosenthal, E. I. J., "Yohanan Alemano & Occult Science" in ed. Y. Maeyama & W. G. Saltzer, ΠΡΙΣΜΑΤΑ *Naturwissenschaftsgeschichtliche Studien (Festschrift for Willy Hartner)* (Frank Steiner Verlag, Wiesbaden 1977) pg 349–361.
Rossi, P., "The legacy of Ramon Lull in sixteenth century thought" Medieval & Renaissance Studies V (1961) pg 183–213.
Roth, C., *History of the Jews in England* (Clarendon: Oxford 1942).
Rothstein, M., "Etymology, Genealogy, and Immutability of Origins" Renaissance Quarterly XLIII (1990) pg 332–347.
Rotondo, A., *Studi e Ricerche di Storia ereticale italiano del Cinquecento* (Edizione Giappichelli, Turin 1974).
——, "Guillaume Postel e Basilea" Critica Storica X/1 (1973) pg 114–159.
Rowland, Ingrid D., *The Culture of the High Renaissance Ancients and Moderns in Sixteenth Century Rome* (CUP, Cambridge, 1998).
——, *The Scarith of Scornello* (UCP, Chicago 2004).
Rubin, M., "The Language of Creation or the Primordial Language: a case of cultural polemics in Antiquity" Journal of Jewish Studies XLIX (1998) pg 306–333.
Rusconi, R., "An Angelic Pope before the Sack of Rome" in [ed.] M. Reeves, *Prophetic Rome in the High Renaissance Period* (Clarendon, Oxford 1992) pg 157–187.
Saenger, P. & van Kampen, K. [eds.], *The Bible as Book The First Printed editions* (British Library, London 1995).

Salibi, K. S., "The Maronite Church in the Middle Ages and its Union with Rome." Oriens Christianus XLII (1958) pg 92–104.

——, "The Maronites of Lebanon under Frankish and Mamluke Rule" Arabica IV (1957) pg 288–303.

——, *Maronite Historians of Mediaeval Lebanon* (Beirut 1959: 2nd ed. Naufal Group, Beirut/Paris 1991).

Salviati, G. B., "Postel, Galatino e l'Apocalypsis Nova" in *Guillaume Postel 1581–1981 Actes du Colloque international d'Avranches 5–9 sept 1981* (G. Trédaniel, Paris 1985) pg 7–108.

Sauchau, E., *Verzeichnis der syrischen Handschriften der königlichen Bibliothek zu Berlin II* (Berlin, 1899).

Schmidt, N., "Traces of early acquaintance in Europe with the Book of Enoch" Journal of the American Oriental Society XLII (1922) pg 44–52.

Schmitt, C. B., "Perennial Philosophy: from Agostino Steuco to Leibniz" Journal of the History of Ideas XXVII (1966) pg 505–532.

Scholem, G., "Zur Geschichte der Anfänge der christlichen Kabbala" in *Essays presented to Leo Baeck* (East and West Library, London 1954) pg 158–193. English translation in [ed.] Joseph Dan, *The Christian Kabbalah Jewish Mystical Books and their Christian Interpreters* (Harvard College Library, Cambridge Mass. 1997) pg 17–51.

Scholem, G. G., *Major Trends in Jewish Mysticism* (Schocken, New York 1961) (3rd Rev. Ed.).

——, *Kabbalah* (Keter, Jerusalem 1974).

Schönfelder, J., *Syrische Handschriften. Verzeichniss der Orientalischen Handschrifte den K. Hof- und Staatsbibliothek in München* (Otto Harrassowitz, Wiesbaden 1875/1970).

Schonfield, H. J., *An Old Hebrew Text of St Matthew's Gospel* (T & T Clark, Edinburgh 1927).

Schur, N., "The Samaritans as described in Christian Itineraries (14th to 18th Centuries)" Palestine Exploration Quarterly L (1986) pg 144–155.

Schwarzfuchs, Lyse, *Le Livre hebreu à Paris au XVIe siècle* (Bibliothèque nationale, Paris 2004).

Schweizer, J., "Ein Beitrag zu Wilhelm Postels Leben und zur Geschichte des Trienter Konzils und der Inquistion" Römische Quartalschrift für christliche Altertumskunde und für Kirchengeschichte XXIV (1910) pg 100ff.

Schwer, P., "Die syrische Wiedergabe der neutestamentlischen Eigennamen" Zeitschrift für die altestamentlische Wissenschaft XXXI (1911) pg 267–303.

Screech, M. A., "The Illusion of Postel's Feminism" Journal of the Warburg and Courtauld Institute XVI (1953) pg 162–170.

Secret, F., "Les Jésuits et le Kabbalisme chrétien à la Renaissance" Bibliothèque d'Humanisme et Renaissance XV (1954) pg 139–144.

——, "G. Postel et les courants prophétique de la Renaissance" Studi Francesi III (1957) pg 375–395.

——, "Les Dominicains et la Kabbale chrétienne à la Renaissance" Archivum Fratrum Praedicatorum XXVII (1957) pg 329–336.

——, *Le Zôhar chez les Kabbalistes Chrétiens de la Renaissance* (Librairie Durlacher, Paris 1958).

——, "Qui était l'Orientaliste Mithridates" Revue des Études juives XVI (CXVI) (1958) pg 96–102, 91.

——, "L'Emithologie de Guillaume Postel" in [ed.] E. Castelli, *Umanismo e Simbolismo* (CEDAM, Padova 1958) pg 381–437.

——, "Le Symbolisme de la Kabbale chrétienne dans la 'Scechina' de Egidio da Viterbo". Archivo di Filosofia (Rome. Instituto di Studi Filosofia 1958) pg 131–154.

——, [ed.], *Egidio da Viterbo. Scechina e libellus de litteris hebraicis* (Edizione nationali dei Classici, Roma 1959).

——, "Une texte mal connu de Simon Luzzato sur la Kabbale" Revue des Études juives CXVIII (1959/60) pg 121–128.

———, "Notes sur Guillaume Postel (VII G. Postel et Sébastien Munster)" Bibliothèque d'Humanisme et Renaissance XXII (1960) pg 377.

———, "Postel censeur des livres hébreux à Venice" Bibliothèque d'Humanisme et Renaissance XXII (1960) pg 384–5).

———, "Le Voyage en Orient de Pierre Duchastel Lecteur de François Ier" Bibliothèque d'Humanisme et Renaissance XXIII (1961) pg 121–126.

———, "Theseus Ambrosius et Postellus 'Ambolateus Doctor Medicinae'" Bibliothèque d'Humanisme et Renaissance vol. XXIII (1961) pg 130–13.

———, "Postel, témoin de la destruction des Talmuds à Rome en 1559" Bibliothèque de Humanisme et Renaissance XXIII (1961) pg 358–9.

———, "La Place de Postel dans la littérature de voyages" Bibliothèque d'Humanisme et Renaissance XXIII (1961) pg 362–366.

———, "G. Postel et les études arabes" Arabica IX (1962) pg 36.

———, "Aegidiana Hebraica" Revue des Etudes juives CXXI (1962) pg 409–416.

———, "Les Grammaires hébraïques d'Augustinus Justinianus" Archivum Fratrum Praedicatorum XXXIII (1963) pg 269–279.

———, "L'Herméneutique de G. Postel" in Archivio di Filosofia, Umanismo e Ermeneutica (CEDAM, Padova 1963) pg 91–118.

———, "Une lettre à Oporin (1553)" Bibliothèque de Humanisme et Renaissance XXV (1963) pg 216–221.

———, "Girolamo Seripando et la Kabbale" Rinascimento (second series) III (1963) pg 251–268.

———, "La Rencontre d'Andreas Masius avec Postel à Rome" Revue d'Histoire ecclésiastique LIX (1964) pg 485–489.

———, "Benjamin Nehemia ben Elnathan et G. Postel à la prison de Ripetta en 1559" Revue des Études juives CXXIV (1965) pg 174–176.

———, "Nouvelles Précisions sur Flavius Mithridates Maitre de Pic de la Mirandole et Traducteur de Commentaires de Kabbale" in L'Opera e il Pensero di G. Pico della Mirandola nella Storia dell' Umanismo (Instituto Nationale di Studi sul Rinascimento, Florence 1965) Vol. II pg 169–187.

———, "Notes sur Guillaume Postel" Bibliothèque de Humanisme et Renaissance XXVIII (1966) pg 691–701.

———, "La Réponse de G. Postel a Teseo Ambrogio" Bibliothèque d'Humanisme et Renaissance XXVIII (1966) pg 698–699.

———, "Egidio da Viterbo et quelques-uns de ses contemporains". Augustiniana XVI (1966) pg 371–385.

———, Guillaume Postel (1510–1581) et sa Interprétation du Candélabre de Moyse (B de Graaf, Niewkoop 1966).

———, L'ésotérisme de Guy le Fèvre de la Boderie (Librairie Droz, Genève 1969).

———, [ed.], Guillaume Postel, Le Thresor des Propheties de l'Univers (Martinus Nijhoff, La Haye 1969).

———, "Filippo Archinto, Girolamo Cardano, et Guillaume Postel" Studi francesci XIII (n. 37) (1969) pg 73–76.

———, Bibliographie des Manuscrits de Guillaume Postel (Droz, Geneva 1970).

———, [ed.], Guillaume Postel, Apologies et Rétractions. Manuscrits inédits publiés avec une introduction et des notes par François Secret (B de Graaf: Niewkoop 1972).

———, "Un Manuscrit retrouvé de G. Postel" Bibliothèque d'Humanisme et Renaissance XXXV (1973) pg 87–99.

———, "Notes sur Egidio da Viterbo" Augustiniana XXVII (1977) pg 205–237.

———, "Postel et la Graecia Mendax" Bibliothèque d'Humanisme et Renaissance XXXIX (1977) pg 125–135.

———, [ed.], Postelliana Bibliotheca humanistica et reformator (B. de Graaf, Niewkoop 1981).

———, Kabbalistes Chrétien de la Renaissance. Nouvelle edition mise à jour et augmentée (Arche, Milano 1985).

——, in "Postel et l'origine des Turcs" in [ed.] Kuntz, *Postello, Venezia e il suo Mondo* (1988) pg 301–306.

——, [ed.], *Guillaume Postel. Paralipomènes de la vie de François Ier Traduction avec introduction et des notes* (Arché, Milan 1989).

Sed, N., "Le Sefer Yesira. L'Edition critique, Le Texte primitif La Grammaire et La Métaphysique" Revue des Etudes juives CXXXIII (1973) pg 513–528.

Sed-Rajna, G., "Une Diagramme kabbalistique de la Bibliothèque de Gilles de Viterbe" in ed. G. Nahon and C. Touati, *Hommages à Georges Vajda* (Editions Peeters, Louvain 1980) pg 365–376.

Segal, L. A., *Historical Consciousness and Religious Tradition in Azariah de' Rossi's Me'or 'Einayim* (Jewish Publication Society, Philadelphia 1989).

Segesvavy, V., *L'Islam et la Réforme* (Edition L'Age d'Homme, Lausanne 1977).

Seiming, P. O., *Syrische 'Eniane und Griechische Kanones* (Verlag der Aschendorffschen Verlagsbuchhandlung, Münster in Westf. 1932).

Setton, K. M., "Lutheranism and the Turkish Peril" Balkan Studies III (1962) pg 133–168.

Sheppard, L. [ed.], *The New Liturgy* (DLT, London 1970).

Signorelli, Gi, *Il Cardinale Egidio da Viterbo Agostiniano, Umanista e Riformatore 1469–1532* (Libreria Editrice Fiorentina, Firenze 1929).

Smitskamp, R., *Philologia Orientalis. A description of books illustrating the study and printing of oriental languages in Europe* (3 vols.) (E. J. Brill, Leiden 1976–91).

Sola, J. C., "El P. Juan Bautista Eliano un documento autobiográfico inédito" Archivum Historicum Societatis Iesu IV (1935) pg 291–321.

Spinks, B. D., *The Sanctus in the Eucharistic Prayer* (C.U.P., Cambridge, 1991).

Spector, S. A., *Jewish Mysticism. An Annotated Bibliography on the Kabbalah in English* (New York/London 1984).

Starabba, R., "Guglielmo Moncada, Ebreo Convertito siciliano del Secola XV" Archivio Storico siciliano n.s. III (Palermo, 1878) pg 15ff.

Steinmann, M., *Johannes Oporinus. Ein Basler Buckdrucher um die Mitte der 16 Jahrhunderts.* Basler Beiträge zur Geschichtswissenschaft n. 105 (Helbing & Lichtenhahen, Basle-Stuttgart 1967).

Steinmetz, D. [ed.], *The Bible in the Sixteenth Century* (Duke UP, Durham 1996).

Steinschneider, M., *Die hebräischen Handschriften der K. Hof- und Staatbibliothek in München, Munich 1895* (Reprint: Verlag Harrassowitz, Wiesbaden).

——, *Verzeichniss der orientalischen Handschriften der K. Hof- und Staatsbibliothek in München* (New Edition: O. Harrassowitz, Wiesbaden 1970).

Stephens, W. E., "The Etruscans and the Ancient Theology in Annius of Viterbo" in [eds.] P. Brezzi et al., *Umanismo a Roma nel Quatrocento* (Columbia UP, New York 1984) pg 309–322.

Stinger, C. L., *The Renaissance in Rome* (Indiana University Press, Bloomington 1985).

Stow, K. R., "The Burning of the Talmud in 1553 in the light of Sixteenth century Catholic attitudes to the Talmud" Bibliothèque d'Humanisme et Renaissance XXXIV (1972) pg 435–459.

——, *Catholic Thought and Papal Jewry Policy 1555–1593* (Jewish Theological Seminary of New York, 1977).

Striedl, H., "Der Humanist Johann Albrecht Widmanstetter (1506–1557) als klassischer Philologe" in *Festgabe der Bayer. Staatsbibliothek für E. Gratzl* (Otto Harrassowitz, Wesbaden 1953) pg 96–120 & pg 101–102.

——, "Die Bücherei des Orientalisten Johann Albrecht Widmanstetter" in [ed.] H. J. Kisslig and A. Schmaus, *Serta Monacensia Franz Babinger zum 15. Januar 1951 als Festgruss dargebracht* (E. J. Brill, Leiden 1952) pg 200–244.

——, "Geschichte der Hebraica-Sammlung der Bayerischen Staatsbibliothek" in H. Franke [ed.] *Orientalisches aus Münchener Bibliotheken und Sammlungen* (Franz Steiner, Wiesbaden 1957) pg 1–37.

Strohmeyer, V. B., "A Prolegomenon to the study of the Armenian Material in Teseo Ambrogio's Alphabetic Compendium" in [ed.] J. J. Weitenberg, *New Approaches to Medieval Armenian Language and Literature* (Rodopi, Amsterdam-Atlanta 1995) pg 167–177.

——, "The Armenian Manuscripts in the Personal Library of Teseo Ambrogio degli Albonesi" in [eds.] H. Palandjian, A. Tonoyan et al., *Festschrift Prof. Dr. Dora Sakayan zum 65 Geburtstag* (Diocese of the Armenian Church of Canada, Montreal 1996) pg 145–158.

——, *The Importance of Teseo Ambrogio degli Albonesi's Selected Armenian Materials for the development of the Renaissance's Perennial Philosophy and an Armeniological Philosophical Tradition* (Yerevan, 1998).

Strothman, W., *Die Anfänge der Syrischen Studien in Europa. Göttinger Orientforschungen I Reihe: Syriaca Band 1* (Harrossowitz, Wiesbaden 1971).

Suermann, H., *Die Gründsgeschichte der Maronitischen Kirche* (Harrassowitz, Wiesbaden 1998).

Tigerstedt, E. N., "Ioannes Annius and Graecia Mendax" in [ed.] C. Henderson, *Classical, Mediaeval, and Renaissance Studies in honour of Berthold Louis Ullman (Vol. II)* (Edizioni di Storia e Letteratura, Rome 1964) pg 293–310.

Tinguely, F., *L'Ecriture de Levant à la Renaissance. Enquête sur les voyageurs français dan l'Empire de Solomon Le Magnifique* (Droz, Geneva 2000).

Troncanelli, F., *La Città dei Segreti. Magia, Astrologia e Cultura Esoterica a Roma (XV–XVIII)* (Franco Angel, Milan 1985).

Ullendorff, E., Beckingham, C. F., *The Hebrew Letters of Prester John* (OUP, Oxford 1982).

——, *Ethiopia and the Bible* (Schweich Lectures 1967) (OUP, London 1968).

Ursu, J., *La Politique orientale de François 1er* (Champion, Paris 1908).

Vaccari, A., "Una Bibbia araba per il primo Gesuita venuto al Libano" Mélanges de l'Université Saint–Joseph X (fasc. 4) (1925) pg 79–104.

Vadja, G., "A Christian Kabbalist reads the Law" Revue des Études juives CXXXVII (1978) pg 258–259.

Vallone, V., "Pietro S. detto il Galatino" *Letteratura e Storia Meridionale. Studi Offerti ad Aldo Valone I* (Biblioteca dell' Archivum Romanum CCXIV Florence, 1989) pg 87–105.

Various, *Guillaume Postel 1581–1981 Actes du Colloque International d'Avranches 5–9 setembre 1981* (Editions de la Maisnie, Paris 1985).

——, *Kabbalistes chrétiennes.* Cahiers de l'Hermétisme (Albin Michel, Paris 1979).

Vasoli, C., "Da Marsilio Ficino a Francesco Giorgio Veneto" in his *Filosofia e Religione nella Cultura de Rinascimento* (Guida Editori, 1988) pg 233–256.

——, "Ermetismo e Cabala nel tardo Rinascimento e nel primo '600'" in [ed.] Fabio Troncanelli, *La Città dei Segreti. Magia, Astrologia e Cultura Esoterica a Roma (XV–XVIII)* (Franco Angel, Milan, 1985) pg 103–118.

——, "Giorgio B. Salvati, Pietro Galatino e la edizione di Ortona—1518—del De Arcanis Catholicae Fidei" in *Cultura Humanistica nel Meridione e la Stampa in Abruzzo. Atti del Convegno su Cultura Umanistica nel Meridone e la Stampa in Abruzzo* (L'Aquila, 1984) pg 183–210.

——, "Giorgio Benigno Salviati". In [ed.] M. Reeves, *Prophetic Rome in the High Renaissance Period* (Clarendon, Oxford 1992) pg 121–156.

——, "Un 'precedente' della 'Virgine Veneziana': Francesco Giorgio Veneto e la clarissa Chiar Bugni" [ed.] Kuntz, *Postello, Venezia, e il suo Mondo* pg 203–225.

——, *Profezia e Ragione* (Studi sulla Cultura di Cinquecento e del Seicento, Napoli 1974).

——, "Hermeticism in Venice. From Francesco Giorgio to Agostino Steucho" in [eds.] Carlos Gilly, Cis van Heertum, *Magic, Alchemy and Science in 15th–18th century: The Influence of Hermes Trismegistus* (CenroDi, 2002).

Vervliet, H. D. L., *Cyrillic and Oriental Typography in Rome at the end of the Sixteenth Century: An Inquiry into the Later Work of Robert Granjon 1578–90* (Poltroon Press, Berkeley 1981).

Vocht, H. De, "Andreas Masius (1514–1573)" in *Miscellanea Giovanni Mercati* (Studi e Testi CXXIV) Rome (1946) pg 425–441, pg 431.

Voci, A. M., "Un 'Ipotesi sulla Genesi della Scechina di Egidio da Viterbo". Critica Storica XX (1983) pg 130–137.

Voet, L., *The Golden Compasses. A History and Evaluation of the Printing and Publishing Activities of the Officina Plantiniana at Antwerp* (trans. R. H. Kaye, Vangendt & Co, Amsterdam 1972).

Vogel, E. G., "Über Wilh. Postel's Reise in der Orient" Serapeum XIV (1853) pg 49–58.

Vööbus, A., *The Apocalypse in the Harklean Version* (CSCO: 400, Subs 56 1978).

Vosté, J. M., "Mar Johannan Soulaqa, premier patriarche des Chaldéens, martyr de l'union avec Rome († 1555) Trois poesies inédites de 'Abdisho' de Gazertha." Angelicum VIII (1931) pg 187–234.

——, "Missio Duorum Fratrum Melitensium O. P. in Orientem saeculo XVI, et relatio, nunc primum edita, eorum quae in istis regionibus gesserunt" Analecta Ordinis Praedicatorum XXXIII (fasc. IV) (1925) pg 261–278.

Walker, D. P., *The Ancient Theology* (Duckworth, London 1972).

Walz, A., "Zur Lebensgeschichte des Kardinals Nikolaus von Schonberg" in *Mélanges Mandonnet Études d'histoire littéraire et doctrinale du Moyen Age* (J. Vrin, Paris 1930) Vol. II, pg 371–387.

Weil, G., *De Guliemi Postelli vita et indole. Vie et caractère de Guillaume Postel.* Paris 1892 (New edition by François Secret, Archè, Milano 1987).

Weil, G. E., *Élie Lévita Humaniste et Massorète 1469–1549* (E. J. Brill, Leiden 1963).

——, "L'Archétype du Massoret ha-Massoret d'Élie Lévita" Revue d'Histoire et Philologie religieuses XLI (1961) pg 147–158.

Weinberg, J., "Azariah dei Rossi: Towards a reappraisal of the Last Years of his Life" Annali della Scuola Normale Superiore di Pisa 3d ser. VIII (1978) pg 493–511.

——, "Azariah de' Rossi and Septuagint Traditions" Italia V no. 1–2 (1985) pg 7–35.

——, "An Apocryphal Source in the Me'or 'Einayim" Journal of the Warburg and Courtauld Institute LVI (1993) pg 280–284.

——, (trans) *Azariah de' Rossi The Light of the Eyes* (CUP, Cambridge 2004).

——, *Azariah de' Rossi's Observations on the Syriac New Testament* (Warburg Institute, London 2005).

Weiss, R., "England and the Decree of the Council of Vienne on the Teaching of Greek, Arabic, Hebrew, and Syriac" Bibliothèque d'Humanisme et Renaissance XIV (1952) pg 1–9.

——, "An unknown Epigraphic Tract by Annius of Viterbo" in *Italian Studies presented to E. R. Vincent* (CUP, Cambridge 1962) pg 101–120.

——, "Traccia per una Biografia di Annio da Viterbo" in Italia Medievale e Umanistica V. (1962) pg 425–441.

Weiss, T., *Zur ostsyr. Laut- u. Akzentlehre auf Grund der ostsyr. Massorah HS des British Museum* (Stuttgart, 1933).

Wesselius, J. W., "The Syriac Correspondence of Andreas Masius" in ed. René Lavenant, *V Symposium Syriacum 1988* (Orientalia Christiana Analecta CCXXXVI) (Pont. Institutum Studiorum Orientalium, Rome 1990) pg 21–30.

Whittaker, J., "Giles of Viterbo as Classical Scholar" in *Egidio da Viterbo e il suo tempo Egidio da Viterbo O.S.A. e il suo tempo. Atti del V Convegna dell' Instituto Storico Agostiniano, Roma—Viterbo 20–23 ottobre 1982* (Analecta Augustiniana, Rome 1983) pg 85–105.

Wilkinson, Robert J., "Emmanuel Tremellius' 1569 Edition of the Syriac New Testament" Journal of Ecclesiastical History Vol. LVIII/1 January 2007 pg 9–25.

——, *The Kabbalistic Scholars of the Antwerp Polygot Bible* (E.J. Brill, Leiden 2007).
——, *The Origins of Syriac Studies in the Sixteenth Century.* Unpublished Doctoral Thesis. University of the West of England 2003.
Williams, R., *On Christian Theology* (Blackwell, Oxford 2000).
Wind, E., "Michelangelo's Prophets and Sibyls" in [ed.] George Holmes, *Art and Politics in Renaissance Italy* (British Academy, OUP, London, 1993) pg 263–300.
Winjman, H. F., *An outline of the Development of Ethiopian Typography in Europe* (E. J. Brill, Leiden 1960).
Wirszubski, C, "Franceso Giorgio's commentary on Giovanni Pico's kabbalistic theses" Journal of the Warburg and Courtauld Institutes XXXVII (1974) pg 145–156.
——, "Giovanni Pico's Book of Job" Journal of the Warburg and Courtauld Institute XXXII (1969) pg 171–199.
——, *Pico della Mirandola's Encounter with Jewish Mysticism* (Harvard University Press, Cambridge Mass. 1989).
——, "Giovanni Pico's Companion to Kabbalistic Symbolism" *Studies in Mysticism and Religion presented to Gershom Scholem* (Jerusalem, 1967) pg 353–362.
Wright, W. W., *Catalogue of the Syriac manuscripts in the B.M.* (London, 1870).
Yates, F. A., *The Occult Philosophy in the Elizabethan Age* (Routledge, London 1979).
Yérasimos, S., "Le Turc en Occident. La connaissance de la langue *Turque en Europe: XVe–XVIIe siècles*" in [ed.] Michèle Duchet, *L'Inscription des Langues dans les relations de Voyages (XVIe–XVIIIe siècles) Actes du Colloque de décembre 1988 à Fontenay aux Roses* (ENS, Fontenay/St. Cloud 1992) pg 191–210.
Young, J., *A Catalogue of the mss in the Library of the Hunterian Museum in the University of Glasgow* (Glasgow, 1908).
Zinguer, I., "Exotisme au Philologie dans les récits de voyages juifs de la Renaissance" in [ed.] M. Duchet, *Inscription des Langues dans les Relations de Voyage (XVIe–XVIIIe siècles)* (ENS, Fontenay/St. Cloud 1992) pg 177–189.
——, "Juifs et Karaites aux XVIe et XVIIe siècles" in [ed.] Ilana Zinguer, *Miroirs de l'Altérité et Voyages au Proche-Orient* (Slatkine, Geneva 1991) pg 55–64.
——, "Tabourot des Accords et les Charactères samaritains" in *Tabourot, Seigneur des Accords Actes du Colloque Dijon 1988* (Dijon, 1990) pg 146–147.
Zuurmond, R., "The Ethiopic Version of the New Testament" in [eds.] B. D. Ehrman & M. W. Holmes, *The Text of the New Testament in Contemporary Research* (Eerdmans, Michigan 1995) pg 142–156.

INDEX